THE ULTIMATE
HOUSE PLANT
HANDBOOK

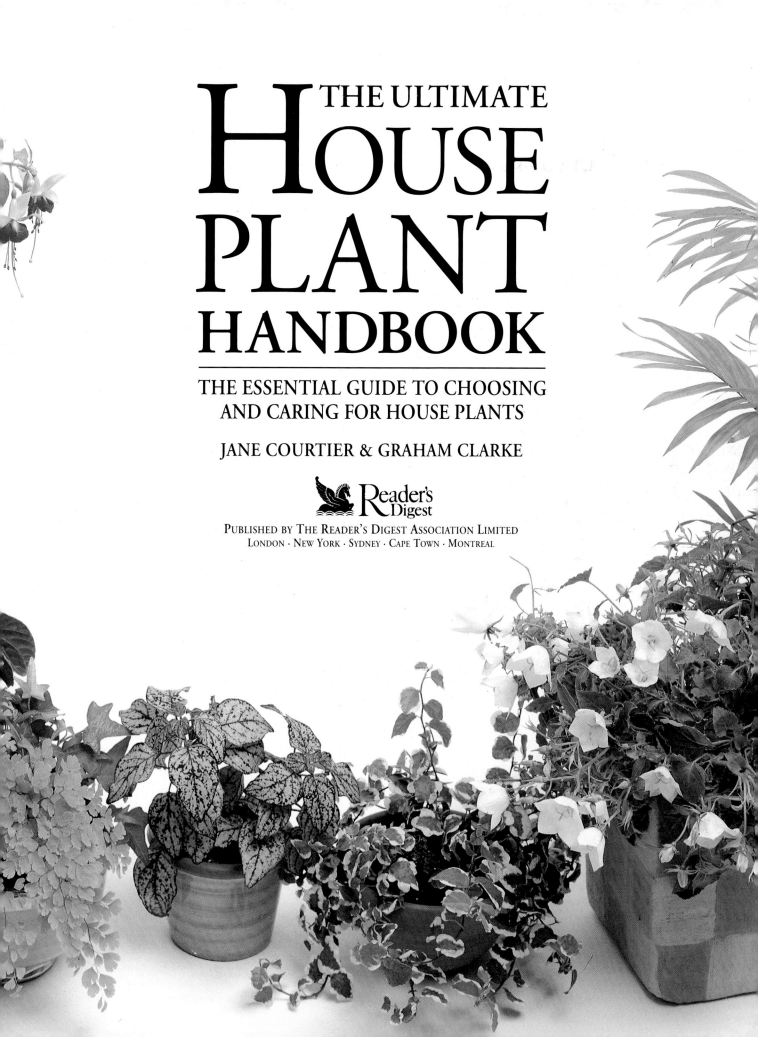

THE ULTIMATE
HOUSE
PLANT
HANDBOOK

THE ESSENTIAL GUIDE TO CHOOSING
AND CARING FOR HOUSE PLANTS

JANE COURTIER & GRAHAM CLARKE

Reader's Digest

PUBLISHED BY THE READER'S DIGEST ASSOCIATION LIMITED
LONDON · NEW YORK · SYDNEY · CAPE TOWN · MONTREAL

A READER'S DIGEST BOOK
Published by The Reader's Digest Association Limited
Berkeley Square House
Berkeley Square
London W1X 6AB

Conceived, edited and designed by
MARSHALL EDITIONS
170 Piccadilly, London W1V 9DD

Copyright © 1997 Marshall Editions Developments Limited

ISBN 0-276-42285-6

A CIP catalogue for this book is available from the British Library

PROJECT EDITOR Gwen Rigby
ART EDITOR Frances de Rees
PICTURE EDITOR Zilda Tandy
DTP EDITORS Mary Pickles, Kate Waghorn, Lesley Gilbert
COPY EDITOR Jolika Feszt
INDEXER Caroline Sheard
MANAGING EDITOR Lindsay McTeague
PRODUCTION EDITOR Emma Dixon
EDITORIAL DIRECTOR Sophie Collins
ART DIRECTOR Sean Keogh
PRODUCTION Bob Christie

Printed and bound in Italy

CONTENTS

INTRODUCTION

PLANTS HAVE A VERY SPECIAL PLACE IN OUR homes. They are living ornaments that grow and develop; they undergo subtle changes through the seasons, presenting an ever-varying display. They respond to and repay our care and attention. A thriving plant is a source of pride to its owner, and it imparts a feeling of well-being to any room. And for those who spend a lot of time indoors, plants in the home provide a wonderful and all-important link with nature and the world outdoors.

A person need not be a horticultural expert in order to derive pleasure from indoor plants, but some knowledge of a plant's preferences for its growing conditions and the requirements for its maintenance will help it to thrive. And that is where you will find this book of immeasurable help. Here you will learn what it takes to ensure that your plants prosper: the ideal temperature and humidity and light conditions, their natural growth cycle, and whether or not they

must have a rest period. The more you know about your house plants, the more you will appreciate them.

Not only can this book help you to keep the plants you already have in good health, it is an invaluable guide to finding new plants that will suit the conditions in your home as well. The information in The Plant Directory section will alert you to the basic needs of a wide range of plants – from the familiar foliage and flowering plants to the exotic orchids. Armed with the book, you will have a better chance of success with any plant. Disappointing impulse buys can be kept to a minimum and you will be able to appraise a plant that has eye-catching colour, a sweet scent or an unusual appearance with a knowledgeable eye.

A final word of advice and encouragement: if you find a plant that you want very badly, but feel cautious about it in terms of its specific needs, by all means take a chance and buy it – unless it is prohibitively expensive. Compare the price of a

Small cacti are mostly inexpensive to buy, so it is easy to make a collection. But the difficulty is how to display the little plants to advantage – a problem attractively solved here by massing them in a wire basket.

Orchids are the epitome of glamour and the exotic to most people. But they are fairly easy to grow, given the right conditions, and the pride and delight of bringing such an exquisite plant into bloom in the home will far outweigh the care and attention it demands.

potted plant with that of a bouquet of cut flowers. Chances are, the plant will give you your money's worth even if it lasts for only a few months.

You can never be certain in advance how well a plant will do; you have to try it. Some plants are wonderfully (and unpredictably) cooperative. They just don't seem to understand the rules, and they appear to be determined to thrive in the most unexpected places and under the least auspicious of growing conditions.

However, if a plant is failing, consider moving it to another position. For example, a plant that doesn't like draughts can be moved from, say, an entrance hall to an area that has similar light but is more protected. You will be either pleasantly surprised by a dramatic recovery, or you will have to try yet another spot; you may even have to admit defeat. But whether you are adventurous or not with your indoor gardening, take pride in your efforts and above all enjoy your house plants.

Miniature cyclamens, primulas and ivies, planted together in a ceramic trough, can bring the colour and scent of spring into the home long before it arrives outdoors.

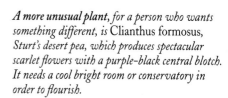

A more unusual plant, for a person who wants something different, is Clianthus formosus, *Sturt's desert pea, which produces spectacular scarlet flowers with a purple-black central blotch. It needs a cool bright room or conservatory in order to flourish.*

Crocuses (left) *are another welcome, easy-to-grow reminder of spring. Plant up a handful of corms in a small pot for a splash of colour.*

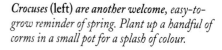

HOW TO USE THIS BOOK

THE FIRST CHAPTER OF THIS BOOK TELLS YOU how to decorate your home with plants, and how to take advantage of their shapes and special features, such as flowers and foliage. You will learn how to choose the right plant for every room in your house, and you will find ideas for the many different kinds of containers that can be used for indoor plants, plus information on supports for plants that trail and climb.

Chapter 2, The Plant Directory, is an exhaustive reference guide to more than 300 indoor plants. It gives details of each plant's requirements – temperature, humidity, lighting conditions, repotting, origin and more. The first part of the directory covers the most popular house plants and illustrates each specimen in full-colour; the second part deals with some of the more unusual plants.

CHAPTER 1
Decorating with Plants

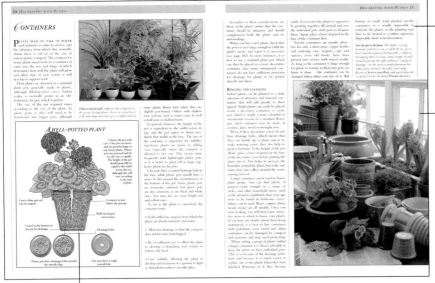

Informative text covers both the technical and decorative aspects of using plants in the home.

Attractive illustrations show a wide range of plants in different situations and act as inspiration for your own planting.

Diagrams and drawings explain technical matters and methods.

CHAPTER 2
The Plant Directory: Feature spreads

Some of the plants most often grown in the home are discussed on eight double-page entries.

Annotation describes the features to look out for on a healthy plant and also those features that will tell you the plant is ailing.

Several other, often surprisingly different, species in the genus are shown and described.

A typical plant is depicted, one half in full health, the other showing the result of neglect and attack by pests and diseases.

The care and culture of the various species mentioned is set out in a clear, detailed manner.

All you need to know about caring for plants is clearly set out in Chapter 3. It begins with a simple explanation of how plants work, and goes on to point out how light, temperature and humidity affect them. You will find the necessary information about feeding, watering, training and potting, as well as some more unusual techniques, such as growing plants hydroponically and providing supplementary lighting.

Propagation by a wide variety of means is fully covered. And there is a wealth of valuable, illustrated instruction about plant pests and diseases and how to combat them. A series of easy-reference charts summarizes the relevant information about all the individual plants that are profiled in The Plant Directory. And a concise glossary explains some of the less-familiar technical terms used throughout the book.

CHAPTER 2
The Plant Directory

Plants are listed alphabetically under their scientific names, and the family names and most frequently used common names are also given.

The introductory text describes the plant and, in some instances, varieties and related species.

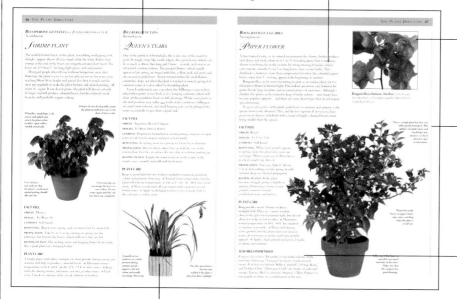

On full-page entries there is a second photograph, which is either a detail of the plant or shows another variety or related species.

Annotation around the plant gives tips for growing or information about possible pests and diseases.

The names are given of some other varieties of the plant or related species you might like to grow.

Photographs show plants at the size and in the condition you are likely to buy them.

CHAPTER 3
Caring for Plants

Easy-to-follow, step-by-step illustrations demonstrate the correct way to look after your plants.

All aspects of plant care are covered by simple and authoritative text. Charts give all the information about every plant in the directory at a glance.

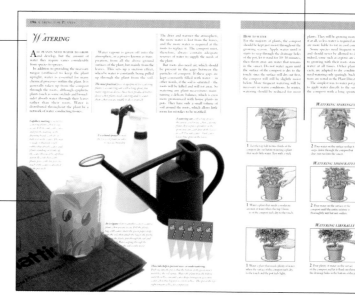

Annotated photographs show and describe some of the equipment you can use to do a specific job.

DECORATING WITH PLANTS

WALK INTO ANY GARDEN CENTRE or shop with a reasonable selection of indoor plants and you will see evidence of the huge diversity of plant shapes and forms that exist. Among these shapes you will find some that are more appealing to you than others, but you will also need to bear in mind how suitable they are for the positions you have to fill in your house.

A tall, striking, 'architectural' plant may be called for to provide a dramatic feature in a prominent position in a large, simply furnished living room. A smaller, more crowded room may be better served by low-growing foliage and flowering plants grouped together on a windowsill or table. No matter how attractive a particular specimen appears in the shop, always try to imagine it in your own home before giving way to impulse and buying it.

Plant shapes fall into six principal groups, but there is some overlap among the groups.

UPRIGHT

A plant such as *Sansevieria trifasciata*, mother-in-law's tongue, would be defined as upright, with its dramatic tall, sharp spikes. Such plants have no hint of spreading or trailing stems to soften the outline, even after several years' growth.

BUSHY

Many indoor plants are classified as bushy. They may have several stems or just one main stem, which divides low down into several branches. The branches spread out to form a more or less rounded, bushy shape, which is well furnished with foliage. *Dieffenbachia maculata*, dumb cane, has a bushy habit, as do pot chrysanthemums. But with the latter, it is the way the raisers treat the plants, rather than their natural habit of growth, that gives them their form.

TRAILING

Soft stems cascade down, sometimes concealing the plant's pot entirely. In some

Plants give a room an inviting air. Here a bushy fern and round-headed standard azalea lead the eye to the staircase wall, which is lightly clothed in a lax-stemmed climber.

PLANT SHAPES

Dieffenbachia maculata

Ficus pumila

Chamaerops humilis

Ficus benjamina

Monstera deliciosa

Sansevieria trifasciata

instances, the stems are prostrate, such as those of *Zebrina pendula*, wandering Jew, or *Ficus pumila*, the creeping fig.

The stems of other plants strike out upwards to begin with, then bend over gracefully as they develop, giving the effect of a fountain. The ever-popular *Chlorophytum comosum*, spider plant, has this appearance, although it is not just the grassy foliage that produces the effect. As plants start to mature, they produce plenty of 'baby' plants on the ends of long, pliable stems; these cascade down to make the plant a true trailer.

CLIMBING

A climber generally has lax stems, which will trail if they are not supplied with supports, but which will scramble eagerly upwards when they are able to. Sometimes these plants need encouragement to start climbing, often nothing will stop

them. They may have twining stems, clinging tendrils or aerial roots to support them in their upward quest.

STANDARD

Standards are tree-like plants that have a main stem and a branching head. *Ficus benjamina*, a popular example, also has an attractive weeping habit, hence its common name of weeping fig.

ARCHITECTURAL

The term 'architectural' applies to forms that are unusual and dramatic. The shape and outline of such plants is bold and eye-catching, and architectural plants are usually grown as stand-alone specimens. They are always large plants, tending to be tall rather than spreading, such as *Chamaerops humilis*, the European fan palm, which has big, boldly cut, fan-shaped leaves and sturdy, hairy stems.

FOLIAGE PLANTS

GROWN MAINLY FOR THEIR LEAVES, foliage plants may also produce flowers. Sometimes these flowers are an added short-term attraction. Sometimes they are insignificant. Occasionally they detract from the appearance of the plant and are best pinched out while in bud.

Foliage plants may be valuable for the shape, texture or colour of their leaves. They are normally of year-round value in the home, although a few, such as caladiums, die back in winter.

LEAF SHAPE

There are literally dozens of different leaf shapes, some of which are particularly attractive and striking. Leaf size, too, varies widely and, together with the shape, plays an important part in the overall effect created by the plant.

Among the many shapes to be found are the bold, hand-like leaves of *Fatsia japonica*, Japanese aralia; the deeply incised leaf fans of *Howea belmoreana*, the curly palm; the heart-shaped foliage of *Philodendron scandens*, the heartleaf philodendron; and the sharp spikes of *Yucca elephantipes*, the spineless yucca.

The huge leaves of *Monstera deliciosa* develop slits and holes that give the plant its common name, Swiss cheese plant; and the foliage of *Syngonium podophyllum* is responsible for the names of goosefoot and arrowhead plant. The needle-like leaves of *Asparagus densiflorus* 'Sprengeri' make it look like a fern.

Many leaves are divided into leaflets, such as the narrow, scalloped fingers of *Dizygotheca elegantissima* and the umbrella-rib leaves of *Schefflera arboricola*, the umbrella tree.

The margins of leaves may be waved, crenulated, serrated or toothed; the bases and tips of each leaf differ in their shapes and patterns. The size of leaves can range from the tiny, bright green pinheads of *Nertera granadensis*, the bead plant, to the extravagant foliage of *Monstera deliciosa* and *Ficus lyrata*, the fiddle-leaf fig.

LEAF TEXTURE

Glossy, leathery, corrugated, downy, velvety, spiny, waxy – the texture of leaves can differ as much as their shape and colour and can give fascinating visual, as well as tactile, effects. The boldly marked foliage of *Begonia rex*, painted-leaf begonia, has short, stiff hairs all over the surface, which gives it a rough, sandpaper texture. In contrast, the hairs on the foliage of *Gynura* 'Purple Passion', the purple passion vine, are soft, producing a plush effect that gives the plant the common name of velvet plant.

The veins stand out prominently on the backs of the leaves of *Begonia rex*, whereas the raised veins of *Maranta leuconeura*, the prayer plant, appear on the top surface of the leaf. In

Chamaedorea elegans

Asparagus densiflorus 'Sprengeri'

Saintpaulia spp.

Pelargonium crispum

Jasminum polyanthemum

Kalanchoe blossfeldiana

Impatiens walleriana

Syngonium podophyllum

Dracaena marginata 'Tricolor'

Cyclamen persicum

Spathyphyllum wallisii

Camellia japonica

Nerium oleander

between the raised veins, tiny hairs give the maranta leaf a satiny look and feel.

Peperomias have deeply corrugated, wrinkled leaf surfaces, as do many pileas, including *Pilea cadieri*, the aluminum plant. The leaves of the rubber plant, *Ficus elastica*, are thick, glossy and leathery. At the other end of the scale, the delicate, paper-thin, translucent foliage of *Caladium* x *hortulanum* has given it the common name of angel-wings.

LEAF COLOUR

If asked what colour leaves are, most people would unhesitatingly reply 'green'. The majority of leaves may be predominantly green, but that is by no means the whole story. Even among plants with completely green foliage, there are many different shades and subtleties of colour. Some greens are so dark as to be almost black – as in the rubber plant *Ficus elastica* 'Black Prince' – while the delicate foliage of *Adiantum raddianum*, the delta maidenhair fern, is the fresh, pale green of springtime.

Leaves can be variegated with gold, cream or white, sometimes around the margin of the leaf, sometimes over its entire surface. These markings may take the form of irregular splashes or mottling, or they may occur in a distinctive pattern. The leaf veins are often highlighted by a contrasting colour, and sometimes the leaves are so strongly variegated that they appear to be yellow or white with green markings. Many ivies are attractively variegated: *Hedera helix* 'Little Diamond' has small leaves with silvery edges, and the much larger leaves of *H. algeriensis* 'Gloire de Marengo' are mottled all over with several shades of green, grey, cream and white.

Variegation in shades of pink and red may also occur. *Dracaena marginata* 'Tricolor' has long slender leaves picked out with fine cream lines and a bright pink edge. In *Maranta leuconeura erythroneura*, the herringbone plant, the leaves are fascinatingly marked, with bright red veins and an irregular backing of pale green or yellow to the central rib.

The green colouring in leaves is chlorophyll, which is essential for plants to be able to make their food satisfactorily. However, some plants seem to be able to survive with very little chlorophyll, which gives rise to interesting and unusual leaf colours. *Iresine herbstii*, the bloodleaf plant, for example, is so called because its foliage and stems are a bright red. And some varieties of *Begonia rex* have leaves of pink, red, silver and purple, with no green to be seen.

The delicate, paper-thin leaves of caladium are often white or cream with a pink central flush and perhaps just a fine margin of green or green veins. Easier to grow are *Coleus blumei*, the cheerful flame nettle, and *Codiaeum variegatum pictum*, known with good reason as Joseph's coat. Both of these can be found with leaves vividly patterned in a wide range of brilliant – and often gaudy – shades of red, yellow, orange and brown. The chlorophyll in these non-green plants is present, but it is well masked by the other pigments.

FLOWERING PLANTS

JUST AS THERE IS AN ENORMOUS range of leaf types, shapes and colours among foliage plants, so the number of flowering plants is immense. Flowers appear in all colours of the spectrum. They may be small individually but carried in large numbers to produce their effect, or they may be large and bold enough for a single flower stem to be the centre of attention. There is, too, a vast array of shapes from the simple, five-petalled trumpets of jasmine or daisy-like cinerarias to the curious appearance of some members of the orchid family. Double, single, pendant, trumpet-shaped, star-shaped, pouched or rosette-forming – the choices are endless.

Spring provides enchanting and colourful plants for the house. Mass pots of bulbs with miniature cyclamens, African violets and primroses to make a heartwarming display.

Sometimes a plant is grown not for its flowers but for the leafy, flower-like bracts that may be far more colourful and eye-catching than the true flowers. *Euphorbia pulcherrima*, the poinsettia, for example, has only small yellow flowers in the centre of its showy red, cream or pink bracts and the scrambling bougainvillea also relies on papery, brightly coloured bracts for its charm. Insignificant flowers may be

followed by colourful and interesting fruits as is the case with *Solanum capsicastrum*, the Christmas, or false Jerusalem cherry.

Most flowers are grown for their colour and appearance, but some are enjoyed mainly for their scent. Twining white jasmine can perfume a whole room, and the sweet scent of the waxy cream trumpets of stephanotis is almost over-powering. Gardenias are not easy plants to bring into bloom indoors, but the white-fading-to-cream, double or semi-double blooms are intensely fragrant.

Many spring bulbs – narcissi, hyacinths and crocuses among them – can be flowered indoors, where their delicate perfume can be more easily appreciated than when they are grown in the garden. *Narcissus tazetta* 'Paperwhite' is a particularly good choice for fragrance and is simple to grow, flowering six weeks after planting with no cold, dark period necessary.

By their nature, flowering plants tend to have a limited season of interest. The length of the flowering period can vary considerably. Some plants, such as orchids, have extremely long-lasting flowers: others have flowers whose individual lives are brief, but because new flowers are

constantly opening to replace the older ones, the period of interest is prolonged.

Many plants have attractive foliage and look good even when the flowering season is over. The pineapple-like blooms of *Aphelandra squarrosa*, the zebra plant, last for several weeks, but when they die, the dark green leaves with their herring-bone pattern of white veins ensure that the plant is still highly decorative.

Yellow and orange calceolarias, slipper flowers (right), *complement the glowing golden wood of an antique chest of drawers and mirror.*

A striking clivia (left) *with its fan of leaves and head of orange flowers is bold enough to stand alone.*

BUYING PLANTS

Indoor plants are available from a wide range of outlets, including supermarkets, florists, petrol stations and greengrocers as well as garden centres. Always buy from an outlet where the plants are regularly and well cared for, otherwise you are asking for disappointment. As a general rule, garden centres and nurseries will give you the widest choice and the most reliable plants.

In winter, protect the plant from cold weather on its journey home, preferably enclosing it entirely in a plastic sleeve or cardboard box made for the purpose. Once home, settle the plant in the position you have selected for it and avoid the temptation to keep moving it from place to place. Be prepared for it to look a little unhappy for a short spell as it adjusts to the different environment of your house; it is not unusual for a few leaves to fall or flower buds to drop off. As long as you have chosen a position that provides a suitable temperature, humidity and light level for the particular species, it will soon recover and start to grow happily.

When buying plants, pick medium-sized, robust, healthy plants with no obvious signs of damage, pests or disease.

Test the compost surface with your finger: it should be just moist. Reject specimens that are bone-dry or sodden.

Look at the base of the pot to see whether roots are protruding from the drainage holes. A lot of visible root means the plant should have been repotted and its growth is likely to have been checked.

Flowering plants should have plenty of developing buds and not too many fully open flowers.

Avoid plants from display units near doorways. They are likely to have been subjected to fluctuating temperatures.

CHOOSING THE RIGHT PLACE

EVERY HOME WILL PROVIDE A surprisingly wide variation in environments, and it is important to select the right plant for the right place. This does not only mean choosing the plant that looks best in a particular position; it also means finding plants that will be happy in the conditions provided. The major variables are light levels and temperature; these are dealt with in more detail in Chapter 3.

Living rooms are probably the most popular areas for plant displays, since these are the rooms in which we tend to relax and enjoy our surroundings. Many plant lovers, though, like to have decorative plants in virtually every room of the house. Of course, each house will be different, but there are some general points that apply to most homes.

HALLWAYS

The hallway is normally the first part of your home a visitor sees, and plants help to create a pleasant, welcoming atmosphere. It can be a difficult position for plants, however, since it is often narrow, restricting the room for plant displays, and receives little natural light. Hallways are usually cooler than the living areas of the house. Opening and closing the front door causes draughts and temperature fluctuations, and if the stairway is situated in the hall, warm air will tend to rise, causing an updraught. The front door is sometimes used only by visitors; if so, plants near it tend to be forgotten.

LIVING ROOMS

These rooms are generally fairly light, with plenty of windows, and they often face the sun. They are usually quite large rooms, where taller, architectural plants can be most easily accommodated. They

A bedside table is the ideal place for an exotic orchid (above); *what better way to greet the morning than by gazing at the perfect blooms.*

Nothing could be more inviting than the prospect of a meal under a leafy vine in a garden room (left) *full of colourful plants such as abutilon and campanula, which love the light.*

are normally comfortably warm while the family is home, but the temperature may drop considerably at night and if the house is empty during working hours in the winter. Time-controlled air conditioning or heating can also cause wide fluctuations in temperature.

Heating also provides a dry atmosphere, and most plants will appreciate some extra humidity.

KITCHENS

Many families spend a lot of time in the kitchen, and while you are likely to be busy there preparing meals and

clearing up, plants help to create a welcoming, pleasant environment. A large kitchen may also be used for eating in and as a general family room where many activities are carried out. This sort of kitchen tends to be kept evenly warm and is often reasonably light; it is therefore suitable for many types of plants.

Older houses or flats may have small, cramped kitchens which often face away from the sun and have small windows. Temperatures in these tend to fluctuate widely, rising considerably during cooking but cooling down quickly afterwards.

Humidity levels in kitchens are often high, due to steam from cooking, washing up and so on, so plant leaves can quickly become coated with greasy, sticky deposits and thus need frequent cleaning. Consequently, tough, glossy-leafed specimens may do better than those with soft, delicate foliage.

The kitchen is primarily a working area. Plants must not get in the way and should never compromise safety when people are working around hot surfaces.

Wicker pot covers tie in with the wicker furniture in this living room (right). *Foliage plants, which need less light, stand at the back, while the pelargonium enjoys a bright spot near the window.*

Bright light, warm colours and plants, such as bamboo, orchid and bromeliad, which thrive in a warm, humid atmosphere (below), *make this a bathroom to luxuriate in and enjoy.*

GARDEN ROOMS AND CONSERVATORIES

Increasing numbers of houses now have conservatories or garden rooms, not just for growing plants but as extra living space. Most modern conservatories are carpeted and furnished and can be heated if necessary, but the high light levels they enjoy still make them excellent places for a wide range of plants.

Temperatures can become extremely high in summer, and ventilation and

blinds or some other form of shading are usually necessary to prevent leaf scorch and to lower the temperature to a more comfortable level. In cooler climates, an unheated conservatory will be cold in winter and so is likely to be unsuitable for many indoor plants, although some heat will be obtained from adjoining rooms.

BEDROOMS

Although the bedroom may be the room in the house where we spend most hours, we are asleep and unappreciative of the delights of plants for most of the time. Many bedrooms face east, and the bedroom windowsill is a popular place for a few undemanding plants. A special effort needs to be made to remember to water them, since they are easily forgotten in the often-rushed morning routine.

BATHROOMS

Although most bathrooms receive little sun, modern bathrooms have the advantage of being evenly warm throughout the day, with high levels of humidity, providing good conditions for plant growth. Light levels are often good, with frosted or obscured glass giving the bright, diffused light favoured by many plants.

But beware, in many houses the temperature will rise rapidly when a bath is run or the shower is used, then fall quickly, leading to the cool, moist conditions that make plants prone to fungal disease.

CHOOSING THE RIGHT PLACE

NOTES FOR ROOM PLAN

The rooms in every house differ in their aspect, their size, how well they are heated, the lighting and so on, and this will affect your choice of plants. This plan gives you a few ideas for plants that are likely to suit particular rooms.

BEDROOM

Cool to moderately warm, good light. Choose easy-to-care-for plants that can put up with a little neglect.

Cyclamen persicum
Fatshedera lizei
Fuchsia hybrids
Jasminum polyanthum
Maranta leuconeura erythroneura
Pelargonium x *hortorum*
Saintpaulia hybrids
Spathiphyllum wallisii

BATHROOM

Moderate warmth; good diffuse light; periods of high humidity.

Adiantum raddianum
Asplenium nidus
Calathea makoyana
Carex morrowii 'Variegata'
Chamaedorea elegans
Chlorophytum comosum 'Vittatum'
Cissus antarctica
Cyperus alternifolius
Epipremnum aureum
Ficus pumila
Maranta leuconeura erythroneura
Nephrolepis exaltata
Peperomia scandens
Philodendron scandens

ENTRANCE HALL

Fairly cool; poor to moderate light. Plants must not be fragile.

Aglaonema commutatum
Aspidistra elatior
Chlorophytum comosum 'Vittatum'
Cissus antarctica
Clivia miniata
Fatsia japonica
Hedera helix
Tradescantia fluminensis

Ocimum basilicum is one of the most decorative and flavoursome culinary herbs. It is an annual and needs warmth and the best light you can give it.

Clivia miniata, with its deep green strap-shaped leaves and glowing orange flowers, is a striking plant. The cool shade of a hall will prolong its flowering period.

Chlorophytum comosum 'Vittatum' is easy to grow. Its greatest need is for bright light without direct sun. When mature, it will show to great advantage against the light from a window.

Cyclamen persicum prefers a cool room with bright filtered light and will thrive despite a little neglect. It is a good plant for a bedroom, where its care may be overlooked.

Cyperus alternifolius likes light shade and its roots must be kept constantly wet, so it is a good plant for a bathroom since you are less likely to forget to water it.

Cissus antarctica will adapt well to quite low light and prefers to be kept cool, so it is ideal for an entrance hall.

KITCHEN
Warm; humid; poor to moderate light. Use temporary plants that can be replaced regularly.

Begonia rex
Chrysanthemum x *morifolium*
Coleus blumei
Epipremnum aureum
Hedera helix
Herbs
Impatiens walleriana
Saintpaulia hybrids
Tradescantia fluminensis 'Variegata'
Zebrina pendula

LIVING ROOM
Warm; good light; adequate space for specimen plants and groups.

Begonia rex
Codiaeum variegatum pictum
Dieffenbachia maculata
Dracaena marginata
Euphorbia pulcherrima
Ficus benjamina
Ficus elastica 'Robusta'
Ficus lyrata
Hydrangea macrophylla
Kalanchoe blossfeldiana
Monstera deliciosa
Philodendron bipinnatifidum
Rhododendron simsii
Yucca elephantipes

CONSERVATORY OR SUNROOM
Heated all year; bright light. Take advantage of the good conditions to grow some more exotic specimens.

Abutilon pictum 'Thompsonii'
Aechmea fasciata
Aeschynanthus speciosus
Allamanda cathartica
Anthurium scherzerianum
Bougainvillea glabra
Caladium x *hortulanum*
x *Citrofortunella microcarpa*
Columnea x *banksii*
Datura x *candida*
Gloriosa superba 'Rothschildiana'
Orchids
Passiflora caerulea
Peperomia scandens
Philodendron scandens
Strelitzia reginae

Impatiens walleriana is a cheerful, free-flowering temporary plant. Set on a kitchen table at which the family has its meals, it brings the summer indoors.

Columnea x *banksii* enjoys bright light but not direct sun. It flowers profusely in winter and early spring, and is good in a hanging basket.

Bougainvillea glabra will thrive in the warmth and bright light of a sunroom, and will bloom throughout summer and autumn.

Dracaena marginata is an excellent plant for a living room. It will tolerate a fairly wide variation in temperature and needs bright filtered light.

Hydrangea macrophylla provides a welcome temporary splash of colour among the more permanent plants. When flowering is over, the plant can be put on the patio or planted outdoors.

Ficus elastica 'Robusta' with its sturdy straight stems and big shiny leaves will grow into a tall specimen plant in time. It will thrive in a wide variety of conditions and is largely trouble-free.

FILLING THE SPACE

THE MOST MAGNIFICENT PLANT CAN lose its impact if it is positioned wrongly. Choose a place that provides the conditions it likes and it will thrive – but you should also choose a place where it will be shown to its best advantage.

SPECIMEN PLANTS

Many plants can be successful when displayed on their own, as single specimens. These are normally fairly large subjects, with a bold outline or dramatic foliage – the so-called architectural plants. Such plants can make an excellent focal point, particularly if spotlights are used for highlighting. *Ficus elastica*, the rubber plant, is perhaps less popular than it once was, but its relative *Ficus benjamina*, the weeping fig, makes a splendid specimen plant. *Ficus lyrata*, the fiddle-leaf fig, has a less elegant shape, but its large, boldly curved leaves provide a point of interest.

A well-grown *Dracaena marginata*, the Madagascar dragon tree, with its tree-like form and spiky foliage, looks especially good in a simply furnished, modern room, as do many of the palms, such as *Howea belmoreana*, the curly palm, and *Chamaedorea elegans*, the parlour palm. In older-style houses, plants with softer, more rounded and less aggressive outlines are often more appropriate.

Climbing plants, trained up supports, can also make excellent specimen plants, and their eventual height can be controlled. *Monstera deliciosa*, *Philodendron scandens* and *Epipremnum aureum* will all make large and statuesque specimens.

Specimen plants are best displayed where they do not have to compete for attention with elaborate furnishings: give them some space to themselves. Plain walls allow the foliage and outline of the plant to be properly appreciated; patterned wallpaper tends to create a confused effect unless the pattern is very subtle. Light-coloured walls display most plants well, although pale and variegated leaves may show up better against darker backgrounds.

Use lighting to complement the plant and give it a new dimension after dark. Completely different effects can be achieved with low-level and high-level spotlights, and backlighting can give dramatic results when used with boldly cut foliage. Glossy-leafed plants are given extra sparkle with artificial lighting, but the foliage must be kept clean and bright.

Specimen plants are normally placed on the floor for the most satisfactory effect, although smaller plants can be set on low tables. Choose a decorative pot that will balance the height and width of the plant so that it does not appear to be top-heavy.

PLANT GROUPS

Grouping a number of different plants together has several advantages. It enables you to create a satisfying display

Large architectural plants need large modern uncluttered spaces to show to greatest advantage (left). *This fine* Ficus benjamina *is well placed; it is the focus of attention at the entrance to the two minimally furnished and neutral-coloured rooms, and at the same time draws them together.*

A deep windowsill in a more traditional type of house (right) *calls for completely different treatment, with several plants grouped together. The grouping is not, however, random. The busy patterning of the pots and jugs is given unity by their colouring and is offset by the block of red of the cyclamen and the colour accent provided by the purple African violets.*

with contrasting or complementary foliage types; short-term flowering plants can add welcome colour and interest, since they can be removed or replaced when their blooms die back; plants with ungainly shapes or leggy stems can more easily be disguised. And a plain-leafed plant that would look dull planted alone in a pot makes its own valuable contribution when set among other foliage or flowering plants.

Not only do plant groups often look better, they tend to grow better too, for a humid microclimate that provides excellent growing conditions is created within the group. It is also easier to look after plants when they are together than when they are dotted around the room: you are less likely to overlook them, and watering is less of a chore. Plants that are grouped together should all enjoy roughly similar conditions of warmth and humidity. Light is less important because it is easier to accommodate varying needs by strategic positioning.

The easiest way to create a group is simply to bring together plants in their

HANDLE WITH CARE

Some indoor plants need to be treated with caution, especially if there are children or pets in the home. A number of species are poisonous if eaten, and others can cause skin irritation or scratches. Children are probably unlikely to eat many indoor plants, but brightly coloured berries are tempting. Cats, particularly, and some dogs may chew a wide variety of plants, though they rarely seem to come to any harm.

Unpleasant skin rashes can be experienced after handling a number of plants, such as *Primula obconica*, by people who are allergic to them, but you do not need to have an allergy to suffer from the spines of cacti – even the silky-seeming hairs of *Cephalocereus senilis*, old man cactus, hide vicious barbs. The tips of sharp, spiky leaves, such as those of some aloes, which may also bear spines, can also injure people. Be particularly careful not to position such plants at eye level, and remember that the eye level of children and animals is lower than your own.

COMMON POISONOUS PLANTS

Capsicum annuum	Ornamental chilli pepper: poisonous berries
Datura x *candida*	Angel's trumpet: all parts poisonous
Dieffenbachia spp.	Dumb cane: sap causes painful swelling of mouth and throat
Euphorbia pulcherrima	Poinsettia: poisonous sap
Nerium oleander	Oleander: all parts extremely poisonous
Solanum capsicastrum	False Jerusalem cherry: poisonous berries

individual pots, arranging them on a windowsill or table top. The pots should be similar: plain terracotta ones are usually more pleasing than a range of different-coloured or patterned pot containers.

Saucers are necessary for effective watering and to prevent furniture being spoiled by drips; if you do not want individual saucers, the plants can be placed together on a large tray. If the tray is half-filled with pebbles or gravel, you can easily increase the humidity around the group by pouring water into the tray to just below the top of the gravel. Or you can put the plants in a deeper, ornamental container that will cover the individual pots entirely (see page 24).

Ready-planted groups in decorative containers can be found in many shops and garden centres. Do not expect these plants to have a long life, however. They are planted closely in small containers for instant effect and are chosen more for their appearance than for their similarity of needs. They should be regarded as short-term decoration, although individual plants can usually be saved if the group is dismantled and replanted once it begins to look jaded.

CHOOSING PLANTS FOR GROUPS

PLANT GROUPS USUALLY WORK BEST if they have some sort of theme – colour, texture or shape – rather than being a haphazard mixture. Groups of plants from within the same family are often successful: cacti, for example, or air plants or spring bulbs. One advantage of this method is that all the plants will enjoy the same growing conditions. You may wish to compose your group entirely of the same species of plant, perhaps contrasting varieties and a range of flower or leaf colours, such as are found among *Saintpaulias*, African violets, or *Coleus blumei*, flame nettles. Or you may prefer the massed effect of three identical poinsettia plants or florists' chrysanthemums.

With foliage plants, using a range of different shades of green can be effective, and a strongly variegated form is emphasised by displaying it among plants with plain leaves. The colour of the variegation can be echoed by flowering plants, with the white markings of the weeping fig *Ficus benjamina* 'Starlight', for example, being picked up by a white chrysanthemum or white campanula. Colours in the plant group can also be used to reinforce the colour scheme of the room itself, or of a particular ornament or painting. Contrasts can be used effectively, with pale green walls forming a background for a group of dark green foliage plants enlivened with a brilliant scarlet poinsettia or a striking yellow kalanchoe, for instance.

Different-textured leaves also make interesting companions. Several species and varieties of peperomia and pilea have rippled or corrugated foliage, some with variegation and stripes as well. *Asparagus densiflorus* 'Sprengeri' makes a bright green haze to contrast with the sharply upright spikes of the pineapple, *Ananas comosus*, or the leathery strap-like leaves of a clivia.

The softly furry leaves of *Columnea gloriosa* and *Gynura* 'Purple Passion' just ask to be stroked, but spiky dracaenas and cordylines warn off all would-be touchers.

One of the most pleasing ways to arrange a group of plants with different forms is to create a triangular shape, with one or two tall plants and a number of lower, more spreading types below them. The apex of the triangle can be in the centre of the group or to one side of it. If all the plants are much the same height, it is sometimes a good idea to raise one of the pots to vary the level of the group.

FINDING THE RIGHT PLACE

The windowsill is probably the most popular place for any indoor plant, but some, especially plant groups, deserve a more prominent position. A large group, with one or two tall specimens, is ideal for a place on the floor near patio doors, where the plants help to link the house with the garden outside and will enjoy good light. Smaller groups may occupy a display table or take the central position on a dining table.

A fireplace is sometimes the focal point of a room, and in summer the hearth can house an attractive collection of indoor plants. A colour theme of reds, yellows and oranges, which mimic the flames, or

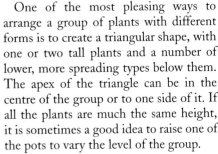

Plants with several different leaf shapes in shades of white, green and cream are harmoniously combined in this arrangement for a hall. The tall, pale orchid provides the focus of attention with the other, lower-growing plants grouped about its base.

cool blues, greens and white emphasising the summer season both work well. In summer the mantelpiece is also a good position for plants, particularly trailing varieties. A mirror behind the display doubles the effect, but extra care must be taken with the arrangement of the plants in this instance.

Always take the plants' needs, as well as their aesthetic effect, into account when choosing their position. A group of plants may well brighten up a dark corner, but they will not stay in good condition for long unless supplementary lighting is used.

Do not position plants where people walking past will continually brush against them; it is not only likely to damage the plants but it will also soon become irritating. And make sure that plants are safe and secure – not likely to topple over or drip on to expensive furniture, carpets or electrical equipment.

A rough-textured sunny wall and brilliantly coloured pots form a pleasing setting for this group of various cacti, a partridge-breasted aloe and a succulent, all of which look quite different but have similar growing requirements – an important consideration when you are grouping plants.

African violets, massed in a shallow china bowl and ranging from pale to deep mauve and pink to ruby red, are the ideal choice of plants here. They echo both the colours and the old-fashioned charm of the antique porcelain figurine, drawing the eye to it and at the same time providing a glowing pool of colour among the otherwise cool neutrals of the room.

CONTAINERS

PLANTS NEED TO TAKE UP WATER and nutrients in order to survive, and the substance from which they normally obtain these is soil or, in the case of indoor plants, compost. The compost for house plants needs to be in a container of some sort, the size and shape of which determines how well the plant will grow and what type of root system it will develop to support itself.

Most plants are obtained in a standard plant pot, generally made of plastic, although *Rhododendron simsii*, Indian azalea, is normally grown in an old-fashioned clay pot, which it prefers.

The size of the pot required varies according to the size of the plant. As plants grow, so they will need to be transferred into bigger pots, although

A blue textured wall emphasises the cool greens in this group of foliage plants; the use of several bowls of the same shape and colour gives it added cohesion.

some plants flower best when they are slightly pot-bound. Others with shallow root systems, such as many cacti, do well in half pots or shallow bowls.

In general, however, the height of the pot is equivalent to the width across its top, and the pot tapers to about two-thirds that width at the base. The size of the container is important for stability; top-heavy plants are prone to falling over, especially when the compost is allowed to dry out. This occurs more frequently with lightweight plastic pots, so it is better to plant tall or large, top-heavy plants in clay pots.

Clay pots have a central drainage hole in the base, while plastic pots usually have a series of slits around the circumference of the bottom of the pot. Some plastic pots are terracotta coloured, but green pots are also common, as are black and white ones. You may also see some bright red and yellow ones.

As far as the plant is concerned, the container must

● Hold sufficient compost from which the plant can absorb nutrients and water.

● Allow for drainage so that the compost does not become waterlogged.

● Be of sufficient size to allow the plant to develop a branching root system to balance the head.

● Give stability, allowing the plant to develop and maximise its exposure to light so that photosynthesis can take place.

A WELL-POTTED PLANT

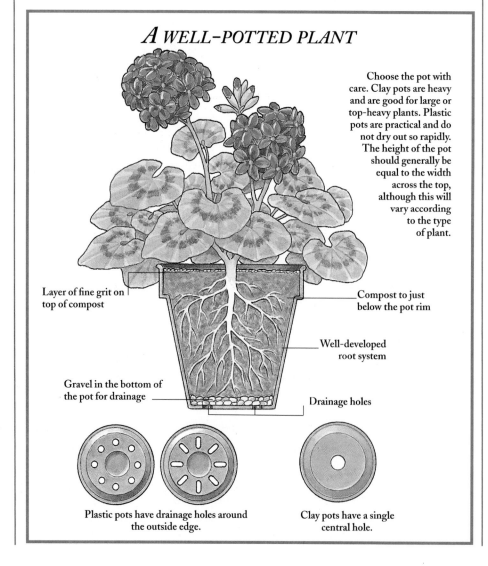

Choose the pot with care. Clay pots are heavy and are good for large or top-heavy plants. Plastic pots are practical and do not dry out so rapidly. The height of the pot should generally be equal to the width across the top, although this will vary according to the type of plant.

Layer of fine grit on top of compost

Compost to just below the pot rim

Well-developed root system

Gravel in the bottom of the pot for drainage

Drainage holes

Plastic pots have drainage holes around the outside edge.

Clay pots have a single central hole.

Secondary to these considerations are those of the plant's owner that the container should be attractive and should complement both the plant and its surroundings.

When you buy a new plant, check that the pot it is in is large enough to fulfil the plant's needs, and repot it if necessary (see page 202). In most instances, it is best to use a standard plant pot which can then be placed in a more decorative container, since many ornamental containers do not have sufficient provision for drainage for plants to be potted directly into them.

RINGING THE CHANGES

Indoor plants can be planted in a wide selection of attractive and unusual containers that will add greatly to their appeal. Single plants can easily be placed inside a decorative container, or cache pot, which is simply a more colourful or ornamental version of a standard flower pot. Such containers may be made of ceramic, glass, wood or wrought iron.

Most of these decorative covers do not have drainage holes, which means that they can double up as plant saucers to make watering easier; they also help to protect furniture. If the height of the pot allows, place a layer of gravel in the base of the decorative cover before putting the plant into it. This helps to increase the humidity around the plant, but make sure water does not collect around the roots, causing root rot.

Larger containers can be used to house plant groups. You can find plenty of purpose-made troughs in a range of styles, and other household items, such as the attractive washbowls that years ago were to be found in bedrooms everywhere, can be used. Brass, copper, china, wood, wicker are all suitable. Once you start looking, you will find many attractive items in which to house your plants. If you have any doubts about their being waterproof, it is best to line containers with polythene; even metal and china containers can be damaged by compost and moisture and may need protecting.

When setting a group of plants within a larger container, it is always advisable to keep the plants in their individual pots. This is so because of the drainage problems and because it is much easier to replace one or two plants when they have finished flowering or if they become sickly. If you want the plants to appear to be growing together, fill around and over the individual pots with peat to disguise them. Again, place a layer of gravel in the base of the container first.

Novelty containers are usually attractive for only a short time: copper kettles and watering cans, teapots, cups and saucers, even old boots, have been pressed into service with mixed results. As long as the container is large enough for plants to remain in their own pots, no harm is done – the container can be changed when when you tire of it. But beware of small, ready-planted novelty containers; it is usually impossible to extricate the plants, so the planting may have to be treated as a rather expensive, disposable short-term decoration.

Suit the pot to the plant. The shallow-rooting primulas' pink flowers are set off by the low green bowl, and the impact of the hyacinths is enhanced by ranging them in a long ceramic trough. A small terracotta pot has the right earthy feel – and good drainage – for the cactus; a sturdy aluminium bin makes a fine contrast to the yellow and orange flowers of Justicia pauciflora, *and a green glass pot is a perfect foil for the dainty* Primula obconica.

BOTTLE GARDENS AND TERRARIA

PLANTS GROWN IN A SEALED GLASS container create their own, separate, virtually self-sustaining environment. A well-planted bottle garden or terrarium is attractive and easy to look after, but both the container and the plants must be chosen with care.

A wide range of containers is suitable, including carboys, sweet jars, goldfish bowls, fish tanks and even large brandy glasses. Try to choose one with a stopper so that it can be sealed, although clear plastic or self-clinging food wrap can be stretched tightly over the top of some glasses and jars. Specially made bottles are available for planting, but they are sometimes tinted green, which interferes with the growth of the plants. Choose clear glass or the lightest tint you can find. Terraria are like miniature old-fashioned

greenhouses in appearance, are easier to plant and extremely attractive, although they tend to be expensive. Plastic versions are cheaper, but they may not have the same appeal as the glass ones.

A terrarium shaped like an old-fashioned greenhouse with open sides is easier to plant and water than a bottle. It is also easier to care for plants and replace them when they become too large.

PLANTS FOR THE BOTTLE GARDEN

Bottle gardens and terraria are ideal for delicate plants that like high humidity and will thrive away from the draughts and dry air of open rooms. The plants need to be slow-growing or your container will soon be swamped. Flowering plants should, on the whole, be avoided, since dead flowers may be difficult to remove and will soon rot.

Buy small specimens and check them carefully for any signs of pests or diseases before planting; remove any damaged stems or foliage cleanly.

Suitable plants include:
Adiantum raddianum and *A. hispidulum*, maidenhair ferns
Begonia bowerii, miniature eyelash begonia
Cryptanthus spp., earth stars
Ficus pumila minima, miniature creeping fig
Fittonia verschaffeltii and *F. v. argyroneura*, painted and silver net leaf;
Pellaea rotundifolia, button fern
Peperomia caperata 'Little Fantasy', emerald ripple peperomia;
Pilea nummularifolia, creeping Charlie
Selaginella kraussiana and *S. martensii*, creeping club mosses.

PLANTING A BOTTLE GARDEN

1 Use a funnel of heavy paper or cardboard to pour the gravel, charcoal and peat-based compost into a narrow-necked bottle.

2 'Landscape' the soil to form a slight slope; then, with a teaspoon tied securely to a cane, scoop out a hole for the first plant in the place you have planned for it.

3 Holding the plant carefully between two canes, manoeuvre it through the neck of the bottle and into the hole you have just made in the compost.

4 Firm the soil around the plant's roots by gently pressing it down with a cotton reel tied to a cane. Repeat the process until all the plants are in their chosen positions.

Once the planting is complete and the plants have been watered, set the bottle close to a window where it will receive bright light but no direct sun.

PLANTING

First, wash out the container with water and detergent; then fill it with water that contains some bleach or disinfectant to kill off any fungus spores and rinse it thoroughly. Make sure that the inside of the container is completely dry before planting it.

Start by pouring in gravel until there is a layer about 2.5cm/1in deep in the bottom. (With a narrow-necked bottle, use heavy paper or cardboard rolled into a funnel to pour in the gravel.) Add a thin layer of charcoal pieces to keep the soil sweet, then add 5–8cm/2–3in of peat-based compost. Landscape this to produce a slight slope for added interest.

You will find it much easier to plant up the bottle if the opening is large enough for your hand to pass through. For planting up narrow-necked bottles, you will either have to buy special tools or improvise by tying a fork, a teaspoon and a cotton reel to long canes to use as planting and firming tools.

Plan the arrangement of the plants before you start to plant them. Take into account whether the garden will be viewed from one side only or all around. Remove the plants from their pots and tease out the roots; wash off some of the soil and trim the roots if necessary. Scoop a hole in the compost with the teaspoon, insert the plant by holding it between two canes, and firm it gently into place with the cotton reel.

AFTERCARE

When planting is finished, cover the surface of the compost with a thin layer of fine sand. Trickle some water down the sides of the bottle to wash any soil off the glass and moisten the compost; lightly mist spray the plants in a terrarium. Leave the container open for a few hours after planting, then replace the stopper; if there is no stopper, stretch some self-clinging plastic film or food wrap over the mouth of the container or close the door of a terrarium.

If the inside of the glass mists over and will not clear, ventilate the container for a short while. Changes in temperature will bring about temporary condensation, but once the garden has settled down, neither watering nor regular ventilation should be necessary. Keep the bottle garden or terrarium in a position where it receives good bright light but not direct sunlight.

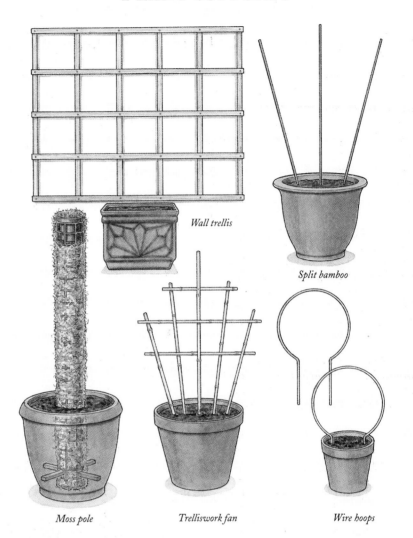

PLANT SUPPORTS

Wall trellis

Split bamboo

Moss pole

Trelliswork fan

Wire hoops

Many plants need supports to keep them shapely, to hold up flowering stems, or because they are climbers. Any type of support should be as unobtrusive as possible.

Climbers that produce aerial roots, such as *Monstera deliciosa*, the Swiss cheese plant, will grow well around a moss pole or a synthetic substitute. To encourage the roots to grow into the moss, the pole should be kept moist by frequent misting or by watering it through a tiny thumb pot set in the top of the moss. A deep container filled with soil-based potting mix is necessary to provide adequate stability for a tall pole.

Jasmine and other climbers look attractive trained around wire, plastic or cane hoops. This keeps the plant neat and encourages flowering by bending the shoots down and slowing the flow of the sap. Two hoops set at right angles will form a plant ball.

Trelliswork, of wood, wire or plastic, can take the form of a fan inserted into a pot or can be attached permanently to a wall to support scrambling plants. A free-standing trellis covered with a vigorous climber makes an attractive room divider.

Split bamboo stakes are useful as a temporary support or for training a wayward stem. Green stakes are the least conspicuous; cut them so they do not show above the plant. Use soft twine or plant ties to attach stems gently to their supports; a figure-eight loop prevents stem damage.

$\mathcal{T}$HE PLANT DIRECTORY

$\mathcal{T}$HE PLANT DIRECTORY IS DIVIDED INTO TWO SECTIONS. The first part deals in depth with the most popular indoor plants, and the second part covers some of the less common subjects. All the plants in the main directory are illustrated with specially taken photographs. In the Secondary Plant List, in order to cover the maximum number of plants, only some are illustrated. However, the same comprehensive information is given for the plants in both sections.

Two pages from the main directory are shown below. They contain most of the elements that appear in all the entries, and to help you use the information to the full, these elements are clarified in the accompanying notes.

Botanical name Plants are listed alphabetically by their botanical name.

Family name Knowing what family a plant belongs to helps you understand its requirements and allows you to discover other indoor plants to which it may be related.

Common name This is the name by which the plant is most popularly known.

FACT FILE
Origin Tells you the geographical area in which the plant originated.
Height Gives the height most average specimens, kept in good growing conditions, are likely to reach in the home within two or three years. The ultimate height will, of course, be determined by the size of container, level of care and any pruning carried out, so this is only a rough guide.
Compost Indicates whether the plant prefers a soil-based or peat-based (soil-less) compost. Where peat-based compost is specified, the new peat-substitute composts may also be used.
Repotting Explains the best time of year to move the plant into a larger container, and gives an idea of how often this should be done. Where you are advised to repot 'as necessary' this means when the roots are showing through the base of the pot, or a plant is overcrowded in its container.
Propagation Gives the main methods of increasing the plant in the home. Details are given where a method is difficult for the home gardener, or where specific requirements such as a heated propagator are necessary.
Keeping plants Requirements such as pruning and training, pinching out growing tips and deadheading are mentioned here, as well as additional information about standing the plant outdoors during the summer. An estimate of the plant's probable lifespan is also given where this is relevant.

BELOPERONE GUTTATA (SYN. *JUSTICIA BRANDEGEANA*)
Acanthaceae

$\mathcal{S}$HRIMP PLANT

The reddish brown bracts of this plant, resembling overlapping roof shingles, appear almost all year round, while the white flowers that emerge at the end of the bracts are insignificant and short-lived. The leaves are 2.5–8cm/1–3in long, light green, oval and pointed.

Disregard people who tell you to throw beloperone away after flowering: the plant is easy to care for and can survive for many years, reaching 90cm/3ft in height and spread. It is best to pinch out the stem tips regularly to make the plant bushier, and annual pruning will renew its vigour. If you do not prune, the plant will almost certainly be larger and will produce colourful bracts, but the relatively weak branches will probably require staking.

If bracts do not develop fully, prune the plant in midwinter, just as the show of bracts ends.

Whiteflies, mealybugs, scale insects and aphids may attack the plant in hot weather; spray with a suitable insecticide.

Loss of leaves may indicate that the plant is rootbound; annual potting should alleviate this.

Overwatering can encourage the leaves to turn yellow. Do not water again until the soil has dried out completely.

FACT FILE
ORIGIN Mexico.
HEIGHT To 90cm/3ft.
COMPOST Soil-based.
REPOTTING Repot every spring, and cut stems back by about half.
PROPAGATION Take 8-cm/3-in tip cuttings in spring; use the prunings, but remove the bracts, which will rot if they are left.
KEEPING PLANTS The arching stems and hanging flower heads make this a good plant for a hanging basket.

PLANT CARE
A bright place, with direct sunlight for short periods during spring and summer will help to produce colourful bracts. ● Minimum winter temperature of 16°C/60°F; ideally 22°C/72°F at other times. ● Keep fairly dry during winter, and moist, not wet, at other times. ● Feed every 2 weeks in summer with a weak solution of fertiliser.

BILLBERGIA NUTANS
Bromeliaceae

$\mathcal{Q}$UEEN'S TEARS

One of the prettiest of bromeliads, this is also one of the easiest to grow. Its tough, strap-like, tooth-edged, olive green leaves, which can be as much as 40cm/16in long and 13mm/^{1}/2in wide, arch over in an attractively random fashion. The pendant flowers, which usually appear in late spring, are tinged with blue, yellow, pink and green and are encased in pink bracts. Nectar formed within the small flowers sometimes drops out when the plant is touched or moved, giving it its common name; it is also called the friendship plant.

A much underrated, easy-care plant, this billbergia is seen to best effect when grown at eye-level, as in a hanging container, which will show off the pendulous bracts to full advantage. While most plants in elevated positions may suffer as a result of dry conditions, billbergias are much more tolerant, and small hanging pots can be plunged into water occasionally to give them a good soak.

FACT FILE
ORIGIN Argentina, Brazil, Uruguay.
HEIGHT To 40cm/16in in flower.
COMPOST Proprietary bromeliad or orchid potting compost, or equal parts of soil-based compost and peat or leaf mould.
REPOTTING In spring, move to a pot up to 13cm/5in in diameter.
PROPAGATION Detach offsets when they are half the size of the parent plant. Let the cut surface dry for a day or so before potting up.
KEEPING PLANTS Empty the water reservoir in the centre of the rosette once a month and refill with fresh water.

PLANT CARE
Keep in good light but out of direct sunlight to maintain good leaf colour and promote flowering. ● Normal room temperature, but the plant will tolerate temperatures as low as 2°–4°C/36°–40°F for a short while. ● Water moderately all year round, with rainwater or cool boiled water. ● Apply weak liquid fertiliser every 2 weeks both to the soil and as a foliar spray.

A month or two outdoors in a shady position during summer greatly improves the leaf colour and usually encourages flowering.

The olive green leaves may become reddish if the plant is placed in direct sunlight.

Illustration A typical plant of the size and form you are likely to find available for sale in garden centres and nurseries is shown.

Introduction This provides a full description of the plant's main features and also mentions some of the varieties and allied species that may be available.

Second illustration On full-page entries, a detail is shown of an interesting feature of the plant, or else another variety or related species is pictured.

Annotation Tips on cultivation or information about pests and diseases that may affect the plant are given in the annotation around the main illustration.

BOUGAINVILLEA GLABRA
Nyctaginaceae

PAPER FLOWER

A true tropical exotic, in its natural environment this showy climber produces such dense and vivid colour on 4.5-m/15-ft trailing stems that it outshines almost everything else in the vicinity. Its strong twining branches, which carry narrow, smooth, 8-cm/3-in-long leaves, have vicious barbs. This drawback is, however, more than compensated for when the colourful papery bracts, some 4cm/1½in long, appear at the beginning of summer.

Bougainvillea can be most frustrating to grow as an indoor plant, for it is reluctant to flower in limited light. Fine indoor specimens can, however, be grown beside large windows and in conservatories or sunrooms. Although a climber, this plant can be trained to keep it bushy indoors – wire hoops have become popular supports – and there are some dwarf types that do not require special training.

Bougainvillea glabra, with purple-pink bracts in summer and autumn, is the species most easily obtained. This, and the less vigorous *B. x buttiana*, have given rise to dozens of hybrids with a range of highly coloured bracts, many being smaller than the species.

FACT FILE

ORIGIN Brazil.

HEIGHT To 4.5m/15ft.

COMPOST Soil-based.

REPOTTING When new growth appears in spring, move the plant into a pot one size larger. When a pot size of 20cm/8in is reached, simply top-dress it.

PROPAGATION Not easy. Take 8–10-cm/3–4-in stem cuttings in late spring or early summer; keep in a heated propagator.

KEEPING PLANTS If the plant becomes straggly, prune it lightly in autumn. Flowering is better if new growth is wound around established stems and tied in.

PLANT CARE

Bougainvillea needs 4 hours of direct sunlight daily. Place in a sunny window close to the glass for maximum light, but do not allow it to bake in hot weather. ● Minimum winter temperature of 10°C/50°F. Set outdoors in summer if possible. ● Water well during active growth, but the plant must not stand in water; do not water in winter until new growth appears. ● Apply a high-potash feed every 2 weeks in spring and summer.

ALSO RECOMMENDED

Bougainvillea glabra 'Alexandra' is rose pink and one of the most free-flowering. 'Variegata' has leaves bordered with cream. *B. x buttiana* hybrids 'Killie Campbell', 'Orange King', and 'Golden Glow' ('Hawaiian Gold') are shades of gold and orange; 'Jamaica Red' is crimson; 'Surprise' ('Mary Palmer') is rose purple or white or a combination of the two.

Bougainvillea x buttiana 'Amethyst', seen close up here, has bracts with a papery quality that enclose its insignificant flowers.

This is a tough plant that does not suffer greatly from pests. But aphids, red spider mites and mealybugs may attack it, so check often for signs of infestation.

Water left on the leaves or papery bracts may cause scorching when the plant is in full sun.

Yellowing of the leaves is caused by too much moisture at the roots. Make sure that the compost has good drainage.

PLANT CARE
The information is always given in the following order.

Light This tells you whether a plant needs bright, moderately bright or shaded conditions. 'Direct sun' or 'full sun' means a plant can be exposed to sunlight all day, all year round. 'Some direct sun' means it benefits from several hours of sun a day but does not require day-long exposure. 'No direct sun' means that damage is likely to occur to leaves or flowers if sunlight is allowed to fall on the plant, particularly through glass. 'Filtered' or 'diffuse' light means sunlight should be filtered by a blind or lightweight curtain.

Temperature Where plants are not very specific in their temperature requirements, 'average' or 'normal' room temperature is advised. This means ordinary, comfortable living conditions both winter and summer – usually about 18°–21°C/65°–70°F. Minimum recommended temperature is sometimes given; this is the lowest temperature possible for healthy growth and development, but plants will not necessarily be damaged by an occasional dip below this point.

Watering The advice to water the plant freely, moderately or sparingly is self-explanatory. Keeping the compost moist means that it should be neither saturated nor allowed to dry out so that it shrinks away from the sides of the pot.

Feeding Explains the type of fertiliser to use and when and how often it should be applied.

Other points Any other special needs such as increasing the level of humidity are noted here.

ALSO RECOMMENDED
This gives suggestions for additional related plants you might consider growing.

ABUTILON PICTUM 'THOMPSONII'
Malvaceae

$\mathcal{S}$POTTED FLOWERING MAPLE

Originating as it does in tropical to warm temperate areas, particularly South America, where it grows in lightly wooded terrain, this is a tender plant related to the mallows. The genus is made up of about 150 shrubs, perennials and annuals, which are grown for their bell-shaped, drooping flowers and maple-like leaves on long stalks.

This form has attractive green and yellow mottled leaves 8–13cm/3–5in long and with three to five lobes. Its red- and orange-veined flowers are 5–8cm/2–3in long and open from spring to autumn. In the wild, the plant will grow into a large shrub, but as an indoor pot plant, it is best kept to 60cm–1.2m/2–4ft. Abutilons are long-lasting, making them useful as semi-permanent feature plants. And since they need plenty of direct sunlight they do particularly well in front of a window.

All abutilons respond well to pruning, and you should not be afraid to use the secateurs when a plant grows beyond its allocated space. Cut back spindly growth in early spring; remove any thin shoots that crowd the centre of the plant and reduce others by a third.

FACT FILE

ORIGIN Brazil.

HEIGHT To 2.1–3m/7–10ft.

COMPOST Soil-based.

REPOTTING Move plants into a pot one size larger each spring, until a 23-cm/9-in pot is reached. Top-dress large plants annually.

PROPAGATION Take 10-cm/4-in tip cuttings in spring and summer and root in equal parts of sand and peat at a temperature of 15°–18°C/59°–65°F.

KEEPING PLANTS Deadhead regularly during the summer. Pinch out growing tips occasionally to maintain bushy growth.

PLANT CARE

Direct sunlight, which will enhance the leaf variegation. ● Winter temperature of 7°–13°C/45°–55°F; the plant may lose some or all of its leaves during this dormant period. ● Little water in winter; water freely in summer. ● Apply a weak liquid fertiliser every 2 weeks from early spring to late summer. ● Large plants can be top-heavy, so ensure that containers are large enough to prevent them falling over.

ALSO RECOMMENDED

Abutilon x *hybridum* is the name given to a group of hybrids that are generally available from garden centres and shops. Look for *A.* x *h.* 'Savitzii', with the palest of green leaves, and 'Cannington Red', with golden yellow foliage and striking rose red blooms. 'Pink Lady' has bright pink flowers with deeper pink veins and 'Kentish Belle' bears vibrant orange flowers.

Abutilon x hybridum *'Red Belle' will grow into a large free-flowering shrub with deep red flowers up to 5cm/2in long that look like Chinese lanterns.*

Flowers appear between the leafstalk and the stem, so buy bushy plants with plenty of side shoots.

Check the leaves regularly for signs of infestation by aphids, whiteflies, red spider mites and cyclamen mites.

Give the plant as much direct sunlight as possible, or leaf and flower colour will be dull.

Mealybugs and root mealybugs both attack abutilons. Check the plant carefully for these pests.

ACALYPHA HISPIDA
Euphorbiaceae

*R*ED-HOT CAT'S TAIL

Guaranteed to be a conversation piece, this exotic plant is one of a few species in the genus to produce conspicuous tail-like flowers. The tiny, bright red blooms, which emerge from the leaf axils usually in late summer and autumn, can reach 30–46cm/12–18in in length. They droop in tassels, without petals and resemble lengths of chenille, hence the plant's other common name of chenille plant. The bright green, slightly hairy, pointed oval leaves are 13–20cm/5–8in long and 8cm/3in wide. *Acalypha hispida* 'Alba' is an attractive white-flowered form.

The plant will form a shrub 1.8m/6ft tall if allowed to grow unchecked. Even if it is kept to just half this size, you should still give it plenty of space. Acalyphas require a high level of humidity.

Dull green leaves with tiny brown spots are the first signs of red spider mites. Keep the atmosphere moist to discourage the pest.

Watch out for mealybug infestation. If you spot the cotton-like coating, pick off the bugs and spray the nest areas with insecticide.

Flowers may appear all year round given the right conditions.

FACT FILE

ORIGIN Java, Papua New Guinea.

HEIGHT To 1.8m/6ft.

COMPOST Soil-based.

REPOTTING Cut back in early spring to 25cm/10in above a leaf and repot into a pot one size larger.

PROPAGATION Take 8–10-cm/3–4-in stem cuttings in spring and establish them in equal parts of sand and peat at 24°C/75°F.

KEEPING PLANTS Acalypha is naturally bushy, so there is no need to pinch out growing tips. Prune the plant annually or renew it from cuttings and discard the old one. Plants are not worth keeping longer than 2 years.

PLANT CARE

Bright filtered sunlight. ● Minimum temperature of 15°C/59°F in winter with, ideally, 21°C/70°F in the growing season. ● Plenty of water in summer; less in winter. ● Stand the pot on a tray of damp pebbles and mist the foliage regularly, except when the plant is in flower. ● Apply a weak liquid fertiliser every 2 weeks from early spring to late summer.

ACALYPHA WILKESIANA
Euphorbiaceae

*C*OPPER LEAF

This plant is grown chiefly for its highly coloured leaves which vary enormously and come in tints of coppery green, mottled and streaked with purple, red and copper, giving it its best-known common name. Other names include match-me-if-you-can, beefsteak plant, fire dragon plant and Jacob's coat. Varieties include 'Can Can', with mainly magenta, mauve and cream leaves, and 'Marginata', with heart-shaped olive green leaves tinged with bronze and edged with carmine.

Like *Acalypha hispida*, this plant can reach 1.8m/6ft. The leaves are about 13cm/5in long and 5cm/2in wide.

FACT FILE

ORIGIN Java, Papua New Guinea.

HEIGHT To 1.8m/6ft.

COMPOST Soil-based.

REPOTTING In late spring, or at any other time if growth has been rapid, move plants into pots one size larger when roots fill the pots.

PROPAGATION In early spring plant 8–10-cm/3–4-in tip or stem cuttings in equal parts of sand and peat. Keep at 24°C/75°F.

KEEPING PLANTS Do not pinch out the growing tips, since this plant is naturally bushy. Discard untidy plants after 2 seasons.

PLANT CARE

Bright filtered light to retain leaf colour. ● Minimum winter temperature of 16°C/60°F; up to 27°C/80°F in summer. ● Plenty of water at all times, particularly in summer when the soil dries out more quickly. ● High humidity: stand the plant on a tray of damp pebbles and mist the foliage regularly. ● Apply a standard liquid fertiliser every 2 weeks during the active growing period.

Check for mealybugs and red spider mites, both of which attack acalyphas.

Reduce the plant's size by half each spring to encourage plenty of new stems and highly coloured leaves.

Keep the compost moist at all times, but plants will wilt if the compost becomes sodden.

ACHIMENES
Gesneriaceae

*C*UPID'S BOWER

There are more than 50 hybrid varieties of achimenes, which are more frequently grown than the species. They are among the most colourful and floriferous pot plants, producing abundant white, pink, purple, blue or yellow flowers throughout the summer. These appear on short stalks from the leaf axils and comprise a narrow tube flaring out into five broad lobes. Each flower lasts only a few days, but the flowering period is extensive. Leaves are generally rich to dark green, slightly hairy, heart-shaped and with toothed edges. Because achimenes have weak stems, they are ideal for a hanging basket, where they can trail.

All achimenes grow from small caterpillar-like rhizomes, which can be started into growth by dipping them in hot water before planting them – hence the unromantic common name of hot-water plant.

Direct sunlight over a long period may scorch the tender leaves, causing small brown spots to appear.

Aphids occasionally attack the fleshy growth at the growing tips.

Dormant tubers will survive the winter in any cool, dry place, but exposure to frost will kill them.

Do not water plants during the dormant period – this will start them into growth at the wrong time.

FACT FILE

ORIGIN Guatemala; hybrids.

HEIGHT To 30cm/12in.

COMPOST Peat- or soil-based.

REPOTTING In early spring set 3–4 tubers horizontally, 13mm/$\frac{1}{2}$in below the surface of the compost in a 10-cm/4-in pot at a minimum of 10°C/50°F.

PROPAGATION Divide tubers when repotting or take 8-cm/3-in tip cuttings in early summer.

KEEPING PLANTS If allowed to dry out, even briefly, the plant will return to dormancy. But do not let flowering plants stand in water or the root system will quickly start to rot.

PLANT CARE

Bright indirect sunlight. ● An average temperature of 18°C/65°F in the growing season; the plants will flag above 27°C/80°F. ● Water freely, particularly when the plant is in flower. ● Apply a high-potash liquid feed every 2 weeks in the flowering season.

ADIANTUM RADDIANUM
Adiantaceae

*D*ELTA MAIDENHAIR FERN

Taken together, the four commonly grown species of adiantums are the most popular of all pot-grown ferns, with *Adiantum raddianum* the most widely grown. They are called maidenhair ferns because the leafstalks are shiny, thin and black, much like human hair.

The plants grow from rhizomes, which spread horizontally and quickly just beneath the surface of the soil. The fronds are some 20–38cm/8–15in long and are divided into many small triangular leaflets, known more correctly as pinnae. Adiantums are very long-lasting and will reach a height of 30–38cm/12–15in and a width of 60cm/2ft or even larger.

FACT FILE

ORIGIN Tropical America.

HEIGHT To 38cm/15in.

COMPOST Open, peaty mixture.

REPOTTING Repot annually in spring. Pack the compost lightly; good drainage is essential.

PROPAGATION In spring, divide the clump, leaving a section of rhizome attached to each piece; pot up separately.

KEEPING PLANTS As needed to keep plants moist in summer and once a week in winter, submerge the pot in water for 10 minutes, then drain.

PLANT CARE

No direct sunlight; adiantums do well in bathrooms and shaded parts of a conservatory or sunroom. ● Winter temperature of 10°C/50°F, with a maximum in summer of 24°C/75°F. ● The roots must be kept moist at all times. ● To improve humidity, stand the pot on a tray of damp pebbles and mist the foliage twice a day. ● Apply a weak liquid fertiliser every 2 weeks from early spring to late summer.

If the fronds dry up, cut them off and spray the plant with water daily until new shoots appear.

Keep plants out of draughts and away from radiators.

Cut the plant right back if the leaflets drop off; maintain watering and humidity to encourage new growth.

Scale insects and mealybugs may attack this plant; check the fronds regularly for signs of infestation.

AECHMEA FASCIATA (SYN. *BILLBERGIA RHODOCYANEA*)
Bromeliaceae

Urn Plant

The natural home of this plant is near the floor of the rain forest, where water from the tree canopy drips on to the tough, leathery, strap-shaped leaves. These often grow to 30cm/12in in length and they combine in the centre of the plant to form a natural, water-retaining vase shape, from which the common name of silver vase plant is derived.

In mature plants 3–4 years old, a central, pointed, pink flower stalk some 15cm/6in long emerges from the centre of the leaves. The top of the stem opens into many bracts, and in summer the actual flowers, which are small and blue, bloom on short stalks that arise between the bracts. They last for up to six weeks, after which the inflorescence gradually fades and shrivels and the rosette dies. At the same time, the plant produces two or three smaller spikes, or rosettes, which can be detached and potted on as separate plants.

Aechmea cylindrata *produces a tall spike of flowers, enclosed in decorative bracts, that rises high above the rosette of leaves.*

FACT FILE

ORIGIN Brazil.

HEIGHT To 50cm/20in.

COMPOST Equal parts peat and peat-based compost, with a little fresh sphagnum moss; free drainage is essential.

REPOTTING Repot every other year.

PROPAGATION Once the offsets at the base of the plant have grown to a viable size, after 4–6 months, remove them in spring and pot them on into rich, barely moist compost. Or cut out the old rosette, allowing the new offshoots to develop instead.

KEEPING PLANTS Despite its exotic appearance, this plant is easy to care for. Simply ensure that neither the water well nor the compost dry out.

PLANT CARE

A tolerant plant, taking either direct or subdued sunlight. ● Minimum winter temperature of 13°C/55°F with, ideally, 27°C/80°F in the growing season. ● Water twice a week with rainwater if possible, keeping 2.5cm/1in depth of water in the well at all times. ● Do not feed this plant in the conventional way; instead, mist the leaves with weak liquid fertiliser occasionally in the spring and summer.

ALSO RECOMMENDED

Aechmea fasciata 'Purpurea' has striking maroon leaves and silver markings; the grey-green leaves of 'Variegata' are striped along their length with cream-yellow.

If flowers, or even the bract spikes, fail to appear, move the plant to a position receiving more light.

This plant may be attacked by aphids, scale insects and mealybugs; check regularly for signs of infestation.

Overwatering or too low a temperature will cause the flower stem to rot; empty the rosette occasionally and allow the compost to dry out.

If the leaves develop brown tips and then shrivel, it is an indication that the plant is too hot and dry; increase watering.

AEONIUM ARBOREUM 'ATROPURPUREUM'
Crassulaceae

*P*URPLE TREE AEONIUM

This plant has dark bronze, spoon-shaped leaves some 5–8cm/2–3in long, but the species plant has leaves of a fresh green colour and the variety 'Schwartzkopf' has almost black leaves. All form strong woody stems, which branch out freely and from which rosettes develop. The rosettes regularly shed some of the lower leaves, leaving the stems scarred at the points where the leaves were attached.

Panicles of small, bright yellow star-shaped flowers form from the centres of the rosettes at the ends of the branches on mature four- to five-year-old plants. These blooms appear from winter through to spring, but once a rosette has flowered, it dies and must be cut out. Aeoniums require a lot of sunshine and fairly dry growing conditions.

FACT FILE

ORIGIN Spain, Portugal, Morocco, Sicily, Sardinia.

HEIGHT To 90cm/3ft.

COMPOST Two parts soil-based to one part coarse sand or perlite.

REPOTTING Move into a pot one size larger every spring. Newly potted plants should be firmly pressed into the potting mixture.

PROPAGATION Sow seed, or take leaf or stem cuttings in spring or summer.

KEEPING PLANTS Use terracotta rather than plastic pots, since mature plants tend to become top-heavy and fall over; stake tall plants.

PLANT CARE

Full sunlight all year. ● Minimum winter temperature of 10°C/50°F; temperatures up to 24°C/75°F at other times. ● Keep the compost moist during the growing period, on the dry side at other times; leaves will shrivel if it gets too dry. ● Apply a weak liquid fertiliser every 2 weeks during the growing period. ● Let the plant rest in winter.

As the plant grows taller, it may require staking.

Overwatering encourages soft, untypical growth, which is likely to droop.

Too little light will result in sparse rosettes and elongated, prematurely falling leaves.

AESCHYNANTHUS LOBBIANUS
Gesneriaceae

*L*IPSTICK VINE

This epiphytic plant is closely related to, and resembles, columneas. It is ideal for use in a hanging basket, since its habit is to sprawl and a simple flower pot cannot always confine it adequately.

The plant originates in tropical rain forests, where it thrives in the high humidity. In the wild its woody stems follow the line of the often moss-covered tree branches, while the roots grow down into any suitable material. The pale green, fleshy, elliptical leaves are up to 5cm/2in wide and 10cm/4in long. During the spring and summer, clusters of 6 to 20 flowers bloom on, or very near, the tips of the stems, which can extend to 60–90cm/2–3ft. The long, blood-red flowers with yellowish throats, arise from deep purple 'lipstick cases'.

Aeschynanthus speciosus, the basket plant, has yellow-orange flowers, marked with red; *A. marmoratus* is not grown for its flowers, which are greenish yellow, but for its attractive foliage – mottled shiny and dark green on the upper surface, and flushed with red below.

Aphids may attack the plant; check it regularly for signs of infestation.

If the stems are pinned to the compost they often branch and make side shoots. The more growing tips, the more flowers.

FACT FILE

ORIGIN Malaysia, Borneo, Java.

HEIGHT To 60cm/2ft.

COMPOST Coarse sphagnum moss, or a mixture of equal parts coarse peat, perlite and leaf mould.

REPOTTING When the roots fill the pot, move the plant into a pot one size larger, or cut it back by one-third and repot it in the same pot.

PROPAGATION Take 10–15-cm/4–6-in tip cuttings in summer.

KEEPING PLANTS If kept in humid conditions, this plant does not have a rest period and so will require watering and attention all year round.

PLANT CARE

Bright light, with up to 2–3 hours of direct sunlight in winter; filtered light in summer. ● Normal room temperature. ● Plenty of water when the plant is in flower, less at other times. ● Raise the level of humidity by standing the pot on a tray of damp pebbles and misting the foliage daily. ● Apply a weak liquid fertiliser at every watering.

AGAVE AMERICANA
Agavaceae

CENTURY PLANT

A group of succulent plants grown for their 'architectural' appeal, agaves are often referred to as century plants as a result of the mistaken belief that flowers appear only once every 100 years. In reality, plants will flower when they reach about 10 years of age; indoors, this is unlikely. This species grows so big that it can be used as a house plant only when young – the leaves of a fully grown specimen may exceed 1.8m/6ft.

The plant forms a stemless open rosette of blue-grey leaves with needle-sharp points on the tips, so it must be kept out of the way of passers-by and children, and gloves should be worn when inspecting it. In spite of these drawbacks, this agave is magnificent when grown as a specimen. Several variegated forms are available.

FACT FILE

ORIGIN Mexico.

HEIGHT Rosette to 1.8m/6ft and flower spike to 7.5m/25ft outdoors.

COMPOST Soil-based, with coarse sand or perlite added for drainage.

REPOTTING In spring, move into a pot one size larger; top-dress plants that have reached maximum convenient pot size.

PROPAGATION Detach offsets 8–10cm/3–4in long from the base of the plant. Leave them to dry for a day or two before potting them up.

KEEPING PLANTS In good conditions plants will last for many years. If they flower, the rosette will die.

PLANT CARE

A sunny position at all times. ● Minimum winter temperature of 10°C/50°F; normal room temperature at other times. ● Allow the top two-thirds of the compost to dry out before watering. ● Apply a weak liquid fertiliser every 2 weeks from early spring to late summer.

Old leaves around the base eventually dry up and can be pulled off, often leaving scars on the woody stem.

During the summer, place agaves outdoors in a sunny place.

Mealybugs may leave their telltale signs – tufts of white, waxy wool – on the leaves; root mealybugs may also infest the plant's roots, which will check its growth.

AGLAONEMA 'SILVER QUEEN'
Araceae

PAINTED DROP TONGUE

Although often sold as *Aglaonema crispum* and called Chinese evergreen, this is a hybrid whose parent plants came originally from the subtropical forests of Southeast Asia, and an important quality of most aglaonemas is their ability to thrive in poor light.

A. 'Silver Queen' is a compact, low-growing plant, with leaves some 13–15cm/5–6in long, on short stems produced at soil level. It gains its name from the leaves, which are green only at the margins and along the main veins, the rest of the leaf being silvery white and cream. As the plant ages, it loses some of the lower leaves and develops a short, trunk-like stem. Small, insignificant, petal-less flowers appear in summer or autumn and are carried on a short stem at the top of which is a 5-cm/2-in-long arum-like spathe. Sometimes small, orange poisonous berries are formed.

This plant likes warmth; a cold draught will soon damage the leaves.

Mealybugs and root mealybugs may attack aglaonemas.

Leaf spot disease may infect the plant, and botrytis fungus may appear if conditions are too cool.

FACT FILE

ORIGIN Southeast Asia.

HEIGHT To 90cm/3ft.

COMPOST Open, peaty mixture.

REPOTTING Repot in spring when necessary. Do not use a pot that is too large, since this plant grows best when its roots are confined.

PROPAGATION In spring, divide the root clump; take tip cuttings or use sections of the old plant's stem. Young plants need high humidity.

KEEPING PLANTS Do not grow this plant where there are children or pets; the sap and berries are poisonous.

PLANT CARE

Subdued light. ● Minimum winter temperature of 15°C/59°F with normal room temperature at other times. ● Water freely in summer; in winter keep the compost just moist. ● Apply a weak liquid fertiliser with every watering from early spring to late summer.

ALLAMANDA CATHARTICA
Apocynaceae

*G*OLDEN TRUMPET

Although this plant is often referred to as the golden trumpet 'vine' – it is after all a climber – its habit when grown in a pot is to sprawl or lean. Its demand for warmth, a humid atmosphere and plenty of sun means that it is a plant for the sunroom or conservatory, although it can be used in other rooms, then moved on when it becomes too large. If grown in large containers, climbing allamandas can be trained on a trellis or wire support to cover a wall; they are most attractive when encouraged to grow up into the roof space.

   Allamandas are spectacular when in flower and were it not for their rather weak constitution would undoubtedly be seen more often. The glossy, dark green, oval leaves are 10–15cm/4–6in long and are borne on long stems. The flaring, buttercup-yellow trumpet blooms of *Allamanda cathartica* appear throughout summer and autumn and can be as much as 10cm/4in wide.

Leaves yellow and drop naturally. Prune any naked stems by half to encourage new leaf buds to break.

Check for mealybugs and scale insects, both of which attack this plant.

In damp conditions, collar rot fungus can attack the soft, fleshy stem. Scatter horticultural grit on the compost around the stem to help prevent it.

Honeydew, the sticky dark secretion from aphids, can be unsightly. If seen, wash the leaves with slightly soapy water.

FACT FILE

ORIGIN Guyana, Brazil.

HEIGHT To 2.4m/8ft and more with a similar spread.

COMPOST Soil-based.

REPOTTING Move into a pot one size larger each spring.

PROPAGATION Take 8–10-cm/3–4-in tip cuttings in early spring.

KEEPING PLANTS To keep the plant healthy, cut it back to roughly half its size just before growth resumes after the winter rest.

PLANT CARE

Bright light, with 3–4 hours of direct sunlight. ● A minimum of 13°–15°C/55°–59°F in winter. ● Water moderately in the growing season; sparingly in winter. ● Stand the plant on a tray of wet pebbles and mist it daily during summer. ● Apply a weak liquid fertiliser every 2 weeks from early spring to late summer. ● In smaller rooms, train this plant over a wire framework; although the stems are tough, they are flexible so are easy to wind and unwind.

ALOCASIA SANDERIANA
Araceae

*K*RIS PLANT

Alocasias are not easy to find, but they are worth looking for if you want a spectacular specimen plant. The erect, thick stems of *Alocasia sanderiana* carry arrow-shaped leaves 30–40cm/12–16in long and 15cm/6in wide. They are of a metallic silver-green, broken by yellowish grey veining, with scalloped edges and a fine white margin; the undersides have a purplish tinge. The rather insignificant petal-less flowers are held on a spadix within a typical arum-like spathe.

   This attention-grabbing plant is, unfortunately, not really happy in normal room conditions and should be returned to a conservatory to recuperate after a few months. A rest period is required in winter, during which the compost should be allowed to become almost dry between waterings and feeding can cease completely.

FACT FILE

ORIGIN Philippines.

HEIGHT To 76cm/30in with a similar spread.

COMPOST Soil-based, with added peat or leaf mould.

REPOTTING Repot annually in spring.

PROPAGATION Divide in spring. Pot up the suckers that form around the plant; or take cuttings of the rhizomes.

KEEPING PLANTS Alocasia is equally good as a solitary specimen plant or as part of a group of house plants.

PLANT CARE

Bright light preferred; avoid direct sunlight in summer. ● A minimum of 18°C/65°F in winter; warm room temperature at other times, preferably above 21°C/70°F. ● Keep the compost moist during the active growth period; reduce watering in winter. ● Humidity is appreciated, so mist the leaves frequently, and stand the plant on a tray of moist pebbles. ● Feed every 2 weeks with a weak liquid fertiliser.

Check the leaves for mealybugs and red spider mites, both of which attack this plant.

Wiping or sponging dust from the metallic-looking surface can damage the leaves. It is better to spray them with water to clean them.

ALOE BARBADENSIS (SYN. *A. VERA*)
Liliaceae

*M*EDICINE ALOE

Aloes are slow-growing succulents found mainly in the African bush, and they display diverse size and habits. Many have leaves that are fiercely armed with hooked teeth and spines.

Aloe barbadensis, today more frequently known as *A. vera,* is a rambling and rather untidy plant that has appreciably larger rosettes of growth than *A. variegata*. It is a good indoor plant and lives up to its common name in that the sap from a broken leaf has amazing curative and restorative qualities when rubbed on sores and bruises and even when used on the hair. As its other common name, burn plant, indicates, it can also be used to alleviate the pain from burns. It has long been cultivated and has now become naturalised in many countries around the world, where it is used both in medicines and in cosmetics.

The plant forms a stemless clump of dagger-shaped grey-green leaves, faintly spotted with white and edged with soft teeth in shades of pink and red. The leaves are 30–60cm/1–2ft long and 5–8cm/ 2–3in wide. A stalk up to 90cm/3ft long carries tubular 2.5-cm/1-in-long yellow flowers in spring.

FACT FILE

ORIGIN Northeast Africa, Arabia.

HEIGHT To 60cm/2ft.

COMPOST Soil-based with added sand.

REPOTTING Repot young plants into a pot one size larger in spring each year. When maximum convenient pot size has been reached, top-dress the plant instead.

PROPAGATION In spring, remove the lateral shoots, or offsets, when the leaves are just beginning to form rosettes. Sticky sap exudes from the shoot, so leave it for two days to dry before planting in a just-damp mixture of compost and sand at normal room temperature.

KEEPING PLANTS This aloe is a long-lived, hardy plant, which is virtually trouble-free.

PLANT CARE

A bright position, with some direct sunlight in winter. ● Water by immersing the pot for 10 minutes; do not let water collect in the rosettes of leaves. Allow the compost to dry out almost completely before rewatering. In winter, water every 3–4 weeks. ● Feed monthly in spring and summer with high-potash fertiliser.

ALSO RECOMMENDED

Aloe jucunda is a pretty plant, which forms 8-cm/3-in-wide rosettes of almost stemless spiny green leaves blotched with cream. *A. humilis,* the spider or hedgehog aloe, has incurving, 10–15-cm/4–6-in-long, spiny blue-green leaves. The leaves of *A. h.* 'Globosa' are slightly smaller.

If the leaves turn brown and dry, the plant has not received enough water. Soak the pot thoroughly in a bucket of water for an hour and then drain it.

Overwatering, particularly in winter, will make black marks appear on the leaves and cause the plant to rot.

Check the leaves for scale insects, which attack this plant.

Mealybugs and root mealybugs both infest this plant. Check the leaves regularly for signs of these pests, and if the plant looks sickly scrape away the top 13mm/½in of compost and make sure there are no insects on the roots.

Aloe jucunda
produces a single spike of pale rose pink and white flowers from the centre of each rosette.

ALOE VARIEGATA
Liliaceae

Partridge-Breast Aloe

All aloes grow well at normal room temperature and are particularly suited to houses with central heating, since they are tolerant of dry air. The most popular dwarf species for indoor cultivation is *Aloe variegata*, which is especially easy to grow and usually does better in the home, even on a windowsill, than in a greenhouse.

The plant produces tight, spiralling rosettes of smooth-edged, V-shaped green leaves up to 15cm/6in long and 4cm/1½in wide. The leaves are marked with irregular paler bands of colour, which give the plant its most frequently used common name. It is also known as the tiger aloe, pheasant's wings and kanniedood aloe, which translates as the aloe that cannot be killed – a tribute to its hardiness. Coral pink flowers appear during late winter and early spring on stems up to 30cm/12in long growing from the leaf axils. The flowers are at their best after the plant has been given a winter rest.

If the plant is grown in too shady a position, the foliage will become pale and soft.

Avoid wetting the leaves when watering; moisture lodging in the leaf axils can cause rotting.

This plant will rarely shed leaves and so it will eventually become top-heavy and prone to toppling over.

FACT FILE

ORIGIN South Africa.

HEIGHT To 30cm/12in.

COMPOST Soil-based with added sand.

REPOTTING In spring, move into a pot one size larger or top-dress plants that are in pots of maximum desired size.

PROPAGATION Take offsets from around the base of the plant. Use a mixture of compost and sand to start them off.

KEEPING PLANTS Shade from strong sunlight in summer.

PLANT CARE

A bright position, with filtered sunlight. ● Maximum temperature of 10°C/50°F during the winter rest period; otherwise, normal room temperature. ● Keep the compost moist during the spring and summer and on the dry side at other times. ● Feed occasionally with a high-potash fertiliser.

ANANAS BRACTEATUS VAR. *TRICOLOR*
Bromeliaceae

Red Pineapple

The common edible pineapple, *Ananas comosus*, is the best known and commercially the most important member of this genus. Its spiny-leafed relative *A. bracteatus* var. *tricolor* is much more ornamental, however, and is sought after as a pot plant for its dramatic foliage and occasional brown, edible fruits. It forms stiff, pointed rosettes of bronze green leaves with yellow margins. The sword-like leaves can be 6.5cm/2½in wide and can grow to more than 90cm/3ft long, so the plant needs plenty of space. Always wear gloves when handling it, since the spines are sharp.

When the plant is five or six years old, a pink fruiting spike may be produced that contrasts attractively with the foliage. The fruit takes several months to form, usually maturing in spring.

FACT FILE

ORIGIN Southern Brazil, Paraguay.

HEIGHT To 90cm/3ft.

COMPOST Proprietary bromeliad compost; or equal parts by volume of coarse sand and peat moss plus half a part of leaf mould.

REPOTTING Move into a pot one size larger every second spring. Once the plant has reached the desired size, simply top-dress it each spring.

PROPAGATION Use good-sized offsets from around the base of older plants and set them in a mixture of peat moss and coarse sand or perlite. Warm conditions in filtered sunlight or a propagator are needed to induce offsets to root.

KEEPING PLANTS Mature plants may become top-heavy, so as they grow repot them into clay pots, which are heavier.

PLANT CARE

A bright position, with some direct sunlight. ● Minimum winter temperature of 18°C/65°F. ● Allow the top two-thirds of the compost to dry out before watering. ● Stand the plant on a tray of moist pebbles or plunge it into moist peat to keep humidity high. ● Apply a weak liquid fertiliser every 2 weeks from early spring to late summer.

If plants are kept in direct sunlight for short periods only, the variegated leaves will take on a rich pink colour.

If the leaf tips become brown, or the leaves shrivel, the atmosphere is too dry and warm. Increase humidity and move the plant to a cooler position.

Ananas is prone to few diseases, but may be attacked by scale insects; check regularly for signs of infestation.

ANTHURIUM SCHERZERIANUM
Araceae

Flamingo Flower

The flamingo flower, also known as tailflower, is spectacularly colourful from spring right through to mid-autumn. Each inflorescence, which can last for almost two months, comprises a large, waxy, scarlet palette-shaped spathe from which a narrow, curly, orange spadix emerges. The pointed dark green leaves, up to 18cm/7in long, are equally handsome. When the plant is not in flower, the leaves harmonise with those of other tropical plants suitable for shady spots. Indeed, setting this plant in a group of other plants can help to support the flower stalks without the need for unsightly staking. In addition, tropical plants like high humidity and placing them together raises the humidity.

Anthurium scherzerianum does not grow quickly and may prove difficult for the beginner. It needs careful monitoring to make sure the conditions are right and must be free from draughts and variations in temperature.

FACT FILE

ORIGIN Guatemala, Costa Rica.

HEIGHT To 23cm/9in.

COMPOST Peat-based, with added sphagnum moss. Good drainage is essential.

REPOTTING Move into a pot one size larger every spring until a pot size of 13–15cm/5–6in is reached, then top-dress annually.

PROPAGATION Divide crowded clumps in spring, ensuring that each piece has some roots attached and a growing point. Establish in humid conditions.

KEEPING PLANTS When grown in ideal conditions, this plant should last for many years.

PLANT CARE

Strong, indirect sunlight in winter; some shade in summer. ● Minimum winter temperature of 10°C/50°F; an ideal upper summer temperature of 22°C/72°F. ● Keep the compost moist during the active growth period; be more sparing with water in winter. ● Mist leaves daily during summer. ● Feed with a weak liquid fertiliser every 2 weeks while growth is evident.

Anthurium andraeanum has large waxy spathes, which shine as though they have been varnished. Its deep green, heart-shaped leaves provide a brilliantly colourful focal point in a group of foliage plants.

ALSO RECOMMENDED

Although not easy to find, there are cultivars with darker red, pink, white and spotted spathes. *Anthurium scherzerianum* 'Rothschildeanum' has a red spathe spotted with white and a yellow spadix, while *A.s.* 'Wardii' has a dark red spathe, with a long red spadix and, unusually, red stems as well.

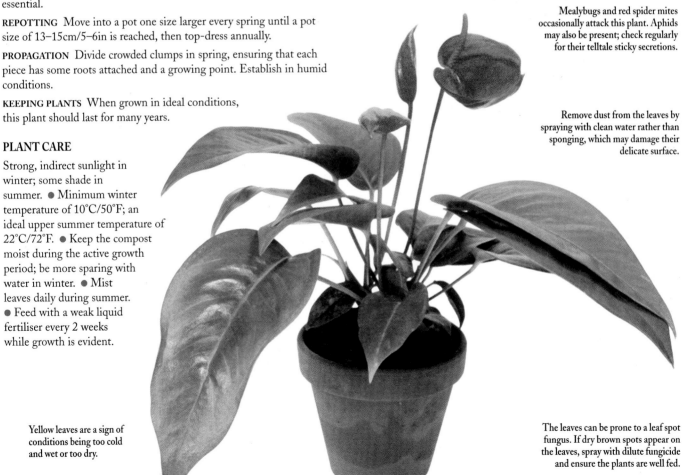

Inflorescences may require staking; attach them to thin canes with soft twine or plastic-covered wire.

Mealybugs and red spider mites occasionally attack this plant. Aphids may also be present; check regularly for their telltale sticky secretions.

Remove dust from the leaves by spraying with clean water rather than sponging, which may damage their delicate surface.

Yellow leaves are a sign of conditions being too cold and wet or too dry.

The leaves can be prone to a leaf spot fungus. If dry brown spots appear on the leaves, spray with dilute fungicide and ensure the plants are well fed.

APHELANDRA SQUARROSA 'LOUISAE'
Acanthaceae

ZEBRA PLANT

One of the most attractive indoor plants, this compact aphelandra is truly a dual-purpose specimen – its fabulous foliage catches the eye when the dramatic yellow bracts are absent. In the wild it thrives in the high humidity and regular downpours of the rain forest, and it has adapted well to indoor conditions but will not flourish unless humidity is high. The stem is stout and fleshy, and the 20–25-cm/8–10-in-long leaves are broadly elliptical, dark greyish green and heavily striped in the vein areas with silvery white. Insignificant tubular yellow flowers peep through a much more impressive four-sided, cone-shaped spike of yellow bracts, tinged red – hence the plant's other common name, saffron spike. To add to the pleasure the plant gives, these bracts are long-lasting, often looking good for six or seven weeks.

Sciarid flies, or fungus gnats, can be a nuisance if the compost mixture becomes excessively wet and sour.

Watch out for scale insects and for aphids, which are drawn to the bracts and young foliage.

Falling leaves are a sign that the plant has been allowed to dry out.

FACT FILE

ORIGIN Brazil.

HEIGHT To 30cm/12in.

COMPOST Soil-based, with peat moss or leaf mould added.

REPOTTING Repot once a year, at any time other than the coldest winter months. Pot the plant firmly.

PROPAGATION Take tip cuttings and sideshoots in spring.

KEEPING PLANTS Plants that have flowered should be cut down to a pair of lower leaves in spring, or they will become too tall.

PLANT CARE

Bright to semi-shaded conditions; no direct sunlight. ● Minimum winter temperature of 13°C/55°F, normal room temperature at other times. ● Water plentifully during the period of active growth. Give less water for a few weeks after flowering to allow the plant to rest, but never allow the compost to dry out completely. ● Maintain a humid atmosphere by standing the plant on moist pebbles, or plunge it into moist peat. ● Apply full-strength liquid fertiliser every 2 weeks from early spring to late summer.

APOROCACTUS FLAGELLIFORMIS
Cactaceae

RAT'S TAIL CACTUS

A popular plant that is easy to care for, the rat's tail cactus produces long streamers of narrow, fleshy, bright green ribbed stems, covered with many rows of fine, prickly spines in radiating clusters. Striking cerise-pink trumpet-shaped flowers 8cm/3in long appear in spring, usually in good quantity. The flowering season extends for some two months, and individual blooms may last for a week. The plant is fast growing.

Display *Aporocactus flagelliformis* in a hanging basket or on a shelf near a window that offers good light, positioning it where no one will brush against it, since the spines are very difficult to remove from the skin and the lengthening stems can soon overbalance a free-standing pot. The rat's tail cactus can also be displayed in an indoor cactus garden with its long stems trailing through an arrangement of sand and rocks.

FACT FILE

ORIGIN Mexico.

HEIGHT To 5–10cm/2–4in; stems to 90cm/3ft or more.

COMPOST Two-thirds soil-based to one-third leaf mould.

REPOTTING Repot every year after flowering. When plants are in 15–23-cm/6–9-in pots, simply top-dress annually.

PROPAGATION Take 15-cm/6-in tip cuttings in early summer. Allow them to dry for a day or two then insert them in a peat and sand mixture. Seed can be sown in spring.

KEEPING PLANTS Set the plant outdoors in summer, in a sheltered sunny spot where it will receive occasional rain.

PLANT CARE

Bright sunlight. ● Winter rest temperature of 7°–10°C/45°–50°F with normal room temperature at other times. ● Allow compost to dry between thorough waterings, but water more sparingly in the rest period following flowering. ● Good drainage is essential; do not allow the plant to stand in water. ● Apply a high-potash fertiliser every 2 weeks from midwinter until flowering stops.

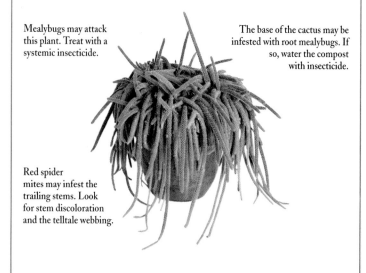

Mealybugs may attack this plant. Treat with a systemic insecticide.

The base of the cactus may be infested with root mealybugs. If so, water the compost with insecticide.

Red spider mites may infest the trailing stems. Look for stem discoloration and the telltale webbing.

ARALIA ELEGANTISSIMA see DIZYGOTHECA ELEGANTISSIMA

ARAUCARIA HETEROPHYLLA (SYN. *A. EXCELSA*)
Araucariaceae

*N*ORFOLK ISLAND PINE

Discovered on the southern Pacific island by Sir Joseph Banks in 1793, this handsome conifer reaches a height of 60m/200ft in its natural habitat. As a pot plant, however, it will grow to a more suitable 90cm–1.8m/3–6ft. It is a slow grower and after reaching this height is past its best. The Norfolk Island pine is appealing because of its horizontally held branches covered with 13-mm/¹/₂-in-long needles, which are bright green in the spring and turn dark green over time. The plant should last for many years and can be used as a Christmas tree.

Araucaria requires a bright, well-lit position and enjoys a spell outdoors on mild days. It likes freely circulating air, but not central heating or warm air conditioning. In summer it needs an even more humid atmosphere, so mist the foliage frequently.

Aphids and mealybugs can attack this plant. Watch for signs of infestation and spray with a suitable insecticide.

Dry, yellowing needles indicate that conditions are too hot and dry. Move the plant to a cool, well-ventilated position, water it and mist more frequently.

FACT FILE

ORIGIN Norfolk Island.

HEIGHT To 1.8m/6ft or more.

COMPOST Soil-based.

REPOTTING Move into a pot one size larger every 2–3 years, or when roots show on top of the compost. Top-dress plants more than 90cm/3ft tall in spring.

PROPAGATION By seed or stem cuttings taken by specialist growers.

KEEPING PLANTS Remove bare lower branches. General pruning is not advisable, but it will encourage bushier growth if the plant becomes straggly.

PLANT CARE

A bright position, with some direct sunlight. ● Winter temperature of 4°C/40°F; otherwise normal room temperature. ● Keep the compost moist except in winter, when less water is needed. ● Mist-spray every 3 days. ● Apply a liquid fertiliser every 2 weeks in summer. ● Keep well away from radiators or heaters.

ARDISIA CRENATA
Myrsinaceae

*C*ORAL BERRY

Few suppliers of house plants stock this small erect shrub because it is so slow-growing. It is, however, an attractive plant and is easy to care for. In nature, it reaches 1.5–1.8m/5–6ft, practically double the height it can attain indoors. The leathery leaves are a glossy deep green, up to 10cm/4in long and 5cm/2in wide, and the tiny, white or pale pink flowers are slightly fragrant. They grow from the leaf axils at the lower part of the foliage in summer and are followed by 6-mm/¹/₄-in round red berries – by far the most attractive feature of the plant. The berries, on almost horizontal stalks, usually appear at the beginning of winter and remain until the onset of flowering the following season.

The coral berry, marlberry or spiceberry will last for three or four years and even longer, though it easily loses its vigour. To retain a compact, bushy shape, prune the plant each spring before flowering.

FACT FILE

ORIGIN Southeast Asia.

HEIGHT To 90cm/3ft.

COMPOST Soil-based.

REPOTTING When the roots have filled the pot, move the plant to a container one size larger at any time of year.

PROPAGATION Sow seed in spring, or take stem cuttings in spring or early summer. Ardisias can also be air-layered. None of these methods is easy.

KEEPING PLANTS If only a few berries are produced, use a small brush to pollinate the flowers the next time the plant is in bloom. Replace the plant when it begins to become spindly.

PLANT CARE

A bright position with some direct sunlight. ● Minimum winter temperature of 7°C/45°F; at other times 7°–16°C/45°–60°F is best. ● Never let the compost dry out. ● Maintain humidity by misting regularly, or stand the pot on a tray of damp pebbles. ● Apply a weak liquid fertiliser every 2 weeks from early spring to late summer; once a month at other times.

If the plant is reluctant to flower, increase humidity in spring when the buds are forming.

Flowers drop before the fruits have set if the plant is too cold or is in a draught; move it to a warmer place.

Red spider mites may attack this plant; watch out for mottled leaves and webbing on the foliage.

Check the plant for mealybugs if white woolly patches form on the leaves and in the leaf axils.

ASPARAGUS DENSIFLORUS 'SPRENGERI'
Liliaceae

ASPARAGUS FERN

Relatives of the lily, this plant and *Asparagus densiflorus* 'Myers' are frequently, but incorrectly, called ferns on account of their finely divided foliage, which is actually modified stems or branches. In its natural habitat – temperate savanna and warm temperate forests – *A. densiflorus* will scramble through and up stronger-stemmed plants, but the two cultivars most often grown indoors make excellent plants for hanging baskets. They produce fleshy roots, often with pronounced tubers on them, which store water and see the plants through brief periods of water shortage; the insignificant flowers are followed by reddish berries.

A.d. 'Sprengeri', the emerald-feather fern, with its drooping stems clothed in 2.5-cm/1-in-long needle-like 'leaves', makes an excellent trailing plant; a well-grown mature specimen can have a spread of 90cm/3ft. Arguably more attractive is *A.d.* 'Myers', which has needle-like branchlets arranged around its stems like plumes, hence its common name of foxtail fern.

FACT FILE

ORIGIN South Africa.

HEIGHT Stems up to 90cm/3ft long.

COMPOST Soil-based.

REPOTTING Repot annually in spring. Leave the surface of the compost well below the rim of the pot; the thick, tuberous roots force the compost up as they grow.

PROPAGATION In spring, divide old overcrowded clumps that have lost their vigour with a sharp knife. Try to retain as many of the roots as possible.

KEEPING PLANTS Asparagus is a long-lived plant; cut out faded fronds to keep the plant looking decorative.

PLANT CARE

Bright filtered sunlight; avoid deep shade. ● Minimum winter temperature of 10°C/50°F; normal room temperature at other times. ● Water thoroughly, allowing the compost to dry out a little between waterings; water sparingly in winter. ● Feed every 2 weeks from spring to early autumn with a standard liquid fertiliser.

If leaves drop off, the plant has either received too much direct sunlight or the compost has been allowed to dry out.

Erratic or too much watering may cause the roots to rot.

Scale insects or red spider mites will attack the plant if conditions are too dry.

ASPIDISTRA ELATIOR
Liliaceae

CAST-IRON PLANT

This is the only species of aspidistra in cultivation; although it is occasionally described as *Aspidistra lurida*, this is an entirely different plant. *A. elatior* is sometimes known as the parlour plant because it was popular with the Victorians, who also prized it for its ability to stand up to poor conditions – hence the name cast-iron plant.

Stemless, it sends up its 30–46-cm/12–18-in oval, dark green, arching leaves from a fleshy, creeping rootstock. It can flower in late winter or early spring, but this event is not frequent. The dull purple, star-shaped blooms are produced at soil level (in nature they are pollinated by snails) and often go unnoticed as a result.

Aspidistras are seen at their best as lone specimens, and a mature plant in an ornamental stand looks very dignified in a hallway or a bay window (which should not receive direct sunlight). Although aspidistras are quite expensive to buy, they are virtually 'everlasting'.

Split and damaged leaves may be caused by overfeeding; if the leaves start to split, reduce the amount of fertiliser by half.

If the plant is too close to a heat source or receives direct sunlight, brown patches may form on the leaves.

Speckled leaves often indicate that the plant has been given either too much or too little water.

Aspidistras may be attacked by red spider mites, scale insects and mealybugs. Check regularly for signs of these pests.

FACT FILE

ORIGIN China.

HEIGHT To 76cm/30in.

COMPOST Soil-based.

REPOTTING Pot on only when essential until a 30-cm/12-in pot is required.

PROPAGATION Divide overcrowded clumps in spring. Single pieces or clusters of leaves with roots can be potted up; the latter will produce a better plant more quickly.

KEEPING PLANTS Old plants are best left in their original pots; remove new shoots and some roots if necessary. Set outdoors in a sheltered spot in summer.

PLANT CARE

Moderate light, without direct sunlight. ● Minimum winter temperature of 10°C/50°F, with a maximum of 21°C/70°F. ● Water moderately, allowing the compost almost to dry out between waterings. ● Feed every 2 weeks during the growing season but do not overfeed. ● Wipe leaves free of dust periodically.

ASPLENIUM NIDUS
Aspleniaceae

*B*IRD'S NEST FERN

The broad, fluted, strap-like fronds of this fern are a shiny fresh green, with a dark central vein. The foliage grows in the form of a rosette, from the centre of which new fronds unfurl. In its natural habitat the plant grows as an epiphyte in moist tropical rain forests, and in these conditions fronds can reach 1.2m/4ft in length. Asplenium makes an excellent house plant; it is a relatively quick grower.

An ideal place indoors is warm, humid, partly shaded and well away from draughts, but aspleniums can tolerate home heating if sufficient humidity is provided. Even large fronds are relatively fragile and should be handled as little as possible. There are no named varieties. *Asplenium australasicum*, commonly grown in Australia and New Zealand, is a very similar plant.

FACT FILE

ORIGIN Southeast Asia, Australia.

HEIGHT To 60cm/2ft in a pot indoors.

COMPOST Peat-based, with some added loam and coarse sand.

REPOTTING Repot in spring, when the roots fill the pot. The roots tend to cling to the side of the pot, so it may be necessary to break the pot to release the root ball.

PROPAGATION This fern can only be raised from spores.

KEEPING PLANTS Stand the plant outdoors in summer in mild climates. Clean the fronds by wiping them gently with a damp cloth or put the plant under the shower. Do not use leaf shine.

PLANT CARE

Medium light, no direct sun; turn the pot regularly to ensure even growth. ● Normal room temperature with a minimum winter temperature of 16°C/61°F. ● Keep the compost moist, especially in the growing period. ● Stand the pot on damp pebbles. ● Apply a weak liquid fertiliser every 2 weeks in spring and summer.

Damaged or dried fronds can be cut off at the base.

If scale insects – on both sides of the leaves – or aphids attack the plant, spray with soapy water, followed by clean water.

Brown spots on the fronds may indicate that the plant is in a position that is draughty or too cold. Move it to a warmer, more protected place.

BEAUCARNEA RECURVATA (SYN. *NOLINA RECURVATA*)
Liliaceae

*P*ONY TAIL PLANT

Originally from the desert of southern Mexico, this bizarre-looking succulent is most unusual and eye-catching. The bottle-shaped woody stem, which serves as a water reservoir, adds to the plant's odd appearance and gives rise to its common names of bottle palm and elephant foot. From this bulbous stem spring several slim, downward-curving 'pony tails' of grey-green leaves up to 90cm/3ft long. Clusters of small white flowers are sometimes produced on older plants.

Beaucarnea recurvata grows slowly, but it is easy to keep and should live for several years. It is ideal in a modern room setting and, since it prefers dry air, will thrive in houses with built-in heating. It likes a sunny position, as well as fresh air, so should be sited near a window.

Check for scale insects and red spider mites, which may attack the plant.

If the leaf tips turn brown, trim back the damaged leaves, but do not decimate the plant.

Limp, pale leaves and soft stems indicate overwatering. Stand the pot on dry newspaper for a day or two, changing the paper when it gets wet. Do not water again until the top of the compost has dried out.

FACT FILE

ORIGIN Mexico.

HEIGHT To 3m/10ft or more.

COMPOST Soil-based, mixed with leaf mould or peat and sand.

REPOTTING Repot every 2–3 years, always ensuring good drainage. Keep this plant in a pot relatively small for the plant's size.

PROPAGATION Sow seed or take offsets in spring or summer, with an air temperature of 24°C/75°F, but propagation is not easy for the amateur.

KEEPING PLANTS Fading leaves can be gently peeled off. Put the plant in a sheltered spot outdoors in summer.

PLANT CARE

Bright light, preferably full sun, all year round. ● Minimum winter temperature of 10°C/50°F. ● Keep the compost moist from early spring to late autumn, but do not let the plant stand in water. ● Feed with a weak liquid fertiliser every 4 weeks during summer.

BEGONIACEAE

*B*EGONIAS

Begonia × *hiemalis* (tuberous), the winter-flowering begonia, has reddish stems up to 46cm/18in long. The most widely seen are the Elatior hybrids such as 'Heidi' (*right*).

The begonia family contains more than 900 species and 10,000 hybrids and cultivars. Some are grown mainly for their flowers, others for their leaves, but most of the flowering types also have attractive foliage. Plants range in size from tiny ground creepers to climbers 3m/10ft high. In general, they do not need much direct sunlight, so most of them make suitable indoor plants.

Begonias bear male and female flowers, sometimes in clusters and sometimes separately. Male flowers last for only a few days, but usually compensate for this by being more striking, often having several layers of petals. Female flowers have four petals and are distinguished by a winged or strongly angled seed pod; they also remain on the plant for weeks or even months.

Since the genus is so large and diverse, it is best divided into three groups, distinguished by the root structure. The first group has fibrous-rooted plants, which grow from a tangle of fine roots that will fill a pot quickly. The second contains the rhizomatous begonias, most of which have a thick, fleshy rhizome that crawls over the surface of the compost, sending down roots as it goes. The final group comprises the tuberous begonias, which are characterised by swollen underground stems, or tubers; they are deciduous and have an annual period of dormancy.

Flowers are usually borne in groups of 3 – a large central male and two smaller female flowers.

Fleshy erect stems up to 2.5cm/1in thick.

Soft dark green leaves 15–20cm/6–8in long, with paler green veining.

Tuber (swollen underground stem) just on the surface of the compost.

ALSO RECOMMENDED

Begonia 'Corallina de Lucerna' (fibrous) is a vigorous plant up to 1.8m/6ft high. The big lance-shaped glossy leaves are spotted with white and deep red below; flowers in large clusters are deep pink to bright red.

Begonia × *tuberhybrida* is the most popular tuberous begonia. The 30-cm/12-in-tall fleshy-stemmed plants carry large and showy single, semi-double and double blooms in a wide range of colours.

Begonia sutherlandii (tuberous) is 15–20cm/6–8in high, with pendulous deep pink stems and red-edged bright green leaves. It bears dainty salmon-pink flowers for 8 months of the year from early spring.

Young shoots distorted by tarsonemid mites chewing them.

The leaves and stems of deciduous begonias start to fall off as the growing seasons nears its end. Do not pull these away from the tuber, since this could damage it; wait for the stems to fall away naturally.

Botrytis fungus will attack plants in cool, damp conditions. Remove and destroy infected leaves and move the plant to a warmer spot; treat with a fungicide if severely affected.

Overwatering, coupled with low temperatures, causes leaves to wilt and turn brown.

Most begonias are prone to powdery mildew on leaves, leafstalks and stems. Spray regularly with a suitable fungicide.

When potting or repotting, sprinkle compost around the roots, rhizome or tuber and tap the pot to settle the mixture; do not compact it with your fingers.

Begonia masoniana (rhizomatous), the iron cross begonia, has deeply puckered leaves. They are bright green, with a mahogany-red cross resembling the German iron cross in the centre.

Begonia rex (rhizomatous) has decorative heart-shaped foliage with zones of silver, pink, purple, cream and near black on the corrugated leaf surfaces. Many named forms are available.

FACT FILE

ORIGIN Tropical America, Africa, Asia; hybrids.

HEIGHT To 46cm/18in and more.

COMPOST Peat-based, or peat- and soil-based in equal parts by volume.

REPOTTING Fibrous: Move plants into pots one size larger every spring until 15–20-cm/6–8-in pots are reached, then top-dress annually instead. **Rhizomatous:** Shallow-rooted and best grown in shallow pots. Move into a pot one size larger only when the rhizome has covered much of the surface of the compost. **Tuberous:** Move semi-tuberous types into pots one size larger each spring.

PROPAGATION Fibrous: Take 8–10-cm/3–4-in stem cuttings of non-flowering shoots in spring or summer. **Rhizomatous and tuberous:** Sow seed, divide or take leaf or stem cuttings in spring or summer.

KEEPING PLANTS All begonias suffer in dry air, so increase humidity by standing pots on moist pebbles, particularly if the temperature rises above 18°C/65°F.

PLANT CARE

Fibrous: Foliage plants require bright light, not direct sun; flowering plants need up to 4 hours' direct sunlight. ● Minimum winter temperature of 13°C/55°F; otherwise, normal room temperature. ● Allow the top 2.5cm/1in of the compost to dry out between waterings; water less frequently in winter. ● Apply a weak liquid fertiliser every 2 weeks during the period of active growth. **Rhizomatous and tuberous:** Bright, filtered light; plants that lose their top growth do not require light during dormant periods. ● Minimum winter temperature of 13°C/55°F ● Let the top 2.5cm/1in of compost dry out between waterings; do not water dormant plants. ● Apply a high-potash liquid feed every 2 weeks in the period of active growth.

PESTS & DISEASES

Begonias are affected by root knot eelworm; tarsonemid mites; weevils; powdery mildew and botrytis.

BELOPERONE GUTTATA (SYN. *JUSTICIA BRANDEGEANA*)
Acanthaceae

*S*HRIMP PLANT

The reddish brown bracts of this plant, resembling overlapping roof shingles, appear almost all year round, while the white flowers that emerge at the end of the bracts are insignificant and short-lived. The leaves are 2.5–8cm/1–3in long, light green, oval and pointed.

Disregard people who tell you to throw beloperone away after flowering: the plant is easy to care for and can survive for many years, reaching 90cm/3ft in height and spread. It is best to pinch out the stem tips regularly to make the plant bushier, and annual pruning will renew its vigour. If you do not prune, the plant will almost certainly be larger and will produce colourful bracts, but the relatively weak branches will probably require staking.

If bracts do not develop fully, prune the plant in midwinter, just as the show of bracts ends.

Whiteflies, mealybugs, scale insects and aphids may attack the plant in hot weather; spray with a suitable insecticide.

Loss of leaves may indicate that the plant is rootbound; annual potting should alleviate this.

Overwatering can encourage the leaves to turn yellow. Do not water again until the soil has dried out completely.

FACT FILE

ORIGIN Mexico.

HEIGHT To 90cm/3ft.

COMPOST Soil-based.

REPOTTING Repot every spring, and cut stems back by about half.

PROPAGATION Take 8-cm/3-in tip cuttings in spring; use the prunings, but remove the bracts, which will rot if they are left.

KEEPING PLANTS The arching stems and hanging flower heads make this a good plant for a hanging basket.

PLANT CARE

A bright place, with direct sunlight for short periods during spring and summer will help to produce colourful bracts. ● Minimum winter temperature of 16°C/60°F; ideally 22°C/72°F at other times. ● Keep fairly dry during winter, and moist, not wet, at other times. ● Feed every 2 weeks in summer with a weak solution of fertiliser.

BILLBERGIA NUTANS
Bromeliaceae

*Q*UEEN'S TEARS

One of the prettiest of bromeliads, this is also one of the easiest to grow. Its tough, strap-like, tooth-edged, olive green leaves, which can be as much as 40cm/16in long and 13mm/^{1}/2in wide, arch over in an attractively random fashion. The pendant flowers, which usually appear in late spring, are tinged with blue, yellow, pink and green and are encased in pink bracts. Nectar formed within the small flowers sometimes drops out when the plant is touched or moved, giving it its common name; it is also called the friendship plant.

A much underrated, easy-care plant, this billbergia is seen to best effect when grown at eye-level, as in a hanging container, which will show off the pendulous bracts to full advantage. While most plants in elevated positions may suffer as a result of dry conditions, billbergias are much more tolerant, and small hanging pots can be plunged into water occasionally to give them a good soak.

FACT FILE

ORIGIN Argentina, Brazil, Uruguay.

HEIGHT To 40cm/16in in flower.

COMPOST Proprietary bromeliad or orchid potting compost, or equal parts of soil-based compost and peat or leaf mould.

REPOTTING In spring, move to a pot up to 13cm/5in in diameter.

PROPAGATION Detach offsets when they are half the size of the parent plant. Let the cut surface dry for a day or so before potting up.

KEEPING PLANTS Empty the water reservoir in the centre of the rosette once a month and refill with fresh water.

PLANT CARE

Keep in good light but out of direct sunlight to maintain good leaf colour and promote flowering. ● Normal room temperature, but the plant will tolerate temperatures as low as 2°–4°C/36°–40°F for a short while. ● Water moderately all year round, with rainwater or cool boiled water. ● Apply weak liquid fertiliser every 2 weeks both to the soil and as a foliar spray.

A month or two outdoors in a shady position during summer greatly improves the leaf colour and usually encourages flowering.

The olive green leaves may become reddish if the plant is placed in direct sunlight.

BOUGAINVILLEA GLABRA
Nyctaginaceae

𝒫APER FLOWER

A true tropical exotic, in its natural environment this showy climber produces such dense and vivid colour on 4.5-m/15-ft trailing stems that it outshines almost everything else in the vicinity. Its strong twining branches, which carry narrow, smooth, 8-cm/3-in-long leaves, have vicious barbs. This drawback is, however, more than compensated for when the colourful papery bracts, some 4cm/1½in long, appear at the beginning of summer.

Bougainvillea can be most frustrating to grow as an indoor plant, for it is reluctant to flower in limited light. Fine indoor specimens can, however, be grown beside large windows and in conservatories or sunrooms. Although a climber, this plant can be trained to keep it bushy indoors – wire hoops have become popular supports – and there are some dwarf types that do not require special training.

Bougainvillea glabra, with purple-pink bracts in summer and autumn, is the species most easily obtained. This, and the less vigorous *B. x buttiana*, have given rise to dozens of hybrids with a range of highly coloured bracts, many being smaller than the species.

Bougainvillea x buttiana *'Amethyst', seen close up here, has bracts with a papery quality that enclose its insignificant flowers.*

FACT FILE

ORIGIN Brazil.

HEIGHT To 4.5m/15ft.

COMPOST Soil-based.

REPOTTING When new growth appears in spring, move the plant into a pot one size larger. When a pot size of 20cm/8in is reached, simply top-dress it.

PROPAGATION Not easy. Take 8–10-cm/ 3–4-in stem cuttings in late spring or early summer; keep in a heated propagator.

KEEPING PLANTS If the plant becomes straggly, prune it lightly in autumn. Flowering is better if new growth is wound around established stems and tied in.

PLANT CARE

Bougainvillea needs 4 hours of direct sunlight daily. Place in a sunny window close to the glass for maximum light, but do not allow it to bake in hot weather. ● Minimum winter temperature of 10°C/50°F. Set outdoors in summer if possible. ● Water well during active growth, but the plant must not stand in water; do not water in winter until new growth appears. ● Apply a high-potash feed every 2 weeks in spring and summer.

ALSO RECOMMENDED

Bougainvillea glabra 'Alexandra' is rose pink and one of the most free-flowering. 'Variegata' has leaves bordered with cream. *B.* x *buttiana* hybrids 'Killie Campbell', 'Orange King', and 'Golden Glow' ('Hawaiian Gold') are shades of gold and orange; 'Jamaica Red' is crimson; 'Surprise' ('Mary Palmer') is rose purple or white or a combination of the two.

This is a tough plant that does not suffer greatly from pests. But aphids, red spider mites and mealybugs may attack it, so check often for signs of infestation.

Water left on the leaves or papery bracts may cause scorching when the plant is in full sun.

Yellowing of the leaves is caused by too much moisture at the roots. Make sure that the compost has good drainage.

BROMELIACEAE

BROMELIADS

This group of some 2,000 species in more than 50 genera, ranging from pineapples to Spanish moss, provides us with some exciting and colourful indoor plants. Typically, they produce wide rosettes of more or less leathery, strap-shaped leaves, often striped or patterned and with a central zone that becomes brightly coloured at flowering time. Flower heads on stout stems, with numerous small flowers, are borne between long-lasting colourful bracts.

There are two types of bromeliad, epiphytic and terrestrial. In the wild, epiphytic plants grow on trees or rocks. They have small, weak root systems, and they obtain much of their nourishment from the air and from the detritus that collects within their leaves. Some of the most beautiful of the epiphytic bromeliads, such as *Aechmea fasciata*, the urn plant, are easy to grow. It is typical of most bromeliads in having a water-holding vessel formed by the bases of the leaves. Air plants, *Tillandsia* spp., are epiphytic bromeliads that live by absorbing water from the atmosphere and trapping dust particles between the tiny scales on their foliage. Among the terrestrial types – those that live in the ground – are *Cryptanthus*, *Dyckia*, *Nidularium*, *Neoregelia* and one of the most widely seen genera, *Ananas*, the pineapple, several species of which make good house plants.

Guzmania lingulata, scarlet star, is a commonly found terrestrial bromeliad. It has smooth, glossy strap-shaped leaves up to 18in/46cm long, which overlap at the base to form a central well, or urn, that holds water. At almost any time of the year it may bear white flowers, which are almost hidden by the scarlet star-shaped bracts that give this plant its common name.

The scarlet star-shaped bracts conceal small white flowers.

Long strap-shaped leaves overlap at their bases to form an urn that holds water.

ALSO RECOMMENDED

Cryptanthus bivittatus is a small species that grows in the ground and thrives in terraria. It forms a rosette of 5–8cm/2–3in-long leaves, with spiny edges, which are striped dark green and in strong light become tinged with pink.

Nidularium billbergioides, another terrestrial bromeliad, forms an upright rosette of glossy light green leaves about 30cm/12in high. The flower spike comprises white flowers, up to 5cm/2in wide, enclosed in bright yellow bracts.

If flowers, or even the bract spikes, fail to appear, move the plant to a location that receives more light.

If the thick leaves develop brown tips and then shrivel, that is an indication that the plant is too hot and dry; increase watering accordingly.

Bromeliads may be attacked by aphids, scale insects and mealybugs; check regularly for signs of infestation.

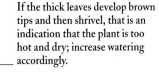

Overwatering or too low a temperature will cause flower stems to rot; empty the well in the centre of the rosette and allow the soil to dry out before rewatering.

Neoregelia 'Meyendorffii' is a cultivar typical of most neoregelias, with the leaves arranged in a rather flat rosette. During the flowering period the leaves change colour to a striking scarlet.

Tillandsia cyanea, an air plant, can be planted in compost. Its grass-like leaves form a rosette up to 30cm/12in wide, and in early summer it bears a spectacular flower head with blue flowers held between bright pink bracts.

FACT FILE

ORIGIN Southern US to Tropical America, Africa.

HEIGHT 10cm–1.8m/4in–6ft.

POTTING MIX Equal parts of peat and peat-based, with some fresh sphagnum moss. Good drainage is essential.

REPOTTING Repot every 2 years. Since rooting systems are not extensive, fairly small pots are suitable.

PROPAGATION Remove good-sized offsets from the base of the plant in spring and pot them in rich, just-moist potting compost.

KEEPING PLANTS Ensure that neither the plant's urn nor the soil is allowed to dry out. Put plants outside in summer, particularly in mild climates, since they love the rain.

PLANT CARE

These are tolerant plants, which can take either direct or subdued sunlight. ● Average room temperature is suitable for growth, with a minimum winter temperature of 13°C/55°F. A temperature of about 24°C/75°F is needed for flowering. ● Water twice a week with tepid rainwater or soft water. Do not overwater bromeliads, although the vessel, or urn, which is the plant's growing point, must be kept full of water at all times. ● Mist the leaves with weak liquid fertiliser occasionally in spring and summer.

AIR PLANTS

Most of these types of epiphytic bromeliads should not be planted in compost, since this would rot the small roots, which are used more for support than for feeding the plant. Instead, wrap the bottom of the plant and any roots in sphagnum moss and wire the plant to a piece of wood or cork. Hang the plant up and spray the moss and leaves twice a day year-round to keep them moist. *Tillandsia* spp. and *Neoregelia tristis* do well grown this way.

PESTS & DISEASES

Bromeliads may be attacked by aphids, scale insects and red spider mites. Check regularly for these pests and spray with insecticide; remove scale insects by hand.

BROWALLIA SPECIOSA 'MAJOR'
Solanaceae

SAPPHIRE FLOWER

The violet-blue blooms of this plant, sometimes known as the bush violet, are carried in the leaf axils of slender, semi-trailing stems. They are trumpet-shaped, opening out to a flat-faced bloom about 5cm/2in wide, and have an attractive white throat. Plants may be bought in flower from midsummer right through the autumn and winter; winter-flowering plants are probably the most popular. The rather drooping foliage is ovate and mid-green. The stems can be supported by thin canes to give a bushy plant, or they can be allowed to trail gracefully. The tips of the stems should be pinched out regularly to keep the plant reasonably compact. Browallias are difficult to keep in good condition for a further flowering season and are usually discarded once flowering has finished.

Browallia speciosa 'Blue Troll', with a compact habit, and *B.s.* 'White Troll', its counterpart with white flowers, are the most popular varieties.

FACT FILE

ORIGIN Colombia.

HEIGHT To 60cm/2ft.

COMPOST Soil-based.

REPOTTING Not usually done.

PROPAGATION Easily grown from seed sown in spring or summer.

KEEPING PLANTS Discard after flowering.

PLANT CARE

Bright light with some direct sun. ● Prefers cool conditions of 10°–16°C/50°–60°F. ● Keep the compost just moist and mist the foliage occasionally. ● Apply a standard liquid fertiliser every 2 weeks throughout the flowering period. ● Remove flowers as they fade.

To extend the flowering period, pick off the flowers as they fade.

Keeping the plant in a cool room will ensure the flowers last as long as possible.

The slender stems often need staking to produce a bushy, upright plant.

BRUNFELSIA PAUCIFLORA (SYN. *B. CALYCINA*)
Solanaceae

YESTERDAY-TODAY-AND-TOMORROW

This plant's strange common name arises from the rapidly changing appearance of the flowers: they open deep purple and fade to lavender the next day, then to white. The flowers are fragrant, about 5cm/2in wide with a central white eye, and even though they are short-lived individually, there are always plenty more blooms to follow. Given the right conditions, brunfelsias can flower at any time of year.

Leaves are long and lance-shaped, glossy mid- to deep green and leathery. Stems should be pruned back in early spring to produce well-shaped plants, and growing tips pinched out throughout the season to keep the plant bushy. Brunfelsias will flower better if they are put in a sheltered place outdoors during warm summer weather, a practice that helps to ripen the wood.

Flowers appear in clusters at the tips of the stems, opening one by one and changing colour day by day.

The leathery leaves are sometimes attacked by scale insects; check the undersides regularly.

Mist foliage regularly in the growing season.

Allow the surface of the compost to dry out between waterings in winter.

FACT FILE

ORIGIN Tropical America, West Indies.

HEIGHT To 60cm/2ft.

COMPOST Soil-based.

REPOTTING Every spring, move to a pot up to 20cm/8in maximum. Do not overpot; plants flower better when the roots are confined.

PROPAGATION Take soft stem cuttings in spring and early summer.

KEEPING PLANTS Prune in early spring and pinch out growing tips during the flowering season to keep the plant bushy.

PLANT CARE

Bright light with some direct sunlight. ● Give moderate warmth, with a minimum of 10°C/50°F in winter. ● Keep the compost moist in the growing season but water more sparingly in winter. ● Apply a standard liquid fertiliser every 2 weeks while the plant is actively growing.

CALADIUM × *HORTULANUM*
Araceae

*A*NGEL-WINGS

An exception to the rule that foliage house plants are decorative all year round, this hybrid tuberous-rooted plant dies down in autumn and remains dormant over the winter. This, together with the fact that the plants are not easy to grow – they require high temperature and high humidity – leads to many of them being discarded after their first season.

The large, 30–40-cm/12–16-in heart-shaped leaves, which are carried on long, arching stalks, are paper thin and spectacularly marked. The range of varieties is wide, and leaf colours vary from white with green edges and crimson veins, as in 'White Queen' shown here, through rose pink with green margins, to spotted and marbled red, pink, white, orange and green. Arum-like flowers may be produced, but these are insignificant compared with the foliage. The plant is also commonly known as elephant's-ears.

FACT FILE

ORIGIN Tropical South America, West Indies; hybrids.

HEIGHT To 60cm/2ft.

COMPOST Peat-based.

REPOTTING Repot in spring; add plenty of pot shards to ensure good drainage.

PROPAGATION When repotting, break off small tubers from the parent and pot them up separately, at the same depth as they are thick, to produce new plants.

KEEPING PLANTS Allow the compost to dry out completely when the foliage dies down. Keep it dry until spring, when repotting takes place.

PLANT CARE

Bright light, but no direct sunlight.
● Warm conditions: at least 16°C/60°F, but 21°C/70°F is better. ● Keep the compost moist throughout the growing season and mist the foliage daily. ● Stand the plant on a dish of moist pebbles to raise the humidity.
● Apply half-strength liquid fertiliser every 2 weeks during the period of active growth.

ALSO RECOMMENDED

Caladium × *hortulanum* 'Pink Beauty' has green leaves with red ribs and pink marbling in the centre. The leaves of 'Carolyn Morton' are bright pink with red ribs and broad, dark green edges, while the bushy 'Frieda Hempel' has bright red leaves, red ribs and dark green margins.

Caladium leaves have magnificent coloration which differs from variety to variety and within the leaves on a single plant. And the paradoxically fragile translucency of the leaves increases their attractiveness. In addition, their shape and huge size are reminiscent of an elephant's ears.

Paper-thin leaves are available in a spectacular range of colours and need to be protected from cold and draughts at all times.

Keep the tuber virtually dry during the winter and restart it into growth in warm conditions (about 24°C/75°F) in spring.

Direct sunlight will scorch the delicate foliage.

Keep the humidity high by misting the foliage and standing the pot on a tray of damp pebbles.

CALATHEA MAKOYANA
Marantaceae

PEACOCK PLANT

The 'eyes' and the very fine lines of this plant's decorative foliage create the appearance of a peacock's tail and give it its most widely used common name, peacock plant. It is also sometimes known as cathedral windows. Calatheas are closely related to marantas (see page 107) but are rather more delicate.

Leaves are thin, oval in shape and about 30cm/12in long. They are light green, feathered with fine, dark green lines running from the midrib to the edge of the leaf, and with elongated, irregularly shaped blotches occurring at intervals. The underside of the leaves is also marked and tends to be a pinkish maroon rather than green. The foliage is held upright on long slender stems.

Yellowing and browning of the leaves is often caused by dry air. Mist regularly and stand the plant on a tray of moist gravel to raise humidity.

The undersides of calathea leaves are an attractive maroon colour.

Never allow the compost to dry out during the growing season.

FACT FILE

ORIGIN America, West Indies.

HEIGHT To 90cm/3ft.

COMPOST Peat-based or soil-based with one-third peat moss or leaf mould added.

REPOTTING In spring every year, or every other year, move the plant into a pot one size larger.

PROPAGATION Divide and repot an established plant in spring.

KEEPING PLANTS Calatheas are fairly long-lived, given the right growing conditions.

PLANT CARE

Light shade; no direct sun. ● Keep in evenly warm conditions with a minimum temperature of 16°C/60°F. ● Water freely with warm, preferably lime-free, water during the growing season, more sparingly in winter. ● Mist the foliage regularly. ● Give the plant plenty of standard liquid fertiliser every 2 weeks in the growing period.

CALCEOLARIA x HERBEOHYBRIDA
Scrophulariaceae

SLIPPER FLOWER

Calceolaria's curious pouch-shaped flowers have given rise to several common names for these hybrid plants, among them pocketbook plant and slipperwort. The brightly coloured flowers are often yellow spotted with red or brown, but orange and red varieties with darker blotches are also available. Flowers are normally borne in spring, in clusters on tall stems that rise above the roughly heart-shaped, light green, downy foliage.

The compost needs to be kept moist at all times, since these plants are difficult to revive if they are ever allowed to dry out. The flowering season will be extended if they are kept in moderately cool conditions.

Calceolaria x *herbeohybrida* 'Anytime Mixed' is an early-flowering strain which if sown in summer will produce flowering plants in early winter. However, as its name implies, it can be sown virtually all year round and will flower four to five months later.

FACT FILE

ORIGIN South America; hybrids.

HEIGHT To 46cm/18in.

COMPOST Peat-based.

REPOTTING None.

PROPAGATION Plants can be raised from seed sown in summer and autumn for flowering the following spring; best left to professionals.

KEEPING PLANTS Discard after flowering.

PLANT CARE

Bright light, but no direct sunlight. ● Keep in a fairly cool room at about 7°C/45°F at night, 16°C/60°F during the day. ● Water plentifully and regularly. ● Provide humid conditions by standing the plant on a tray of wet pebbles or peat moss.

Always choose a plant with plenty of unopened buds. The flowering season should extend for about a month in the right conditions.

Check the undersides of the leaves regularly for aphids and spray with a contact insecticide if they are present.

Keep in a cool position that is free from draughts.

CALLISIA REPENS
Commelinaceae

CALLISIA

This easily grown callisia is related to tradescantia and is similar in appearance. It produces trailing stems up to 60cm/2ft long, which start erect but droop as they mature. The stems are densely clothed in oval, pointed, rather fleshy bright green leaves.

Callisia elegans (syn. *Setcreasea striata*), the striped inch plant or wandering Jew, has leaves striped with white down their length; the undersides of the leaves, which are visible because of the plant's trailing habit, are purple.

Like many plants that are easy to grow and to propagate, these two are often treated with disdain, but well-grown specimens make attractive subjects for hanging baskets. Set three or four plants around the edge of a pot to make a well-filled basket. After two or three years plants begin to look jaded and straggly and are best replaced; new plants are easily raised from cuttings.

FACT FILE

ORIGIN South and Central America, USA (Texas).

HEIGHT To about 10cm/4in; stems trail to 60cm/2ft.

COMPOST Either peat- or soil-based.

REPOTTING Generally unnecessary.

PROPAGATION Take 5-cm/2-in stem cuttings in spring and summer.

KEEPING PLANTS Pinch out stem tips regularly to keep the plant compact. Replace the plant with a rooted cutting when it becomes leggy – usually after about 2 years.

PLANT CARE

Bright light. ● Cool or moderately warm room, with a minimum winter temperature of 10°C/50°F. ● Keep the compost moist during the growing season, but allow the surface to dry out between waterings in the winter rest period. ● Mist the foliage occasionally. ● An application of liquid fertiliser every 10 to 14 days in summer helps to keep the foliage dense and the growth compact.

Excessively dry conditions may cause brown marks on the foliage. Mist the plants to increase humidity.

Red spider mites are sometimes attracted to the tips of the stems, where their fine webbing can be seen. Increase humidity to combat this pest.

Bright light with direct sun helps to prevent plants becoming straggly.

CALLISTEMON CITRINUS
Myrtaceae

CRIMSON BOTTLE BRUSH

Although this attractive and unusual indoor plant will grow well in normal room conditions, it is ideal for a conservatory or sunroom, where it can be allowed to develop into a moderately large shrub. The flower spikes have no petals but consist of tightly packed, bright red stamens with yellow tips. These 10-cm/4-in spikes have the appearance of a particularly colourful bottle brush. Leaves are long, narrow and pointed, giving the plant a rather spiky appearance.

Flowering occurs in summer; once it is over, move the plant outdoors into a sunny, sheltered position to help ripen the wood for good flowering the following season. Bring it back indoors when the nights start to become cold. Callistemons need a winter rest period during which they should be kept cool and watered moderately.

The brilliantly colourful, erect flower spikes are topped with a little tuft of leaves.

A bright, sunny position is essential for good flowering.

Soil-based compost suits this plant best. Be careful not to overwater, especially in autumn and winter.

FACT FILE

ORIGIN Australia.

HEIGHT To 1.2m/4ft.

COMPOST Equal amounts of soil-based compost, leaf mould and coarse sand.

REPOTTING Repot in spring. Increase the size of pot until the plant is as large as you desire, then top-dress annually.

PROPAGATION Sow seed in spring or take semi-ripe cuttings in early summer.

KEEPING PLANTS Cut back by about half immediately after flowering, to keep the plant compact.

PLANT CARE

Strong, bright light with several hours of direct sun. ● Normal room temperature; keep cool during the winter rest period, with a minimum temperature of 8°C/47°F. ● Keep the compost thoroughly moist in spring and summer; water moderately in winter. ● The plant prefers low humidity and good ventilation.

CAMELLIA JAPONICA
Theaceae

*C*AMELLIA

In the home, the beautiful waxy blooms of this winter- and early spring-flowering shrub can be appreciated at close quarters, and they are secure from damaging frosts. The flowers may be single, double or semi-double, carried in clusters or singly, depending on variety. They may be white, pink or red, or a combination of either pink and white or red and white, and may be about 13cm/5in wide. The glossy, dark green leathery leaves are carried on woody branches and tend to curl under slightly from the tips and sides.

Camellias are ideal plants for a cool, airy room or conservatory since they do not like the hot, dry conditions of heated houses. They need regular misting and should be set on a tray of gravel to raise the humidity, especially when the buds are forming. Do not move flowering plants; the buds are likely to drop off if you do.

FACT FILE

ORIGIN China, Japan, India, Indonesia.

HEIGHT To 3m/10ft or more.

COMPOST Equal parts of lime-free soil-based potting mix, peat moss and coarse leaf mould.

REPOTTING When necessary, move the plant into a pot one size larger after flowering until maximum practical size is reached; thereafter, top-dress at the end of the rest period.

PROPAGATION Take semi-ripe cuttings in early summer; difficult for the amateur.

KEEPING PLANTS Stand outdoors in a sheltered place in summer; bring under cover in late autumn.

PLANT CARE

Bright light but no direct sun. ● Must have cool conditions of 7°–16°C/45°–60°F. ● Keep the compost evenly moist when the buds are forming. After flowering, allow the surface of the compost to dry out between waterings. ● Mist-spray daily. ● Give a liquid feed every 10 to 14 days during the growing season.

Stand the plant outside in summer to encourage buds to form.

Check the undersides of the leaves for scale insects and push off any scales with a fingernail.

Buds will drop if compost dries out during the flowering season.

CAMPANULA ISOPHYLLA
Campanulaceae

*S*TAR OF BETHLEHEM

This trailing plant is ideal for a hanging basket or any position where its long stems, studded with blue bell-like flowers, can be allowed to trail. The soft, pale green leaves are heart-shaped, but in good conditions are almost hidden by the clusters of star-shaped blooms. Stems reach up to 30cm/12in in length.

Flowers are generally light blue, although a white variety is available; *Campanula isophylla* 'Stella Blue' and 'Stella White' are the varieties most frequently offered. Also known as falling stars and bellflower, this campanula is easy to grow, demanding only a fairly cool room and regular watering throughout the growing season.

Check the young leaves for the presence of aphids; treat with a contact insecticide.

If humidity is too high, grey mould may occur; treat with a fungicide.

Display plants in a hanging basket or on a tall pot stand; allow stems to trail gracefully.

Reduce watering and keep the plant cool during the winter.

FACT FILE

ORIGIN Italy.

HEIGHT To 15cm/6in, trailing stems to 30cm/12in long.

COMPOST Soil-based.

REPOTTING When roots appear on the surface of the compost, move plants to pots one size larger up to a maximum of about 13cm/5in.

PROPAGATION Take soft tip cuttings in spring and summer or grow on from seed.

KEEPING PLANTS Campanulas do not like too much humidity. Cut back stems after flowering and reduce watering in the winter.

PLANT CARE

Bright light but no direct sun. ● Cool conditions up to 16°C/60°F. ● Water regularly during the growing season. ● Apply a standard liquid fertiliser every 2 weeks while the plant is in flower. ● Remove faded blooms to encourage a long flowering season.

CAPSICUM ANNUUM
Solanaceae

*O*RNAMENTAL PEPPER

Grown for its brightly coloured fruits, rather than its foliage or flowers, this plant is a variety of the chilli pepper and is also often called the ornamental chilli pepper. The mid-green leaves are oval and pointed, and white, star-shaped flowers appear in summer and early autumn. Stand the plant outdoors in summer to ensure good pollination. The usually cone-shaped fruits, which are held erect, change colour from green through yellow and orange to red. There are purple varieties as well, and also some that have round, ball-shaped fruits similar to the false Jerusalem cherry, *Solanum capsicastrum* (see page 137). The fruits ripen in autumn and winter, which accounts for their most usual common name in the northern hemisphere – Christmas pepper.

Keep plants out of the reach of children who may be tempted to sample the fruits, for like the chilli pepper, the fruits of all species are intensely fiery and are not pleasant to eat. Juice from the fruits can cause painful burning and stinging of the delicate skin near the eyes and mouth, so be sure to keep your hands away from your face after handling them.

Capsicum annuum 'Holiday Cheer' *has round berries that change from cream through yellow and purple to holly red; fruits at various stages on the same plant give a multi-coloured effect.*

FACT FILE

ORIGIN South America.

HEIGHT To 30cm/12in.

POTTING MIX As provided.

REPOTTING Usually none.

PROPAGATION Sow seed in early to mid-spring in peat-based compost.

KEEPING PLANTS Usually discarded after fruiting.

PLANT CARE

A brightly lit, sunny position is required. ● Fairly cool conditions, about 13°C/ 55°F. ● Keep the compost moist at all times, particularly during the flowering period. ● Mist the foliage regularly. ● Stand the plant in an open sheltered position outdoors in summer to aid pollination and fruiting.

ALSO RECOMMENDED

Capsicum annuum produces either cone-shaped or round fruits, according to the variety. *C.a.* 'Red Missile' has large, tapered fruits that are brilliant red when ripe; *C.a.* 'Fireball' has round fruits, maturing from cream through orange to scarlet on compact plants.

Juice from the berries is a powerful irritant, so take care when handling them.

If leaves look papery and fine webbing can sometimes be seen, check for red spider mites. Stand the plant on moist gravel to increase humidity, which helps to combat this pest.

Hot, dry air leads to foliage shrivelling and falling and encourages attack by red spider mites. Mist the foliage regularly.

CAREX MORROWII 'VARIEGATA'
Cyperaceae

*J*APANESE SEDGE GRASS

The sedges are usually found growing outdoors in boggy soil at the sides of rivers and ponds, but one variety, *Carex morrowii* 'Variegata', makes a useful indoor plant. The narrow, grassy leaves, striped pale green and white, arise from a rhizomatous root to make a gracefully arching fountain of foliage up to 46cm/18in long.

Plants are easy to grow and are not fussy about conditions, although they prefer a cool, humid atmosphere. They are useful plants for groups, where their slender, upright, grassy foliage contrasts well with broad-leafed plants that have more rounded shapes.

FACT FILE

ORIGIN Japan.

HEIGHT To 30cm/12in.

COMPOST Soil-based preferably.

REPOTTING Repot in spring, when the roots can be seen growing through the base of the pot.

PROPAGATION Divide plants into two or three clumps at any time during the growing season; very small clumps will not grow well.

KEEPING PLANTS This plant is long-lived and if given even minimum attention will thrive for years.

PLANT CARE

Bright filtered light helps to ensure well-coloured foliage. ● Cool to moderately warm conditions; winter temperature of 10°–16°C/50°–60°F. ● Keep the compost moist but not waterlogged. ● Mist the foliage frequently at temperatures of 18°–21°C/65°–70°F. ● Apply standard liquid fertiliser every 4 weeks in spring and summer.

The grassy foliage makes a graceful arching shape.

The variegation of the leaves is more marked when plants are grown in bright light with some direct sun.

Keep the compost just moist but never saturated.

CATHARANTHUS ROSEUS
Apocynaceae

*R*OSE PERIWINKLE

This plant is related to the blue-flowered periwinkles, *Vinca* spp., but produces white, pale violet or pink star-shaped flowers with a deeper-coloured throat. The oval leaves are bright green and shiny, and flowers are produced in profusion at the tips of the stems. This periwinkle forms a rounded, shrubby plant with a flowering season that lasts all summer and into autumn.

Catharanthus roseus aroused much interest some years ago when its wild form was found to produce a drug useful in the treatment of leukaemia. It is not a demanding plant to grow, but is not widely available at garden centres, although it fairly easy to raise from seed.

Shiny, healthy-looking oval leaves have a light-coloured midrib.

Star-shaped flowers, with slightly reflexing petals, are about 2.5cm/ 1in wide and are often carried in large numbers.

Seedlings produce the healthiest, most free-flowering plants.

A well-grown plant can quickly fill a 13-cm/5-in pot. Pot on as necessary to keep the plant growing strongly.

FACT FILE

ORIGIN Madagascar.

HEIGHT To 25cm/10in.

COMPOST Soil or soil-based.

REPOTTING Move vigorous plants into pots one size larger as necessary.

PROPAGATION Sow seed in a warm sheltered spot in late winter or early spring, or in a warm greenhouse in winter. Soft tip cuttings can be taken in spring and early summer.

KEEPING PLANTS Not easy to bring into flower again, so plants are often discarded after flowering.

PLANT CARE

Bright light with some direct sun will encourage good flowering. ● Moderate warmth with a minimum temperature of about 10°C/50°F. ● Keep the compost moist throughout the flowering period and mist the leaves occasionally. ● Apply a standard liquid fertiliser every 10 to 14 days.

CATTLEYA SPP.
Orchidaceae

CATTLEYA

Many species of orchids are becoming increasingly popular as plants to grow in the home, cattleyas among them. They are not as difficult to grow as many people believe, and the exotic, waxy, long-lasting flowers are very rewarding. There are several species and varieties of cattleya suitable as house plants. All are epiphytic – in the wild they do not grow in soil but on the stems of other plants, receiving moisture and nutrients from the atmosphere and from rain. In cultivation, they are grown in a special orchid compost, often consisting of a mixture of bark, sphagnum moss and osmunda fibre.

Cattleyas produce swollen pseudobulbs with long, strap-shaped leaves. Flowers in shades of pink and red, often splashed with yellow, and with a frilled lower lip, arise in clusters or singly on long stems. The flowers may be up to 13cm/5in wide and can last for more than a month; after flowering, plants rest for about six weeks.

Among the species available are *Cattleya intermedia*, with clusters of rose pink and deep purple blooms in late spring or early summer; and *C. labiata*, which produces groups of large flowers in shades of pink and red marked with yellow in early winter.

FACT FILE

ORIGIN Tropical South America, Mexico, West Indies.

HEIGHT To 60cm/2ft.

COMPOST Special orchid compost available from specialist growers.

REPOTTING Move into a pot 5cm/2in larger when the pseudobulbs appear crowded.

PROPAGATION After the rest period, divide overcrowded plants into two, using a sharp knife to cut through the rhizomes (the stems that join the pseudobulbs together at the base).

KEEPING PLANTS Do not spray cattleyas; it may injure new growth and will mark flowers.

PLANT CARE

Bright light but no direct sunlight. ● Warm conditions, with a minimum temperature of 16°C/60°F. ● Water frequently during the growing period, sparingly during the rest period. ● Mist the plant regularly, especially in temperatures over 21°C/70°F and stand the pot on a tray of moist pebbles – humidity must be high. ● Give a foliar feed every 3 or 4 waterings during the period of active growth.

ALSO RECOMMENDED

Many hybrids and named varieties have larger flowers than the species. Among them are *Cattleya* Bob Betts 'White Wings', a large-flowered, spring-blooming plant, and *C.* Nigritian 'King of Kings', which produces many-flowered clusters of splendid lavender-coloured blooms. *C.* 'Guatemalensis', with small salmon pink flowers in spring, is a natural hybrid.

Pseudobulbs are swollen stem bases from which the leaves and flower stems arise. Wait until the pot is crowded with pseudobulbs before repotting, otherwise flowering will be adversely affected.

Flowers consist of three sepals and three petals, the lower one of which is tubular and frilled to form a lip. Remove flowers as they fade.

Allow the compost to dry out between waterings, and give a rest period with very little water for about 6 weeks after flowering. Use lime-free water if possible.

Old, shrivelled pseudobulbs may remain on the plant for several years. They do not need to be removed.

The hybrid 'Violacea' is a charming small-flowered cattleya. Its pale-coloured flowers are borne in abundance and it produces 3 or 4 blooms to a stem.

CHAMAEDOREA ELEGANS
Palmae

PARLOUR PALM

One of the most popular palms for the home, *Chamaedorea elegans* (also known as *Neanthe elegans*) has long, arching leaves divided into pairs of leaflets either side of the central midrib. It eventually develops a short trunk, and after three or four years may produce sprays of tiny yellow flowers. It remains a small, compact plant and is easy to look after. Young plants are particularly suitable for bottle gardens or terraria. Because of their slow growth rate, older, larger plants can be very expensive; small young plants are a better buy. Chamaedorea is also known as the good luck, or dwarf mountain, palm.

FACT FILE

ORIGIN Mexico, Guatemala.

HEIGHT To 6ft/1.8m after several years.

COMPOST Soil-based mixed with half the amount of peat.

REPOTTING Necessary only when the roots have completely filled the pot; firm the compost gently but thoroughly around the roots.

PROPAGATION From seed. Practicable only by specialists.

KEEPING PLANTS Plants will survive for many years if good growing conditions are provided.

PLANT CARE

Moderately bright light or light shade. ● Minimum winter temperature of 10°–13°C/50°–55°F. ● Keep the compost moist during the growing season; allow the top one-third to dry out between waterings in winter. ● Mist the foliage regularly and stand the plants on a tray of moist pebbles to increase humidity. ● Apply half-strength liquid fertiliser monthly during the growing period only.

Brown tips to the leaves are usually caused by an excessively dry atmosphere. Increase the humidity.

Sprays of tiny yellow flowers may appear on a 3- to 4-year-old plant if it is grown in good light.

Dry-looking leaves with a silvery or mottled appearance may indicate attack by red spider mites. Maintain a humid atmosphere to combat this pest.

CHAMAEROPS HUMILIS
Palmae

EUROPEAN FAN PALM

There are several other fan palms, but this is the only one that is native to Europe. The large, deeply divided, fan-shaped fronds give the plant its other frequently used common names: dwarf fan palm and hair palm. Each dark green leaf measures about 60cm/2ft across and consists of a number of stiff, spiky segments radiating from the base. The leaf stalk, which is generally 30–60cm/1–2ft long, is sharply toothed.

The plant makes a bushy, architectural shrub which is generally not difficult to grow in normal room conditions. Where temperatures fall below 13°–16°C/55°–60°F in winter, water this palm sparingly and allow the top half of the compost to dry out between waterings.

Even well-established plants do not produce flowers or fruit when grown indoors.

Take care when handling the palm: the leaf stems are covered with sharp teeth.

The long, stiff leaf segments often become shaggy and split at their tips.

FACT FILE

ORIGIN Western Mediterranean countries.

HEIGHT To 1.2m/4ft.

COMPOST Soil-based.

REPOTTING In spring, move into a pot one size larger every second year until desired size has been reached, then top-dress annually.

PROPAGATION Sow fresh seed in a propagator, or carefully separate 20–25-cm/8–10-in suckers with roots from the parent plant and pot them up individually.

KEEPING PLANTS Well cared for, this palm can survive for several years.

PLANT CARE

Bright light with some direct sun, although the plant will tolerate light shade. ● Minimum temperature 10°C/50°F. ● Keep the compost moist at all times in the growing period, but do not allow the pot to stand in water. ● Apply a liquid feed every 10 to 14 days in summer.

CHLOROPHYTUM COMOSUM 'VITTATUM'
Liliaceae

*S*PIDER PLANT

Probably because it is so easy to grow and propagate, the spider, or ribbon, plant is one of the most popular of all plants both in homes and offices. The grassy, ribbon-like leaves, which form an arching clump, are 15–30cm/6–12in long and are green, with central bands of creamy white.

In spring and summer, sprays of small white flowers are produced on long, yellow, wiry stems that cascade gracefully down from the parent plant. Spider plants are especially attractive in hanging baskets or wall-mounted pot holders. The flowers are followed by clusters of baby plants, each producing a miniature clump of variegated leaves. Roots soon develop on these plantlets, which can be removed from the parent and potted up individually.

FACT FILE

ORIGIN South Africa.

HEIGHT To 25cm/10in.

COMPOST Peat-based or peat-substitute.

REPOTTING Move into a container one size larger when roots start to appear through the base of the pot.

PROPAGATION Pot up baby plantlets when they start to develop roots, or divide the rosettes in spring.

KEEPING PLANTS These are hardy plants and will go on for years, provided they are given good growing conditions and are repotted when necessary.

PLANT CARE

Bright light is essential for well-coloured leaves; too much direct sunlight will scorch the foliage. ● Minimum temperature 7°C/45°F. ● Keep the compost moist at all times in spring and summer; water more sparingly in winter. ● Feed with a standard liquid fertiliser every 10 to 14 days from early spring to late autumn.

Brown tips to the leaves develop if the compost is allowed to dry out or if the air is excessively hot and dry. Mist the foliage occasionally.

The plant needs good light to ensure the best colour contrast on the variegated leaves.

Instead of being allowed to cascade from the parent plant, flowering stems can be trained around a cane hoop.

CHRYSALIDOCARPUS LUTESCENS
Palmae

*B*UTTERFLY PALM

This upright palm produces tall, bamboo-like stems topped with arching fronds which are divided into leaflets in more or less opposite pairs. The fronds are pale yellow-green and up to 1.2m/4ft long. Previously called *Areca lutescens*, this palm is also sometimes known as the areca palm, golden feather palm or yellow palm.

With its bold, striking outline, chrysalidocarpus makes a good specimen plant. It is fairly slow-growing, so large specimens tend to be expensive to buy.

The cane-like stems of mature plants are marked with notches, indicating the positions of previous leaf stalks.

Old fronds at the base of the plant turn brown and shrivel, and should be removed. Their removal leads to the development of the typical reed-like stems.

Mottled, greyish, dry-looking leaves may indicate attack by red spider mites. Keep the pests at bay by providing a humid atmosphere.

FACT FILE

ORIGIN Madagascar.

HEIGHT To 1.5m/5ft or more after several years.

COMPOST Soil-based.

REPOTTING Move into a pot one size larger every other year in spring. Top-dress annually once the pot is as large as desired.

PROPAGATION When repotting, detach suckers (ideally those some 30cm/12in high with good root growth) complete with roots from the base of established plants and pot them up individually.

KEEPING PLANTS These palms are hardy and will last for many years.

PLANT CARE

Bright filtered light. ● Minimum temperature of 13°C/55°F. ● Keep the compost moist at all times during the growing season. In winter reduce watering in lower temperatures. ● Mist the foliage daily to maintain a humid atmosphere. ● Apply liquid fertiliser every 2 weeks in the growing season.

CHRYSANTHEMUM* x *MORIFOLIUM
Compositae

*F*LORISTS' CHRYSANTHEMUM

A popular short-term flowering plant, the florists' chrysanthemum (*Dendranthema* x *grandiflorum* as it is currently known) requires specialist production techniques from the commercial grower. Deep green, aromatic, lobed leaves are set on short stems topped with double, semi-double or single flowers in a wide range of colours: white, cream, red, orange, yellow and pink. Anemone-centred flowers are also available, as are fine-petalled 'spiders', and 'spoons' with rolled petals opening out at the ends. Most florists' chrysanthemums consist of several cuttings inserted around the edge of a pot; because the compost is filled with roots, plants tend to dry out quickly.

In nature, the flowering time of chrysanthemums is controlled by day length: they are 'short-day' plants that flower naturally in late summer and autumn. Commercial growers manipulate artificial lighting to bring plants into flower throughout the year, but they are probably most popular as autumn and winter plants. (Buy only plants that are already showing colour in the buds; others may not open.)

Plants are also treated with dwarfing chemicals to keep them compact; without these chemicals most varieties would flower at 90cm–1.2m/3–4ft high. Since these are only temporary indoor plants, they can sometimes successfully be planted out in the garden in mild climates, where they will revert to their full height and natural flowering season the following year.

FACT FILE

ORIGIN Northern temperate zones; hybrid.

HEIGHT To 30cm/12in.

COMPOST Not applicable.

REPOTTING None.

PROPAGATION Tale soft stem cuttings to produce garden plants; it is not possible for the home gardener to produce successful house plants.

KEEPING PLANTS Discard after flowering, or plant outdoors.

PLANT CARE

Moderately bright light without direct sun. ● Flowers last best in reasonably cool conditions of 13°–16°C/55°–60°F. ● Keep the compost moist at all times.

ALSO RECOMMENDED

Chrysanthemum frutescens (syn. *Argyranthemum frutescens*), the white marguerite, has masses of daisy-like flowers with a bright yellow central disc. It can grow to 90cm/3ft, but on pot plants – best bought from a specialist grower in early spring – the growing shoots are usually pinched out and the plants are about 46cm/18in high.
        C.f. 'Etoile d'Or' has lemon yellow petals, and 'Mary Wootton' rose pink petals.

A wide variety of flower types and shapes is available, though the doubles are probably the most popular.

Compact, low-growing plants are produced by the use of dwarfing compounds. Surviving plants will eventually return to their natural height.

Chrysanthemum frutescens, *the white marguerite, is one of the most floriferous and rewarding of summer-flowering plants.*

The colourful flowers should last for several weeks in reasonably cool, bright conditions.

Water frequently to keep the compost thoroughly moist.

CISSUS ANTARCTICA
Vitadacae

*K*ANGAROO VINE

A fast-growing, scrambling plant, this cissus can cover large areas of trellis with its bright green, healthy-looking leaves and is useful as a screen or room divider. The pointed, oval leaves are shiny, with toothed edges, and are carried on tough stems that climb upwards and outwards rapidly, clinging to any support by means of curling tendrils. *Cissus antarctica* can also be grown in hanging baskets and allowed to trail. *C.a.* 'Minima' is probably better for this, since it has a more spreading growth habit. These plants are suitable for a wide range of conditions and are popular because of their adaptability.

Cissus rhombifolia 'Ellen Danica', the quick-growing grape ivy, has handsome, glossy three-lobed leaves and is an excellent plant for a hanging basket or for growing up a trellis to form a room divider.

FACT FILE

ORIGIN Australia.

HEIGHT To 3m/10ft.

COMPOST Soil- or peat-based.

REPOTTING Move up in spring, when roots have filled the pot.

PROPAGATION Take young tip cuttings in spring and early summer; strip off the lower leaves, dip in hormone rooting powder, insert into a mixture of peat and sand, and enclose the pot in a plastic bag. Roots should form within 6–8 weeks.

KEEPING PLANTS Pinch shoot tips back to keep plants within bounds; if they become bare at the base, cut them well back in spring.

PLANT CARE

Ideally, bright light but no direct sun, but the plant will adapt to a wide range of light conditions. ● Cool conditions, with a minimum of 7°–10°C/45°–50°F in winter. ● Keep the soil moist throughout the growing season; allow the surface to dry out between waterings in winter. ● Liquid-feed every 10–14 days in spring and summer. ● Provide a suitable support before stems become tangled or misshapen.

ALSO RECOMMENDED

Cissus rhombifolia (often sold as *Rhoicissus rhomboidea*), the grape ivy, has leaves that are a deep green, although young shoots are covered in fine hairs, which gives them a silvery appearance. Tendrils are forked at the tips. The variety 'Ellen Danica' has attractively lobed leaflets.

Cissus discolor is much more unusual, and more difficult to grow. The velvety, spear-shaped leaves are marked with silver and pink in a similar fashion to those of *Begonia rex*. This plant needs warm conditions and high humidity to do well.

Train the plant up a trellis, netting or moss pole. Make sure supports are firmly fixed, since the weight of the foliage on well-grown plants can easily cause them to topple over.

Cissus needs good light but should be protected from direct sun, which causes scorch marks on the leaves. The plant will tolerate light shade.

Aphids often attack young shoots. Inspect them regularly during spring and early summer and treat with a contact insecticide if the pests are present.

Mist the foliage regularly to keep it healthy. Brown leaf tips indicate that the atmosphere is too dry.

x *CITROFORTUNELLA MICROCARPUS*
Rutaceae

CALAMONDIN

Citrus plants make attractive shrubs particularly suitable for a sunroom or conservatory. This cross between a tangerine (mandarin) and a kumquat – also found under the name of x *Citrofortunella mitis* – is one of the best to grow indoors, since it makes a compact tree that bears flowers and fruits while still young.

The glossy, dark green, oval leaves are aromatic when crushed and are carried on woody branches which, unlike those of many other species of citrus, are spineless. White, star-shaped, fragrant flowers are borne mainly in summer but may appear sporadically at any time of year. They are followed by small round fruits, carried in clusters of two or three at the tips of the branches, which tend to bend down the stems as they develop. The fruits ripen slowly, changing from deep green to orange, and measure about 4cm/1½in in diameter; they are decorative and, although very bitter, are sometimes used in jams. Flowers and fruits are often seen on the tree at the same time, adding to its interest.

To ensure fruiting, pollinate the flowers with a soft brush if the plant is indoors. Pollination is improved by standing the plant outdoors in summer.

Yellowing or mottled leaves may indicate nutrient deficiency. Apply a foliar feed containing trace elements.

Scale insects can be a problem. Check the undersides of the leaves, pushing off any scales with a fingernail.

Attack by red spider mites can be combated by misting to increase humidity and by standing the pot on moist gravel.

FACT FILE

ORIGIN Hybrid.

HEIGHT To 1.2m/4ft.

COMPOST Soil-based.

REPOTTING Move the plant into a pot one size larger every spring until the maximum convenient size is reached; thereafter top-dress annually.

PROPAGATION Difficult; take semi-ripe cuttings in early summer.

KEEPING PLANTS Stand outdoors in a sheltered place in summer; bring it under cover in late autumn.

PLANT CARE

Bright light with several hours of direct sun daily. ● Minimum winter temperature of 10°C/50°F. ● Allow the surface of the compost to dry out between waterings. ● Mist the foliage frequently and stand the pot on a tray of moist gravel to increase humidity. ● Give a high-potash liquid feed every 10–14 days in the growing season.

CLERODENDRUM THOMSONIAE
Verbenaceae

BLEEDING HEART VINE

This climbing plant can be trained up a trellis or around a hoop, or allowed to trail from a hanging basket or raised pot. It can also be kept bushy by regularly pinching out the tips of shoots. The deep green ovate leaves are attractively veined, but the plant's chief glory is the striking red-and-white flowers, which consist of a white lantern-shaped calyx from which the bright scarlet blooms with prominent stamens emerge. The flowers are produced from spring to autumn in clusters at the ends of the stems. *Clerodendrum thomsoniae* 'Variegatum', with variegated, marbled green leaves, is sometimes available.

FACT FILE

ORIGIN Tropical West Africa.

HEIGHT To 2.4m/8ft.

COMPOST Soil-based.

REPOTTING When the compost is filled with roots, move to a pot one size larger in spring; top-dress when maximum convenient pot size is reached.

PROPAGATION Take stem cuttings in late spring, pot up in a mixture of equal parts of coarse sand and peat moss; move to a soil-based mix after 3–4 months.

KEEPING PLANTS Prune in spring, just as the plant is starting into growth; cut back the stems by about half to keep it at a manageable size indoors.

PLANT CARE

Bright light is required for good flowering, but protect from direct sunlight. ● Moderate warmth during the growing season, but keep warm (17°–29°C/62°–85°F) in winter. ● Keep the compost moist throughout the flowering season; water sparingly in the winter rest period. ● Mist frequently with tepid water from spring onwards. ● Apply standard liquid fertiliser every 2 weeks in the growing season.

The striking red-and-white flowers are produced most freely in warm, humid conditions.

The plant flowers best when slightly pot-bound.

Pinch out the shoot tips occasionally to keep the plant tidy.

The twining stems can be trained up supports or left to trail from a hanging basket.

CLIVIA MINIATA
Amaryllidaceae

KAFFIR LILY

Although this is a long-established favourite, it often fails to flower indoors, usually because it has not been given a winter rest. The long, strap-shaped, deep green leaves overlap at the base, rather like those of a leek, then fan out at the top. In late winter or early spring a tall flower stem, carrying a head of about 10–15 trumpet-shaped flowers, pushes out from between the leaves. The flowers are usually orange with yellow throats, but deeper reddish shades and yellow or cream varieties are sometimes available.

The roots of clivias are thick, fleshy and rather brittle, and plants flower best when slightly pot-bound. Offsets are produced on established plants, and while these can be removed and used for propagation, they will produce an impressive specimen with a number of flower heads if they are allowed to remain.

FACT FILE

ORIGIN South Africa.

HEIGHT To 46cm/18in.

COMPOST Soil- or peat-based.

REPOTTING The fleshy roots soon appear to crowd the pot, but plants should be repotted only every 3–4 years. Instead, top-dress in late winter.

PROPAGATION Carefully detach offsets complete with roots from the parent and pot up individually.

KEEPING PLANTS Cut out embryo fruits that form after the flowers drop; pull withering flower stalks off the plant.

PLANT CARE

Bright light with some direct sun in spring. ● A winter rest period is essential, with a temperature of around 10°C/50°F for 6–8 weeks from late autumn. ● Keep the compost moist during the growing season, and water very sparingly during the rest period. ● Give a liquid feed every 12–14 days during the growing season.

ALSO RECOMMENDED

Clivia miniata 'Striata' has variegated leaves but is difficult to find.

Wipe the glossy, deep green leaves with a damp cloth occasionally to keep them looking fresh.

Snap off the flower head once all the blooms have faded, but wait until the flower stem begins to shrivel before pulling it gently from the plant.

Fluffy white mealybugs can sometimes be found between the leaf bases. Use a systemic insecticide to deal with any infestation.

The thick, fleshy roots often appear on the surface of the compost, but do not repot the plant until it is essential. It will flower best when the roots are restricted.

If the plant is not given a cool winter rest period, the flower stalk may not develop properly or flowers may fail to form.

The flower stem of Clivia miniata *bears an umbel of some 12–15 fragrant, trumpet-shaped flowers in a cheery, soft orange.*

CODIAEUM VARIEGATUM PICTUM
Euphorbiaceae

*C*ROTON

Another name for this popular plant is Joseph's coat, and a look at the range of forms available will soon explain why. The tough, leathery leaves are, indeed, of many colours, largely yellow-and-green mottled or veined with rosy pink, red or orange. Their shapes, too, vary enormously from long and pointed to short and broad; from slender, wavy-edged ribbons to deeply lobed and fiddle-shaped. The plant forms a small, sturdy shrub, often with a bare lower stem.

In some forms the colours remain the same; in others they darken with age. Mature plants may produce insignificant, fluffy cream-coloured flowers.

Codiaeum 'Golden Bell', a recently developed variety, has long, square-ended yellow, green and pink leaves, some with smaller leaflets growing from them.

FACT FILE

ORIGIN Malaysia, Pacific Islands, Northern Australia.

HEIGHT To 90cm/3ft.

COMPOST Soil-based.

REPOTTING Move into a pot one size larger in spring; when maximum desired size is reached, top-dress instead.

PROPAGATION Take tip cuttings in spring.

KEEPING PLANTS Plants are naturally bushy, so should not need pruning. But if they become too large cut them well back in early spring and use the prunings for propagation.

PLANT CARE

Bright light with some direct sun.
● Warm conditions with a minimum of 13°C/55°F in winter. ● Keep the compost evenly moist during the growing period. Reduce watering in winter, but do not allow the compost to dry out completely. ● Mist often and stand the plant on a tray of moist pebbles. ● Liquid-feed every 2 weeks during the growing season.

ALSO RECOMMENDED

Many varieties are available which are often sold unnamed. *Codiaeum variegatum pictum* 'Aucubifolium' has green, laurel-like leaves spotted with yellow; 'Craigii' has deeply lobed leaves with yellow veins. The leaves of 'Reidii' are suffused with red, yellow and pink and the veins are deep red. 'Bravo' has lightly lobed leaves splashed with yellow.

Keep the plants in bright light to ensure the best foliage colour and to avoid a bare lower stem where leaves have fallen prematurely.

Check the undersides of the leaves, especially along the midrib, for scale insects. If you find any, scrape them off with a fingernail.

Colours fade if the light is poor, especially in winter; move the plant to a brighter position.

Mealybugs and red spider mites both attack this plant; high humidity will help to keep the latter pest at bay.

The range of different shapes and colour combinations of codiaeum leaves is vast.

COELOGYNE CRISTATA
Orchidaceae

Coelogyne

This orchid produces two strap-shaped, slightly arching leaves from each of the rounded or egg-shaped pseudobulbs, which are tightly clustered. Flower stalks some 30cm/12in long arise from the pseudobulbs in winter or early spring and carry 6–8 scented white flowers with golden yellow markings on the lip and undulating petals.

Coelogynes are not the easiest orchids to grow in the home. They require high humidity during the growing season and a short winter rest period in order to produce their flowers. The pure white-and-gold flowers are, however, carried in quite large numbers on established plants, making coelogyne's cultivation a tempting prospect. It grows well mounted on a log or bark or in a hanging wooden basket, where its long, drooping flower stems will show to best advantage.

FACT FILE

ORIGIN Himalayas.

HEIGHT To 30cm/12in.

COMPOST Use only special orchid compost, which usually consists of shredded bark, osmunda fibre and sphagnum moss.

REPOTTING Repot in spring every 3–4 years. The plant resents disturbance.

PROPAGATION Cut off part of the rhizome together with a small number of pseudobulbs and pot up in special orchid compost.

KEEPING PLANTS With proper care, this orchid will last for many years.

PLANT CARE

Bright filtered light at all times. ● Minimum winter temperature of 13°C/55° during the day, 7°C/45°F at night. In summer, keep the temperature below 24°C/75°F. ● To water, stand plants in water for 10 minutes. Always keep the compost moist in the growing period. During the rest period, water just sufficiently to prevent the compost drying out completely. ● Mist the foliage regularly to ensure high humidity. ● Apply a foliar feed every 2 to 3 waterings.

A 6-week winter rest period is essential to ensure good flowering.

Pseudobulbs become wrinkled and yellow after flowering, but the new ones are shiny and light green. Take care not to splash the pseudobulbs when watering.

COLEUS BLUMEI
Labiatae

Flame Nettle

Known today as *Solenostemon scutellarioides*, but usually offered as *Coleus blumei*, this plant is cheap and easy to grow. These qualities, together with its brilliantly coloured foliage, have made it a popular, if fairly short-lived, house plant. The toothed leaves are usually ovate or heart-shaped, although some varieties have lance-shaped, or interestingly lobed or contorted foliage. The square, fleshy stems are typical of the mint family. Spikes of small blue flowers are often produced, but these are rather insignificant and detract from the foliage, so they are usually removed.

Foliage colours vary from green with yellow markings to intense reds, brilliant yellows and oranges, deep maroon and brown. Leaves may be edged or veined with contrasting colours or simply splashed with several different colours; some varieties have no green on the leaves at all. No wonder the plant is also called the painted nettle.

If winter temperatures fall much below 13°C/55°F, leaves may wilt and fall.

Pinch out the stem tips occasionally to keep plants bushy, and remove flower spikes when they appear.

If aphids attack the soft young foliage, spray with insecticide or soapy water, or pinch out and destroy the affected shoot tips.

Lower leaves fall in poor light, or if the plant is short of water.

FACT FILE

ORIGIN Tropical Africa, Asia.

HEIGHT To 60cm/2ft.

COMPOST Soil-based.

REPOTTING Move the plant into a larger pot as necessary during the growing season.

PROPAGATION In spring, sow seed or take stem cuttings. In late summer, take cuttings which should be overwintered in a greenhouse.

KEEPING PLANTS Discard the plant when it becomes leggy.

PLANT CARE

Bright light with some direct sun is essential for good leaf colour; intense summer sun will scorch the foliage. ● Moderately warm rooms, with a minimum of 13°C/55°F. ● Keep the compost evenly moist at all times, using lime-free water if possible. ● Mist the foliage regularly. ● Liquid-feed every 2 weeks during the growing season.

COLUMNEA x *BANKSII*
Gesneriaceae

*G*OLDFISH PLANT

Several species of columnea are available, but not all are easy to grow as indoor plants. *Columnea* x *banksii* is one of the most tolerant. Its dark green leaves are smooth and almost succulent. They are carried in opposite pairs along trailing stems that can reach 90cm/3ft or more, making this columnea an ideal plant for a hanging basket.

The bright red tubular flowers, about 6.5–8cm/2½–3in long, have yellow throats, with the upper petals forming a hood. They are borne in profusion in winter and early spring and occasionally in other seasons as well.

FACT FILE

ORIGIN Tropical America; hybrids.

HEIGHT Stems trail to 90cm/3ft or more.

COMPOST Peat-based.

REPOTTING Repot in spring, when the roots fill the pot.

PROPAGATION In spring or summer take cuttings from stems that are not flowering. Root them with bottom heat or sow seed in spring.

KEEPING PLANTS In good conditions, plants will last for several years.

PLANT CARE

Columneas need bright light but not direct sun. ● Warm conditions, with a minimum of about 13°C/55°F in winter. ● Keep the compost just moist, allowing the top third to dry out between waterings. Reduce watering in lower winter temperatures. ● A humid atmosphere must be maintained at all times. Mist the foliage with tepid water daily. ● Liquid-feed with a high-potash fertiliser every 10–14 days during the growing season.

ALSO RECOMMENDED

Columnea gloriosa has leaves that are densely covered with fine brownish hairs and produces large, striking, orange-red hooded flowers with yellow throats. The leaves of *C.g.* 'Purpurea' are covered with purple hairs.

Among the many hybrids are 'Alpha', with bright yellow flowers freely produced sporadically throughout the year, and 'Chanticleer', one of the easiest and most popular varieties, with a compact, branching habit and orange flowers produced all year. 'Mary Ann' produces unusual deep pink blooms at intervals during the year, and 'Stavanger' has smooth, glossy leaves and large, orange-red flowers.

Columnea gloriosa *has slender stems that tend to trail to about 90cm/3ft before they branch. It bears brilliant orange-red single flowers, which can be 8cm/3in long; they are followed by large white berries.*

The bright orange-red hooded flowers give columneas their common name of goldfish plant.

Smooth-leafed varieties are easier to grow than the hairy-leafed types.

All columneas need the high humidity provided by frequent misting.

Small brown spots on the leaves can be caused by misting with cold water; use tepid water instead.

CORDYLINE AUSTRALIS
Agavaceae

Cabbage Tree

Cordylines are sometimes confused with dracaenas, to which they are related, and *Cordyline australis* may be offered as *Dracaena indivisa*. It makes a fountain-shaped plant, with long, narrow, arching leaves on top of a short, stout stem. It has something of the appearance of a palm tree, and plants in this group are often known as 'false palms'. Also known as palm lily, grass palm, New Zealand cabbage palm and fountain dracaena, *C. australis* is an architectural plant, popular in modern settings.

Leaves are sword-shaped and leathery, mid- to dark green, and up to 90cm/3ft long. The variety *C.a.* 'Purpurea' has deep, rich purple-bronze leaves and *C.a.* 'Atropurpurea' has a purple flush at the base and up the centre of the leaf. Small white flowers in long panicles appear on mature plants, but are rarely produced in the home. It is a long-lived, fairly tolerant plant, and can withstand lower temperatures than other cordylines.

FACT FILE

ORIGIN New Zealand.

HEIGHT 1.8–3m/6–10ft or more.

COMPOST Soil- or peat-based.

REPOTTING Move into a pot one size larger every spring. Once the maximum desired pot size is reached, top-dress annually with fresh compost.

PROPAGATION In spring, sow seed, or take shoot tip cuttings from basal or stem shoots. Cut back overgrown plants and use 5-cm/2-in sections of the old stems with growth buds as cuttings.

KEEPING PLANTS The plant will benefit from a spell in the shade outdoors in summer.

PLANT CARE

Bright indirect sunlight; the plant will stand some shade. ● Minimum winter temperature of 10°C/50°F. ● Keep the compost moist during the growing season but allow it to dry out slightly between waterings in winter. ● Give a balanced liquid fertiliser every 2 weeks in spring and summer.

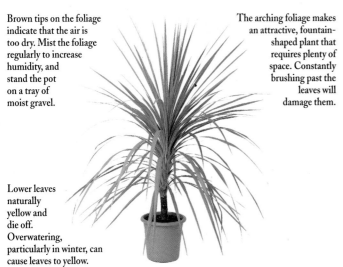

Brown tips on the foliage indicate that the air is too dry. Mist the foliage regularly to increase humidity, and stand the pot on a tray of moist gravel.

The arching foliage makes an attractive, fountain-shaped plant that requires plenty of space. Constantly brushing past the leaves will damage them.

Lower leaves naturally yellow and die off. Overwatering, particularly in winter, can cause leaves to yellow.

CORDYLINE TERMINALIS
Agavaceae

Good Luck Plant

Also known as ti tree or ti plant and red dracaena, *Cordyline terminalis* is sometimes incorrectly sold as *Dracaena terminalis*. It has more or less lance-shaped leaves up to 60cm/2ft long and 10cm/4in or so wide. Young foliage is pinkish red, gradually becoming deep coppery green. Several attractively coloured varieties are available, including *C.t.* 'Rededge', probably the most popular, with leaves streaked and outlined in red and a relatively compact habit. 'Baptistii' is flushed with red and yellow, and 'Kiwi' has leaves of mid-green, light green and cream, edged and flushed with pink. As the plant grows, the lower leaves fall to produce a plant with a rosette of foliage at the top of a long stem. It will last for several years.

The broad leaves have long leaf stalks and spread out like a fan from the central stem.

Dry air causes brown edges on the foliage. Regular, frequent misting is required.

Bright, filtered light is needed for the most intense leaf colour.

Watch out for aphids on the young leaves, particularly on the undersides. Treat with a contact insecticide.

FACT FILE

ORIGIN Polynesia.

HEIGHT 90cm–3m/3–10ft.

COMPOST Soil- or peat-based.

REPOTTING In spring, move into a pot one size larger until maximum required pot size is reached; thereafter top-dress annually.

PROPAGATION In spring, separate suckers from the base, pot them up individually and keep in warm, humid conditions until established. In early summer, cut the stems from old plants into 5-cm/2-in sections, each with a bud, and insert into seed compost with added sharp sand.

KEEPING PLANTS This is a long-lived plant in favourable conditions.

PLANT CARE

Bright conditions with filtered sun. ● Minimum winter temperature of 13°C/55°F. ● Keep the compost evenly moist during the growing season. Allow the surface to dry out between waterings in winter. ● Mist the foliage regularly. ● Feed with a balanced liquid fertiliser every 2 weeks in spring and summer. ● Protect from draughts.

CRASSULA ARBORESCENS (SYN. C. COTYLEDON)
Crassulaceae

CHINESE JADE PLANT

Most crassulas are low-growing, but some make small bushy shrubs. In their native habitat – the drier areas of South Africa – day temperatures can be high with a huge drop at night, causing heavy dew. The flowers of most crassulas are tiny, but they may appear in very large numbers.

The Chinese, or silver, jade plant can grow to 1.2m/4ft high and, with its thick, trunk-like stem and many branches, which are symmetrical in mature specimens, it makes a perfect miniature 'tree'. No training or pruning is required. The 2.5–5-cm/1–2-in-wide fleshy leaves are almost round and grey-green, rimmed with red. Flowers rarely appear indoors, but if you are lucky you will see them – tiny stars in white through to pink, carried in clusters during spring.

Crassula arborescens 'Variegata' is an attractive, slower-growing variegated form, with yellowish leaf markings.

Grey mould may develop if the plant is overwatered or drainage is inadequate.

Mealybugs may attack this plant; check for signs of the white waxy wool on leaves and stems.

If the plant is limp, wilting or discoloured, knock it out of its pot and check for root mealybugs or weevil grubs. Waterlogging could also cause these symptoms.

Brown, shrivelled or shrunken patches on leaves are caused by underwatering or the roots being dry for too long.

FACT FILE

ORIGIN South Africa (Cape Province, Natal).

HEIGHT To 1.2m/4ft.

COMPOST Soil-based, with some added peat.

REPOTTING Move into pots one size larger each spring. Once plants are in 20-cm/8-in pots, top-dress annually instead.

PROPAGATION Take tip cuttings in spring or summer.

KEEPING PLANTS Stand the plant in a sunny window and set it outdoors in summer to toughen up the stems and improve leaf colour.

PLANT CARE

Bright light, with some direct sunlight. ● Minimum winter temperature of 7°C/45°F, with normal room temperature at other times. ● Water liberally during spring and summer, but allow the compost to dry out between waterings. ● Apply a weak liquid fertiliser every 2 weeks from spring to autumn.

CRASSULA OVATA (SYN. C. PORTULACEA)
Crassulaceae

JADE TREE

Similar in many respects to its close relative *Crassula arborescens*, this succulent has glossy, dark green, spoon-shaped fleshy leaves which grow from a tree-like trunk. It may produce pretty, but short-lived, pink or white flowers in spring.

C. ovata likes the warm, dry atmosphere of a heated home and does not require much attention. If it is necessary to prune the plant, dust the wounds with sulphur or cigarette ash to stem the flow of sap. Mist the leaves occasionally to clean them. The jade tree, or money tree as it is sometimes called, is a slow grower and should last for many years.

FACT FILE

ORIGIN South Africa (Namaqualand to Transvaal).

HEIGHT To 90cm/3ft.

COMPOST Soil-based and perlite or sand in a ratio of 3:1.

REPOTTING Move only when necessary, probably every other year. Once plants are in 20-cm/8-in pots, top-dress annually instead.

PROPAGATION Sow seed in a propagator or root individual leaves or stem cuttings in a peat/sand mixture at room temperature. Allow cuttings to dry out for a few days before planting.

KEEPING PLANTS Stand the plant outside in summer in a sunny, protected spot.

PLANT CARE

Bright light, with some direct sunlight. ● Minimum winter temperature of 7°C/45°F; this plant can withstand high temperatures. ● Water 2 or 3 times a week in spring and summer, once a month in winter. ● Apply a high-potash fertiliser every 2 weeks from spring to autumn only.

Leaves drop in winter if the room is too warm; move the plant to a cooler position.

If the plant becomes spindly, move it to a brighter position.

Check stems and roots regularly for mealybugs; check roots for signs of weevil grubs.

CROCUS HYBRIDS
Iridaceae

*D*UTCH CROCUS

The crocuses most commonly seen in the home are Dutch hybrids, which have larger and more striking flowers than the species. The leaves are striped green and white, and the cup-shaped flowers, which appear in winter and early spring, may be white, yellow, bronze, purple or striped.

Dry corms are offered for sale in late summer, and ready planted pots are available from late autumn onwards. Among the best for growing indoors are 'Pickwick', shown here, which is pale silver-lilac with deep lilac stripes and a bright orange stigma, and the silvery, amethyst blue 'Little Dorrit', one of the largest of all crocuses. 'Queen of the Blues' has large flowers of soft ageratum blue with a paler edge.

FACT FILE

ORIGIN Hybrids.

HEIGHT To 10cm/4in.

COMPOST Soil-based or bulb fibre.

REPOTTING Plant several corms together in early autumn; set them just below the surface of the potting mixture. Corms must be 'wintered' for about 10 weeks and brought into a warm room only when the flower buds are visible.

PROPAGATION Remove cormlets from adults when repotting. Otherwise, sow ripe seed; plants will take 3–4 years to flower.

KEEPING PLANTS After flowering, either let the corms dry out in the pot and keep them until the next autumn, or plant them out in the garden. They will not bloom again indoors.

PLANT CARE

Filtered sunlight. ● Cool conditions, with a maximum temperature of 24°C/75°F. ● Keep the compost moist at all times. ● Apply weak liquid fertiliser every 4 weeks from planting to the start of flowering.

It is better to mass crocuses of one variety in a shallow bowl, rather than to mix them, because they tend to bloom at different times.

CROSSANDRA INFUNDIBULIFORMIS
Acanthaceae

*F*IRECRACKER FLOWER

This striking plant, also known as *Crossandra undulifolia*, is a small shrub from the rain forests of southern India and Sri Lanka. Its shiny, dark green leaves with wavy edges are held in opposite pairs and are 6.5–13cm/2½–5in long. From spring to late autumn, the flowers – in shades of yellow, orange and red – rise in twos and threes from upright tufts of green bracts. Each has a tube-shaped base, but flares out into a lobed disc up to 4cm/1½in wide. Even young specimens will flower readily, but after about two years they tend to lose their vigour and should be replaced. The form 'Mona Walhead' has salmon pink blooms; those of *C. pungens* are yellow.

Crossandras are good for groups, since they flourish best when surrounded by other plants and enjoy humid conditions.

Check for red spider mites; regular misting will help to discourage this pest.

A reluctance to flower may mean that the plant is in too shady a position. Move to a brighter place and pinch out some leaf growth to stimulate flower buds.

Falling leaves and a drooping appearance may indicate that the plant is standing in a cold draught; move it to a warmer place.

FACT FILE

ORIGIN India, Sri Lanka.

HEIGHT To 38cm/15in.

COMPOST Soil-based, with added peat.

REPOTTING Repot each spring, in a pot one size larger. Ensure good drainage since waterlogging can be fatal to the plant.

PROPAGATION Take 5–8-cm/2–3-in-long tip cuttings in spring and root them in a heated propagator.

KEEPING PLANTS Stand the plant outdoors in the sun in summer.

PLANT CARE

Bright filtered light, avoiding direct sunlight. ● Stable year-round temperatures no lower than 18°C/65°F. ● From spring to autumn water thoroughly, allowing the compost almost to dry out before giving more; water sparingly in winter. Water should be tepid.
● Stand the plant on a tray of moist pebbles for extra humidity, and mist regularly. ● In spring and summer, feed every 2 weeks with a high-potash liquid fertiliser.

PRIMULACEAE

CYCLAMENS

A t one time only experts could grow first-class cyclamens, but that has changed with the recent introduction of modern F1 hybrid varieties, which are available mainly as pot plants and as seed from the larger seed houses. *Cyclamen persicum* hybrids, florists' cyclamen, are dramatic, vigorous and free-flowering; they are no longer seasonal flowers that appear only in autumn. Hybridists have made it possible for cyclamens to flower all year round, but these plants tend to be most popular during the winter months.

There are large types, typically reaching 30cm/12in in height and spread, and intermediates, growing to 23cm/9in; both will often have more than 30 flowers on the plant at a time. Many varieties are available, and the colour of their swept-back petals ranges from white to pink, salmon, red and purple; bicoloured flowers are also found. Some cyclamens have frilled petals, and a few varieties have fragrant flowers. More recently, miniature strains have been developed with small leaves and charming little long-stemmed flowers in white, many shades of pink, red, mauve and bicolours. In some varieties of both larger and miniature cyclamens, the leaves are marbled with silver or a different shade of green or have a silver margin.

Although usually treated as annuals, cyclamens can last for several years if the tubers are dried off in the late spring and rested during the summer months.

Cyclamen persicum hybrids are so numerous and so varied – many are not even named – that it is difficult to recommend one over another. More important when buying a plant is its condition.

Fresh-looking and upright stems, leaves and flowers.

Plenty of well-formed flower buds visible among the leaves.

Leaves are well-formed and attractively marked.

Cyclamens do not mix well with other plants, but they are excellent long-lasting specimen plants for a cool room.

ALSO RECOMMENDED

The foliage of some cyclamens may be heavily marbled or bordered with silver and pale green. Still other plants have plain deep green leaves.

Cyclamen flowers may be striped. Above, cerise petals of a large cyclamen have a paler pink stripe. Most plants have flowers that spread sideways, almost like wings.

Frilled petal edges provide a striking variation to the brilliant orange-pink flowers of this intermediate-sized cyclamen with stems 18–20cm/7–8in long.

Aphids and red spider mites may attack this plant; check regularly for signs of their presence.

Yellowing leaves with brown patches are a sign of botrytis. Grey mould may soon appear and can quickly kill the plant. Cut away affected leaves or stems, and move the plant to a better ventilated place.

If leaves become stunted and hard, the plant may be infested with cyclamen mites, which look like dust on the underside of the leaves. There is no effective control, and the plant should be destroyed.

Yellowing, falling leaves are an indication that the plant is in a position that is too warm.

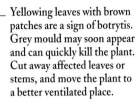

FACT FILE

ORIGIN Mediterranean regions to Iran, Europe; hybrids.

HEIGHT 13–30cm/5–12in, with a similar spread.

COMPOST Soil-based.

REPOTTING In midsummer, when growth has started, repot rested plants with the tuber only half-buried. Use the same size pot each year; cyclamens flower best if they are slightly pot-bound.

PROPAGATION Divide the tuber into sections at potting time. Alternatively, sow seed from late summer to early winter. The earlier this is done, the stronger the plant will be for the first season of flowering. Most varieties take up to 18 months to flower; miniatures may take only half this time. The temperature must be about 21°C/70°F for germination – the highest this plant will ever require.

KEEPING PLANTS After the leaves die down, dry the plant out slightly and rest it in a cool, frost-free place until new growth starts.

PLANT CARE

Bright filtered light away from direct sunlight. ● A cool temperature of 13°–18°C/55°–65°F all year. ● Do not pour water on to the tuber, since this will cause it to rot. Water from below, but do not leave the plant standing in water for longer than 10 minutes or so; it does no harm to allow the leaves to droop slightly before applying water. ● Feed with standard liquid fertiliser every 2 weeks while the plant is in bud and flower. ● As flowers fade, remove the entire stalk by twisting it off at the base. Remove any yellowing or damaged leaves in the same way. Do not cut the stems.

PESTS & DISEASES

Cyclamens are prone to infestation by aphids, red spider mites and cyclamen mites. If the soil is too wet and ventilation is poor, they may suffer from fungal diseases, particularly botrytis.

The sweet-scented deep pink flowers with fringed borders make this miniature cyclamen extremely attractive. These tiny plants are among the most charming.

Miniature cyclamens, which are 8–13cm/3–5in high, have dainty flowers and petite foliage. They will bloom well some 7–9 months from sowing.

CYMBIDIUM HYBRIDS
Orchidaceae

*C*YMBIDIUMS

Of all the orchids suitable for growing in homes, cymbidiums are the most easy-going and adaptable. A handful of species are in cultivation as indoor plants, but these have largely been replaced by the thousands of hybrids, which are available with flowers in widely differing sizes. The smaller hybrids are best for heated rooms and produce flowers some 4–8cm/1½–3in across. Flower colours, too, are varied, from white, green and yellow to pink, red and maroon; those of *Cymbidium* 'Mem Rosl Greer', shown here, are a creamy pink with a deeper spotted centre. The waxy blooms generally have elliptical petals radiating from a prominent, differently coloured, three-lobed centre.

Cymbidiums produce clumps of pseudobulbs, which are surrounded by leathery strap-like leaves. Flower spikes appear from around the bases of the pseudobulbs, mature gradually and bear one or many flowers along the length of the spike. A mature plant may bear as many as 100 blooms in a season. To encourage flowering, cymbidiums need cool temperatures and a rest period for four to six weeks in late autumn. After that, they can be returned to their normal position.

FACT FILE

ORIGIN Tropical Asia, Australia; hybrids.

HEIGHT 76cm–1.5m/30in–5ft.

COMPOST Special orchid compost: a mix of fibrous peat or osmunda fibre, perlite and/or grit, and small pieces of charcoal to aid drainage.

REPOTTING Repot every 3 or 4 years.

PROPAGATION Sow seed or divide mature plants after flowering. Divide the pseudobulbs with a sharp knife; select bulbs with shoots and pot up 3–4 to a pot, discarding any dead growth.

KEEPING PLANTS Set plants outdoors to rest in summer. The sun will ripen the plants and encourage them to flower later in the year.

PLANT CARE

Filtered light in summer; direct sunlight in winter. ● Minimum winter temperature of 7°C/45°F; slightly cooler than normal room temperature at other times. ● Water every day in summer, preferably in the morning, using tepid rainwater if possible. Water once or twice a week in spring and autumn, and once every 2 weeks in winter. ● Stand the pot on a tray of moist pebbles to increase humidity. ● Apply a weak liquid fertiliser every 2 weeks in summer; do not feed while the plant is resting.

ALSO RECOMMENDED

Cymbidium 'Minuet' has flower stems about 38cm/15in long, each bearing up to 20 brown, green or yellow flowers, which are 2.5–4cm/1–1½in across. *C.* 'Peter Pan' bears fewer flowers, but they are exotically coloured greenish yellow, with the lip spotted with a deep maroon brown.

Aphids may attack flower spikes and buds, particularly during winter; spray with insecticide.

Look for signs of red spider mites; while not common on cymbidiums, these pests will infest plants if they are kept in dry conditions.

Mosaic virus will occasionally get a hold on this plant, causing the leaves to become mottled and yellow. There is no cure, so the plant should be destroyed. Failure to take immediate and swift action will enable aphids to spread the virus to other plants.

Cymbidium *'Western Rose' is one of the most exotic-looking cultivars of this orchid. It has sprays of large dusky pink flowers, each with a spotted creamy lip.*

CYPERUS ALTERNIFOLIUS
Cyperaceae

UMBRELLA PLANT

The name *cyperus* derives from the Greek for sedge, and the umbrella plant, palm or grass, is one of the few aquatic plants suitable for growing indoors, where with reasonable care it will do well. It will, with time, adapt itself to almost any location. The plant forms clumps of rather thin, pale green, grassy leaves, which radiate from the tops of the stems and are not in themselves particularly attractive. But the petal-less flowers, enclosed in tiny bracts and arranged in umbrella-like flower heads, add much to the plant's appearance.

Cyperus alternifolius is usually available during the summer. It has an almost Oriental quality and suits uncluttered, modern interiors. *C.a.* 'Variegatus' is an attractive variety with leaves striped with white or, often, completely white.

FACT FILE

ORIGIN Madagascar, Mauritius.

HEIGHT 60cm–1.2m/2–4ft, with a spread of up to 90cm/3ft.

COMPOST Soil-based, with charcoal added to keep the soil fresh and to lessen odours caused by souring compost.

REPOTTING Move into a pot one size larger each spring.

PROPAGATION When the plant fills the pot, remove it from the pot. Make an initial knife cut across the clump, then tear it apart by hand. Plant up sections individually.

KEEPING PLANTS As stems die, cut them off to allow for new growth.

PLANT CARE

Full, bright sunlight or light shade. ● Minimum winter temperature of 10°C/50°F, with constant room temperature at other times. ● The pot should stand in a pan of shallow water at all times; it can be immersed in water to the top of the pot. ● Apply weak liquid fertiliser monthly from spring to autumn, or push fertiliser tablets into the soil around the roots.

Pale leaf colouring, unsightly blotches on the leaves, or the plant's failure to produce many stems may indicate that its position is too shady.

Mealybugs may infest the green flowers at the top of the plant.

Aphids and whiteflies may attack young leaves; check regularly for signs of these pests.

If leaves develop brown patches or edges, make sure the plant is receiving enough water.

DAVALLIA FEJEENSIS
Davalliaceae

RABBIT'S FOOT FERN

Practically all other ferns require a good deal of humidity, but this elegant and vigorous example does not and so thrives indoors. The unusual creeping rhizome, rather like a rabbit's or hare's foot, which grows over the edge of the pot, is the main feature of the plant. These brown rhizomes, which are covered with white-tipped hairs, can extend to 90cm/3ft, and if several plants are placed in a hanging basket or in a pot on a high window ledge, they will in time take on an almost spider-like appearance. Dark wiry stalks emerge from the rhizomes, and these produce light green, triangular, leathery fronds as much as 30cm/12in long. Plants lose and then replace their leaves once a year.

If the fronds turn brown or become sparse, the conditions are too hot or dry. Raise the humidity level around the plant and water it more regularly.

Aphids and scale insects tend to attack this plant; check frequently for signs of infestation.

FACT FILE

ORIGIN Fiji.

HEIGHT To 46cm/18in.

COMPOST Peat- or soil-based.

REPOTTING In spring move the plant into a pot one size larger; top-dress a mature plant. The root system is shallow, so use a half-pot.

PROPAGATION In spring, take sections of rhizome, each with some roots and frond growth. Plant the sections in a mixture of peat and sand, then water and place in a propagator. Keep out of direct sunlight.

KEEPING PLANTS Plants will last for 5 or 6 years if well cared for.

PLANT CARE

Bright light at all times but not direct sunlight. ● Minimum winter temperature of 13°C/55°F, with normal room temperature at other times. ● Water thoroughly during the growing period but do not allow the plant to become waterlogged. In winter, allow the top of the compost to dry out between waterings. ● Stand the pot on a tray of moist pebbles to increase humidity, and mist the plant regularly. ● Apply weak liquid fertiliser every 2 weeks throughout the year.

DIEFFENBACHIA MACULATA (SYN. *D. PICTA*)
Araceae

*D*UMB CANE

This plant is grown almost entirely for its attractive shape and striking foliage, although it does produce insignificant spathe flowers. Some of the more robust forms can reach a height of about 1.8m/6ft in six years or so, but dieffenbachias are grown principally as compact plants that seldom get out of hand if confined to reasonable-sized pots. Dieffenbachia leaves, which can be up to 25cm/10in long, are usually green, and the more commonly seen forms have patches, blotches or variegations in shades of white, cream, yellow or pale green, giving rise to the frequently used common names of leopard lily or spotted dumb cane.

All parts of this plant are poisonous; the sap has a most unpleasant effect on the mouth and throat, causing swelling, pain and temporary loss of speech, a fact reflected in the name dumb cane. Wear gloves when handling dieffenbachias and wash your hands well afterwards.

Dieffenbachia maculata *'Camilla', which grows to only about 38cm/15in high, is a smaller plant than the species. It has cream leaves edged in rich green.*

FACT FILE

ORIGIN Brazil; hybrids.

HEIGHT 46cm–1.8m/18in–6ft.

COMPOST Soil- and peat-based in equal quantities.

REPOTTING Move in summer, when the plant has become too big for its pot.

PROPAGATION Take 8–13-cm/3–5-in-long stem cuttings with a node or eye in spring or summer; place them horizontally, half submerged, in a peat and sand mixture. Keep at a temperature of 21°–24°C/70°–75°F.

KEEPING PLANTS Cut back, hard, plants that are too tall; new growth will sprout from the cut.

PLANT CARE

Fairly light, but shaded from direct sun. ● Minimum winter temperature of 15°C/59°F, with normal to high room temperature at other times. Keep away from heat sources and out of cold draughts. ● In spring and summer water generously; in winter water less and use tepid water. ● Stand the plant on a tray of damp pebbles and mist the foliage when the temperature is high. ● In spring and summer apply weak liquid fertiliser with each watering; feed only every second watering at other times.

ALSO RECOMMENDED

Dieffenbachia maculata 'Exotica' has deep green leaves, regularly blotched with cream and pale green. 'Rudolph Roehrs' has creamy white leaves when young, but develops pale green spots, with a green midrib and margins. In the variety 'Tropic Snow', the leaves are splashed with creamy white along the main veins. *D. seguine* is similar in many respects to *D. maculata*, but is more vigorous, with longer, narrower dark green leaves.

D. x *bausei* is a fairly robust hybrid, growing to 90cm/3ft in height. Leaves are 30cm/12in long, and are yellow-green with dark green blotches and margin and numerous small white spots.

The colour in variegated leaves will suffer if the plant does not receive sufficient light, and growth will be spindly.

Falling leaves may mean that the atmosphere is too cool or too damp.

Leaf scorch can occur if the plant has been placed too near to a heat source, or has been left in strong, direct sunlight. Remove scorched leaves, since they will not recover.

Aphids and symphalids may infest both the plant and the compost; check regularly for signs of these pests and spray with insecticide if necessary.

If the plant is overwatered, the stems may rot.

DIMORPHOTHECA SINUATA (SYN. *D. AURANTIACA*)
Compositae

STAR OF THE VELD

In the wild this plant is a shrubby perennial, but as an indoor plant it is best treated as an annual, and makes a colourful summer-flowering potted plant for the conservatory or sunroom.

Dimorphothecas, or African daisies, are spreading plants, and this species will form a mound up to 30cm/12in high. The coarsely toothed oblong leaves, some 8cm/3in long, are aromatic and the daisy-like flowers, which open from early summer to autumn, can be as much as 5cm/2in wide. They are generally bright orange-yellow, sometimes with a purplish tinge at the base of the petals.

Recent hybrids have been bred in many different colours. Among the best are the compact 'Salmon Queen' with salmon pink flowers, the aptly named 'Glistening White' with 18-cm/7-in stems, and 'Giant Orange' (sometimes called 'Goliath') with larger-than-normal, bright orange-yellow flowers.

FACT FILE

ORIGIN South Africa.

HEIGHT To 30cm/12in.

COMPOST Soil-based, with added coarse sand for good drainage.

REPOTTING Not required.

PROPAGATION Sow seed in winter or spring, or take stem cuttings in midsummer for overwintering.

KEEPING PLANTS Usually treated as an annual.

PLANT CARE

Bright light with full sun. ● Warm room temperature, with good ventilation, in summer; a minimum winter temperature of 10°–13°C/ 50°–55°F for overwintering plants. ● Water sparingly at all times – overwatering may cause the stems to rot. ● Feed every 2 weeks from spring to autumn with a half-strength solution of liquid fertiliser.

Good ventilation is essential for this plant; in damp conditions, botrytis – grey mould – may develop.

Dimorphothecas require full sunlight to ensure blooming. In good conditions, the plant will be covered with flowers from late spring through to autumn.

DIONAEA MUSCIPULA
Droseraceae

VENUS'S FLY TRAP

Carnivorous plants generally come from areas where their roots are unable to obtain sufficient nutrients from the soil, so they have developed a way of absorbing nutrients from animals, live or dead. Plants such as dionaea feed on small insects by trapping them and then digesting the contents of their bodies.

Venus's fly trap – the only species in this genus – is arguably the most interesting insect-eater, not for its appearance, but more for its action. It is a perennial with rosettes of heart-shaped leaves 8–15cm/ 3–6in long that are hinged in the middle and armed with sharp teeth. Inside the leaf are many bristles and, more importantly, three particular hairs which when touched trigger the leaf to close up, trapping any insect attracted by the plant's secretions. The action is immediate, and the leaves may stay shut for as long as two weeks, after which they open again and reset themselves for the next victim. In summer, clusters of white flowers, some 2cm/³⁄₄in wide, appear on short stems.

If the leaves and stems become limp, it may mean that the plant is being kept too dry. Water it well; even then the plant may not recover.

At times of the year when there are few insects for the plant to feed on, it can look pale and limp. Feed it with small pieces of raw meat.

FACT FILE

ORIGIN USA (North and South Carolina).

HEIGHT 8–20cm/3–8in.

COMPOST Half peat, half sphagnum moss.

REPOTTING Not necessary.

PROPAGATION In spring divide the rhizome, planting each piece separately; or sow seeds in autumn, in peat mixed with spaghnum moss. In both instances, cover with plastic until the new plants are established.

KEEPING PLANTS Dry rooms can be fatal, so cover the plant with a plastic dome, which will retain humidity.

PLANT CARE

Bright light with some direct sunlight. ● Minimum winter temperature of 10°C/50°F; normal room temperature at other times. ● Stand the pot in a shallow container of rainwater and keep the compost moist at all times. In winter cover the pot with a plastic dome and keep the compost just moist. ● From spring to autumn, if there are no flies about, feed occasionally with newly swatted insects or small pieces of meat.

DIPLADENIA × *AMABILIS* **see** *MANDEVILLA* × *AMOENA*

DIZYGOTHECA ELEGANTISSIMA
Araliaceae

False Aralia

Sometimes sold as *Schefflera elegantissima* or *Aralia elegantissima*, this is a graceful shrub with a slim, mottled stem from which grow palm-like, leathery, serrated leaves about 8cm/3in long and 13mm/½in wide. An interesting feature of the plant is the manner in which the character of the leaves alters as they mature. The young, delicate, filigree copper brown foliage changes to coarser dark green, almost black leaves, which are much more typical of the Araliaceae family to which the plant belongs.

False, or finger, aralias are beautiful enough to stand alone, but in the tropical islands of their native habitat they grow with cordylines, crotons, cycas and epipremnums, and indoors they can be used in a similar collection of tropical plants to add height and grace. For the best effect, plant two or three to a pot. Flowers are not produced on pot specimens.

FACT FILE

ORIGIN New Caledonia, Polynesia.

HEIGHT To 1.8m/6ft.

COMPOST Soil-based.

REPOTTING Move into a pot one size larger in spring, only when the roots have filled the pot.

PROPAGATION New plants can be raised from fresh seeds or stem cuttings in spring, but both operations are difficult for amateurs.

KEEPING PLANTS Dizygothecas do best in a warm conservatory and can last for 5 years or so. Prune in spring to improve the shape or promote bushiness.

PLANT CARE

Bright light, but avoid direct sunlight. ● Year-round warmth, with a minimum winter temperature of 16°C/60°F. ● Thoroughly soak the compost with each watering, but allow it almost to dry out before rewatering. ● Improve humidity by standing the pot on damp pebbles and misting the plant each day. ● Apply a weak liquid fertiliser every 2 weeks between spring and autumn.

Drooping leaves are a sign of overwatering.

Aphids and mealybugs may attack this plant; check for signs regularly.

Falling leaves may mean that the plant is too dry at the roots. Water well and improve the humidity level.

DRACAENA FRAGRANS 'MASSANGEANA'
Agavaceae

Corn Plant

A popular and hardy house plant, *Dracaena fragrans* is one of the more tolerant of the dracaena group; it originates in tropical Africa, but is sufficiently hardy to grow farther east in the higher altitudes of Ethiopia. As a house plant, it will withstand a variety of temperatures and conditions as long as it has adequate humidity.

The straight *D. fragrans* produces rosettes of strong, plain green curving leaves 60cm/2ft long, and 10cm/4in wide. As it grows, the plant sheds its lower leaves, so after a few years it will probably consist of a cluster of attractive leaves on top of a stout bare stem, occasionally with a leafy side branch or two. Occasionally scented yellow flowers are produced; these are followed by orange-red berries.

The variegated form 'Massangeana' is much more widely grown, mainly for its attractive leaves, each of which carries a central corn-yellow band and is bordered by narrower yellow stripes.

If the plant is too cold or damp, botrytis may get a hold; look for brownish spots on the leaves.

The plant sheds older, lower leaves from time to time. If younger leaves turn yellow and droop, the plant is being kept too dry and hot. Water well and increase the frequency of misting.

Rotting stems and leaves are an indication of overwatering.

Red spider mites and scale insects may attack the plant; check for signs regularly.

FACT FILE

ORIGIN Upper Guinea, Ethiopia, tropical Africa.

HEIGHT To 1.5m/5ft.

COMPOST Soil- or peat-based.

REPOTTING Repot every 2 or 3 years, in spring.

PROPAGATION Take 8-cm/3-in tip or stem cuttings in spring or late summer, or air-layer.

KEEPING PLANTS This plant does not like draughts, so stand it in a protected spot. It grows slowly and should last for several years.

PLANT CARE

Bright light, but not long periods of direct summer sun. ● This plant can stand fluctuating temperatures, with a minimum of 13°C/55°F. ● Keep the compost moist; water once or twice a week in the active growing period; less in winter. ● Stand the pot on a tray of damp pebbles and mist the plant often, but not while it is in the sun. ● Apply a weak liquid fertiliser every 2 weeks from spring to autumn.

DRACAENA MARGINATA
Agavaceae

*M*ADAGASCAR DRAGON TREE

This exotic-looking plant produces leaves from its base. Over the years, the lower leaves fall so, as the plant grows, it develops a slender ringed trunk. On top of these stems are dense tufts of spiky, 30–40-cm/12–16-in-long, deep green leaves with fine red or purple edgings. In its native habitat it can be quite a substantial plant, growing to a height of 2.7m/9ft or more; indoors it will reach a more suitable 1.8m/6ft after several years. This is perhaps the easiest dracaena to grow indoors, since it is slow-growing and tolerant of varying room conditions and different degrees of humidity.

Dracaena marginata 'Tricolor', called by some the rainbow plant, has cream-striped leaves with a red edging. The variety 'Colorama' has a lighter leaf, with a narrow edge of red, an inner band of cream and a light and dark green central stripe.

The plant's growth rate will slow down and more leaves than normal will fall off if the temperature is too low.

The lower leaves will droop if conditions are too dry; water and spray more frequently.

Mealybugs may lodge in the leaf axils; check for signs regularly.

FACT FILE

ORIGIN Madagascar.

HEIGHT To 1.8m/6ft.

COMPOST Soil-based with added peat.

REPOTTING Pot up very 2 or 3 years, in spring.

PROPAGATION Take 8–10cm/3–4in stem cuttings in spring; leave for 24 hours before planting them in a sandy rooting mixture.

KEEPING PLANTS In warmer areas this plant will appreciate a spell outdoors in summer, but place it in a sheltered position.

PLANT CARE

Bright light to bring out the leaf colour, but avoid direct sunlight in summer. ● Minimum winter temperature of 13°C/55°F, up to 22°C/72°F at other times. ● Water once or twice a week from spring to autumn; less in winter. ● Humidity is not as crucial with this plant as it is with *Dracaena fragrans*, but it will benefit from a twice-weekly misting between spring and autumn. ● Feed every 2 weeks during the active growing period with a weak liquid fertiliser.

DRACAENA SANDERIANA
Agavaceae

*B*ELGIAN EVERGREEN

The most dainty of the dracaenas, *Dracaena sanderiana* is a slow-growing, slender, upright shrub from the tropical rain forests of Cameroon. It is sometimes called ribbon plant, on account of its narrow, slightly twisted leaves of deep grey-green with broad creamy white margins that grow to 23cm/9in long and 2.5cm/1in wide, and is perfect where space is limited. The plant rarely branches from the base, so three or four specimens should be planted together in a large planter to create an interesting mass of spiky foliage. Provided it is not scaldingly hot, this plant can tolerate standing close to a heater, but cold draughts can be detrimental.

FACT FILE

ORIGIN West Africa.

HEIGHT To 90cm/3ft.

COMPOST Soil-based.

REPOTTING Repot only when necessary. Once plants are in 13-cm/5-in pots, top-dress with fresh compost annually.

PROPAGATION Take stem, tip and basal cuttings in spring. Stem cuttings, 8–10cm/3–4in long, will root readily if set upright in a peat and sand mixture and kept warm. Root tip cuttings in a propagator; basal shoots with some roots will grow if enclosed in a plastic bag.

KEEPING PLANTS Keep the plant in a protected spot.

PLANT CARE

Bright, filtered light enhances the leaf colour. ● Minimum winter temperature of 10°C/50°F; normal room temperatures in summer. ● Water plentifully when in active growth, more sparingly in winter. ● Feed every 2 weeks from spring to early autumn with weak liquid fertiliser.

Mealybugs may inhabit the leaf axils, and scale insects may attach themselves to the leaves and stems; check regularly for signs of these pests.

Rotting stems and leaves are an indication of overwatering.

ECHINOCEREUS PECTINATUS
Cactaceae

ℋEDGEHOG CACTUS

One of the so-called desert cacti, the hedgehog cactus has a columnar stem that can eventually reach 25cm/10in in height and 8cm/3in across, although it usually remains smaller than this when it is grown indoors. Being a slow grower, it may take as long as five years to reach a height of 8cm/3in, and it will begin to branch from the base only when it is about 13cm/5in high. The broad, medium-green ribs are covered with areoles, each of which bears about 25 short, radial white spines in an unusual formation that resembles the teeth of a comb. They are so closely packed as to give the plant a white appearance. All species of echinocereus, about 15 of which are in general cultivation as indoor plants, bloom only when they are a few years old. The freely produced cup-shaped flowers of the hedgehog cactus are deep pink, covered with soft spines on the outside, and up to 8cm/3in wide.

Scale insects and mealybugs attack this plant; check often for signs of infestation.

Thin, elongated stems may result from too little light during the growing period, or too much warmth in winter. These stems may not flower freely.

Corky patches on the stems may be caused by insect damage, sudden chilling, physical injury or underwatering during the growing period.

If the plant rots from the base, it has been kept too wet, usually in winter when it is resting.

FACT FILE

ORIGIN Central Mexico.

HEIGHT To 25cm/10in.

COMPOST Soil- or peat-based, both with added perlite or sand.

REPOTTING If the roots fill the pot, move the plant to a pot one size larger in spring or replant in the same pot, using fresh compost.

PROPAGATION In spring or summer, remove a branch from a mature plant. Allow the cutting to dry for 3 days, then insert the base into sand or cuttings mix and keep it out of direct sunlight for a month.

KEEPING PLANTS Stand the plant outdoors in the sun in summer.

PLANT CARE

Full sunlight all year round to stimulate flowering. ● Temperatures of 2°–4°C/35°–40°F during the winter rest. Light frost can be endured as long as the compost is completely dry. ● Barely moisten the compost, and allow the top two-thirds to dry out before rewatering in the growing period; do not water in winter if plants are kept below 4°C/40°F. ● Apply a high-potash liquid feed every 2 weeks to a plant in peat-based compost, every 4 weeks to one in soil-based compost.

EPIPHYLLUM ACKERMANNII
Cactaceae

𝒪RCHID CACTUS

The epiphyllums grown as house plants are almost all hybrids; their wild-plant parents are found as epiphytes in the tropical rain forests. The true orchid cactus, now renamed *Nopalxochia ackermannii* but still generally known as *Epiphyllum*, produces cup-shaped crimson blooms, 10–15cm/4–6in wide, all year round. It is, however, rarely seen today, having been surpassed in flower colour by the many hybrids that have been created. The species and the hybrids have leafless stems, up to 60cm/2ft long and 5cm/2in wide, which are notched at the edges and segmented.

The newer hybrids bloom prolifically, mainly in spring. The flowers may be white, cream, yellow or orange, all shades of pink and red, or even bicoloured and can be large (up to 15cm/6in wide) or small. Those with smaller flowers look good in hanging baskets with their stems trailing.

FACT FILE

ORIGIN Mexico; hybrids.

HEIGHT To 60cm/2ft.

COMPOST Half peat, half soil-based, with added perlite or sand.

REPOTTING This plant flowers best if slightly pot-bound. In spring, move into a pot one size larger until a 15-cm/6-in pot is reached; thereafter top-dress instead.

PROPAGATION Detach 10–15-cm/4–6-in sections of stem in spring or early summer. Allow to dry for 2 days, then plant in compost as above.

KEEPING PLANTS Cut back old stems when they become too long. Put the plant outdoors in a sheltered spot from late spring to early autumn.

PLANT CARE

Bright, filtered light; no direct sunlight. ● Minimum winter temperature of 4°C/40°F; normal room temperature at other times. ● Water generously while plant is growing; moderately at other times. ● Stand the pot on a tray of damp pebbles to increase humidity and mist daily in warm room conditions. ● From early spring until flower buds are well developed, feed every 2 weeks with a high-potash liquid fertiliser. Stop feeding for 4 weeks, then resume until early autumn.

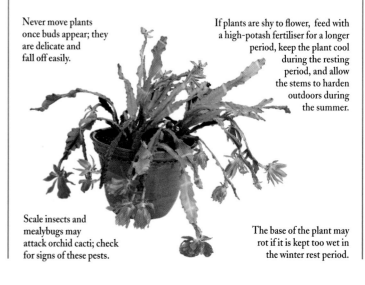

Never move plants once buds appear; they are delicate and fall off easily.

If plants are shy to flower, feed with a high-potash fertiliser for a longer period, keep the plant cool during the resting period, and allow the stems to harden outdoors during the summer.

Scale insects and mealybugs may attack orchid cacti; check for signs of these pests.

The base of the plant may rot if it is kept too wet in the winter rest period.

EPIPREMNUM AUREUM
Araceae

*D*EVIL'S IVY

The golden pothos, taro vine or devil's ivy, as it is commonly known, is one of the most remarkable of all foliage plants. Epipremnums come in many shapes and sizes and may be displayed as climbers or as trailing plants. There are about 10 species in this genus with aerial roots, each with a characteristic tendency to wrap itself around the nearest object.

Epipremnum aureum (syn. *Pothos aureus, Scindapsus aureus*) is highly decorative, with mustard and green variegation on the 15-cm/6-in-long heart-shaped leaves. It is tolerant of a wide range of conditions, although when placed far from the light source the variegation is affected. Indoors it should not be allowed to exceed 1.8–2.4m/6–8ft in extent, but it can grow five times as high in the wild, where plants produce flowers rather like those of the arum; pot plants, however, do not flower.

FACT FILE

ORIGIN Solomon Islands.

HEIGHT To 1.8–2.4m/6–8ft.

COMPOST Soil-based.

REPOTTING Move the plant to a pot one size larger each spring, but do not overpot.

PROPAGATION Take 10–13-cm/4–5-in stem cuttings with two good leaves attached at any time of year, or tip cuttings when pruning in spring. The plant can also be layered.

KEEPING PLANTS Although slow to start, this plant is an excellent climber and will last for many years. Pinch out the growing tips regularly to promote bushy growth and prune the plant in early spring to reduce its size.

PLANT CARE

Bright, indirect light. ● Minimum winter temperature of 10°C/50°F, with normal room temperature at other times.
● Allow the top two-thirds of the potting mixture to dry out between waterings.
● During the growing period, apply weak liquid fertiliser every 2 weeks.

ALSO RECOMMENDED

Epipremnum aureum 'Marble Queen' is an attractive alternative, but can be difficult to care for. *E.a.* 'Tricolor', as the name suggests, has leaves marbled with three colours: pale green, yellow and cream.

Epipremnum aureum 'Marble Queen' has beautiful leaves, boldly streaked and marbled with soft green and white.

Wet, brown patches on leaves indicate infection by botrytis; destroy any such leaves.

Aphids may attack young plants, and mealybugs may infest both young and old plants. Check regularly for signs of the pests.

Stems will rot at the base if the plant is constantly overwatered.

EPISCIA CUPREATA
Gesneriaceae

FLAME VIOLET

The creeping or trailing stems of *Episcia cupreata*, from which emerge nodeless red or green stolons bearing new plants at their tips, will rapidly cover the surface of a shallow pan or trail from a hanging basket. The oval, hairy leaves, 5–8cm/2–3in long and 2.5–5cm/1–2in wide, have toothed edges and are arranged in a rosette; their colouring ranges from deep bronze green to bright green, usually with silvery markings around the veins.

The 2.5-cm/1-in-long flowers, which appear in spring and continue until autumn, are bright red and tubular. They flare out at the tip into lobes that may be fringed at the edges. Deep in the centre of the tube – which is lined with soft hairs – lies a yellow 'eye'. Although in the wild the plants are shielded from the fierce sun by the leaf canopy, they need bright light to flower well in the home.

Watch out for aphids, which may infest young leaves.

Humidity must be high, or leaves will develop brown edges and flower buds will shrivel.

FACT FILE

ORIGIN Colombia, Venezuela.

HEIGHT To 15cm/6in.

COMPOST Equal parts of peat and perlite to ensure good drainage, plus some sphagnum moss if available.

REPOTTING Move into a pot one size larger only when roots fill the current pot.

PROPAGATION Detach plants that develop at the ends of the stolons and pot up individually. Single leaves with short stalks will also root.

KEEPING PLANTS These shallow-rooting plants do best in wide-topped pans and hanging baskets in which the offsets can trail down.

PLANT CARE

Bright light, no direct sunlight. ● Warm conditions; minimum winter temperature of 13°C/55°F. ● Water generously during the growing season, more sparingly in winter. Do not wet leaves at night. ● Stand the pot on a tray of moist pebbles to provide added humidity. ● Every 2 weeks apply a weak liquid fertiliser to actively growing plants.

EUPHORBIA MILII VAR. *SPLENDENS*
Euphorbiaceae

CROWN OF THORNS

There are about 2,000 known species in the spurge family, and this is one of the easiest to grow indoors. For a succulent shrub, it is not fussy. It readily produces bright green leaves and, from late winter until early autumn, clusters of tiny flowers surrounded by two cheery red bracts. In the form *lutea*, the bracts are yellow. Flowering can be almost continuous if plenty of good, bright light is provided.

In its native habitat the plant grows happily in granite crevices, reaching up to 1.8m/6ft, but as an indoor plant it rarely achieves this height. The woody stems are about as thick as a little finger and carry sharp spines, most of which are around 2cm/¾in long; wear gloves when handling the plant. The relatively few leaves are bright green, elliptical and are up to 6.5cm/2½in wide.

FACT FILE

ORIGIN Madagascar.

HEIGHT To 60cm/2ft.

COMPOST Soil-based, with sand or perlite added to improve drainage.

REPOTTING Repot every 2 years; once a plant is 5 or 6 years old, simply top-dress it.

PROPAGATION In spring or summer take 8-cm/3-in stem cuttings. Dip the cut ends into tepid water to halt the flow of sap, then leave them for 24 hours to dry before inserting them into compost.

KEEPING PLANTS Prune if necessary before new growth appears in spring, but beware: when cut, the plant exudes a poisonous white latex. Do not allow it to come into contact with the eyes or mouth.

PLANT CARE

Full sunlight, but shade it from very strong summer sun. ● Minimum winter temperature of 13°C/55°F; normal room temperature at other times. The plant likes warm, dry conditions. ● Allow the surface of the compost to dry out between waterings; water sparingly in winter. ● Apply a weak liquid fertiliser every 2 weeks while in bloom.

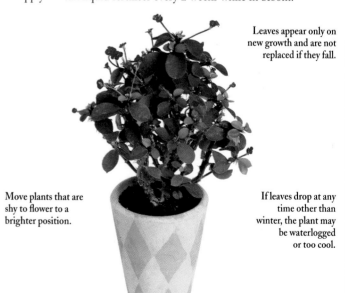

Leaves appear only on new growth and are not replaced if they fall.

Move plants that are shy to flower to a brighter position.

If leaves drop at any time other than winter, the plant may be waterlogged or too cool.

EUPHORBIA PULCHERRIMA
Euphorbiaceae

*P*OINSETTIA

Most people treat the poinsettia (also called Christmas star, Mexican flame leaf or lobster plant) as an annual, purchasing a new plant at the beginning of the traditional winter flowering period and discarding it at the end. But in suitable climates, it can be planted in the garden after its use indoors. The plant's leaves are pale green and the small greenish yellow flowers uninteresting, but the vibrantly coloured bracts can be magnificent. These are, in fact, coloured leaves that develop at the top of the stems in autumn, and they can be as long as 25cm/10in. Initially only the striking, brilliant red version was common, but there are now varieties with pink, creamy white and bicoloured bracts.

FACT FILE

ORIGIN Mexico.

HEIGHT 38–90cm/15in–3ft.

COMPOST Peat-based.

REPOTTING Repot every year in midsummer; but do not overpot.

PROPAGATION Take 10–15-cm/4–6-in stem cuttings from the top of the plant in midsummer. Seal the ends in hot water, let them dry out for 24 hours, then insert them into sandy compost.

KEEPING PLANTS See box above right.

PLANT CARE

Keep young plants in bright filtered light; direct winter sun will not harm mature plants. ● A winter temperature of 15°–21°C/59°–70°F; cooler when the plant is not in colour. ● Keep the compost moist in winter and spring; reduce watering after flowering. ● Apply weak liquid fertiliser every 2 weeks from mid-autumn to late spring.

ALSO RECOMMENDED

Euphorbia pulcherrima 'Diva' has brick red bracts. On 'Rosea' the bracts are pale pink, darkly veined. They are salmon pink on 'Pink Peppermint', strong lemon yellow on 'Lemon Drop'.

KEEPING PLANTS

In spring, when the plant has finished flowering, cut it back to 10–15cm/4–6in. Store it in a warm place, and keep the compost almost dry until new growth appears, usually after about 2 months. Then, in early summer, water the plant well and when growth restarts, repot it in fresh compost in the same-sized pot.

Beginning in mid-autumn it is essential to keep a poinsettia in total darkness for 14 hours each day if the coloured bracts are to appear. For 2 months, cover the plant with a black plastic bag in the early evening and remove it the following morning, while increasing watering and feeding. When the bracts begin to show colour, leave the plant uncovered.

Nurseries use a growth retardant to limit the size and bushiness of the plants sold in shops, but this is not possible for the home grower, and plants kept for a second or third year will inevitably be larger.

Red spider mites and mealybugs may attack this plant; check for signs regularly. Increase humidity and watering to help deter the mites.

A milky sap leaks from wounds to the stem and leaf stalks. It may stain clothing. Keep it from contact with the eyes or mouth.

Euphorbia pulcherrima *'Ecke's White' has cream bracts. Also in the Ecke range are 'Top White' and 'Hot Pink'.*

If leaves fall without wilting, the light is insufficient or the temperature too low.

When leaves wilt and then fall, the plant is being overwatered; allow the compost to dry out before watering again.

EXACUM AFFINE
Gentianaceae

GERMAN VIOLET

A member of the gentian family, this plant also goes under the names of Arabian and Persian violet. It is a small plant, with a height and spread of 15–20cm/6–8in, and has 2.5-cm/1-in-long, glossy olive green leaves. In late spring countless mauve-purple or white scented flowers, each with a yellow eye, appear and continue to bloom until late autumn. *Exacum affine* 'Rococo' has double lavender-blue flowers. Although it is generally treated as an annual, exacum is a biennial, and is raised commercially from seed sown in early autumn or early spring and is sold as an indoor plant. For an eye-catching effect, mass several plants that are just coming into flower in a large bowl.

FACT FILE

ORIGIN Socotra (Gulf of Aden).

HEIGHT To 20cm/8in.

COMPOST Peat-based.

REPOTTING In spring, move overwintered plants into pots one size larger.

PROPAGATION In winter or spring, sow seed on the surface of an open peaty or sphagnum-rich compost in a shallow 10-cm/4-in pot.

KEEPING PLANTS Pinch off blooms as they fade to prolong flowering. If the plant withers after flowering, discard it, but if you want to overwinter it, prune it back hard to maintain its bushiness.

PLANT CARE

Bright, filtered light but not strong direct sunlight. ● Normal room temperatures; a minimum of 10°C/50°F if plants are overwintered. ● Keep the compost moist, never sodden. ● Place the pot on a tray of damp pebbles to increase humidity. ● Feed every 2 weeks throughout the year with weak liquid fertiliser.

If flowers fail to appear, move the plant to a warmer position and increase the humidity.

The flowers will fade and quickly die if the rootball ever becomes dry.

Wilting plants may mean that they are in a draughty position.

x FATSHEDERA LIZEI
Araliaceae

TREE IVY

This cross between two plants of different genera but the same family (known as a bigeneric hybrid) was raised by a French nursery just before World War I, using *Fatsia japonica* 'Moseri', the Japanese fatsia or aralia, as one parent and *Hedera helix* var. *hibernica*, Irish ivy, as the other. The habit and shape of x *Fatshedera lizei* show the characteristics of both parents. The broad spread of the fatsia has been enlarged, and the stem of the ivy has been strengthened. The leaves are shiny, with a tough leathery texture and the ivy shape has been enlarged: leaves may be up to 13cm/5in wide. From the ivy the plant has also inherited a partially climbing habit and so needs some form of support, such as a moss pole. For the best effect, set three or four plants around the edge of a single pot. Indoor plants do not often flower.

Aphids may infest the soft growing tips.

Leaf loss is natural on older plants; if the plant becomes unattractive and leggy, take cuttings and start new plants.

Mealybugs and red spider mites may attack this plant; spray with insecticide and increase watering and humidity.

If conditions are too cool, shady or damp, botrytis mould may affect the leaves. Remove any diseased leaves, spray with fungicide, and improve the growing conditions.

FACT FILE

ORIGIN Hybrid.

HEIGHT To 2.4m/8ft.

COMPOST Soil-based.

REPOTTING Each spring, move into a pot one size larger. Once the plant has reached maximum desired size, top-dress annually instead.

PROPAGATION Take 8–10-cm/3–4-in tip cuttings in spring or early summer.

KEEPING PLANTS Pinch out growing tips to encourage bushiness; prune in spring if necessary to restrict the plant's size. In summer put the plant outdoors in a sheltered spot, out of direct sunlight.

PLANT CARE

Medium shade to bright filtered light; avoid extremes. ● Minimum winter temperature of 7°C/45°F, not above 15°C/59°F at other times. ● Keep the compost moist in the growing season, water less often in winter. ● Spray the leaves with water every other day. ● Feed with weak liquid fertiliser every 2 weeks in the period of active growth.

FATSIA JAPONICA
Araliaceae

JAPANESE FATSIA

Also known as Japanese aralia and false castor-oil plant, this has been a popular garden and indoor plant since Victorian times. When it is grown outdoors, it will make a large shrub 1.8–2.4m/6–8ft high and with a spread of some 1.2m/4ft. Indoors it can be kept much smaller, since it can withstand quite drastic pruning. It does best in cool rooms, porches or conservatories, since in high temperatures the stems and the glossy, lobed and pointed leaves become soft and sappy, easily damaged and prone to attack by pests. More typical plants, with leathery light green, hand-shaped leaves, often as much as 40cm/16in wide, develop under cooler conditions. Creamy white flowers, followed by shiny black berries, may appear in autumn.

Mealybugs, red spider mites and aphids may attack this plant; check regularly for signs of these pests.

Loss of the oldest, lower leaves is normal on mature plants.

Botrytis mould may affect the leaves if the plant is in too cool, shady or damp a place; remove damaged leaves, spray with fungicide, and move the plant to a better position.

FACT FILE

ORIGIN Japan, Korea.

HEIGHT To 1.8m/6ft.

COMPOST Soil-based.

REPOTTING In spring move the plant into a pot one or two sizes larger. Once it has reached its maximum size, top-dress annually.

PROPAGATION In spring take basal or side shoots as cuttings; keep them warm and humid inside a plastic bag or propagator.

KEEPING PLANTS Cut back by half in spring if necessary; pinch out growing tips to encourage dense growth. Stand the plant outdoors in a sheltered, shady position in summer. It should last for many years.

PLANT CARE

Bright light with some shade; no strong summer sun. ● Minimum winter temperature of 7°C/45°F; not above 15°C/59°F at other times. ● Keep the compost moist at all times. ● Spray with water every 2 days; in warm weather stand the pot on a tray of moist pebbles. ● Apply standard liquid fertiliser every 2 weeks in spring and summer. ● Clean the leaves with a damp sponge; do not use leaf shine.

FAUCARIA TIGRINA
Aizoaceae

TIGER JAWS

The fleshy, greyish green leaves of *Faucaria tigrina* are 5cm/2in long, spotted with many tiny white dots, and are distinctly jaw-like, complete with soft, tooth-like spines. It is a small succulent plant from dry areas of South Africa, where it grows in rock crevices. In its natural habitat, faucaria gains moisture from dews caused by rapid changes in night temperature, and from humid winds off the sea.

This plant makes a low-growing, star-shaped rosette. In summer and autumn, golden yellow, stalkless flowers reminiscent of daisies emerge from the rosette. They are up to 6.5cm/2½in wide and tend to open most fully in the afternoon.

FACT FILE

ORIGIN South Africa (Cape Province).

HEIGHT 5–10cm/2–4in.

COMPOST Soil-based and perlite or grit, to aid drainage, in a ratio of 2:1.

REPOTTING Move every 2 or 3 years in spring, when the plant has completely covered the surface of the compost.

PROPAGATION Divide overcrowded clumps in late spring or early summer; if a rosette has no root attached, allow it to dry for 24 hours before inserting it in a sand-loam mix.

KEEPING PLANTS The plant has relatively little root, so it is best planted in a shallow pan or half-pot.

PLANT CARE

Bright light; requires 3–4 hours of sunlight daily to ensure flowering. ● Minimum winter temperature of 10°C/50°F; normal room temperature at other times. ● Water copiously in summer and autumn; keep plants almost dry in winter. ● Apply a weak liquid fertiliser every 4 weeks to actively growing plants.

Mealybugs may infest the leaves; look for the tufts of waxy wool and scrape them off with a fingernail.

Root mealybugs leave wool tufts on the roots of the plant; every few weeks, gently knock it out of its pot and check for this pest.

Overwatering during the winter rest period will cause rotting at the base of the plant and limp growth.

MORACEAE

Ficus

This is a large and diverse genus of plants that are generally natives of the warmer parts of the world. Most ficuses have evergreen foliage, although there are some variegated forms. Many make excellent indoor plants, and a suitable ficus can be found for any indoor situation. *Ficus* is the Latin word for the edible fig, and that plant is one of this group, which includes trees, shrubs and climbers. Most of these plants are tolerant of a wide range of temperatures, and they adapt well to different conditions in the home, although they seldom flower or fruit in containers.

One of the most common indoor plants is the rubber plant, *Ficus elastica*, and its many improved hybrids such as 'Decora', which has oval, glossy dark green leathery leaves up to 30cm/12in long. The leaves emerge from a rust-red protective sheath, and the vein on the underside of the leaf is also red. The sturdy *F.e.* 'Robusta' is shown here.

Among other species commonly found in the home are *F. benjamina*, the weeping fig; and *F. pumila* (*F. repens*), the creeping fig, which is ideal for a hanging basket or as ground cover. Several less well known species are also available, such as *F. rubiginosa*, the Port Jackson, or rusty, fig and *F. microcarpa* (*F. retusa*), Indian laurel. *F.m.* 'Hawaii', with variegated leaves, is often sold as *F. benjamina*. *F. benghalensis*, the banyan tree, has leaves and stems covered with fine reddish hairs.

Ficus elastica 'Robusta' is a sturdy plant with leaves that are larger and rounder than those of 'Decora'. The shiny, leathery leaves are up to 30cm/12in long and have a pronounced mid-rib. When well cared for, this ficus can reach 3m/10ft in a pot. It does not fruit until it is about 30 years old.

When cleaning or handling young leaves, be very careful; they are easily damaged, and the scars will remain for the plant's entire life.

The central stem tends to grow straight, without branching, although branching will occur if the growing tip is removed.

ALSO RECOMMENDED

Ficus deltoidea var. diversifolia is the only species commonly grown indoors that regularly produces fruit (albeit inedible). It forms a much-branched small tree up to 90cm/3ft tall with thick dark green leaves.

Ficus pumila, the creeping or climbing fig, grows to about 10cm/4in high, but will trail to over 60cm/2ft. It thrives in damp shade and has thin, heart-shaped leaves, which are usually pale green and puckered.

Ficus lyrata, fiddle-leaf fig, has 30-cm/ 12-in-long, glossy dark green leaves. In the wild, it starts as an epiphyte and becomes a tree up to 12m/40ft high, but in a pot it can easily be kept to a modest 90cm/3ft.

Mealybugs may attack older plants; check regularly for signs of infestation.

When the stem is cut or leaves break off, latex-like sap will bleed from the plant. This can be stopped by applying powdered charcoal or cigarette ash to the wound.

Drooping, lifeless-looking leaves that gradually turn yellow and fall indicate that the plant is being overwatered.

Scale insects can become a problem if left unchecked; inspect stems and leaves regularly – especially the undersides – of all ficus types.

Sooty mould will readily grow on leaves, establishing itself in the excreta of scale insects. Wipe the leaves with soapy water to remove it.

Leaf spot, a fungal disease, causes black spots on the leaves. Spray the plant with a suitable insecticide.

Older leaves turn yellow, then brown naturally and fall.

Prolonged overwatering will cause the roots to rot.

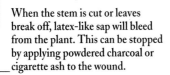

FACT FILE

ORIGIN Tropical and subtropical regions, particularly India and Malaysia.

HEIGHT 10cm–3m/4in–10ft.

COMPOST Soil-based for large-leafed ficuses; peat-based for smaller types.

REPOTTING In spring, move all types into a pot one size larger only when roots fill the pot. Ficuses grow best if slightly pot-bound.

PROPAGATION It is difficult for the amateur to propagate large-leafed types. Plants are slow to root from cuttings because of high water loss from the large leaves, and are better air-layered instead. But this is a slow and difficult process. Small-leafed types, such as Ficus pumila, root easily from tip cuttings taken in spring.

KEEPING PLANTS These are not overly demanding plants, and all ficus species are long-lasting, some exceptionally so, provided the growing conditions are right.

PLANT CARE

Medium to bright light; some direct sunlight will not harm the plants. *Ficus pumila* prefers semishade.
● Minimum winter temperature of 10°–13°C/50°–55°F; normal warm room temperature at other times.
● Allow the top two-thirds of the compost to dry out before rewatering. Do not overwater. ● Apply a weak liquid fertiliser every 2 weeks in spring and summer. ● Spray smaller plants or plants with hairy leaves to clean the foliage. Sponge glossy leaves regularly to clean off any dust. To avoid damage, support the leaf with one hand while sponging it off.

PESTS & DISEASES

Scale insects and mealybugs infest these plants; check regularly for signs of these pests. Plants are also prone to attack by sooty mould.

Ficus benjamina, the weeping fig, has glossy 5–10cm/2–4in tapering leaves. In the wild it is a large tree, but can be kept to 1.8m/6ft in a pot. Stems are often plaited together for decorative effect.

Ficus benjamina 'Starlight' is a variegated form whose leaves are a fresh apple green and white. Like other weeping figs, it has a pronounced graceful drooping habit and is highly ornamental.

FITTONIA VERSCHAFFELTII ARGYRONEURA
Acanthaceae

Silver Net Leaf

Originally from the tropical rain forests of South America, this attractive plant has delicate, oval, olive green leaves with an overall pattern of distinct white veining; hence its other common name of mosaic plant. In summer, insignificant yellow-green flowers may appear which should be removed or they will hinder the plant's growth.

In its natural habitat, the plant grows as a low ground-cover creeper, flourishing in the shady environment. It is quite difficult to grow successfully indoors because it needs a humid atmosphere, with a temperature always above 18°C/65°F – avoid the 'three Ds': direct sunlight, draughts and dry air. The plant is, however, ideal for bottle gardens and terraria and in mixed bowls, where it will spread to about 30cm/12in.

FACT FILE

ORIGIN Peru.

HEIGHT To 15cm/6in.

COMPOST Peat- or soil-based.

REPOTTING Repot each spring in the same pot. The plant is shallow rooting, so shallow bowls or half-pots are best.

PROPAGATION In spring, root 5-cm/2-in stem tip cuttings in warm humid conditions, or layer stems.

KEEPING PLANTS Pinch out growing points regularly to encourage dense growth.

PLANT CARE

Bright position or light shade; avoid direct sunlight. ● Minimum winter temperature of 18°C/65°F; warmer room temperature at other times. ● Use tepid water to keep the compost damp, but never sodden. ● Mist the plant regularly, and stand the pot on a tray of moist pebbles to increase humidity. ● Apply a weak liquid fertiliser once a month in summer.

Shrivelling leaves indicate that the air is too dry or the plant is in direct sunlight. Increase humidity and move to a semi-shady position.

If leaves go yellow, the plant is being overwatered. Remove the damaged leaves and allow the compost to become almost dry before rewatering.

Leaves will drop if the plant is placed in a cool or draughty position.

Aphids may attack this plant; check for their presence regularly.

FREESIA
Iridaceae

Freesia

Hybrid freesias are attractive, sweet-smelling plants which will flower well in the house or a conservatory. The 5-cm/2-in funnel-shaped flowers grow on one side of wiry stems, 30–46cm/12–18in long, which emerge between narrow, strap-like leaves; they are available in white, yellow, mauve, pink, red and orange. 'Super Giant' hybrids are a high-yielding and early-flowering strain in all colours.

Freesias grow from corms, which should be planted up in batches from late summer to early winter for flowering in succession through to the middle of spring. Set the corms 5–8cm/2–3in apart, just covering the tops with compost, followed by a layer of peat 2.5cm/1in deep; for maximum impact, plant six corms in a 13-cm/5-in pot. Keep the pots in a greenhouse or conservatory, and give small amounts of water until growth is visible.

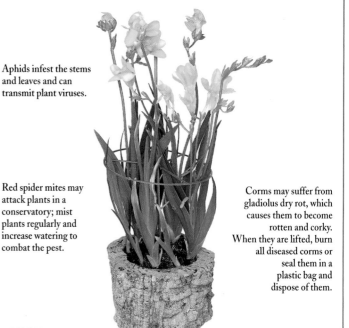

Aphids infest the stems and leaves and can transmit plant viruses.

Red spider mites may attack plants in a conservatory; mist plants regularly and increase watering to combat the pest.

Corms may suffer from gladiolus dry rot, which causes them to become rotten and corky. When they are lifted, burn all diseased corms or seal them in a plastic bag and dispose of them.

FACT FILE

ORIGIN South Africa; hybrids.

HEIGHT To 46cm/18in.

COMPOST Soil-based with added sharp sand.

REPOTTING Pot up dry corms from late summer to early winter.

PROPAGATION Sow seed in mid-spring, avoiding excessively high temperatures, or plant corms from late summer to early winter.

KEEPING PLANTS Support plants by pushing light canes into the compost and stretching string between them. After flowering, allow plants to dry out; in midsummer lift, dry and store the corms.

PLANT CARE

Bright light, with some direct sunlight. ● Minimum temperature of 5°C/41°F from mid-autumn to early spring; cool room temperature at other times. ● Water actively growing plants well; ease off once the flowers fade. ● Apply weak liquid fertiliser every 2 weeks from the time flower buds show until the end of flowering.

FUCHSIA
Onagraceae

Fuchsia

Among the most popular flowering plants, fuchsias are available in tender or hardy form, with numerous perennial and shrubby species and cultivars, all of which have woody stems and small pointed deciduous leaves. Some modern hybrids can grow as tall as 1.8m/6ft outdoors, but in cool greenhouse and indoor conditions, the most suitable are dwarf or hanging varieties.

Plants flower from early spring through to late autumn, producing unique, highly ornamental, pendulous blooms, which consist of a bell-shaped flower surrounded by four sepals, long stamens and an extremely long style. Flowers may be single, semi-double or double in almost every colour except yellow; some of the most attractive have sepals of one colour and petals of another.

Buy small plants in spring and, to increase humidity, stand the pots on trays filled with wet pebbles. In summer, plants that are normally kept indoors will thrive if given short spells outside in bright light, but not direct sun. In winter, the leaves will drop, but the plant will remain alive and dormant if kept in a cool, frost-free place, although fuchsias are often discarded at the end of the season.

FACT FILE

ORIGIN Central and South America, New Zealand; hybrid.

HEIGHT To 60cm/2ft (dwarf varieties).

COMPOST Soil-based, peat and sand in equal quantities.

REPOTTING Repot each spring, in the same pot or one a size larger, up to 13cm/5in diameter.

PROPAGATION Take 8–10-cm/3–4-in-long tip cuttings in spring or autumn and root them in warm conditions.

KEEPING PLANTS Pinch out growing tips in spring and early summer to encourage bushy growth. Cut back stems by two-thirds when the plant stops flowering and overwinter in cool conditions.

PLANT CARE

Bright position, but not full sun. ● Minimum winter temperature of 8°C/47°F; warm room temperatures at other times. ● Water actively growing plants well; in winter, allow dormant plants to dry out between waterings. ● Stand the plant on a tray of damp pebbles to increase humidity. ● Feed with a weak liquid fertiliser once a week between spring and autumn.

ALSO RECOMMENDED

Hundreds of hybrid varieties of fuchsia are now available. 'Cascade' has white sepals streaked with pink, and crimson petals; 'Checkerboard' has white and red sepals, with deep red petals. The sepals of 'Display' are rose pink and the petals cerise, while 'Swingtime' has red sepals and white double petals faintly streaked with pink; both are particularly good for hanging baskets. 'Dollar Princess' has cerise sepals and purple petals, and 'Falling Stars' has red sepals with deep red petals. The flowers of 'Golden Marinka' are all-red, but the foliage is variegated green, white and cream.

If red spider mites attack the plant, spray it with insecticide and increase the humidity around the plant.

Leaves that drop prematurely may mean that the atmosphere is too hot and dry. Increase the humidity and move the plant to a cooler place.

Aphids and whiteflies may attack fuchsias; check frequently for signs of the pests and spray with a suitable insecticide if they are present.

Brown spotting with yellow margins on the leaves may mean that the plant is being overwatered; allow it to dry out before rewatering, and improve the drainage.

When a new plant is purchased, or a greenhouse-grown specimen is brought into a dry room, flowers may shed rapidly. To counteract this, choose plants in bud, not in flower, and put them in a bright, cool location near a window.

Fuchsia *'Little Charmer'*, a *hybrid miniature, is ideal for an indoor hanging basket.*

GARDENIA AUGUSTA
Rubiaceae

GARDENIA

There are several species of gardenia – also called Cape jasmine – but *Gardenia augusta*, also known as *G. jasminoides* and *G. grandiflora*, is the one most commonly seen. This old-fashioned, attractive flowering shrub is not difficult to grow, but it does need particular attention if it is to fill a room with its powerful perfume. It is best regarded as a greenhouse, conservatory or patio plant that is brought indoors when in flower. The delicate buds can suffer during transit, so take great care when moving the plant and make sure that it is well protected within a draught-free carrier.

The glossy, dark, evergreen leaves resemble the foliage of camellia, but gardenia leaves, which can be 10cm/4in long, are softer and less rounded. The flowers are 5–10cm/2–4in wide, single, semidouble or double and startlingly white, fading to creamy yellow before they drop. Mature gardenias may reach 1.2–1.8m/4–6ft indoors, but they are more usually bushy shrubs, often growing only 15cm/6in or so in a year.

FACT FILE

ORIGIN Southern China.

HEIGHT 60cm–1.8m/2–6ft indoors.

COMPOST Equal parts of peat moss and leaf mould; must be lime-free.

REPOTTING Move into a pot one size larger every spring.

PROPAGATION Take 8-cm/3-in tip cuttings in spring or early summer, and root them in a warm propagator.

KEEPING PLANTS Prune in late winter to maintain a good shape. The plant can last for many years in the right conditions.

PLANT CARE

Bright light, with some direct sunlight in winter. ● A constant temperature of 16°C/60°F when buds are forming, otherwise normal room temperatures. ● Water moderately with soft, tepid water in the period of active growth; less frequently in winter. ● Mist daily in warm weather with tepid rainwater – do not wet the flowers. ● Apply an 'acid' liquid fertiliser every 2 weeks from early spring to late summer.

Yellowing leaves may mean that the plant is being kept in too shady a position.

Fumes from domestic gas appliances will cause the plant to wilt and die.

Flowers will fall early if the air around the plant is too dry.

Water with a high lime content causes the foliage to become pale and yellow. Use only lime-free water or rainwater and apply sequestered iron every 2 weeks for a couple of months.

Scale insects, mealybugs, aphids and red spider mites all attack gardenias. If they are present, spray with insecticide and improve humidity.

GERBERA JAMESONII
Compositae

BARBERTON DAISY

The major attraction of this popular summer pot plant, also known as the Transvaal daisy, is its large, showy flowers in shades of purple, crimson, red, orange, pink, yellow, cream and white. Both single and double forms are available. The long-lasting flowers, measuring 5–10cm/2–4in across, have soft furry petals and are borne on stiff, grey-green leafless stems up to 60cm/2ft long.

Recent hybrids, with stems about half the length, are better suited to indoor cultivation. They are generally regarded as annuals and can produce up to six blooms at a time; the 15-cm/6-in-long lobed leaves are woolly on the undersides. Buy hybrid plants in bud in early summer.

Leaf spot fungus shows as large brown spots covered with tiny dots and with a thin, violet-coloured border; eventually the spots coalesce, and the leaves start to shrivel.

Aphids may attack gerberas; check regularly for signs of these pests.

Distorted stems and foliage, particularly with young growth, may be a symptom of infestation by tarsonemid mites.

FACT FILE

ORIGIN South Africa (Transvaal), Swaziland; hybrids.

HEIGHT To 46cm/18in.

COMPOST Peat- or soil-based.

REPOTTING Move up in spring, when dividing plants.

PROPAGATION Divide or take cuttings of non-flowering shoots; most hybrids will flower well the first year. Alternatively, sow seed in early spring. Plants grown from saved seed will revert to longer stems, but there are some seed strains available which will produce dwarf plants.

KEEPING PLANTS In a mild climate, the plant will benefit from a spell outdoors after flowering. Replace the plant after 2 or 3 years.

PLANT CARE

Bright light, with some direct sunlight. ● A temperature of 10°–21°C/ 50°–70°F when in flower. ● Keep the compost moist at all times. ● Mist the leaves occasionally. ● Feed flowering plants once a week with half-strength liquid fertiliser. ● Ensure a good circulation of air around the plant.

GLORIOSA SUPERBA 'ROTHSCHILDIANA'
Liliaceae

GLORY LILY

A vigorous climbing plant that grows from elongated, finger-like tubers, the glory lily has slender stems which bear shiny, lanceolate leaves with twining tendrils at their tips, by which the plant clings to its support. The flowers arise from the leaf axils near the top of the stems; they are carried singly on long stalks and look a little like turk's cap lilies, with reflexed, wavy-edged petals of bright red edged with yellow and with a yellow base. The prominent stamens are arranged like the spokes of a wheel below the petals. The plant flowers all summer; after this the tubers should be dried off for the winter.

The glory lily is an unusual but spectacular indoor plant which is sometimes available from garden centres in flower, although it is more usual to buy dormant tubers from bulb specialists.

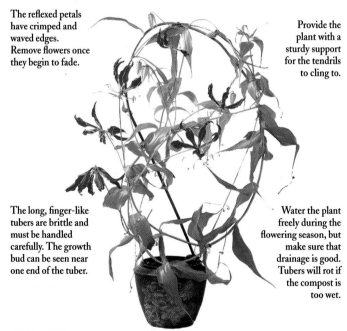

The reflexed petals have crimped and waved edges. Remove flowers once they begin to fade.

Provide the plant with a sturdy support for the tendrils to cling to.

The long, finger-like tubers are brittle and must be handled carefully. The growth bud can be seen near one end of the tuber.

Water the plant freely during the flowering season, but make sure that drainage is good. Tubers will rot if the compost is too wet.

FACT FILE

ORIGIN Tropical Africa.

HEIGHT To 1.2m/4ft or more.

COMPOST Soil- or peat-based, with good drainage.

REPOTTING Handle tubers carefully and pot each in a 15-cm/6-in pot.

PROPAGATION Plant new tubers formed during the growing season, or sow seed in spring.

KEEPING PLANTS After flowering, let the foliage die back; store tubers in a dry place at a minimum of 10°C/50°F until spring, then repot.

PLANT CARE

Bright light, but no direct midsummer sun. ● A warm room with a minimum of 16°C/60°F in the growing period. ● Water newly potted tubers sparingly until shoots emerge, keep the compost evenly moist until flowering finishes, then stop watering. ● Mist the foliage occasionally. ● Apply a high-potash liquid feed every 2–3 weeks when the plant is in active growth.

GREVILLEA ROBUSTA
Proteaceae

SILKY OAK

In its native habitat, this grevillea makes a large tree, but as a pot plant it is seldom more than 1.8m/6ft in height and most plants are much smaller. The finely divided leaves are mid- to dark green, slightly downy on top and silky beneath; they have a fern-like appearance but become less divided as they age. The mature foliage is less attractive than that of young specimens. The silk oak is fast-growing, and where there is room for it can make a striking indoor specimen tree.

A tolerant plant, *Grevillea robusta* thrives best in rather cool conditions. It does not flower in cultivation as an indoor plant.

FACT FILE

ORIGIN Australia.

HEIGHT To 1.8m/6ft.

COMPOST Ericaceous (lime-free).

REPOTTING Repot in spring and also during summer if roots can be seen emerging through the drainage holes in the base of the pot.

PROPAGATION Sow seed in spring and early summer, or take soft stem cuttings in summer.

KEEPING PLANTS The plant is often discarded after 2 or 3 years because the lacy fern-like young foliage becomes less finely divided on older plants and is less attractive.

PLANT CARE

Bright light with some sun, but not direct midsummer sun. Grevillea will also grow well in light shade. ● A minimum winter temperature of 7°C/45°F, with 13°–16°C/55°–60°F in summer. ● Keep the compost evenly moist in spring and summer. Allow the top 2.5cm/1in to dry out between waterings in winter. ● Mist the foliage occasionally, particularly in warm conditions. ● Feed with a balanced liquid fertiliser every 2 weeks in spring and summer.

The undersides of the leaves have a silky feel and appearance, giving the plant its common name.

Check that the growing points on young plants are not damaged when selecting one at a garden centre or nursery.

Infestation by red spider mites is a sign that the atmosphere is too dry. Increase humidity by frequent misting and standing the pot on a dish of damp pebbles.

GYNURA 'PURPLE PASSION'
Compositae

PURPLE PASSION VINE

Thought to be a hybrid between *Gynura procumbens* and *G. aurantiaca*, this foliage plant produces ovate, toothed, more or less holly-shaped leaves on trailing or climbing stems, which are best displayed in a hanging basket or wall pot. The foliage is mid-green, but is covered with dense purple hairs, particularly on the underside; the stems are also hairy, which gives the whole plant an almost fluorescent, velvety appearance, and it is also known as the velvet plant. When the plant is kept in bright light, the colour is often particularly intense and can create a quite startling effect.

Shaggy, orange-yellow, groundsel-like flowers are produced in spring and should be removed, since they are not only unattractive but have an unpleasant smell.

The iridescent purple hairs are most dense on young foliage and shoot tips and the colour is strongest on plants kept in bright light.

Mist the foliage with a fine spray only in warm conditions. The hairs trap the moisture which can lead to rotting.

Stems are twining or semi-twining and can be trained up a trellis or left to trail.

FACT FILE

ORIGIN Hybrid.

HEIGHT Trailing stems up to 1.5m/5ft long.

COMPOST Soil- or peat-based.

REPOTTING In spring, move into a pot one size larger.

PROPAGATION Take soft stem cuttings in spring and early summer.

KEEPING PLANTS Pinch out shoot tips to keep the plant compact. Cut back older plants to 10cm/4in in spring. Discard plants after 2 years.

PLANT CARE

Bright light, for good coloration; some sun, but strong summer sun can scorch the leaves. ● Minimum winter temperature of 10°C/50°F. ● Water moderately in the growing season; less often in winter. ● Stand the plant on a tray of damp pebbles to increase humidity. ● Feed with a balanced liquid fertiliser every 2 weeks during spring and summer.

HAEMANTHUS HUMILIS 'WILSONII'
Amaryllidaceae

HAEMANTHUS

This lily with its pair of grey-green hairy leaves and stem is an unusual house plant. In summer it produces a rather short-lived umbel of pale pink or white flowers on a sturdy stem. The more commonly grown perennial bulb, usually called *Haemanthus katherinae*, is related, but it is now correctly known as *Scadoxus multiflora* ssp. *katherinae*. This bulb has mid-green, wavy-edged leaves up to 30cm/12in long on short stalks, which it retains during the winter. The bright red, showy flowers with prominent stamens are carried in a ball-like umbel at the top of a tall, fleshy stem that is often streaked or flushed with red at the base. The 20-cm/8-in-wide flower head appears in summer.

FACT FILE

ORIGIN Southern Africa.

HEIGHT Flower stems to 30cm/12in.

POTTING MIX Soil-based.

REPOTTING Repot in spring, every 3–5 years, when the bulb is too large for the pot or roots can be seen through the base of the pot and on the surface of the soil. Otherwise, top-dress annually.

PROPAGATION Best grown from offsets. From seed it flowers in about 18 months; division is very slow.

KEEPING PLANTS Haemanthus flower best when undisturbed and may be kept in the same pot for several years.

PLANT CARE

Bright light with some direct sun. ● Average room temperature, with a minimum of 10°C/50°F. ● Water freely in summer and let the surface of the soil dry out between watering; water less in winter. ● Give a high-potash liquid feed every 2 weeks in the growing season.

The globular flower head, consisting of many small flowers, is usually about 10cm/4in wide.

Make sure the neck of the bulb is just above the surface of the compost when potting it.

HEDERA HELIX
Araliaceae

*E*NGLISH IVY

This well-known, fast-growing, climbing plant, although perfectly hardy and widely grown outdoors, makes an excellent indoor plant. The three- to five-lobed, roughly palmate leaves vary considerably in shape and size (from about 2cm/³/₄in to 10cm/4in) according to variety. Stems are tough and wiry and progress upwards, clinging to their support by means of aerial roots; outdoors, they have no problem attaching themselves to brickwork, fences and so on, but usually need to be tied in to canes and supports in the home. In outdoor conditions, the growth of ivy changes to a mature form when the plant has reached the top of its climb. Stems become erect and bushy, leaves entire, and flowers are produced. This does not normally occur with plants grown indoors.

There are dozens of varieties suitable for growing as pot plants, many of them variegated. 'Glacier' has three-lobed leaves mottled grey-green, silver and cream; 'Goldheart' has a large, irregular central blotch of creamy yellow against a dark green background. 'Sagittifolia' has an elongated central lobe, giving the leaves an arrowhead appearance; plain green and variegated forms are available. 'Ivalace' has curled and crimped leaf margins, giving a lacy effect.

FACT FILE

ORIGIN Europe.

HEIGHT Most will climb as high as they are allowed to.

COMPOST Soil- or peat-based.

REPOTTING Move small plants into larger pots when roots emerge through the base of the pot.

PROPAGATION In spring and early summer, take 8–10-cm/3–4-in tip cuttings and root them in water or compost.

KEEPING PLANTS Grow the plant up canes or trellis, tying in the stems, or set several plants in a hanging basket or pot and allow the stems to trail. Pinch out the growing tips to keep the plant neat.

PLANT CARE

Bright light; variegated forms need some direct sun.
● Cool temperatures are required, ideally around 10°C/50°F. ● Allow the surface of the compost to dry out between waterings. ● Mist the foliage frequently.
● Apply a standard liquid fertiliser every 2 weeks in spring and summer.

ALSO RECOMMENDED

Hedera algeriensis, a larger-leafed species with shallowly lobed leaves up to 15cm/6in wide; 'Gloire de Marengo' is mottled grey-green with a white edge to the leaves.

Hedera algeriensis *'Gloire de Marengo' has large leaves, pleasingly variegated with grey-green and white. It is a vigorous grower and, trained over a trellis, makes a good background to flowering plants.*

Take care where you position ivy – the aerial roots will cling firmly to walls and can spoil decorations and furnishings.

Ivy is particularly prone to attack by red spider mites. Check the foliage for mottling or yellow flecking; mist the plant regularly, especially in warm conditions.

Cut out the all-green shoots that are sometimes produced on variegated ivies. Improve the light to maintain leaf coloration.

HEPTAPLEURUM ARBORICOLUM see
SCHEFFLERA ARBORICOLA

HIBISCUS ROSA-SINENSIS
Malvaceae

ROSE OF CHINA

Hibiscus is a shrubby evergreen plant, bearing dark green, ovate leaves with toothed edges. The large, showy flowers, in white and shades of red, orange, yellow and pink, open out to flared trumpets, some 10–15cm/4–6in wide, with a prominent column of fused stamens. On well-grown plants, there will be a succession of flowers from spring to late summer. Single or semi-double varieties are available, and plants can sometimes be bought trained as short standards, but these are expensive. *Hibiscus rosa-sinensis* 'Koenig' is an attractive double-flowered yellow variety; 'Golden Belle' has large, golden yellow single flowers with ruffled petals, while those of 'Surfrider' are yellow with a red eye. The flowers of 'Paramaribo' are rich red, and 'Rosalie' has flowers of a clear rose pink and sharply indented leaf margins.

When conditions suit them, hibiscus are long-lived plants, and they need regular pruning to keep them small enough for the home. Larger plants look good in a sunroom or conservatory.

FACT FILE

ORIGIN Tropical Asia.

HEIGHT To 1.8m/6ft.

COMPOST Soil-based, with a little added peat or peat substitute.

REPOTTING In spring, move into a pot one size larger. When the maximum desired pot size is reached, top-dress annually.

PROPAGATION In late spring and early summer, take 8–10-cm/3–4-in tip or heel cuttings.

KEEPING PLANTS Cut the stems back by half to two-thirds in early spring to keep indoor plants compact.

PLANT CARE

Bright light with some direct sun. ● Normal room temperature in the growing season; allow to rest at 13°C/55°F during the winter. ● Keep the compost thoroughly moist at all times in spring and summer; in winter, allow it to dry out between waterings. ● Mist the foliage frequently and stand the pot on a tray of damp pebbles to increase humidity. ● Feed with a high-potash liquid fertiliser every 2 weeks in summer. ● Try not to move the plant while it is in bud or the buds may drop.

ALSO RECOMMENDED

Hibiscus schizopetalus, known as Japanese lantern or Japanese hibiscus, is a more graceful looking plant with slender arching branches. The drooping pink flowers on long stalks have fringed, turned-back petals with a long stamen column; they can be more than 5cm/2in wide.

Buds will drop if plants are moved to a place with a different temperature. Lack of humidity or allowing the compost to dry out may also cause buds to drop.

The large, trumpet-shaped flowers will fall after a day or two, but more should be produced for a long succession of blooms.

Aphids sometimes attack the young foliage. Treat with a contact insecticide.

Hibiscus rosa-sinensis *'Koenig' has flowers with a double ring of bright yellow petals and, almost hidden within them, a red eye.*

HIPPEASTRUM x *ACKERMANNII* (SYN. *H.* x *ACRAMANNII*)
Amaryllidaceae

Amaryllis

The common name of this plant is a misnomer – *Amaryllis belladonna* is related but is a quite different bulb. Hippeastrums are popular and easily available, and a wide range of varieties exists. The big, fleshy bulbs produce a tall, succulent, hollow green flower stem, usually in spring, although specially treated bulbs are available for winter flowering. Large, strong bulbs may sometimes produce two flowering stems, but one is more usual. The stem bears two to four large, colourful, lily-like trumpets with six petals and prominent curving stamens, which last for several weeks. Flowers are available in red, white, salmon or pink and they may be striped or flushed with a second colour.

Normally the leaves follow the flower stem, although occasionally both are produced together. Leaves are long and strap shaped, mid- to dark green, and they arise in opposite pairs which arch over. Hippeastrum bulbs must be given a rest in autumn and early winter if they are to flower successfully the following year.

FACT FILE

ORIGIN South and Central America; hybrids.

HEIGHT To 60cm/2ft.

COMPOST Soil-based.

REPOTTING Set the bulb in the compost with the top third above the surface. At the end of the rest period, repot the bulb in fresh compost in the same pot.

PROPAGATION Sow seed in spring, or pot up any offsets that appear around the base of the bulb; they will take several years to grow to flowering size.

KEEPING PLANTS A rest in autumn and winter is important to bring plants into flower the following year. Bright light and adequate feeding until leaves die down in mid-autumn are needed for the formation of flower buds.

PLANT CARE

Bright light with some direct sun. ● Fairly cool conditions will ensure the flowers last well; maximum temperature 18°C/65°F. ● Water sparingly until the flower bud appears, then increase watering but allow the surface of the compost to dry out before rewatering. When flowers fade, gradually decrease watering until mid-autumn; then dry out the compost completely: bulbs need a dormant period of 8 weeks. ● Mist the foliage frequently and stand the pot on a tray of moist pebbles. ● Feed with a high-potash fertiliser every 10–14 days from the time the bud appears until autumn. ● The bud may drop if the plant is moved after it has emerged.

ALSO RECOMMENDED

Many hippeastrum cultivars are available for indoor planting. 'Appleblossom' is pale pink and white; 'Red Lion' is a strong, rich red; 'Picotee' is white with a fine red margin to the petals; and 'Bijou' has soft apricot-coloured flowers. There are also double-flowered varieties such as 'Lady Jane', with orange-pink-and-white flowers.

Hippeastrum *'Appleblossom' bears blooms whose huge size is in marked contrast to their delicate pink and white coloration.*

The huge flowers can make plants top-heavy, particularly if they are grown in peat-based compost. Stake the flower stem if necessary, but be careful not to damage the bulb when inserting the stake.

Set the large, fleshy bulb so that the top third is above the level of the compost. Buy only bulbs that are plump and not shrivelled.

Plants that have not been well cared for during the previous season sometimes produce only leaves. This is unlikely to occur with commercially grown bulbs.

HOFFMANNIA REGALIS 'ROEZLII'
Rubiaceae

TAFFETA PLANT

The three species of hoffmannia used as house plants are grown for their striking foliage. Although they do flower, the blooms tend to be insignificant and are hidden among the leaves. These plants are shrubby perennials which are usually fairly short-lived in the home.

Hoffmannia regalis 'Roezlii' has satiny puckered leaves some 15cm/6in long that are purplish green above and purple-red underneath. The leaves of H. ghiesbreghtii are lance-shaped and up to 30cm/12in long; they are a deep reddish green with the veins picked out in silver. The leaves of H.g. 'Variegata' are irregularly marked with dark green, pale silvery green, cream and light pink. H. refulgens has rounded leaves of an almost iridescent coppery green, which are deeply veined, with a puckered, textured surface between the veins. The variety 'Vittata' has silvery veins.

The prominently veined foliage has an almost metallic sheen; the undersides of the leaves are purple-red.

Aphids may attack young leaves; treat the pests with a contact insecticide.

The short-stemmed flowers are quite attractive, but are usually hidden among the leaves.

If the leaves droop, the temperature may be too low. Keep the plant in an evenly warm, draught-free position: it is an ideal subject for a sunroom or conservatory.

FACT FILE

ORIGIN Mexico, Central America.

HEIGHT 30–60cm/1–2ft.

POTTING MIX Soil- or peat-based.

REPOTTING Move into a pot one size larger in spring when roots can be seen emerging through the drainage holes in the base of the pot.

PROPAGATION Take stem cuttings in early summer. Some bottom heat in a propagator will improve rooting.

KEEPING PLANTS Discard plants when they become leggy; this is usually after about 5 years.

PLANT CARE

Bright diffused light. ● Warm conditions, with a minimum temperature of 16°C/60°F. ● Keep the soil just moist during the growing season; allow the surface to dry out between waterings. ● Mist the foliage occasionally with a fine spray. ● Feed with a balanced liquid fertiliser every 2 weeks in spring and summer.

HOWEA BELMOREANA
Palmae

SENTRY PALM

Still sometimes sold as kentia palms, howeas are popular, tolerant, slow-growing house plants; Howea belmoreana is also known as curly palm. They are long-lived, and mature plants produce gracefully arching fronds with short leafstalks from the top of a short trunk. Indoors, each fan may be as much as 30cm/12in wide and 46cm/18in long on older specimens. The leaves of H. forsteriana have longer leafstalks and do not arch as gracefully as those of H. belmoreana. The former has a more spreading habit, but the two are so similar in appearance that they may be confused. Both make bold specimen plants.

FACT FILE

ORIGIN Lord Howe Island, South Pacific.

HEIGHT To 1.8m/6ft or more.

POTTING MIX Soil-based, with a little added peat moss.

REPOTTING Every 2 or 3 years, move into a pot one size larger in spring.

PROPAGATION Sow seed in a heated propagator, but seedlings are slow-growing and propagation in the home is not really practical.

KEEPING PLANTS This long-lived palm will benefit from a spell outdoors in summer.

PLANT CARE

Bright, diffused light; the plant will tolerate shade. ● Normal room temperature, with a minimum of 13°C/55°F. ● Keep the soil moist during the growing season; allow the surface to dry out between waterings in winter. ● Mist the foliage regularly; stand the pot on a tray of moist pebbles. ● Feed with a standard liquid fertiliser every 2 weeks in spring and summer.

The dark green fronds are made up of many arching pinnae, or leaflets, about 4cm/1½in wide.

Refresh dull, dusty foliage by standing the plant under a gentle shower or outdoors in warm summer rain.

Leaf tips tend to turn brown even on healthy plants. Mist the foliage regularly with water to ensure high humidity. Scorch marks may be caused by bright, direct sunlight on the leaves.

Scale insects may attack this plant: look for dark brown, oval scales firmly fixed to the undersides of the leaves. Remove them carefully with a thumbnail. If left, they can cause black sooty mould to develop.

HOYA LANCEOLATA SSP. *BELLA*
Asclepiadaceae

MINIATURE WAX PLANT

The long, slender stems of this plant (usually known just as *Hoya bella*), with their pale grey-green oval or lance-shaped leaves, are upright at first, then arch over to trail gracefully. Flower heads, produced from the tips of the stems in summer, consist of a cluster of up to 10 star-shaped, waxy white flowers with a rose pink, five-pointed centre. The heads hang down, and the plant is best grown in a hanging basket so that the blooms can more easily be appreciated, or trained around a wire hoop and tied in at intervals with soft twine. The flowers are sweetly scented, and drops of sticky nectar often form on them. Do not move the plant when the buds are forming, since this will usually cause them to drop.

H. carnosa, wax plant, is generally easier to grow than *H. bella* and it climbs rapidly. The flowers, which are produced in summer, are similar to those of *H. bella*, but each flower head carries about twice the number of blooms. These are strongly fragrant, and another common name for *H. carnosa* is honey plant. The foliage is thick and fleshy, glossy and mid- to dark green; although several variegated forms are available, they are sometimes more difficult to bring into flower.

FACT FILE

ORIGIN India, Southeast Asia.

HEIGHT Stems trail to around 46cm/18in. *H. carnosa* can reach 4.5m/15ft or more.

COMPOST Peat-based; must be free-draining.

REPOTTING Plants flower best when slightly pot-bound, so move them into pots one size larger in late spring only every 2 years or so.

PROPAGATION Take 8–10-cm/3–4-in stem tip cuttings in late spring.

KEEPING PLANTS Do not remove faded flower heads; flowers will be produced from the same spur in subsequent years.

PLANT CARE

Bright light with some direct sun. ● Warm conditions, with a minimum of 16°C/60°F in winter and a temperature of 18°–21°C/65°–70°F in summer. ● Water moderately in summer, allowing the surface to dry out between waterings; in winter give only sufficient water to prevent the compost drying out completely. ● Mist the foliage regularly, but avoid spraying the flowers. ● Apply a high-potash liquid feed every 2–3 weeks in the growing period.

ALSO RECOMMENDED

Hoya carnosa 'Variegata' has cream-edged leaves. *H. australis* has slightly smaller flowers with a honeysuckle scent.

Plant in a hanging basket or wall pot, so the drooping flower heads can be seen from below.

If stems are weak, leaves pale and widely spaced, and flowers few, move the plant to a lighter, sunny position. But protect plants from scorching caused by direct midsummer sun.

Pick off individual flowers when they fade, but do not disturb the spur from which the flowers arise.

Mealybugs may attack this plant. Remove them with a damp cloth and spray the plant with a suitable insecticide.

Hoya carnosa *produces heavy flower heads that may contain as many as 30 sweet-scented flowers. These start off white and soon turn pale pink with a white and rose centre.*

HYACINTHUS ORIENTALIS
Liliaceae

Hyacinth

Most of the sweet-scented hyacinths that bloom indoors are grown from bulbs specially prepared for forcing, and they will flower several weeks earlier than their normal spring season outdoors.

Leaves are long, strap shaped and mid-green. A single flower spike arises from the bulb, with a fleshy stem and densely packed racemes of fragrant flowers. Many varieties are available in shades of blue, violet, red, pink, apricot, yellow and white; among the most popular are rose pink 'Anna Marie', 'Delft Blue', which flowers very early, and 'City of Haarlem', a soft primrose yellow. Plant treated bulbs as soon as you get them. Set them in a bowl of moist, peaty compost so that the noses show just above the surface. Keep them in cool (4°C/40°F) completely dark conditions for about eight weeks. When the shoots are about 5cm/2in high, bring them into the light and keep them at about 10°C/50°F; once the buds show colour, move the bulbs to their flowering position. If you plant different types of bulbs over a few weeks, they will bloom in succession, giving flowers for about two months.

FACT FILE

ORIGIN Hybrid.

HEIGHT 25–30cm/10–12in.

COMPOST Peat-based, rather than bulb fibre, if you want to keep the bulb to flower outside in future years.

REPOTTING None.

PROPAGATION Pot up offsets from around the base of the bulb.

KEEPING PLANTS Cut down flower stalks after the flowers have faded, but water and feed the bulbs until the leaves die down. Bulbs are not suitable for indoor use again but can be planted in the garden.

PLANT CARE

Bright conditions for leaf and flower development. ● A maximum of 16°C/60°F in the bulbs' flowering position. ● Keep the compost just moist at all times. ● Give a balanced liquid fertiliser every 2 weeks from the time the flower buds are visible until the foliage dies down.

Use a thin cane to support the flowering stem if the large flower head is very heavy.

Malformed flower heads, or flower spikes that do not emerge properly above the leaves, are the result of keeping the bulbs too warm or not completely dark during the cold period.

Different varieties come into flower at different times. For the best effect plant up bowls with several bulbs of the same variety, rather than mixing them.

HYDRANGEA MACROPHYLLA (SYN. *H. HORTENSIS*)
Hydrangeaceae

Hydrangea

These hardy shrubs are usually treated as temporary pot plants and may be discarded after flowers fade. Several cuttings are usually grown in one pot to form a bushy plant. The hydrangea most commonly grown as a pot plant is the hortensia, or mop head type. The large, globular flower heads are made up of sterile florets in shades of blue, pink or white; the colour is determined by the acidity of the compost. In alkaline soils the florets are pink. They turn blue in acid conditions; aluminium sulphate can be given to ensure the blue colour is retained. Not all varieties change colour successfully, some pinks turning a muddy purple, but 'Blue Prince', 'Garten-Baudirektor Kuhnert', 'Holstein', 'Maréchal Foch' and 'Queen Elizabeth' usually have strong, clear colours, whether pink or blue.

If flower heads lose their blue colour and begin to turn purple or pink, the compost has become alkaline. Treat with aluminium sulphate.

Foliage rapidly turns yellow and falls if the compost is allowed to dry out. Pots are usually tightly packed with roots, so water frequently.

FACT FILE

ORIGIN Japan.

HEIGHT To 60cm/2ft.

COMPOST Soil-based; ericaceous (lime-free) for blue varieties.

REPOTTING Repot after flowering, if you wish to try the plant indoors for a second year.

PROPAGATION Take cuttings in late summer; overwinter in a cold frame.

KEEPING PLANTS Plant in the garden if in good condition or, after flowering, repot, cut back the stems by half and continue to water and feed. Put in a cold frame or unheated greenhouse; move into warmer conditions in late winter to bring the plant into leaf and flower early.

PLANT CARE

Bright light, but not direct sun. ● A maximum of 16°C/60°F will help the flowers to last. ● Keep well watered during the growing season; use lime-free water. Water sparingly in winter. ● Give a high-potash liquid fertiliser every 1–2 weeks in the growing season.

HYPOESTES PHYLLOSTACHYA
Acanthaceae

Polka dot plant

A fast-growing foliage plant, the polka dot plant, also known as freckle face, has oval, pointed leaves about 4cm/1¹/₂in long, which are dark green, spotted and splashed with pink. Plants in the 'Splash' series are the most commonly grown, and are so heavily marked that the leaves appear to be pink with green flecks. As well as the popular 'Pink Splash', the deeper-coloured 'Rose Splash' and 'White Splash' are available.

The plant quickly makes a fairly lax bush, and the growing tips should be pinched out regularly to keep it reasonably compact. It is usually discarded after it has become leggy, but soft stem cuttings are easily rooted to provide replacements. The pale lilac flowers are insignificant and flower stems are usually pinched out as they appear.

Commercially grown plants are kept compact by the use of growth-regulating chemicals.

Hot summer sun may cause brown scorch marks on the foliage. Protect plants by filtering the sunlight with blinds or curtains.

Leaves may revert to all-green in poor light. Keep the plant in good, bright light for the best coloration and compact growth.

Pinch out any flower spikes that appear in summer, since they detract from the foliage.

FACT FILE

ORIGIN Madagascar.

HEIGHT Keep to about 30cm/12in by pinching out.

COMPOST Peat-based.

REPOTTING Not usually required.

PROPAGATION Take soft stem cuttings in spring and summer; put several cuttings in a pot for a good display. Sow seed in early spring.

KEEPING PLANTS Discard the plant when it becomes leggy and replace it with newly rooted cuttings.

PLANT CARE

Bright light, with some direct sun, for good leaf colour, but protect plants from scorching by very hot sun. ● Average room temperature, with a minimum winter temperature of 17°C/62°F. ● Keep the compost just moist during the growing season; allow the surface to dry out between waterings. Water more sparingly in cooler winter temperatures. ● Apply a balanced liquid fertiliser every 2–3 weeks during the growing season.

IMPATIENS WALLERIANA
Balsaminaceae

Busy lizzie

Popular and easily grown plants, busy lizzies have fleshy, succulent stems with lance-shaped to oval, toothed leaves. Flat-faced, usually spurred flowers, with a central eye, are carried in profusion in a wide range of colours – white, pink, red, carmine, salmon, orange and lavender, with some bicolours. Plants may flower almost year-round.

There are many different varieties, some of which have larger flowers, darker, bronze foliage or double and semi-double flowers like miniature roses. The more compact, early and free-flowering strains are most commonly produced commercially. New Guinea hybrids have attractive foliage – often with a central yellow stripe on the leaves. They produce plentiful flowers in summer, but they do not bloom so well during the winter.

FACT FILE

ORIGIN Warm temperate regions of Africa and Asia, New Guinea; hybrids.

HEIGHT To 46cm/18in.

COMPOST Peat-based.

REPOTTING Repot only when the compost is filled with roots.

PROPAGATION In spring and summer, take soft stem cuttings, which root easily, or sow seed from early spring to early summer.

KEEPING PLANTS The plant is usually discarded when it becomes leggy. Bright light and regular feeding help to prolong its life.

PLANT CARE

Bright light, but not direct hot summer sun. ● Normal room temperature, with a minimum of 13°C/55°F; for winter flowering 16°C/60°F or higher is necessary. ● Keep the compost moist at all times; reduce watering in winter. ● Give a high-potash liquid feed every 2 weeks in spring and summer to prolong flowering.

If the plant has a mass of foliage but few flowers, it has probably been overpotted. Wait until the compost is filled with roots before repotting, and avoid high-nitrogen fertilisers.

The plant flowers best when slightly pot-bound and so needs frequent watering, especially in warm conditions. Foliage wilts rapidly if the plant is short of water.

IRESINE HERBSTII
Amaranthaceae

BLOODLEAF

The unusual colour of the succulent stems and lance-shaped oval leaves of the bloodleaf is caused by a pigment which masks the normal green chlorophyll of the leaf. Because this plant has such a vibrant colour, it is also called the beefsteak plant. Insignificant flowers are occasionally produced but are best picked off because they detract from the coloured foliage. In the variety 'Brilliantissima', the veins are picked out in pink. 'Aureo-reticulata' has green leaves with yellow-marked veins, although stems and leafstalks are still red.

FACT FILE

ORIGIN Brazil.

HEIGHT To 60cm/2ft.

COMPOST Soil-based, with good drainage.

REPOTTING Repot when roots emerge through the drainage holes in the bottom of the pot.

PROPAGATION Take soft stem cuttings in spring and summer.

KEEPING PLANTS Pinch out the growing tips regularly to keep plants compact and bushy; discard them when they become leggy.

PLANT CARE

Bright light is essential to retain good leaf colour, but shade from direct sun in midsummer. ● Normal room temperature, with a minimum of 13°C/55°F in winter. ● Keep the compost moist at all times in the growing season; reduce watering in winter. ● Mist the foliage occasionally in warm weather. ● Apply a standard liquid fertiliser every 2 weeks during the growing season.

The brilliant leaf colour fades if the plant does not receive sufficient light.

Watch out for aphid infestation of the soft young shoots. Treat with a contact insecticide when necessary.

Regular pinching out of the growing tips helps to keep plants compact. But once they become leggy, they can be replaced by cuttings, which are easy to root.

JASMINUM MESNYI
Oleaceae

PRIMROSE JASMINE

This species was once known as *Jasminum primulinum* and is still sometimes offered under that name. It is a long-lived scrambling, evergreen shrub with mid-green leaves divided into three leaflets. The bright yellow flowers are produced in spring and continue into the early summer; they are usually semi-double or double and are carried singly in the leaf axils. Unlike those of the more popular members of the jasmine family, these flowers are unscented. The stems do not twine and need to be tied to thin canes for support.

Tie the stems to thin canes as they develop. This jasmine is an ideal plant for a conservatory, where it can be trained on a permanent wall trellis.

The yellow flowers have a larger number of petals than other jasmine species, giving them a double or semi-double appearance.

Trifoliate leaves are carried in opposite pairs on square stems and are evergreen in all but the coldest conditions.

FACT FILE

ORIGIN China.

HEIGHT To 3m/10ft.

COMPOST Soil-based.

REPOTTING In late spring, move into a container one size larger. Once the maximum desired pot size has been reached, top-dress annually with fresh compost.

PROPAGATION Take stem cuttings between late spring and late summer; use soft tips in spring and semi-ripe wood later. You can improve the success rate by using a propagator with bottom heat.

KEEPING PLANTS This jasmine is long-lived and needs little attention other than tying in to its support and pruning to limit its size.

PLANT CARE

Bright light with some direct sun. ● Cool room temperature, with a range of 16°–18°C/60°–65°F. ● Keep the compost just moist at all times. ● Give a balanced liquid feed every 2–3 weeks during the growing season.

JASMINUM POLYANTHUM
Oleaceae

CHINESE JASMINE

This vigorous climber with wiry, branching stems is the most popular jasmine grown as an indoor plant. Flowers are carried in winter and spring in large clusters arising from the leaf axils near the stem tips. They have a long tube and open to a small white star. The buds, tubes and, sometimes, the reverse of the petals are deep pink. The intensely fragrant flowers – a single plant will scent a large room – are occasionally followed by small black berries. It may lose its leaves.

FACT FILE

ORIGIN China.

HEIGHT To 3m/10ft.

COMPOST Soil-based.

REPOTTING Repot in summer as necessary; plants flower best when slightly pot-bound.

PROPAGATION Take semi-ripe cuttings in summer or soft stem cuttings in spring.

KEEPING PLANTS Cut out older, flowered stems in summer. Train new growth gently around a hoop to encourage prolific flowering.

PLANT CARE

Bright light with some direct sun. ● Normal to cool temperature, minimum of 7°C/45°F. ● Keep the compost moist in the growing season. Allow the surface to dry out between waterings in winter. ● Mist the foliage regularly. ● When the plant comes into bud, apply a high-potash liquid fertiliser every 2 weeks.

Leaves may turn black if conditions are too cold in winter. Take off the affected leaves and move the plant to a position that is slightly warmer.

Repot only when the compost is filled with roots. Overpotting may cause lush, leafy growth and a failure to flower.

JUSTICIA CARNEA
Acanthaceae

KING'S CROWN

Also known as *Jacobinia carnea*, this is a shrubby plant with ovate or lance-shaped leaves up to 15cm/6in long. Leaves are often slightly furry and rather coarse in appearance. Flowers are produced in late summer and autumn in dense plumes about 13cm/5in long. They are tubular and rosy pink with green bracts and give the plant its other common names, pink acanthus and Brazilian plume flower.

The semi-twining stems can be trained and tied over a trellis for support.

Growing tips should be regularly pinched out to keep the plant compact and bushy.

Tall plumes of shaggy rose pink flowers are carried in late summer and autumn.

Red spider mites can cause mottled, pale foliage with webbing visible around the young leaves. Increase the humidity by more frequent spraying.

FACT FILE

ORIGIN South America.

HEIGHT To 1.2m/4ft but usually kept below this by pinching.

COMPOST Soil-based.

REPOTTING Repot whenever roots appear through the drainage holes in the base of the pot.

PROPAGATION Take stem cuttings in spring from overwintered plants.

KEEPING PLANTS Cut stems back by half after flowering and give the plant a winter rest at about 13°C/55°F. Discard after 2 years.

PLANT CARE

Bright light with some direct sun, especially during the winter. ● A minimum of 13°C/55°F in winter; otherwise, normal room temperature. ● Keep the compost thoroughly moist in the growing season; reduce watering in winter. ● Mist the plant regularly while it is in active growth. ● Apply a balanced liquid fertiliser every 2 weeks from spring to autumn.

CRASSULACEAE

KALANCHOES

This is an extremely varied group of plants, all of which are succulent to some degree; they are grown for either their foliage or their flowers. Because they all have more or less fleshy leaves, they are tolerant of a dry atmosphere and are good plants in heated houses; they will also thrive in a sunny spot where many other plants would wilt and fade. The leaves grow in pairs opposite each other, and the four-petalled tubular flowers are borne in panicles at the ends of the stems.

Probably the most popular species is *Kalanchoe blossfeldiana*, flaming Katy. Its natural flowering season is from late autumn to early spring, but by cutting down the hours of daylight the plant receives in summer, growers can bring it into flower at almost any time of the year. It is a bushy plant with fleshy dark green leaves that are oval with a toothed margin and are often tinged with red at the edges and on the undersides. Small tubular flowers are carried in dense panicles on tall stems rising above the foliage.

Most of the kalanchoes grown as house plants are fairly small, but some, such as *K. beharensis*, velvet-leaf, grow into specimens up to 1.2m/4ft tall. This species has triangular hairy leaves about 15cm/6in long. On the small *K. tomentosa*, the hairs are so fine and soft that they are more like fur. Most of the other species grown indoors have more typically succulent leaves with a smooth surface that is either shiny or has a waxy bloom.

Kalanchoe blossfeldiana hybrids produce dense panicles of up to 50 small flowers that are long-lasting and available in a good choice of colours. The most common is scarlet, but plants with yellow, white, orange and pink flowers, like the hybrid 'Calypso' shown here, are easy to find.

Choose a plant with bright, fresh-looking leaves and flower stems with plenty of unopened buds.

Leaves are fleshy and succulent, and are usually flushed with red when the plant is kept in a sunny position.

ALSO RECOMMENDED

Kalanchoe manginii 'Tessa' is a good plant for a hanging basket. It has reddish wiry stems that bear loose panicles of flowers like dainty drooping bells. The flowers are usually salmon or pink with green tips.

Kalanchoe tomentosa, called panda plant or pussy ears, has rosettes of thick pointed leaves covered with silvery 'fur'. The leaf tips and margins are marked with brown.

Kalanchoe marmorata is commonly known as the penwiper because its blue-green, rounded fleshy leaves are blotched with purple-brown. Panicles of white flowers are sometimes borne.

Mealybugs commonly infest this plant. They appear as white, woolly patches, usually near the leaf stalk. Remove them with a damp cloth or cotton bud as soon as you see them.

The leaves are brittle and can be damaged by careless handling. Tips break away easily, leaving a brown line across the leaf.

Lower leaves will shrivel or turn yellow if the soil is allowed to become too dry.

If the plant droops and wilts for no explicable reason, take it out of its pot and check to see whether root mealybugs are the cause.

Kalanchoe pumila is a low-growing, branching plant. Its oval leaves have toothed edges and a white waxy covering that gives them a bright silver-blue appearance. Little lilac-pink flowers with deeper purplish lines on the petals are produced in clusters in late winter or early spring. It is displayed to best advantage in a hanging basket.

FACT FILE

ORIGIN Madagascar, tropical Africa.

HEIGHT 25–60cm/10–24in indoors; *Kalanchoe marmorata* will reach 1.2m/4ft outdoors.

COMPOST Soil-based with added sand or perlite.

REPOTTING In spring move plants that are not being discarded into pots one size larger.

PROPAGATION Take stem cuttings in spring. Kalanchoes can also be propagated from leaf cuttings and from seed. Home-propagated plants will flower in their natural season – late winter and spring – not necessarily the same flowering season as the plant you bought.

KEEPING PLANTS *K. blossfeldiana* is normally discarded after it has flowered, since it is difficult to bring it into flower again indoors.

A second flowering can sometimes be achieved by giving the plant a rest period after flowering, then standing it on a bright windowsill. In mild conditions, stand the plant outdoors in a well-lit, lightly shaded spot for a spell to encourage it to flower again.

Failure of the plant to flower at the expected time can be caused by exposing it to artificial light.

PLANT CARE

Bright light with some direct sun, especially in winter. ● Normal room temperature, with a minimum of 10°C/50°F. Give plants grown especially for their foliage, such as *K. pumila*, a winter rest at 10°–13°C/ 50°–55°F. ● Water fairly sparingly, allowing the top 2.5cm/1in of the soil to dry out between waterings. Reduce watering in cooler winter temperatures when plants are resting. ● Apply a balanced liquid fertiliser every 3 weeks during the period of active growth and flowering.

PESTS & DISEASES

Kalanchoes may occasionally be attacked by tarsonemid mites, especially strawberry mites, but they are more commonly infested with mealybugs and root mealybugs. Otherwise, kalanchoes are largely trouble-free plants.

LANTANA CAMARA
Verbenaceae

Yellow Sage

The wrinkled, rather coarse, toothed leaves of this lantana, which can be an invasive plant outdoors, are similar to those of sage and give the plant its common name. But the flowers, which bloom between late spring and mid-autumn, are quite different, being more like those of the related verbena. They are carried in flattened or slightly rounded heads, and each flower is small and tubular, with a central eye; buds open from the outside ring of the flower head.

The plant shown here is the plain yellow 'Sundancer', a spreading variety which is good in a hanging basket. But in 'Chelsea Gem', the flowers start yellow then darken through orange to orange-red so, as successive rings of flowers open towards the centre, two or three distinct colours exist within each head. White, lilac, pink, red and many bicoloured varieties are also found.

The flowers are attractive to butterflies when the plant is grown in a place to which they have access.

Lantana is prone to attack by whiteflies. Spray several times with insecticide for good control.

Pinch out the growing tips regularly to keep the plant bushy.

FACT FILE

ORIGIN Tropical America; cultivars.

HEIGHT To 1.8m/6ft, but usually kept to 30cm/12in in the home.

COMPOST Soil- or peat-based.

REPOTTING Repot in spring, only when the compost is tightly packed with roots; flowering is improved when plants are slightly pot-bound.

PROPAGATION Take soft stem cuttings in early summer.

KEEPING PLANTS Rest plants in winter in cool, dry conditions. Cut back stems to 10–13cm/4–5in in late winter, just before the start of new growth. Stand plants outdoors for a spell in summer.

PLANT CARE

Bright light with some direct sun, especially in winter. ● A temperature of about 10°C/50°F in winter, otherwise normal room temperature. ● Keep the compost moist in the growing season; give just enough water to prevent the compost drying out in winter. ● Stand the pot on moist pebbles to increase humidity from spring to autumn. ● Apply a standard liquid fertiliser every 2 weeks in the period of active growth.

LITHOPS LESLIEI
Aizoaceae

Living Stones

This curious, long-lived succulent has the distinct appearance of greyish pebbles, hence its other common names of stone or pebble plant. The fleshy, swollen leaves, arising from a short underground stem, are produced in pairs, but they are fused for virtually their entire length, having only a slit across the top which splits them into two parts, often of unequal size. They are frequently grey with mottled, light brown markings, but occur in many stone-like colours.

After two or three years, daisy-like, bright yellow flowers with many shaggy petals are produced in autumn. These emerge from the split between the leaves and are often larger than the leaves themselves. They rest on the leaf surface and may cover the plant completely. Once the flowers have faded and the seeds have formed, the leaves begin to shrivel and a new pair pushes up through the split to replace them.

FACT FILE

ORIGIN South Africa.

HEIGHT 2.5–5cm/1–2in.

COMPOST Soil-based, with coarse sand added for good drainage.

REPOTTING Repot in late spring after several years, when clumps become crowded. Use a standard-depth pot, rather than a shallow pan, since this species forms relatively long and extensive roots. Spread a layer of grit on the surface of the compost.

PROPAGATION Divide clumps in late spring when repotting, or grow from seed. Seedlings take several years to reach flowering size.

KEEPING PLANTS It is best to grow several lithops together in a fairly large pan to help to keep the potting mix at a constant temperature.

PLANT CARE

Bright light, with several hours of direct sun; give light shade in the height of summer. ● Minimum winter temperature of 10°C/50°F. ● Keep the compost barely moist from spring to autumn, letting the top half dry out between waterings. When the flowers have faded and the old leaves are shrivelling, withhold water until the following spring. ● It is not necessary to feed lithops. ● Good ventilation is essential.

Lithops needs plenty of bright light and is an excellent plant for a sunny windowsill.

Overwatering causes the plant to rot. The fleshy leaves become wrinkled and shrivelled after flowering – a new pair will replace them.

The fleshy leaves vary in colour but are always natural stone shades. They are often mottled.

The large, daisy-like flowers are fairly short-lived but make a colourful sight when they appear.

MAMMILLARIA BOCASANA
Cactaceae

*P*OWDER PUFF CACTUS

The cylindrical or globular stems of this cactus eventually form a large, rounded clump. Many silky white hairs arising from areoles – cushion-like bumps – on the stems cover the plant and give it its powder puff appearance. Each areole also bears one or more yellow-brown, hooked central spines, which are longer and stiffer than the silky hairs. The spines are sharp, so put the cactus where people will not brush against it, hurting themselves and damaging the plant.

Like many mammillarias, this species blooms freely while it is still young. The yellow or creamy white flowers, which are produced in spring in a ring near the tops of the stems, are about 13mm/$\frac{1}{2}$in wide.

FACT FILE

ORIGIN Mexico.

HEIGHT To 5cm/2in.

COMPOST Soil- or peat-based and grit in equal quantities.

REPOTTING Repot after several years, when the clump is overcrowded. Handle the clump by means of a strip of newspaper to protect your hands and to cause minimum damage to the plant. A wide, shallow pan is most suitable.

PROPAGATION In spring and summer, remove offsets from the edge of a clump and pot up separately. Plants can also be grown from seed.

KEEPING PLANTS Plants will last for many years, given proper attention.

PLANT CARE

Bright, direct sunlight. ● Minimum winter temperature of 7°C/45°F. ● Water moderately from spring to autumn, keeping the compost just moist but letting the top 13mm/$\frac{1}{2}$in dry out between waterings. In winter, water just sufficiently to prevent the compost drying out completely. ● Apply high-potash fertiliser once a month during the growing season.

ALSO RECOMMENDED

Mammillaria zeilmanniana, the rose pincushion, produces large numbers of deep cerise flowers in summer.

Many species of mammillaria start out as simple columnar plants, forming clusters and flowering only when they are 4 or 5 years old. But even without flowers, the plants are attractive, with their spiral pattern of spine-bearing areoles.

Stout hooked spines in the centre of each areole catch easily on clothing, often causing damage to the plant's stem.

Too much water can cause the stems to rot and collapse from the base. Never let water remain on the surface of the compost, and water only around the outside of the clump.

Mealybugs – sap-sucking insects covered in waxy white wool – often lodge between the areoles under the spines and are difficult to control. Use a systemic insecticide to deal with them.

MANDEVILLA x *AMOENA* 'ALICE DU PONT'
Apocynaceae

Mandevilla

Many species of mandevilla used to be known as *Dipladenia* and they are still often offered under that name. The most easily available plant is *Mandevilla* x *amoena* 'Alice du Pont', a hybrid resulting from a backcross of *M. amabilis* and *M. splendens*. It has glossy, deep green, ovate leaves on twining stems and large, funnel-shaped flowers, which are carried throughout the summer. The scrolled buds open to pink, with a darker pink throat shading to yellow deep in the throat.

Mandevillas are handsome plants for a sunroom or conservatory, where they can be grown in large tubs. They do well in borders, where they can be trained up a support against a wall. In pots they can be provided with canes or a trellis, or the climbing shoots can be cut back after flowering to keep the plant bushy.

FACT FILE

ORIGIN Brazil; hybrids.

HEIGHT To 3m/10ft when allowed to climb.

COMPOST Free-draining, soil-based compost.

REPOTTING Repot annually in spring until the maximum desired pot size is reached, then simply top-dress with fresh compost.

PROPAGATION Not easy. Take soft stem cuttings in spring and root them in a propagator with bottom heat.

KEEPING PLANTS Cut stems back hard after flowering to keep growth bushy and promote flowering shoots the following year.

PLANT CARE

Fairly bright light, but no direct sun. ● Minimum winter temperature of 13°C/55°F. ● Water plentifully, allowing the surface of the compost to dry out between waterings. Water more sparingly in winter. ● Mist the foliage regularly. ● Give high-potash fertiliser every 2 weeks in the growing season.

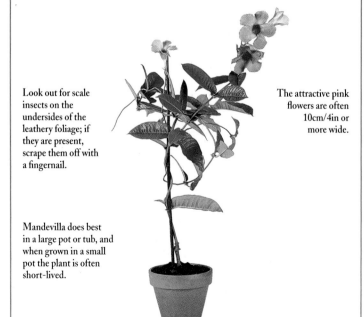

Look out for scale insects on the undersides of the leathery foliage; if they are present, scrape them off with a fingernail.

The attractive pink flowers are often 10cm/4in or more wide.

Mandevilla does best in a large pot or tub, and when grown in a small pot the plant is often short-lived.

MANETTIA INFLATA
Rubiaceae

Firecracker Vine

The freely branching, twining stems of this climber, occasionally sold as *Manettia bicolor* or *M. luteo-rubra*, bear lance-shaped, bright green leaves in opposite pairs. The plant can be trained up canes or a trellis and will also trail attractively when grown in a hanging basket. The colourful, tubular, hairy flowers, arising from the leaf axils on 2.5-cm/1-in stalks, are orange-red tipped with yellow and about 2cm/³/₄in long. They are produced in great profusion for most of the summer and sometimes well into the autumn. This species is also known as the Brazilian firecracker.

FACT FILE

ORIGIN South America.

HEIGHT To 3m/10ft.

COMPOST Soil- or peat-based.

REPOTTING Move into a pot one size larger whenever roots appear through the drainage holes in the base of the pot.

PROPAGATION In spring and early summer, take soft stem cuttings from nonflowering shoots.

KEEPING PLANTS Cut back stems by half in spring to promote new growth and maintain the plant's shape.

PLANT CARE

Bright light with some direct sun. ● A minimum winter temperature of 13°C/55°F; otherwise, normal room temperature. ● Keep the compost moist throughout the growing season; water more sparingly in winter. ● Mist the foliage occasionally. ● Give a high-potash fertiliser every 2 weeks during the period of active growth.

The vigorous, slender twining stems can be trained around canes, up a trellis or even allowed to trail.

Brightly coloured tubular flowers are often carried in such large numbers that they almost obscure the foliage.

The oval leaves usually have short stalks but are sometimes stalkless.

MARANTA LEUCONEURA
Marantaceae

PRAYER PLANT

The brightly marked, attractively feathered foliage of marantas is similar to that of calatheas and ctenanthes, to which they are closely related. Marantas have earned their common name of prayer plant because of the way in which their leaves tend to fold up at night and unfold the following morning, sometimes with a distinct rustling noise. The blunt leaves are oval, strikingly veined and patterned on the surface, often red below, with clasping leaf stalks. Three varieties of *Maranta leuconeura* are commonly grown.

FACT FILE

ORIGIN Brazil.

HEIGHT To 25cm/10in.

COMPOST Soil-based.

REPOTTING In spring, repot when roots appear through the drainage holes in the base of the pot, usually every other year. Marantas have a shallow rooting system and do best in a shallow pot or half-pot.

PROPAGATION Divide clumps by pulling them apart carefully in spring.

KEEPING PLANTS Plants will last for several years provided they are repotted and fed regularly.

PLANT CARE

Moderate light with no direct sun; leaf colours fade and leaves curl in very bright conditions. ● Thrives in temperatures up to 24°C/75°F, with a minimum winter temperature of 16°C/60°F. ● Keep the compost moist throughout the growing season; water sparingly in winter. ● Mist the foliage regularly with lime-free water, and stand the pot on a dish of moist pebbles. ● Apply a balanced liquid fertiliser every 2 weeks during the growing season.

The herringbone plant, Maranta leuconeura erythroneura, *with its shiny dark and pale green leaves with bright red veins, is the most colourful of the marantas.*

ALSO RECOMMENDED

Maranta leuconeura leuconeura, which is often called *M.l. massangeana,* has dark, velvety green leaves with silver veins and a silver central section along the midrib.

M.l. erythroneura, herringbone plant, has dark green, satiny leaves with prominent red veins and irregular yellow-green patches behind the midrib. It is also sold as *M. tricolor.*

M.l. kerchoveana, rabbit tracks, has pale green leaves with lighter veins and irregular purple-brown blotches either side of the midrib which give it its common name. It is much less striking than the other two varieties but is still very popular.

Red spider mites attack the plant in warm, dry conditions. Increase humidity by frequent misting to combat these pests.

The leaves of most varieties naturally fold up and become more erect at night; this does not indicate that there is anything wrong with the plant.

Dust the leaves lightly with a soft, dry cloth or feather duster to avoid spoiling the satiny leaf surface. Do not use a damp cloth to clean the leaves.

Leaf tips and margins become papery and brown if the air is too dry; mist the plants regularly with lime-free water to make sure that chalky deposits do not spoil the appearance of the leaves.

MEDINILLA MAGNIFICA
Melastomalaceae

ℛOSE GRAPE

This is one of the most striking flowering plants grown indoors. It can become extremely large with an equally large spread, but it is not easy to keep and is normally treated as a short-term plant. It needs a big pot or tub and will do best if grown in conservatory conditions.

The angular stems carry pairs of leathery, glossy, dark green, ovate leaves which are stalkless and deeply veined. They are about 30cm/12in long and half as wide. In late spring, long, pendulous flower stalks, which can be up to 46cm/18in overall, are produced from the tips of the branches. The small, rosy pink flowers with yellow stamens are carried in long panicles beneath two or three tiers of bright pink bracts.

This plant is very prone to attack by red spider mites, particularly in warm, dry conditions. Mist the foliage frequently to increase humidity.

The pendulous flower heads are spectacular in spring and early summer. Plants with deeper pink flowers are sometimes available.

Medinilla demands warmth and high humidity, and is difficult to grow well in the home. Conservatory conditions suit it better.

FACT FILE

ORIGIN Philippines.

HEIGHT To 1.2m/4ft.

COMPOST Soil-based, with added peat.

REPOTTING Repot in spring every year until the maximum desired pot size is reached, then top-dress annually with fresh compost.

PROPAGATION Not practical by amateurs.

KEEPING PLANTS Cut back the shoots by about half after flowering and give the plant a winter rest in slightly cooler conditions. Reduce watering but continue to mist the foliage regularly.

PLANT CARE

Bright, filtered light with no direct sun. ● Warm conditions, about 21°C/70°F; a minimum winter temperature of 16°C/60°F. ● Keep the compost moist during the growing season, but allow the surface to dry out between waterings. Water sparingly in winter. ● Mist the foliage frequently and stand the pot on a tray of moist pebbles. High humidity is essential. ● Give a high-potash liquid feed every 2 weeks from the time the flower buds start to form until autumn.

MONSTERA DELICIOSA
Araceae

𝒮WISS CHEESE PLANT

A popular, tolerant foliage plant, monstera can become a large and striking specimen. It has a rather sprawling, scrambling habit and climbs by means of thick, fleshy, aerial roots, which are freely produced from the stem. The young plant bears entire heart-shaped leaves, but if it receives sufficient light as it develops, it will produce deeply cut adult foliage. Characteristic holes and deep splits from the margin almost to the midrib of the large, glossy, deep green leaves are responsible for its other common names split leaf and window plant.

'*Deliciosa*', meaning pleasing, refers to the white spadix that on a mature plant may develop into an aggregate of white berries with a tropical fruit flavour, giving it the common names Mexican bread fruit and fruit salad plant.

Yellowing lower leaves are usually a sign of overwatering. Keep the compost just moist and do not allow the pot to stand in water.

Aerial roots low on the plant can be pushed into the compost where they will help to provide nutrients and moisture. Higher roots can be removed or trained into a moss pole.

FACT FILE

ORIGIN Mexico.

HEIGHT To 3m/10ft.

COMPOST Soil-based, with some added peat.

REPOTTING Repot in spring, when roots fill the pot – usually every other year.

PROPAGATION Take small tip cuttings in spring, or air-layer when the plant becomes too large.

KEEPING PLANTS A moss pole is an ideal support for this plant; try to keep the moss moist and train the aerial roots to grow into it.

PLANT CARE

Fairly good light, but no direct sun. In shade, the leaves will be smaller and less perforated. ● A minimum winter temperature of 10°C/50°F; otherwise, 18°–24°C/65°–75°F. ● Water moderately during the growing season, but allow the surface to dry out between waterings. Give less water in winter. ● Mist the foliage regularly in warm conditions.
● Give a balanced liquid feed every 2 weeks from spring until autumn.

Narcissus SPP.
Amaryllidaceae

Daffodil

Grown as house plants during the winter, these bulbs are a wonderful harbinger of spring, when they flower naturally out of doors. There are dozens of varieties suitable for growing indoors. They can be bought in bud during the winter or as specially treated bulbs. Bulbs can be planted from autumn onwards and will flower long before they would in the garden. Narcissus should be treated in the same way as hyacinths (see page 98). They need a cold, dark period of about eight weeks after planting.

The foliage of narcissus is mid- to pale green, long and strap-shaped. Flowers are in many shades of yellow or white and have several different forms. Perhaps most familiar is the trumpet daffodil, such as 'King Alfred', shown here with its ring of petals backing a long, frilled trumpet. Where the trumpet is as long as the petals, the variety tends to be commonly known as a daffodil, otherwise it is called a narcissus. The trumpet or cup may be the same colour as the petals, or a contrasting shade. Other types have short, flared trumpets; in double varieties, the trumpets are replaced by extra layers of frilly petals. Flowers may be carried singly on the stems or in bunches, and many varieties are sweetly scented. Size varies considerably, from tiny dwarf forms to large-flowered, tall hybrids.

FACT FILE

ORIGIN Temperate zones of Europe, Asia and North Africa.

HEIGHT To 46cm/18in, depending on variety.

COMPOST Peat-based potting compost, rather than bulb fibre, if the bulbs are to be planted out in the garden after flowering.

REPOTTING None. It is not worthwhile trying to grow treated bulbs indoors for a second year.

PROPAGATION Plant offsets produced around the base of the bulb.

KEEPING PLANTS Allow to dry off when the leaves die down, remove bulbs from the pot and store in a cool, dry place until autumn, when they can be planted out in the garden.

PLANT CARE

Keep bulbs in total darkness after planting until the shoots are about 8cm/3in high, then bring them into bright light out of direct sun. ● Keep bulbs at 4°C/40°F during the dark period; bring them into the light at about 10°C/50°F until the buds show colour, then keep at a maximum of 16°C/60°F in their flowering positions. ● Keep the compost just moist until the leaves fade, then allow it to dry out. If you want to plant the bulbs outdoors, do not stop watering until the leaves begin to yellow. ● Apply a high-potash liquid fertiliser every 2 weeks until the leaves start to fade.

ALSO RECOMMENDED

Dwarf varieties are excellent for pot cultivation and include the cyclamineus hybrids 'February Silver', 'February Gold' and 'Tête-à-Tête', the jonquil 'Baby Moon'; and the bunch-flowered tazetta narcissus 'Minnow'.

Among the larger varieties, fragrant 'Paperwhite' is particularly easy to grow and requires no cold, dark period. 'Carlton' is a large, clear yellow; 'Ice Follies' is white with a creamy yellow cup, and 'Fortune' has soft yellow petals and a cup tipped with an intense orange.

'Paperwhite' belongs to the group of hybrids known as Tazetta narcissi, which produce several flowers to a stem. It is particularly easy to grow, requiring no dark, cold period. It flowers some 4 to 6 weeks after planting and has a delicious sweet scent.

Excessive warmth will shorten the life of flowers and may cause buds to shrivel and turn brown, preventing them from opening.

The flowers may be a range of shades of white, cream, yellow and orange; some varieties even have a pink tinge. Contrasting trumpets or cups are particularly attractive.

Keep the plants in a bright position to prevent the stems becoming too tall and leggy. Support the flower stems of tall varieties with green split canes.

Bunch-flowered 'Soleil d'Or' and 'Paperwhite' can be grown in glasses of water or in wet pebbles. They will flower within 6 weeks with no cold, dark period necessary and are deliciously fragrant.

NEOREGELIA CAROLINAE 'TRICOLOR'
Bromeliaceae

*B*LUSHING BROMELIAD

The rosette-forming, strap-shaped leaves of this bromeliad can be 38cm/15in or more long. They are glossy green, striped along their length with creamy yellow and rose pink, and have spiny-toothed edges. Just before flowering, the central leaves that form the water-holding cup turn a brilliant, long-lasting rosy red; the flowers themselves are purplish blue and rather insignificant. The rosette, which is generally only about 23cm/9in high, dies back after flowering, but offsets are freely produced around the base to take its place.

Scale insects are often found on the undersides of the leaves. Scrape them off carefully with a fingernail and treat the plant with a systemic insecticide if the infestation is severe.

The central foliage turns bright red just before the plant flowers. This red coloration and the cream and pink stripes on the foliage develop best in bright light.

Keep the centre of the rosette half-full of water. Drain it once a month by tipping the plant carefully on one side, then refill the rosette.

The base of the plant may rot if it is overwatered. Keep the compost just moist during the summer: do not saturate it.

FACT FILE

ORIGIN Brazil.

HEIGHT 23–30cm/9–12in.

COMPOST Soil-based, with added peat or leaf mould, or soil- and peat-based in equal parts. Both types of compost need coarse sand or shredded bark added for good drainage.

REPOTTING Repot in spring as necessary. Do not overpot.

PROPAGATION Remove offsets in spring and pot up separately. If the offset does not have roots, root it in a propagator with bottom heat.

KEEPING PLANTS Once the main rosette has completely died back after flowering, pot up the offsets that are produced to replace it.

PLANT CARE

Bright light with several hours of direct sun daily for good leaf colour.
● Normal room temperature, with a minimum of 10°C/50°F.
● Keep the compost just moist, allowing the surface to dry out between waterings. Top up the cup in the centre of the rosette with water regularly. ● Mist the foliage daily in summer and stand the pot on a tray of moist pebbles. ● Apply a half-strength solution of balanced liquid fertiliser every 3–4 weeks in summer, pouring it into the centre of the rosette as well as on the compost.

NEPHROLEPIS EXALTATA 'BOSTONIENSIS'
Oleandraceae

*S*WORD FERN

Also known as Boston fern, this is the most commonly grown variety of nephrolepis. It makes a spreading rosette, its bright green, pinnate leaves forming broad trailing fronds up to 1.2m/4ft long, which are upright at first and arch over slightly as they grow. Brown spore cases can be seen on the undersides of the pinnae, or leaflets. The much-divided leaves have given rise to another common name – ladder fern.

Wiry runners carry young plantlets, which root readily to cover the surface of the compost. These ferns are ideally grown in hanging baskets or displayed on a pedestal, where their graceful habit can best be appreciated.

FACT FILE

ORIGIN Tropical and subtropical regions.

HEIGHT 23–30cm/9–12in.

COMPOST Peat-based.

REPOTTING In spring, when roots emerge through the drainage holes in the base of the pot, move the plant into a pot one size larger.

PROPAGATION At any time, cut young plantlets away from the runners and pot up separately.

KEEPING PLANTS This fern will grow steadily all year round, given the right conditions. When the plant has reached the maximum desired size, trim off some of the roots in spring and repot in the same pot.

PLANT CARE

Bright light but no direct sun; the fern will tolerate some shade.
● Normal room temperature, with a winter minimum of 10°C/50°F.
● Keep the compost thoroughly moist, but do not allow the pot to stand in water. If the temperature falls to near the minimum, reduce watering and let the top 2.5cm/1in of compost dry out before rewatering. ● Mist the foliage daily in summer and stand the pot on a tray of moist pebbles. ● Give a balanced liquid fertiliser every 2 weeks when the plant is in active growth.

Scale insects can be troublesome; either scratch them off with a fingernail or treat affected plants with insecticide at quarter strength. Remove any residue by spraying with water.

Increase humidity around the plant by misting regularly. This will prevent the tips of the foliage turning brown.

The brown spore cases carried in two rows on the underside of each pinna are sometimes mistaken for scale insects.

Keep the compost moist at all times. If it dries out in the growing season, the fronds will yellow and die.

NERIUM OLEANDER
Apocynaceae

Oleander

An attractive sun-loving shrub for the home and conservatory, oleander has dark green, narrow, lance-shaped leaves on woody, branching stems. The flat-faced, funnel-shaped flowers are carried at the ends of the stems in groups of eight or so and are up to 5cm/2in wide. Typically, flowers are rose pink, but there are also red, white, apricot, salmon pink and yellow varieties and some double-flowered forms. Oleander is a member of the periwinkle family, and some similarity can be seen in the flowers.

Caution: All parts of this plant are poisonous. Keep it out of the reach of children and animals.

The attractive pink, red, white or yellow flowers are carried in groups of three at the tips of the stems. In some varieties they are fragrant.

The bay-like foliage and rose pink flowers give oleander its other common name of rose bay.

Established plants can make quite large, bushy shrubs; a garden room or conservatory is the ideal place for them.

Scale insects are a common problem. Remove scales found on the undersides of the leaves with a fingernail and spray the plant with insecticide if necessary.

FACT FILE

ORIGIN Mediterranean regions, Asia to Japan.

HEIGHT To 1.8m/6ft.

COMPOST Soil-based.

REPOTTING Repot in spring, when roots emerge through the drainage holes in the base of the pot. Plants do best in large pots or tubs.

PROPAGATION Take stem cuttings in early summer.

KEEPING PLANTS After flowering, put the plant in a sheltered spot outdoors until autumn to ripen the wood for good flowering the following year.

PLANT CARE

Bright light with several hours of direct sun. ● Normal room temperature, with a winter rest at 13°C/55°F and a minimum of 7°C/45°F. ● Keep the compost thoroughly moist in the growing season, especially when the buds are forming. Water more sparingly in winter. ● Apply a balanced liquid fertiliser every 2 weeks in summer.

NIDULARIUM INNOCENTII 'STRIATUM'
Bromeliaceae

Bird's Nest Bromeliad

This bromeliad species is closely related to neoregelia and has a similar appearance. The plant forms a rosette of 30-cm/12-in long, strap-shaped leaves with spiny margins, which are usually purplish green, with a metallic sheen. There are, however, two striped varieties, 'Lineatum' and 'Striatum' (shown here), which are very similar, with white stripes running the length of the leaf; 'Striatum' tends to have broader stripes. In the centre of the rosette, the leaves are much shorter and turn brick red just before the plant flowers in autumn, producing white blooms carried in clusters.

FACT FILE

ORIGIN Brazil.

HEIGHT 23–30cm/9–12in.

COMPOST Soil-based with added peat, or equal parts of soil- and peat-based, both with added coarse sand or shredded bark.

REPOTTING Repot in spring, only when roots fill the compost.

PROPAGATION Pot up offsets individually in spring.

KEEPING PLANTS When it is 3–4 years old, nidularium flowers once only from each rosette, which then dies. Replace it by young offsets.

PLANT CARE

Bright light, but without direct sun. ● Minimum winter temperature of 13°C/55°F, but preferably 16°C/60°F or above. Normal room temperature in summer. ● Keep the compost moist in the growing season, but allow the top to dry out between waterings. In winter, water sparingly. Keep the central cup filled with water; replace the water every 4 weeks. ● Apply half-strength, balanced liquid fertiliser every 3 weeks in the growing season.

The centre of the rosette turns brick red at flowering time, which can be at any time of year but occurs most commonly in autumn.

The undersides of the spiny-toothed leaves are often flushed with purple.

The natural home of nidularium is tropical rain forest, and it needs high humidity to grow well. Mist the plant frequently and stand the pot on a dish of moist pebbles.

OCIMUM BASILICUM
Labiatae

Sweet Basil

A popular aromatic herb for use in the kitchen, basil also makes an attractive house plant. Among the many varieties available are 'Dark Opal' with purple-black foliage, 'Ruffles' and 'Purple Ruffles', with large, strongly undulating and ruffled leaves in purple or green, and 'Crispum', the lettuce-leafed basil, with large, undulating leaves up to 10cm/4in long.

Plants have the typical square stems of the mint family, with ovate leaves carried in opposite pairs. These are normally soft textured, rather fleshy, and light green, with an intense, peppery, clove-like aroma. The plant is a fast-growing, small, lax bush. Heads of hooded white flowers are carried at the tips of the stems, but these are usually pinched out in bud to encourage the production of foliage. Keep the plant bushy by pinching out growing tips regularly.

FACT FILE

ORIGIN Asia.

HEIGHT To 60cm/2ft.

COMPOST Soil- or peat-based.

REPOTTING Pot up when roots emerge from the base of the pot.

PROPAGATION Sow seed in early spring.

KEEPING PLANTS Basil is an annual, but plants can be kept through much of the winter by sowing seed in early summer and pinching out flower buds as soon as they are seen. This will also help to keep them bushy. Stand plants outdoors in warm summer weather.

PLANT CARE

Bright light, with 3–4 hours of sunshine; shade the plant from very hot sun which will scorch the leaves. ● Normal room temperature. ● Keep the compost moist at all times. ● Apply a half-strength balanced liquid fertiliser every 7 days during spring and summer.

If whiteflies are a problem, destroy affected plants and raise new ones from seed. Using an insecticide is not usually worthwhile.

Pinching out the growing tips keeps plants bushy and compact. If the herb is used in the kitchen, this will happen as a matter of course.

Varieties with large leaves, ruffled edges and unusual colours are attractive, but the plain-leafed type has the strongest flavour and aroma.

ODONTOGLOSSUM·GRANDE
Orchidaceae

Tiger Orchid

The striking flowers of this odontoglossum, also known as *Rossioglossum grande*, are made up of petals and sepals of similar colours. Each large, egg-shaped pseudobulb produces a pair of mid-green, lance-shaped leaves some 30cm/12in long. Flower stems are produced from late summer to spring and carry up to seven or eight clear yellow flowers with reddish brown stripes, which give the plant its most frequently used common name. It is also called the clown orchid. The lip of the bloom is white with brown bands. Each flower can be as much as 18cm/7in wide.

Although they originate in tropical America, odontoglossums grow at high altitudes in cool mountainous regions and do not thrive if the temperature is too high.

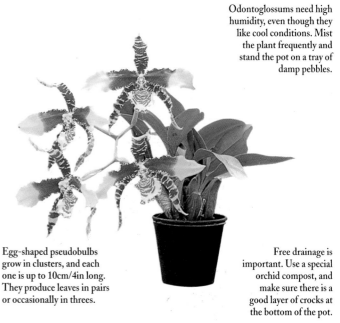

Odontoglossums need high humidity, even though they like cool conditions. Mist the plant frequently and stand the pot on a tray of damp pebbles.

Egg-shaped pseudobulbs grow in clusters, and each one is up to 10cm/4in long. They produce leaves in pairs or occasionally in threes.

Free drainage is important. Use a special orchid compost, and make sure there is a good layer of crocks at the bottom of the pot.

FACT FILE

ORIGIN Mexico, Guatemala.

HEIGHT Flower stems to 30cm/12in.

COMPOST Special orchid compost, usually containing bark, perlite and osmunda fibre or sphagnum moss in varying proportions.

REPOTTING Repot annually in spring or autumn. Use a clay pot and place a good layer of crocks in the base for drainage.

PROPAGATION Divide large clumps into groups of healthy pseudobulbs by cutting through the rhizome with a sharp knife.

KEEPING PLANTS In the right conditions, this is a long-lived orchid.

PLANT CARE

Bright, diffuse light with no direct sun. ● A temperature range of 16°–18°C/60°–65°F. ● In the growing season water thoroughly with lime-free water, but let the surface dry out between waterings. Water less in the winter rest period. ● Apply a half-strength balanced liquid fertiliser as a foliar spray every 2 weeks in the growing season, or use a proprietary orchid fertiliser.

OPHIOPOGON JABURAN
Liliaceae

W̶HITE LILY-TURF

This is the only species of this plant that is grown as an indoor plant. The grass-like foliage, rising directly from the roots, forms a good contrast with the more rounded shapes of other plants. The narrow leathery leaves, up to 46cm/18in long, arch over gracefully to make a fountain-like clump. In late summer or autumn, a flower stem arises from the centre of each tuft. It bears tubular, creamy white or pale lilac nodding blooms, which are sometimes followed by violet-blue berries.

A variegated form with creamy stripes running the length of the leaf is most often seen as an indoor plant. It may be offered as 'Variegatus', 'Argenteo-variegatus' or 'Javanensis', all of which are synonymous with the variety 'Vittatus'. The stripes on the leaves of 'Aureo-variegatus' are a deeper yellow.

Ophiopogon planiscapus *'Nigrescens' is a striking plant with purple-black foliage and flowering stalks, which bear lilac flowers followed by black fruits.*

The heads of nodding flowers are rather similar to those of the garden shrub pieris.

FACT FILE

ORIGIN Japan.

HEIGHT To 50cm/20in.

COMPOST Soil-based, with a little added coarse sand.

REPOTTING Repot annually in spring, when the clump has covered the surface of the compost.

PROPAGATION When the clump fills a 15-cm/6-in pot, divide it carefully in spring and pot up the divisions individually. Or sow seed in spring.

KEEPING PLANTS The plant requires bright light in order to flower. Keep it almost dry during the winter rest period.

PLANT CARE

Bright, diffuse light with no direct sun. ● Average warmth or relatively cool conditions, with a minimum temperature of 10°C/50°F. ● Keep the compost just moist throughout the growing period and water even more sparingly in winter. ● Mist the leaves regularly, especially in warm conditions. ● Apply a standard liquid fertiliser every 2 weeks during the growing season.

ALSO RECOMMENDED

Ophiopogon planiscapus 'Nigrescens' is a hardier plant than *O. jaburan* and can survive in lower temperatures. It is a good ground-cover plant for a large tub in a sunroom or a border in a greenhouse.

Clumps spread by underground rhizomes and will form a thick turf if given sufficient room. Although the leaves are grassy, the plant is a member of the lily family and is related to *Liriope muscari*, which it resembles.

If plants fail to produce flowers, they are probably in too shady a spot. Bright light is necessary for good flowering, but the foliage needs protection from direct, strong sunlight.

ORCHIDACEAE

ORCHIDS

Phalaenopsis **hybrid.** These flat-faced orchids are known as moth orchids because the numerous pale-coloured flowers on arching stems look like moths in flight. Since they are monopodial orchids, aerial roots are produced from the stem, but there are no pseudobulbs. The leaves are thick and fleshy.

Prized for their exotic, long-lasting flowers, orchids are usually regarded as difficult plants that are suitable only for growing under controlled greenhouse conditions, but several species can be grown successfully in the home.

Some species of orchids are terrestrial, growing in soil, but most of those grown as indoor plants are epiphytic and in the wild grow on trees or sometimes rocks. In addition to roots at the base, these orchids usually have aerial roots and need a special compost and container if they are to do well in the home. There are two types of epiphytic orchids: monopodial orchids that produce a single stem from the roots at the base, and sympodial orchids that have many stems arising from a horizontal rhizome. The latter have pseudobulbs – variously shaped swollen stem bases that look like bulbs and store water and food for the plant. Among the best orchids for growing in the home are the epiphytic cymbidiums, cattleyas, coelogynes, dendrobiums, lycastes, miltonias, odontoglossums and vandas. Phalaenopsis are the easiest to grow.

Orchid flowers come in an enormous variety of shapes, sizes and colours, but they always have six petal-like parts, three of which are true petals and three – the topmost one and the lower pair – sepals. The two upper petals are usually larger than the sepals, while the lower petal, or lip, is always a different shape and colour from the others. The flowers are often luscious looking, with a waxy or velvety or sometimes lustrous texture to the petals.

Each showy flower remains attractive for several weeks. Several flowers are borne on one stem, which may be erect or slightly pendulous.

ALSO RECOMMENDED

Cattleyas are probably the best-known orchids. They produce flowers singly or in small groups ranging from rose pink to white and pale lavender, and most have a deeper-coloured curled, frilly lip.

Dendrobiums bear groups of flowers, often fragrant, on short stalks, which grow from tall, usually stem-like pseudobulbs. Flower colour ranges from white to pink, lavender and deep purple.

Miltonias, known as pansy orchids, have velvety, sometimes fragrant blooms in small groups on long stems. Flowers are fairly small and strikingly coloured, with attractive markings on the large, lobed lip.

Colonies of aphids are attracted to young growth and flower stems. They can sometimes be removed with a damp cloth, or they can be treated with a contact insecticide.

If moisture is allowed to lie on the leaves, black spots will appear, and fungus infections may attack the plant.

Mealybugs, with their white waxy coating, can sometimes be found clustered at the base of leaves or flower stalks. A systemic insecticide is usually necessary to control them.

Brown scorch marks on the foliage are caused by direct sun falling on the leaves. Good light is essential, but it must be diffuse.

Unless a thick layer of stones is placed in the bottom of a conventional flowerpot, the soil will become waterlogged and sour, and the roots will rot. Good drainage is essential.

FACT FILE

ORIGIN **Epiphytic orchids:** most common in tropical regions of the world; hybrids.
Terrestrial orchids: most common in temperate zones; hybrids.

HEIGHT Up to 60cm/2ft.

COMPOST Special free-draining orchid medium.

REPOTTING Repot only when roots or clumps of pseudobulbs are almost bursting out of the pot.

PROPAGATION Divide clumps of pseudobulbs into smaller groups; cut through the rhizome that joins them with a sharp sterilized knife.

KEEPING PLANTS Some orchids flower in 18–20 months, others may take 5 or 6 years before they flower. Blooms usually last 3–6 weeks, but some may last up to 12 weeks. Cut off the flowers when they start to fade.

PLANT CARE

Epiphytic orchids: Bright light shaded from direct sun. ● Normal warm room temperature in summer, cooler conditions of 10°–16°C/ 50°–60°F in winter. ● Moisten the medium thoroughly; allow the top 13mm/¹/₂in to dry out between waterings. Water less in cooler winter temperatures. Pseudobulbs will rot if the plant is overwatered. ● Apply a balanced liquid fertiliser every 2 weeks during the growing season. ● Mist foliage regularly and stand pots on a tray of moist pebbles. High humidity is important. ● Good ventilation is essential to these plants.
Terrestrial orchids: Medium light, but generally not direct sunlight. ● Normal room temperature. ● Water actively growing plants moderately; allow the top 2.5cm/1in to dry out before rewatering. Water sparingly for 6 weeks after flowering. ● Stand the pot on a tray of damp pebbles. Mist-spray daily in temperatures over 21°C/ 70°F. ● Apply a foliar feed every 2–3 waterings.

PESTS & DISEASES

Aphids and mealybugs may infest the plants, and if the atmosphere is too dry, red spider mites can be a pest. Orchids can be infected by viruses, especially cymbidium mosaic virus; this cannot be treated and plants must be destroyed.

Oncidiums bear clusters of many small flowers on long slender stems that rise from the base of ovoid pseudobulbs. The large-lipped flowers vary from white to red, pink, yellow, green and brown.

Paphiopedilums Slipper orchids are the only terrestrial orchids that do well in the home. They bear single flowers on long stems; flowers have a pouch-shaped lip and a streaked or spotted top sepal.

OXALIS DEPPEI (SYN. O. TETRAPHYLLA)
Oxalidaceae

LUCKY CLOVER

Tuberous-rooted oxalis, called lucky clover or shamrock plant, often makes a troublesome, invasive plant in the garden, but confined to a pot it can be appreciated for its attractive flowers and foliage. The tubers of *Oxalis deppei* are reputed to be edible.

The leaves, which are carried on weak, slender stems, are typical four-leaf clover leaves. Each lobed leaflet has a V-shaped purple-brown blotch at the base, and together these blotches form a ring in the centre of the leaflets. The five-petalled flowers are pinkish red to purple, usually with a greenish yellow throat, and are held in loose umbels on long stalks in summer. A white-flowered form also exists.

Since this species requires plenty of warmth and sunlight, it makes a good windowsill plant.

The delicate, usually nodding umbels of flowers may be deep rose pink to purple. The white-flowered form is less popular.

Although oxalis is not a true clover, this plant is grown mainly for its 'lucky' four-leafed clover associations. It is also sometimes grown as shamrock, which it resembles.

Many fleshy, tuberous roots are made. They spread rapidly if given sufficient room.

FACT FILE

ORIGIN Mexico.

HEIGHT 23–30cm/9–12in.

COMPOST Soil-based.

REPOTTING Repot in spring, when the tubers fill the pot.

PROPAGATION Divide the clump carefully when repotting or sow seed in spring.

KEEPING PLANTS In time, the clump tends to sprawl and growth becomes leggy and overgrown. The plant is often discarded at this stage, but dividing it and keeping it in good light will prolong its life.

PLANT CARE

Bright light, with some direct sun. ● Cool conditions; a minimum winter temperature of 7°C/45°F. ● Keep the compost just moist in spring and summer, allowing the surface to dry out between waterings. In winter, water more sparingly. ● Mist the plant from time to time. ● Apply a balanced liquid fertiliser every 3 weeks in summer.

PACHYSTACHYS LUTEA
Acanthaceae

LOLLIPOP PLANT

This branching, bushy plant has upright stems, woody at their base, which carry mid- to deep green, lanceolate leaves in opposite pairs. The leaves are heavily veined, giving them a sculpted appearance. Tall flower spikes appear at the ends of the stems in spring and persist throughout the summer. Each white flower is hooded and lasts only a few days, but it is carried in a bright golden yellow, long-lasting bract. The blooms emerge through the bracts, starting from the base of the flower head and opening in succession. The flower heads themselves are reminiscent of those of aphelandra, and the two plants are sometimes confused, although they are, in fact, quite different.

FACT FILE

ORIGIN Tropical America.

HEIGHT To 46cm/18in.

COMPOST Soil- or peat-based.

REPOTTING Repot in spring, when roots show at the base of the pot.

PROPAGATION Take stem cuttings in early summer.

KEEPING PLANTS Pinch out growing tips from time to time to keep the plant bushy. Cut back the stems by a third or more as the plant starts into new growth in spring.

PLANT CARE

Bright light is necessary for flower production, but no direct sun. ● Minimum winter temperature of 13°–16°C/55°–60°F; cool to normal room temperature in summer. ● Keep the compost thoroughly moist in the growing season; water more sparingly in winter. ● Mist the foliage occasionally. ● Apply a high-potash liquid fertiliser every 2 weeks from spring until early autumn.

The flower spikes, with their golden bracts and white flowers, are about 10cm/4in long, and are attractive from spring right through to early autumn.

Plants often fail to flower if they do not get enough light. Move them into a bright position and apply a high-potash fertiliser to encourage flowering.

If the plant is allowed to dry out, the lower leaves will soon fall. Keep the compost constantly moist in the growing season.

Older plants become leggy in time and are best replaced with newly rooted cuttings.

The Sheffield
College
Hillsborough LRC

PELARGONIUM x *HORTORUM*
Geraniaceae

Geranium

Easy-going and colourful for long periods in summer, these are among the most popular indoor flowering plants. *Pelargonium* x *hortorum*, the zonal pelargonium, is the most common type. The stems are fleshy, becoming woody and brittle with age, and branch freely. They carry rounded, lobed and scallop-edged leaves which nearly always have a central brownish ring, or zone, which gives them their name. The foliage has a characteristic fragrance when handled. Flowers are carried in summer, in dense, rounded heads on top of sturdy, erect stems. Each individual flower is simple, five-petalled or double, in a wide variety of shades of white, pink, salmon, scarlet and purple; sometimes they are bicoloured. Dozens of new varieties are bred every year and are available from specialist nurseries.

There are plenty of types with variegated leaves, such as 'Mrs Henry Cox', which has mid-green leaves with a wide, red-flushed zone and creamy margin and bears single pink flowers.

FACT FILE

ORIGIN Warm temperate zones, South Africa.

HEIGHT To 90cm/3ft.

COMPOST Soil- or peat-based.

REPOTTING Repot in spring when roots show through the base of the pot. Flowering is improved if plants are slightly pot-bound.

PROPAGATION Take stem cuttings in spring and early summer. Zonal pelargoniums can also be raised from seed sown in early spring.

KEEPING PLANTS Overwinter in a cool room. To keep the plants reasonably compact and shapely, cut the stems hard back in early spring. This new growth is ideal for use as cuttings. Pinch out the growing tips regularly to encourage bushiness.

PLANT CARE

Bright light with full sun.
● Moderate to cool room temperatures, with a minimum of 7°C/45°F in winter.
● Water sufficiently to make the compost thoroughly moist, then allow the top 2.5cm/1in to dry out before watering again. Water sparingly in winter.
● Apply a high-potash liquid fertiliser every 2 weeks during the growing season.

ALSO RECOMMENDED

Pelargonium x *domesticum*, the regal pelargonium. The leaves are larger than in zonals, lighter in colour, and with a densely scalloped edge. Pinks, purples, white and rose red are the usual flower colours. Individual flowers are large, with frilly edged petals, often marked with a different colour: rose red 'Grand Slam' has the upper petals blotched with a deep strawberry-black colour.

The zonal cultivar 'Robert Fish' is grown mainly for its red, yellow, brown and green leaves. The plant produces small single flowers that are perhaps better removed, since they tend to detract from the foliage.

Lower leaves turn red or yellow in very dry or cool conditions. To some extent this is natural in winter, but check that the plant is receiving sufficient warmth and moisture if a large number of leaves are lost.

Flower heads are composed of many individual flowers; the flower heads tend to shatter if brushed against or moved when in full bloom.

Overwatering will cause the main stem to rot at soil level. Always allow the compost to dry out slightly between waterings.

Pale circles on the leaf surface may indicate attack by the fungus disease rust; check the undersides of leaves for the characteristic powdery brown pustules. Rust is difficult to control; remove and burn affected leaves and spray the plant with an approved fungicide.

PELARGONIUM PELTATUM
Geraniaceae

*I*VY-LEAFED GERANIUM

This species has long, slender, brittle trailing stems and fleshy, brittle, ivy-shaped leaves. Flowers are carried in small clusters and tend to appear more sparsely petalled than those of zonal pelargoniums, although there are double or semi-double varieties. The upper petals often have contrasting markings on them. There is a full range of flower colours in shades of red, orange, pink, salmon, white and purple, with bicoloured varieties such as the red and white 'Rouletta'.

Variegated leaves add to the attraction of these pelargoniums. 'L'Elégante' is a long-established variety, which has mid-green leaves with cream edges that become flushed with purple in cool conditions. Some strains of ivy-leaved pelargonium, such as 'Summer Showers', are now easily raised from seed.

FACT FILE

ORIGIN Warm temperate zones.

HEIGHT Prostrate, trailing to 90cm/3ft.

COMPOST Soil- or peat-based.

REPOTTING Repot in spring, when roots show through the base of the pot. Do not overpot.

PROPAGATION Take stem cuttings in spring and early summer or sow seed in early spring.

KEEPING PLANTS Overwinter in a cool room. Prune stems back hard in early spring to keep the plants reasonably compact and shapely. New growth is ideal for use as cuttings.

PLANT CARE

Bright light, full sun. ● Moderate warmth, with a minimum of 7°C/45°F in winter. ● Give sufficient water to make the compost thoroughly moist; allow the top 2.5cm/1in to dry out before watering again. Water very sparingly in winter. ● Apply a high-potash liquid fertiliser every 2 weeks from the time the buds form until autumn.

High-nitrogen fertilisers given to young plants can cause lush leaf growth and a failure to flower. Do not feed plants until buds are forming; use a high-potash fertiliser.

The trailing stems of ivy-leafed pelargoniums are brittle and easily broken, so handle and position the plants with care.

Corky growths on the leaf surfaces are caused by oedema, the result of overwatering.

PELARGONIUM SPP.
Geraniaceae

*S*CENTED-LEAFED GERANIUMS

Although all pelargoniums have slightly aromatic foliage, a number of species has strongly fragrant leaves in a wide range of unusual scents, and the full fragrance is given off when the leaves are stroked or gently rubbed. The leaf shapes and plant forms are extremely variable. The flowers are usually simple, rather sparse and in pale colours, and it is for their foliage that these plants are grown.

Many types are available. *Pelargonium abrotanifolium* is a slow-growing, woody-stemmed plant with silver, finely cut foliage quite unlike other pelargoniums. *P. capitatum*, rose-scented geranium, has soft furry leaves and pink flowers. *P. crispum*, lemon geranium, shown here, has small scallop-edged leaves. *P. graveolens*, rose geranium, has grey-green, deeply lobed toothed leaves. *P. odoratissimum*, apple geranium, has tall, rather lax stems carrying small, softly hairy, wavy-edged leaves. *P. quercifolium*, oak-leafed geranium, is a tall shrubby plant, with a strong, spicy, peppery scent. *P. tomentosum*, peppermint geranium, has large leaves which are softly hairy and strongly scented.

Pinch out vigorous varieties frequently to prevent the stems becoming overlong. Use the shoot tips as cuttings.

Although many scented-leafed varieties bear flowers, these are usually fairly insignificant and can be removed if desired.

The fragrance is usually released by the slightest touch; lemon-scented varieties, in particular, are intensely aromatic.

FACT FILE

ORIGIN Warm temperate zones.

HEIGHT To 90cm/3ft according to species.

COMPOST Soil- or peat-based, with good drainage.

REPOTTING Repot in spring, when roots show at the base of the pot.

PROPAGATION Take stem cuttings in spring and early summer.

KEEPING PLANTS Pinch out the shoot tips of strong-growing varieties regularly to encourage branching and maintain a bushy shape.

PLANT CARE

Bright light, full sun. ● Moderate warmth, with a minimum temperature of 7°C/45°F in winter. ● Ensure that the compost is thoroughly moist, then allow the surface to dry out before watering again. Water more sparingly in winter. ● Apply a standard liquid fertiliser every 3 weeks from spring to autumn.

PEPEROMIA CAPERATA
Piperaceae

*E*MERALD RIPPLE

The heart-shaped, deep green leaves of this peperomia are borne on fairly long, red-tinged stalks. They are deeply veined and have an attractive, corrugated surface. Tall, white, poker-like flower spikes, also with red stems, emerge above the mound of foliage in summer and early autumn. 'Emerald Ripple' is a compact form that makes a dense mound of leaves. 'Variegata' has almost white leaves with a central splash of mid-green, but the light and dark effect of the corrugated surface does not show up so well on the light-coloured leaf.

FACT FILE

ORIGIN Brazil.

HEIGHT To 25cm/10in.

COMPOST Peat-based.

REPOTTING In spring, move young plants into pots one size larger; it is not usually necessary to repot older plants every year.

PROPAGATION Take leaf or stem cuttings in spring.

KEEPING PLANTS This is a largely trouble-free plant, which lasts well.

PLANT CARE

Moderate light, shaded from direct sun. ● A minimum winter temperature of 10°–13°C/50°–55°F; otherwise normal room temperature. ● Water sparingly, especially in winter, allowing the top half of the compost to dry out before rewatering. ● Mist plants frequently and stand the pot on a dish of moist pebbles. ● Apply a balanced liquid fertiliser every 2 weeks from spring to autumn.

Protect peperomias from strong sun; variegated types need brighter conditions than those with plain leaves.

The tall flower spikes are neither showy nor colourful, but they are produced in abundance and make a graceful addition to the plant.

If the lower leaves and base of the stems turn black, overwatering is the most likely cause. Water these plants sparingly at all times.

PEPEROMIA MAGNOLIIFOLIA
Piperaceae

*D*ESERT PRIVET

This plant is often offered as *Peperomia obtusifolia*, but differs from it in that its growth is more upright and it has more leaves. It forms a small, shrubby, branching plant with smooth, waxy, rather fleshy, rounded leaves carried alternately on the stems. Although growth is largely upright at first, the stems tend to bend downwards as the plant gets older.

The variegated forms are most commonly grown. 'Variegata' has cream-and-green leaves, with the leaves often being almost entirely cream when young but turning a bright lime green as they age. The leaves of 'Green and Gold' are more irregularly marked, with light green centres, a creamy gold mid-region and darker green margins, often with a feathered look.

Variegated leaf forms of this peperomia are most favoured as house plants. Young leaves are often almost entirely cream and become marked with green as they age.

Oedema, which causes corky swellings on the underside of the foliage, is the result of excessive watering. Keep the compost only just moist and never allow the plant to stand in water.

Lower leaves will fall if the conditions are too cold. Water plants sparingly in winter.

FACT FILE

ORIGIN Northern South America, West Indies.

HEIGHT To 20cm/8in.

COMPOST Peat-based.

REPOTTING Repot every 2 years or so, when the compost in the existing pot is filled with roots.

PROPAGATION Take stem tip cuttings in spring and early summer, or leaf stem cuttings in spring.

KEEPING PLANTS Under good conditions, this plant is long-lived.

PLANT CARE

Bright light, but not direct sun. ● Normal room temperature with a minimum of 13°C/55°F; better at 16°C/60°F in winter. ● Keep the compost just moist in summer, allowing the top 2.5cm/1in to dry out before rewatering. Water even more sparingly in winter. ● Mist the plant frequently and stand the pot on a dish of moist pebbles to increase humidity. ● Apply a balanced liquid fertiliser every 2 weeks during the growing season.

PEPEROMIA SCANDENS
Piperaceae

CUPID PEPEROMIA

The trailing forms of peperomia are much less common than the bushy species. *Peperomia scandens*, also known as *P. serpens*, has heart-shaped leaves about 5cm/2in long, which are carried alternately on pinkish stems that can trail up to 1.2m/4ft or be tied to supports to make the plant into a climber. The leaves are fleshy, with a waxy surface.

The form 'Variegata' is the one most commonly offered for sale. It has mid-green leaves with a wide, creamy yellow margin. The young leaves are often almost entirely cream, and the green centre develops gradually as the plant matures. Plants in containers do not often produce flowers.

FACT FILE

ORIGIN South America.

HEIGHT Stems trail or climb to 1.2m/4ft.

COMPOST Preferably peat-based.

REPOTTING Repot only when the compost is filled with roots.

PROPAGATION Take stem tip cuttings in early summer. They should root in 4–6 weeks.

KEEPING PLANTS In good conditions peperomias last for several years.

PLANT CARE

Bright conditions, with shade from direct sun in summer. A little direct winter sunshine helps to intensify the variegation of the foliage. ● Normal room temperatures, with a winter minimum of 13°C/55°F. ● Keep the compost just moist; allow the surface to dry out between waterings. Water less in winter. ● Mist frequently in summer and stand the pot on a dish of moist pebbles to increase humidity. ● Apply a balanced liquid fertiliser every 2 weeks in the growing season.

The foliage requires good, bright conditions to maintain its colouring. Some direct sunshine is beneficial in winter, but be careful not to scorch the fleshy leaves by overexposure to the sun.

Pinch out the shoot tips occasionally to promote branching, and cut the stems hard back in mid-spring.

PHILODENDRON BIPINNATIFIDUM
Araceae

TREE PHILODENDRON

Unlike the more familiar philodendron species, this one does not climb. Instead it makes a sturdy, spreading plant, which eventually develops a stout 'trunk' and can form an impressive architectural specimen. Because of its spread – 1.8m/6ft or more across – it needs plenty of space. It should not be confused with the somewhat similarly named *Philodendron bipennifolium*, horsehead philodendron, which is a climbing species with fiddle-shaped leaves.

The large leaves of *P. bipinnatifidum* are a deep glossy green and are about 90cm/3ft long. When young, they are more or less heart-shaped, with indented margins. As they develop, the indentations become more deeply cut until the leaf appears to be divided into many slender leaflets and takes on an overall arrowhead shape. The leaves are carried on long stalks, arising in a rosette formation from the crown.

Direct sun falling on the leaves can cause brown scorch marks on the foliage.

Juvenile leaves are uncut and more or less heart-shaped.

The appearance of the glossy, dramatic-looking leaves can be enhanced by cleaning them carefully with a damp cloth.

FACT FILE

ORIGIN Brazil.

HEIGHT To 1.2m/4ft.

COMPOST Soil-based with added peat.

REPOTTING Repot in spring or early summer when roots fill the current pot, usually every other year.

PROPAGATION Sow seed in spring in a heated propagator; do not cover the seed.

KEEPING PLANTS Provide a cane for support if needed.

PLANT CARE

Moderate light, shaded from direct sun. ● Average room temperature, with a winter minimum of 13°C/55°F. ● Keep the compost moist at all times during the growing season. Water more sparingly in winter and let the surface of the compost dry out between waterings. ● Mist the foliage occasionally. ● Apply a balanced liquid fertiliser every 2 weeks during the growing season.

PHILODENDRON ERUBESCENS
Araceae

*B*LUSHING PHILODENDRON

This strong-growing, climbing plant has leaves about 25cm/10in long that are shaped like arrowheads. They are a glossy deep green, with a coppery red underside and reddish margins, and are carried on long, purple-red leafstalks; the young stems are also red.

One of the most popular hybrids, 'Burgundy', has *Philodrendron erubescens* as one of its parents. 'Burgundy' is a slow-growing climber, whose long leaves are deep reddish green above and wine red on the undersides; it has glowing red leafstalks. 'Red Emerald' is another commonly grown variety with bright green foliage and red stems.

The wine-red tinge to the glossy dark green foliage and stems is intensified by good light, but plants should be protected from direct, strong sunlight.

Lower leaves that turn yellow and fall usually mean the plant is being overwatered, particularly in winter. Do not let the pot stand in water; do allow the surface to dry out before rewatering.

The thick aerial roots should be carefully trained into the damp moss of a moss pole. Use a piece of wire bent into the shape of a hairpin to hold the roots in place.

FACT FILE

ORIGIN South America.

HEIGHT To 1.8m/6ft or more.

COMPOST Soil-based with added peat.

REPOTTING Repot in spring or early summer when roots fill the pot. Use a large, broad-based pot to prevent the plant becoming top-heavy.

PROPAGATION Take stem tip cuttings in early summer and root them in a mixture of half peat moss, half coarse sand.

KEEPING PLANTS Provide the plant with a moss pole for support.

PLANT CARE

Good to moderate light, shaded from direct sun. ● Average room temperature, with a minimum of 13°C/55°F in winter. ● Keep the compost moist at all times during the growing season. Allow the surface of the compost to dry out between waterings in winter. ● Mist the foliage occasionally. ● Feed with a balanced liquid fertiliser every 2 weeks in spring and summer.

PHILODENDRON SCANDENS
Araceae

*H*EARTLEAF PHILODENDRON

The most popular of the philodendrons, known also as the sweetheart plant, this one is undemanding and extremely easy to grow. The leaves are strongly heart-shaped and a bright, glossy mid-green; when the foliage is young, it has a bronze tinge. The leaves are normally 10cm/4in long although they may double or treble in size as they mature. They are carried alternately on slender twining stems, which will trail, or climb when given support. Trailing plants should have the tips pinched out occasionally to keep the plant bushy and encourage it to branch.

FACT FILE

ORIGIN Tropical America.

HEIGHT Climbs or trails to 1.2m/4ft or more.

COMPOST Peat-based, or soil-based with added peat.

REPOTTING Repot in spring or early summer when the compost is filled with roots. When the maximum desired pot size is reached, top-dress in spring instead.

PROPAGATION In spring and early summer, take stem tip cuttings just below a node and remove the bottom leaves. The cuttings will root easily in a mixture of half damp peat, half coarse sand or perlite.

KEEPING PLANTS The plant can be trained on a trellis or up a moss pole. In each instance, it will need to be tied in initially, although eventually the aerial roots will grow into the moss on the pole. Stems can also be allowed to trail from a hanging basket.

PLANT CARE

Bright light but no direct sun. ● Average room temperatures, with a winter minimum of 13°C/55°F. ● Give sufficient water to keep the compost moist during the growing season; allow the surface to dry out between waterings in winter. ● Mist the foliage occasionally. If the plant is grown on a moss pole, spray the pole every day. ● Apply a balanced liquid fertiliser every 2 weeks in the growing season.

Elongated, straggly stems show that the plant is not receiving sufficient light; move it to a brighter position, but not into direct sun.

Small aerial roots will attach themselves to a moist surface, such as a moss pole. Stems must be tied in to the support when the plant is trained as a climber.

Young shoots are sometimes infested with aphids. If so, treat them with a contact insecticide.

PHOENIX ROEBELENII
Palmae

PYGMY DATE PALM

The arching, mid- to deep green fronds on this slow-growing palm grow from a central crown. The fronds, which are divided into many slender leaflets, are soft, not spiky like those on other date palms, and spread out in a graceful fashion to give the plant a feathery appearance, more delicate than that of other members of the genus. The fronds are covered in a thin layer of white scales.

The slow-growing pygmy date palm makes a good specimen plant, which should be allowed sufficient room to spread to as much as 1.2m/4ft wide when several years old. The long panicles of yellowish flowers are not normally produced on indoor plants.

If the leaflets turn brown and crisp at the tips and margins, the air is too dry. Mist the plant regularly to maintain a humid atmosphere.

Scale insects often infect these plants. Check the undersides of the leaves and remove any scales with a fingernail. Treat with systemic insecticide if the infestation is bad.

The fronds have a feathery appearance and arch outward, giving the plant a graceful outline.

FACT FILE

ORIGIN Laos.

HEIGHT To 1.2m/4ft; usually about 60cm/2ft indoors.

COMPOST Soil-based.

REPOTTING Repot in spring only when necessary, since this plant resents root disturbance. Take care not to damage the roots.

PROPAGATION Suckers are sometimes produced at the base of the plant and can be cut away carefully and treated as cuttings. Plants can also be raised from seed, but take several years to achieve a reasonable size.

KEEPING PLANTS This palm needs a humid atmosphere. Stand the pot on a tray of moist pebbles and mist the foliage regularly.

PLANT CARE

Bright light; will tolerate some direct sun. ● A minimum temperature of 13°C/55°F in winter; normal room temperatures in summer. ● Keep the compost thoroughly moist during the growing season. Give just enough water in winter to prevent the compost from drying out, to give the plants a short winter rest. ● Apply a balanced liquid fertiliser every 2–3 weeks in summer.

PILEA CADIEREI
Urticaceae

ALUMINIUM PLANT

A popular and easily grown plant, *Pilea cadierei* has ovate mid-green leaves about 8cm/3in long, which grow in opposite pairs on the rather fleshy stems. The leaf surface is textured, and the four rows of silvery raised patches between the veins give this pilea the other common name watermelon pilea. The undersides of the leaves have a reddish tinge; new foliage is lighter green in colour.

The plant branches freely, forming a small bush, but it tends to become straggly after a couple of seasons. Frequent pinching out of the growing tips will help to keep it compact. Cuttings are easily rooted, so leggy plants can be regularly replaced. The variety 'Minima' is a dwarf form with smaller leaves.

FACT FILE

ORIGIN Vietnam.

HEIGHT Up to 30cm/12in before plants need to be replaced; 'Minima' grows to about 15cm/6in.

COMPOST Peat-based.

REPOTTING Repot in spring as necessary.

PROPAGATION Take stem tip cuttings in spring or summer.

KEEPING PLANTS Plants are best discarded at the end of the season, and replaced with rooted cuttings. If plants are kept for a second season, cut the shoots back by half in spring.

PLANT CARE

Good light, but shaded from direct sun. ● Minimum of 13°C/55°F in winter; normal warm room temperature at other times. ● Keep the compost just moist during the growing season, allowing the surface to dry out between waterings. Water more sparingly in winter. ● Mist regularly to increase humidity, and stand the pot on a tray of moist gravel. ● Apply a balanced liquid fertiliser every 2 weeks in summer.

The foliage has an attractive quilted appearance, with strongly contrasting silver markings. Keep the plant in good light for the best coloration.

Aphids can often be found thickly clustered on the tips of the young shoots. Pinch out affected shoots or spray with a contact insecticide.

The lower leaves fall naturally, giving older plants a straggly appearance; this will be accentuated by both over- and underwatering.

PILEA PEPEROMIOIDES
Urticaceae

$\mathcal{P}$ILEA

This unusual pilea forms a mound of leaves, each of which rises directly from the roots on a single, unbranched stem. The oval, almost rounded leaves, up to 10cm/4in long, are fleshy and a bright mid-green with a shiny surface. In summer, small, fluffy, yellowish green flowers may be produced, but these are secondary to the foliage.

Another attractive species is *Pilea involucrata*, sometimes incorrectly called *P. spruceana*. This is a bushy, spreading plant with ovate leaves which are strongly textured and quilted on the upper surface. They are dark green with a reddish brown tinge and red undersides. One of the most popular forms is 'Moon Valley' (also sold as *P. mollis*), which has pointed, bright green, puckered leaves with dark bronze veins.

FACT FILE

ORIGIN West Indies.

HEIGHT To 30cm/12in.

COMPOST Peat-based.

REPOTTING Repot in spring when necessary.

PROPAGATION Take stem tip cuttings in spring or summer.

KEEPING PLANTS In order to flower well, the plant needs a cool winter rest period. Discard the plant after 3 or 4 years when it becomes leggy.

PLANT CARE

Moderate to bright light, but shaded from direct sun. ● Warm room temperature, with a minimum of 13°C/55°F in winter. ● Keep the compost evenly moist during the growing season; allow the surface to dry out between waterings. Water more sparingly in winter. ● Apply a balanced liquid fertiliser every 2 weeks during spring and summer. ● Keep the plant out of draughts.

The foliage is brightly coloured, especially in good light conditions.

Some leaves will fall naturally in winter, but cold conditions or overwatering may cause excessive leaf loss. Move an affected plant to a slightly warmer position and allow the compost to dry out between waterings.

PIPER ORNATUM
Piperaceae

$\mathcal{C}$ELEBES PEPPER

Although this climbing plant – sometimes incorrectly offered as *Piper crocatum* – has leaf forms similar to *Philodendron scandens*, the heartleaf plant, it is not as easy to find or to grow. It is, however, worth the search, since the heart-shaped leaves are more attractively coloured, being olive green with silvery pink markings along the veins and red undersides. They are about 10cm/4in long and are carried alternately on slender pink wiry stems.

Also known as the ornamental pepper, the Celebes pepper belongs to the true pepper family, a group of plants that produce one of the world's most important commercial spices.

The heart-shaped leaves have a slightly puckered surface attractively marked with silvery pink.

Stems will trail gracefully if 2 or 3 plants are set in a hanging basket. Alternatively, the stems can be trained up stakes inserted into the pot and tied gently at intervals.

Plants will lose their leaves if the growing conditions are not to their liking. They need warm, humid conditions and resent sudden changes in temperature; do not expose them to draughts.

FACT FILE

ORIGIN Sulawesi.

HEIGHT To 1.5m/5ft.

COMPOST Peat-based, or a mixture of peat- and soil-based.

REPOTTING Repot in spring when the plant has become top heavy, usually only every 2 or 3 years.

PROPAGATION Take stem cuttings in late spring and summer. They are not easy to root, but a heated propagator will help.

KEEPING PLANTS The plant is usually grown up two or three canes – stems must be tied in to the supports – or it can be allowed to trail.

PLANT CARE

Bright filtered sunlight. ● Evenly warm conditions, with a winter minimum of 16°C/60°F. ● Water moderately at all times, allowing the surface to dry out between waterings. ● Mist the foliage regularly and stand the pot on a tray of moist pebbles. ● Apply a balanced liquid fertiliser every 2 weeks in spring and summer.

PLATYCERIUM BIFURCATUM
Polypodiaceae

$\mathscr{S}$TAGHORN FERN

One glance at this plant is sufficient to tell you how it got its common name – the fronds are large and distinctly antler-like, dividing into lobes at their tips. It is also sometimes known as *Platycerium alcicorne* and commonly as elkhorn fern.

The plant has two types of frond. The sterile fronds at the base are more or less kidney-shaped, pale green becoming brown with age, and they clasp their support, which in the wild is normally a tree trunk, since the plants are epiphytes. The frond is slightly curved, and the debris that falls and is trapped behind it rots down to form a source of nutrients for the plant. Fertile fronds up to 90cm/3ft long arise from the sterile frond and are spreading or drooping, branching into antler-like lobes. They are greyish green, covered with a white, felty 'scurf'.

Although the fern can be grown in a pot, it is better in a slatted basket or mounted on a piece of wood or bark, which more closely mimics its natural growing conditions. Wrap the rootball in damp sphagnum moss and tie it to the bark or a wooden plaque with twine.

The large sterile frond will eventually cover the compost and clasp the sides of the pot, making it impossible to water the plant from above.

Handle the plant with care: the white scurf on the fronds is easily damaged.

FACT FILE

ORIGIN Australia.

SPREAD To 60cm/2ft.

COMPOST Moist sphagnum moss mixed with leaf mould.

REPOTTING The clasping sterile frond makes it difficult to repot a plant when it has outgrown its current pot, so mount it or put it in a wooden orchid basket.

PROPAGATION Not practical in the home.

KEEPING PLANTS Mist the leaves frequently with tepid water, but do not allow water into the growing point; this may cause rot to develop.

PLANT CARE

Bright light with some direct sun, but not strong summer sun. ● Minimum of 13°C/55°F. In summer 21°C/70°F is ideal. ● Water well, then allow to dry between waterings. Occasionally plunge the root area into water for several minutes, then drain. Water pot-grown plants from below; tip away water remaining after 15 minutes. ● Feed once a month in summer, either as a spray or in the plunging water.

PLECTRANTHUS COLEOIDES 'MARGINATUS'
Labiatae

$\mathscr{C}$ANDLE PLANT

Plectranthus are easily grown plants, but not as common in garden centres as one might expect – probably because they are so simple to propagate that they tend to be passed from one gardener to another rather than bought. *Plectranthus coleoides*, today more correctly called *P. forsteri*, is a bushy plant with red stems which are upright at first, but soon trail. The ovate leaves are up to 6.5cm/2½in long with toothed margins, broadly edged white in the variety 'Marginatus', which is the one used almost exclusively as an indoor plant. Pale lilac, nettle-like flowers are sometimes produced, but are rather insignificant and are usually removed.

Common names for plants in this genus are confused. *P. oertendahlii*, a prostrate species with rounded, bronze green leaves with cream white or silver veins and red-tinted undersides, is known both as candle plant and Swedish ivy, and *P. australis* is called Swedish ivy in the US.

FACT FILE

ORIGIN New Caledonia, Fiji.

HEIGHT Trailing stems to 30cm/12in.

COMPOST Peat-based.

REPOTTING Repot in spring, but plants are usually replaced annually.

PROPAGATION Take easily rooted stem cuttings from spring to autumn.

KEEPING PLANTS Plants are usually replaced with fresh cuttings at the end of a year. Pinch out growing tips to maintain bushiness.

PLANT CARE

Bright light with some direct sun except in midsummer. ● Minimum temperature 13°C/55°F; average room temperature in summer. ● Keep the compost thoroughly moist all through the growing season; frequent watering is usually necessary. Water more sparingly in winter. ● Mist the foliage occasionally. ● Feed with a balanced liquid fertiliser every 2 weeks in spring and summer.

Leggy stems, with long gaps between the leaves, are common on plants that do not get sufficient light. Plants do, however, naturally grow straggly with age.

The toothed leaves are slightly aromatic when touched. A plain-leafed type exists, but the variegated form is normally grown.

The trailing stems are best displayed in a hanging basket or a pot mounted on a pedestal. Pinch out the growing tips regularly to keep the plant bushy.

PLUMBAGO AURICULATA
Plumbaginaceae

CAPE LEADWORT

A rather straggling semi-climber, blue Cape plumbago produces panicles of sky blue flowers throughout the summer. Both its common and scientific names refer to the fact that it was once thought to cure lead poisoning. It used to be known as *Plumbago capensis* and is still frequently offered under that name.

The mid-green, oval leaves are borne on slender stems and the flowers are carried in heads of up to 20 at the tips of young shoots. They are tubular, opening to a pale blue star, each of the five petals having a thin dark line running down the centre. 'Alba' is a white-flowered variety.

FACT FILE

ORIGIN South Africa.

HEIGHT To 1.2m/4ft.

COMPOST Soil-based.

REPOTTING Repot in spring, in a pot one size larger until maximum desired pot size is reached; thereafter top-dress annually.

PROPAGATION Take stem cuttings of non-flowering shoots in late spring and summer, or sow seed in spring.

KEEPING PLANTS Cut stems back to about 15cm/6in just as the plant is starting into growth in spring – flowers are borne on the current year's growth. Tie the plant in to a trellis or canes, or train it around a hoop. Where the climate is suitable, put the plant outdoors in summer.

If buds fall before the flowers open, conditions are too hot and dry for the plant. Move it to a cooler position, mist the foliage and see that the compost is moist.

PLANT CARE

Bright light with several hours of direct sun. ● Minimum temperature of 7°C/45°F in winter; can tolerate temperatures as high as 32°C/90°F. ● Keep the soil moist at all times in spring and summer; water more sparingly in winter. ● Mist the foliage occasionally. ● Apply a high-potash liquid fertiliser every 2 weeks in spring and summer.

ALSO RECOMMENDED

Plumbago indica, scarlet leadwort, has foliage ranging from soft pink to red. It is a tender species, originating in Southeast Asia, and needs bright filtered light with some sun, a minimum temperature of 16°–18°C/60°–65°F and high humidity. As with *P. auriculata*, flowers are borne on the current year's growth if the plant is cut back in spring; left unpruned, it will bloom in late winter if the situation is warm enough.

Red spider mites can be a nuisance, by causing pale, flecked foliage with webbing on the underside. Spray plants with water regularly.

House plants can be kept neat by training the stems around a hoop, but plumbago is ideal for a conservatory, where it can be allowed to grow over a permanent trellis.

Plumbago indica *is a tender and unusual species that bears lax sprays of red or deep pink flowers in summer.*

PRIMULACEAE

PRIMROSES

Primula obconica is known as poison primrose because the hairs on the foliage can cause a skin irritation. The flowers come in a wide choice of colours.

The large primula family contains a number of popular indoor plants that flower in winter and early spring. Like daffodils, they cheer us by anticipating the flowering of their outdoor relatives.

Among the most commonly grown is the robust *Primula obconica*, the poison primrose, so called because it contains the irritant chemical primin, although the 'Libre' series has been bred to be free of it. Most plants are available as unnamed varieties, but the 'Ariane' series has large flowers and compact foliage, and is available in purplish blue, orange, white, and red-and-white and blue-and-white bicolours.

Commercial varieties of *P. vulgaris* with larger flowers are available in yellow, purple, orange, red, pink and white, all with pronounced yellow eyes. There are double varieties and bicolours. A hybrid of *P. vulgaris* and *P. veris* (the cowslip) is the polyanthus, *P.* x *tommasinii*. The foliage is similar to that of the primrose, but the flowers are carried in umbels on the top of stout, 10-cm/4-in-long stalks.

The species *P. sinensis* and *P. malacoides* are daintier and have smaller flowers. Those of *P. malacoides* are only about 2cm/³⁄₄in wide, but double-flowered and dwarf forms have also been developed.

P. 'Kewensis' is a hybrid that comes true to seed and produces brilliant yellow, long-lasting flowers with a sweet scent from midwinter through to spring.

Flowers are 2.5cm/1in wide and have 5 heart-shaped petals. The indentation at the top of the petals makes it appear as though there are 10 of them. The flowers are borne in umbels on stems up to 30cm/12in tall.

Mid-green, rather coarse rounded to heart-shaped leaves are covered in fine hairs.

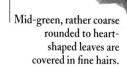

ALSO RECOMMENDED

Primula denticulata, drumstick primula, is a vigorous upright plant. It has a round head made up of tightly packed mauve, purple or purple-pink flowers on a stem up to 46cm/18in long.

Primula 'Kewensis' has wavy-edged, toothed leaves covered with a dusting of fine white powder. Whorls of bright yellow fragrant flowers with a long tube crown the 38-cm/15-in flower stalks.

Primula malacoides, the delicate-looking fairy primrose, has oval, toothed leaves. The small, fragrant flowers, arranged in 3–6 tiers on 46-cm/18-in stems, may be pink, purple or white, with a yellow eye.

Aphids are sometimes found on the young foliage. Pick off affected leaves or spray the plant carefully with a contact insecticide. Not all insecticides are suitable for primulas; read the label carefully.

Limp, yellowing lower leaves may mean the plant has been overwatered. Keep the soil moist, but never let the plant stand in water.

The C-shaped grubs of vine weevils eat the roots, causing wilting and eventual collapse of the plant. By the time they have been discovered, it is usually too late to save the plant, but an insecticidal dust may help.

Hairs on the leaves can trap water, which leads to rotting of the foliage and grey mould. Do not mist the plant.

Primula sinensis, the Chinese primrose, has soft, hairy lobed leaves with toothed edges. The many-flowered stalks start short and lengthen as the frilly-petalled red, white, pink or purple flowers open.

Primula vulgaris, the common primrose, forms a rosette of wrinkled hairy leaves from the middle of which grow pale yellow flowers with deeper yellow eyes, each on a slender single stem.

FACT FILE

ORIGIN Mainly Northern Hemisphere, especially China.

HEIGHT 20–38cm/8–15in.

COMPOST Peat-based.

REPOTTING Move *Primula obconica* and *P. sinensis* into a pot one size larger in early autumn. Do not touch the foliage if you are allergic; use rubber gloves. The other primulas mentioned here should be discarded or, in the case of *P. vulgaris*, planted outdoors.

PROPAGATION Sow seeds in summer and autumn according to type or species, or divide plants after they have finished flowering.

KEEPING PLANTS After flowering, keep plants of *P. obconica* and *P. sinensis* outdoors in a cool, sheltered, lightly shaded location. Water just enough to prevent the soil from drying out. In early autumn remove yellow and dead foliage, repot the plants, bring them indoors and gradually increase the amount of water.

PLANT CARE

Bright light with some direct sun, especially in winter. ● Cool conditions will extend the life of the flowers: 10°–16°C/50°–60°F is the ideal range. ● Keep the compost thoroughly moist at all times during the flowering period: water sparingly in summer.
● Apply a high-potash liquid fertiliser every 1–2 weeks during the flowering season, starting when buds appear ● Wear rubber gloves when handling plants of the hairy-leafed *P. obconica* and *P. sinensis*.

PESTS & DISEASES

Primulas are fairly free from pests and diseases, although vine weevils, aphids and red spider mites may be a nuisance. Plants are more likely to suffer from botrytis and root rot, which are caused by poor cultivation and overwatering.

SAXIFRAGA STOLONIFERA
Saxifragaceae

*M*OTHER OF THOUSANDS

This plant is ideal for a hanging pot, since its main feature of interest is the large number of baby plantlets it produces at the tips of long, slender runners. The rounded leaves, with lightly scalloped edges, are covered with silvery hairs. They are deep olive green on top, with a network of silver veins, while the undersides and leafstalks are wine red. The variety 'Tricolor' has smaller leaves with an irregular, white, pink-flushed margin, and is slower growing.

Plantlets grow on fine, thread-like, red stolons which can be 60cm/2ft or more long, and are generally produced in abundance. The plantlets root easily wherever they touch the compost and soon form a dense mat if allowed to do so. Small, white star-shaped flowers with rather lopsided petals are carried on long spikes in late summer.

Hang the pot in a well-ventilated position, but out of draughts.

The red flush to the foliage is most pronounced when plants are grown in bright light, but shade the leaves from strong, direct sunlight.

The way the plants produce long runners, plus their rather geranium-like leaves, have given them an alternative common name of strawberry geranium.

FACT FILE

ORIGIN East Asia.

HEIGHT To 20cm/8in; stolons trail to 60cm/2ft.

COMPOST Soil-based.

REPOTTING In spring, move into a larger pot if roots are overcrowded.

PROPAGATION Peg down plantlets into pots of compost, where they will quickly form roots; they can be separated from the parent before or after they have rooted.

KEEPING PLANTS Replace plants with young plantlets after 2–3 years.

PLANT CARE

Bright light, with some direct, but not very strong, sun to maintain leaf colouring. ● Cool conditions – 10°–16°C/50°–60°F; a minimum winter temperature of 7°C/45°F. ● Keep the compost moist during the growing season. In winter, water just sufficiently to prevent the compost drying out. ● In a warm position, stand the pot on a dish of moist gravel to increase humidity. Spray foliage occasionally with a fine mist – do not allow drops of water to remain on the leaves.
● Apply a balanced liquid fertiliser every 4 weeks in spring and summer.

SCHEFFLERA ARBORICOLA
Araliaceae

*U*MBRELLA TREE

Now available in a wide range of varieties, *Schefflera arboricola* is also known as *Heptapleurum arboricolum*. It forms a slender tree shape, the upright stem bearing fingered leaves with eight or so 10–15-cm/4–6-in-long oval leaflets which are carried in a circle on leafstalks up to 15cm/6in long. The leaflets near the top of the circle are usually smaller than those at the base. If a tall plant is required, support the stem with a moss pole; aerial roots are produced on mature plants, and these can be inserted into the moss. *S. actinophylla*, syn. *Brassaia actinophylla*, has more leaflets on longer stalks. These leaflets are darker green and can be as much as 30cm/12in long.

FACT FILE

ORIGIN Southeast Asia.

HEIGHT To 1.8m/6ft; more usually 90cm/3ft in the home.

COMPOST Peat-based.

REPOTTING Repot in spring, when roots show through the drainage holes in the base of the pot. A large, unpinched plant will do better in a heavy clay pot to balance the top growth and give extra stability.

PROPAGATION Take stem tip cuttings in spring and summer.

KEEPING PLANTS Clean the large glossy leaves with a damp sponge.

PLANT CARE

Bright light with some direct sun except in midsummer. ● Normal room temperature, with a winter minimum of 13°C/55°F. ● Keep the compost moist but not wet in the growing season. Let the surface of the compost dry out between waterings in winter. ● Mist the plant regularly and stand the pot on a saucer of moist gravel to increase humidity. ● Give a balanced liquid fertiliser every 2 weeks while the plant is in active growth.

Sponge the leaves with lime-free water every 2–3 weeks to remove the dust.

Pinch out the growing tips to produce a bushy, branching plant; an unstopped specimen will quickly become tall and need support.

The leafstalks are normally semi-erect, but will droop if the plant is allowed to dry out. Keep the compost moist, but not waterlogged, from spring to autumn.

Aphids are sometimes found on the young foliage. Pick off affected leaves or spray the plant carefully with a contact insecticide. Not all insecticides are suitable for primulas; read the label carefully.

Limp, yellowing lower leaves may mean the plant has been overwatered. Keep the soil moist, but never let the plant stand in water.

The C-shaped grubs of vine weevils eat the roots, causing wilting and eventual collapse of the plant. By the time they have been discovered, it is usually too late to save the plant, but an insecticidal dust may help.

Hairs on the leaves can trap water, which leads to rotting of the foliage and grey mould. Do not mist the plant.

Primula sinensis, the Chinese primrose, has soft, hairy lobed leaves with toothed edges. The many-flowered stalks start short and lengthen as the frilly-petalled red, white, pink or purple flowers open.

Primula vulgaris, the common primrose, forms a rosette of wrinkled hairy leaves from the middle of which grow pale yellow flowers with deeper yellow eyes, each on a slender single stem.

FACT FILE

ORIGIN Mainly Northern Hemisphere, especially China.

HEIGHT 20–38cm/8–15in.

COMPOST Peat-based.

REPOTTING Move *Primula obconica* and *P. sinensis* into a pot one size larger in early autumn. Do not touch the foliage if you are allergic; use rubber gloves. The other primulas mentioned here should be discarded or, in the case of *P. vulgaris,* planted outdoors.

PROPAGATION Sow seeds in summer and autumn according to type or species, or divide plants after they have finished flowering.

KEEPING PLANTS After flowering, keep plants of *P. obconica* and *P. sinensis* outdoors in a cool, sheltered, lightly shaded location. Water just enough to prevent the soil from drying out. In early autumn remove yellow and dead foliage, repot the plants, bring them indoors and gradually increase the amount of water.

PLANT CARE

Bright light with some direct sun, especially in winter. ● Cool conditions will extend the life of the flowers: 10°–16°C/50°–60°F is the ideal range. ● Keep the compost thoroughly moist at all times during the flowering period: water sparingly in summer.
● Apply a high-potash liquid fertiliser every 1–2 weeks during the flowering season, starting when buds appear ● Wear rubber gloves when handling plants of the hairy-leafed *P. obconica* and *P. sinensis.*

PESTS & DISEASES

Primulas are fairly free from pests and diseases, although vine weevils, aphids and red spider mites may be a nuisance. Plants are more likely to suffer from botrytis and root rot, which are caused by poor cultivation and overwatering.

RHAPIS EXCELSA
Palmae

MINIATURE FAN PALM

Also known as bamboo palm and little lady palm, this is a neat, fairly compact palm of Oriental appearance. The leaves consist of a variable number of deep, glossy green, rather corrugated, deeply veined leaflets up to 30cm/12in long.

The plant forms clumps of slender, strongly upright stems covered with brown fibre. As the lower leaves fall, they leave smooth green scars on the stems, giving them a bamboo-like appearance. A variegated form exists, with leaves striped creamy yellow or white.

FACT FILE

ORIGIN China.

HEIGHT To 3m/10ft.

COMPOST Soil-based.

REPOTTING Repot in spring, every other year at most. Plants grow best when slightly pot-bound.

PROPAGATION Remove suckers – preferably with roots attached – from the base of the plant in spring and pot them up individually.

KEEPING PLANTS This is a slow-growing palm, and with proper care it should last for many years.

PLANT CARE

Bright filtered light. ● Normal to cool room temperature, with a minimum of 7°C/45°F in winter. ● Keep the compost constantly moist in spring and summer. Water less in winter; allow the top 13mm/½in to dry out between waterings. ● Mist the plant frequently, preferably with lime-free water, and stand the pot on a tray of moist pebbles. ● Apply a balanced liquid fertiliser once a month in the growing season.

Brown leaf tips are common. Increasing the humidity by more frequent misting of the foliage will probably help.

Pale, mottled leaves with fine webbing under the tips are signs of red spider mite damage. A more humid atmosphere should discourage the mites.

The number of leaflets to each leaf differs widely. The variegated form tends to be slower-growing than the plain-leafed type.

RHIPSALIDOPSIS GAERTNERI
Cactaceae

EASTER CACTUS

The mid-green stems of this forest cactus are flattened and segmented, about 5cm/2in long and half as wide. The edges are scalloped and bear small areoles with tufts of yellow bristles rather than spines. The tip of each segment produces a new segment from its centre, and the arching, trailing stems that result branch freely. In spring, the segments at the tips of the branches produce flowers with layers of colourful, reflexing petals and petal-like sepals in shades of red or pink. The flowering season lasts for several weeks.

Rhipsalidopsis gaertneri, which has recently been reclassified as *Hatiora gaertneri*, is often confused with schlumbergera, the Christmas cactus (see page 133), which is similar in appearance.

Do not move the plant when it is in bud, or the buds are likely to fall. Even turning the pot around can have this effect.

Dull, limp, wrinkled segments show the plant is short of water. Keep the compost thoroughly moist when the plant is in flower.

The trailing stems are brittle, and segments break off easily. Remove any that are damaged and use undamaged portions for propagation.

FACT FILE

ORIGIN Brazil.

HEIGHT To 30cm/12in, with a similar spread.

COMPOST Peat-based with coarse sand in a ratio of 3:1; good drainage is essential.

REPOTTING Repot in mid-spring, after the rest period, when the compost is filled with roots. A hanging basket is ideal for this plant.

PROPAGATION Break off segments in spring and summer and insert the base into compost, where they will root readily.

KEEPING PLANTS Give the plant a spell outdoors in a sheltered, shady position in summer.

PLANT CARE

Bright filtered sunlight. ● Normal room temperatures, with a winter minimum of 10°C/50°F. Rest the plant in cool conditions after it has flowered for 2–3 weeks. ● Keep the compost moist while the plant is in bloom. For a month after flowering ceases, give just enough water to prevent the compost drying out completely; then increase the amount of water but allow the surface of the compost to dry out between waterings. ● Mist the foliage frequently. ● Apply a high-potash liquid fertiliser every 2 week s from the formation of the buds until flowering is over. Do not feed during the rest period, then give a balanced liquid feed every 4 weeks until flowering begins again.

RHODODENDRON SIMSII AND HYBRIDS
Ericaceae

Indian Azalea

Although they are popular and colourful flowering plants in winter and early spring, many of these hybrid azaleas do not survive in the home for more than one season. They flower best when the roots are restricted, so any plant you buy is likely to be relatively pot-bound. This means that watering has to be frequent to keep the roots constantly moist, a condition the plant requires.

Azalea hybrids make small, spreading shrubs with leathery, dark green, oval leaves that are usually covered in silky, silvery hairs. The stems are woody and bear small clusters of colourful flowers at their tips. The flowers are usually about 2.5cm/1in across and are often double or semi-double, although there are single varieties that have prominent golden stamens. Some varieties have strongly ruffled petals. Colours includes shades of white, pink and red, and some bicolours.

FACT FILE

ORIGIN China, Taiwan; hybrids.

HEIGHT To 60cm/2ft as a pot plant.

COMPOST Peat-based, ericaceous (lime-free) compost.

REPOTTING Pot up after flowering, every 2-3 years; plants flower best when slightly pot-bound. Clay pots are preferable for good drainage.

PROPAGATION Not practical in the home.

KEEPING PLANTS In summer, sink the pot in the soil in the shade outdoors to prevent it drying out and water regularly.

PLANT CARE

Bright light, but no direct sun. ● Cool conditions 10°–16°C/50°–60°F. ● Water copiously with lime-free water, but do not let the pot stand in water. ● Mist-spray the foliage frequently and stand the pot on a tray of moist gravel. ● Apply a high-potash liquid fertiliser every 2 weeks from spring to autumn and sequestered iron or a specialised plant food occasionally.

Hot, dry air causes the flower buds to turn brown and papery and fail to open: it will eventually kill the plant.

If the plant dries out, it may wilt dramatically, with limp leaves and flowers. But if you act fast, you can usually revive it by plunging the whole pot into water.

Yellow leaves with green veins indicate a lime-induced nutrient deficiency. Use a fertiliser specially for lime-hating plants. Make sure that acid compost has been used. Water plants with rainwater in hard-water areas.

RHOEO SPATHACEA 'VARIEGATA'
Commelinaceae

Boat Lily

Although this plant is now known as *Tradescantia spathacea* 'Vittata', it is generally offered in nurseries and garden centres as *Rhoeo spathacea* 'Variegata' and sometimes even *R. discolor*. It is, however, much less common than the well-known tradescantia (see page 144).

The long, fleshy, lance-shaped leaves grow in an erect or slightly spreading rosette from a short stem. The surface of the leaf is glossy green with yellow stripes along its length, and the underside is purple-red. At the base of the outer leaves, small, three-petalled, white flowers peep from within long-lasting, purple, boat-shaped bracts, giving rise to the plant's other common name, Moses in the cradle. Flowering may occur at any time of year.

Avoid draughts or fluctuating temperatures, which slow the plant's development.

The yellow stripes on the surface of the leaves become more pronounced in bright light, but the plant will tolerate a shady position.

Purple, boat-shaped bracts at the base of the leaves enclose numbers of small white flowers.

FACT FILE

ORIGIN West Indies, Mexico.

HEIGHT To 36cm/14in.

COMPOST Peat- or soil-based.

REPOTTING Repot in spring when roots fill the pot; usually 2–3 years.

PROPAGATION Remove offshoots, complete with a few roots, from the base of the plant and pot up individually. The plain-leafed form can be raised from seed.

KEEPING PLANTS Plants normally deteriorate after 4–5 years, but enough sideshoots should be produced to replace them regularly.

PLANT CARE

Moderate light with no direct sun. ● Minimum winter temperature 13°–16°C/55°–60°F; normal room temperature at other times. ● Keep the compost thoroughly moist throughout the growing season. Water less in winter; allow the top half of the compost to dry out between waterings. ● Mist the foliage frequently in summer and stand the pot on a tray of moist gravel. ● Feed with a balanced liquid fertiliser every 2 weeks in the growing season.

SAINTPAULIA SPP.
Gesneriaceae

African Violet

Saintpaulias are one of the most popular of all flowering indoor plants. Hundreds of cultivars have been bred from the species, and new varieties come on to the market each year.

Plants usually form a low-growing rosette of rounded, hairy leaves with lightly scalloped edges and long, fleshy leafstalks. Leaves are mid- to dark green, often with a bluish tinge, and the undersides and leaf stalks may be red. Small clusters of star- or violet-shaped flowers with a pronounced yellow eye are held on stems which rise above the foliage; they may appear throughout the year, often in great profusion.

Modern varieties include doubles and semi-doubles, and flowers with frilly-edged petals. Flower colours range from white and pale pink through all shades of violet and blue to rosy red; there are bicolours and flowers with a contrasting edge to the petals. The 'Chimera' strain has flowers with bold stripes in a variety of colours.

Less widely seen are the forms with variegated leaves. Some varieties are so striking that the flowers come a rather poor second to the foliage. There are also trailing varieties, with drooping stems, and miniature and micro varieties, some of which are only 5cm/2in across when in full flower.

FACT FILE

ORIGIN Tanzania; hybrids.

HEIGHT To 15cm/6in, depending on variety.

COMPOST Peat-based.

REPOTTING Repot in spring, when roots fill the pot. The plant flowers best when slightly pot-bound, so use a pot about one-third the diameter of the plant.

PROPAGATION Take leaf stem cuttings or divide large clumps in spring and summer.

KEEPING PLANTS African violets will last for many years provided their special requirements are met.

Varieties with frilled petals, such as the large-flowered, pale pink 'Marguerite', are among the most attractive saintpaulia hybrids for use in the home.

PLANT CARE

A bright position with no direct sunlight. Filtered winter sunlight or additional fluorescent lighting in winter will encourage year-round flowering; position lights about 30cm/12in above the plants. ● An even temperature of 18°–24°C/65°–75°F. ● Water from below – moderately during the growing season – allowing the surface of the compost to dry out between waterings; water less in cooler winter temperatures. ● High humidity is essential, but the hairy leaves may be damaged by moisture. Stand the pot on a dish of moist gravel; spray foliage with a very fine mist only in warm conditions. ● Apply a dilute high-potash liquid fertiliser every 2 weeks when the plant is in flower and a standard liquid feed at other times.

ALSO RECOMMENDED

Among the best of the miniature hybrids, which seldom grow more than 13–15cm/5–6in across, are *Saintpaulia* 'Little Delight', with white flowers, edged with purple; 'Love Bug', with semi-double, deep red flowers; 'Pip Squeak', with tiny pale pink flowers, and 'Wee Hope', whose flowers are white with a blue centre.

Flower buds will not form when days are short, but extra artificial light from fluorescent tubes should promote winter flowering.

Remove damaged leafstalks and dead flower stalks by twisting them sideways to break off the entire stalk. Do not cut them.

Soft, brown spots on the leaves can be caused by moisture lying on the foliage or by sun falling directly on the plant.

Fluffy, grey mould seen on dying flowers and leaves is botrytis, a fungus disease which starts on dead tissue. It is worst in cold, moist conditions. Remove all dead and damaged parts and move the plant to a slightly warmer position.

Use a long-spouted can to water the plant under the rosette of foliage, or stand the pot in water for 30 minutes. Overwatering will cause the leaves to rot at soil level.

SANSEVIERIA TRIFASCIATA 'LAURENTII'
Agavaceae

*M*OTHER-IN-LAW'S TONGUE

This sansevieria is a popular house plant, well known for its longevity and tolerance of neglect. The fleshy leaves, which grow in a rosette from a thick rhizome, are sword-shaped, sharply pointed, stiff and very tall; they are deep green, with horizontal bands of lighter grey-green in a pattern which gives the plant its other common name of snakeskin, or snake, plant. The margins of 'Laurentii', which is the variety most commonly seen, are deep golden yellow. Sprays of small creamy white flowers appear only occasionally.

The second type of sansevieria is quite different. It is low-growing and forms a rosette of leaves that lie close to the surface of the compost, seldom growing taller than 15–20cm/6–8in.

FACT FILE

ORIGIN South Africa.

HEIGHT To 60cm/2ft.

COMPOST Soil-based.

REPOTTING Move in spring, only when the roots become too congested in the pot – sometimes they will even crack it. Use a clay pot to provide a stable base for the tall leaves.

PROPAGATION Divide the clump, or separate offsets from the base of the plant, using a sharp knife to cut through the rhizome, and pot them up individually. Otherwise cut a leaf into 5-cm/2-in strips and push these, right way up, into a mixture of soil-based compost and coarse sand in a ratio of 2:1. The new plants will not have the golden leaf margins of the parent.

KEEPING PLANTS Sansevieria grows slowly and will last for many years.

PLANT CARE

Bright light; this plant enjoys full sun.
● A minimum winter temperature of 13°C/55°F; average to warm room temperature at other times.
● Water moderately during the growing season; allow the top 2.5cm/1in of the compost to dry out between waterings. Give just enough water in winter to prevent the compost from drying out. Do not splash water into the centre of the rosette of leaves, as it will cause them to rot. ● Apply a balanced liquid fertiliser every 4 weeks in the growing season.

ALSO RECOMMENDED

Sansevieria trifasciata 'Hahnii' forms a low-growing, compact, rather spreading rosette, with the relatively broad leaves reaching only about 15cm/6in long.
S.t. 'Golden Hahnii' has broad yellow leaf margins and stripes on the mid-green leaves. The silvery leaves of *S.t.* 'Silver Hahnii' are mottled with dark green.

Yellow leaves may be caused by rotting at the base of the plant, which is nearly always a symptom of overwatering.

Do not repot plants until the clumps of stems are virtually bursting out of their pots.

A heavy, fairly wide container is necessary to balance the tall top growth, otherwise the plant will topple over frequently, particularly in winter, when the compost must be kept fairly dry.

Sansevieria trifasciata tends to sport, or deviate from the usual type, so many different cultivars exist; this is S.t. 'Craigii', *a mutant of* 'Laurentii'.

SAXIFRAGA STOLONIFERA
Saxifragaceae

Mother of Thousands

This plant is ideal for a hanging pot, since its main feature of interest is the large number of baby plantlets it produces at the tips of long, slender runners. The rounded leaves, with lightly scalloped edges, are covered with silvery hairs. They are deep olive green on top, with a network of silver veins, while the undersides and leafstalks are wine red. The variety 'Tricolor' has smaller leaves with an irregular, white, pink-flushed margin, and is slower growing.

Plantlets grow on fine, thread-like, red stolons which can be 60cm/2ft or more long, and are generally produced in abundance. The plantlets root easily wherever they touch the compost and soon form a dense mat if allowed to do so. Small, white star-shaped flowers with rather lopsided petals are carried on long spikes in late summer.

The red flush to the foliage is most pronounced when plants are grown in bright light, but shade the leaves from strong, direct sunlight.

Hang the pot in a well-ventilated position, but out of draughts.

The way the plants produce long runners, plus their rather geranium-like leaves, have given them an alternative common name of strawberry geranium.

FACT FILE

ORIGIN East Asia.

HEIGHT To 20cm/8in; stolons trail to 60cm/2ft.

COMPOST Soil-based.

REPOTTING In spring, move into a larger pot if roots are overcrowded.

PROPAGATION Peg down plantlets into pots of compost, where they will quickly form roots; they can be separated from the parent before or after they have rooted.

KEEPING PLANTS Replace plants with young plantlets after 2–3 years.

PLANT CARE

Bright light, with some direct, but not very strong, sun to maintain leaf colouring. ● Cool conditions – 10°–16°C/50°–60°F; a minimum winter temperature of 7°C/45°F. ● Keep the compost moist during the growing season. In winter, water just sufficiently to prevent the compost drying out. ● In a warm position, stand the pot on a dish of moist gravel to increase humidity. Spray foliage occasionally with a fine mist – do not allow drops of water to remain on the leaves.
● Apply a balanced liquid fertiliser every 4 weeks in spring and summer.

SCHEFFLERA ARBORICOLA
Araliaceae

Umbrella Tree

Now available in a wide range of varieties, *Schefflera arboricola* is also known as *Heptapleurum arboricolum*. It forms a slender tree shape, the upright stem bearing fingered leaves with eight or so 10–15-cm/4–6-in-long oval leaflets which are carried in a circle on leafstalks up to 15cm/6in long. The leaflets near the top of the circle are usually smaller than those at the base. If a tall plant is required, support the stem with a moss pole; aerial roots are produced on mature plants, and these can be inserted into the moss. *S. actinophylla*, syn. *Brassaia actinophylla*, has more leaflets on longer stalks. These leaflets are darker green and can be as much as 30cm/12in long.

FACT FILE

ORIGIN Southeast Asia.

HEIGHT To 1.8m/6ft; more usually 90cm/3ft in the home.

COMPOST Peat-based.

REPOTTING Repot in spring, when roots show through the drainage holes in the base of the pot. A large, unpinched plant will do better in a heavy clay pot to balance the top growth and give extra stability.

PROPAGATION Take stem tip cuttings in spring and summer.

KEEPING PLANTS Clean the large glossy leaves with a damp sponge.

PLANT CARE

Bright light with some direct sun except in midsummer. ● Normal room temperature, with a winter minimum of 13°C/55°F. ● Keep the compost moist but not wet in the growing season. Let the surface of the compost dry out between waterings in winter. ● Mist the plant regularly and stand the pot on a saucer of moist gravel to increase humidity. ● Give a balanced liquid fertiliser every 2 weeks while the plant is in active growth.

Sponge the leaves with lime-free water every 2–3 weeks to remove the dust.

Pinch out the growing tips to produce a bushy, branching plant; an unstopped specimen will quickly become tall and need support.

The leafstalks are normally semi-erect, but will droop if the plant is allowed to dry out. Keep the compost moist, but not waterlogged, from spring to autumn.

SCHLUMBERGERA × *BUCKLEYI*
Cactaceae

CHRISTMAS CACTUS

The Christmas cactus is sometimes known as zygocactus, and is related to the Easter cactus, rhipsalidopsis. It is a forest cactus, valuable for its freely produced, colourful winter flowers.

It has flattened stems composed of segments, which have sharply toothed margins and small areoles surrounded by brownish bristles. New segments arise from the tips of existing ones, so that eventually arching stems are produced. Flowers are borne at the tips of the stems in winter or early spring; despite the common name, most varieties flower naturally rather later than Christmas in the northern hemisphere. The flowers are tubular, about 5cm/2in or more long, with layers of swept-back petals and prominent stamens. They are generally magenta or rosy red; new varieties are constantly being bred.

Schlumbergera × *buckleyi*, also known as *S. bridgesii*, is a hybrid between *S. truncata* and *S. russelliana*.

FACT FILE

ORIGIN Hybrid.

HEIGHT To 60cm/2ft, with a similar spread.

COMPOST Peat-based, with added coarse sand.

REPOTTING Repot every year, after the rest period, when the roots are showing through the drainage holes in the base of the pot.

PROPAGATION Segments root readily in peat-based cuttings compost.

KEEPING PLANTS Move to a sheltered, shaded position outdoors during the summer months to promote flowering the following winter.

PLANT CARE

Bright light but no direct sun in summer; some winter sun. ● Normal room temperature, with a cooler rest period after flowering and a spell outdoors in summer. ● Keep the compost always moist when the plant is growing; after flowering, water sparingly for 8 weeks until new growth begins in spring, then increase watering. ● Mist the plant regularly and stand the pot on a dish of moist gravel. ● Apply a high-potash liquid fertiliser every 2 weeks during the growing season.

ALSO RECOMMENDED

Schlumbergera truncata, known as claw or crab cactus, is a parent of many of the hybrid schlumbergeras. It has deeply indented edges to the stem sections, with pointed 'claws' at the ends – hence its common names – and bears large flowers with reflexed petals in the autumn.

Schlumbergera truncata, *the crab cactus, has flowers that vary in shape and may be white, almost any shade of red or pink, and bicoloured.*

The leaf segments have smoothly scalloped margins.

Although this plant is a cactus, its home is in humid forests, rather than deserts, so it needs quite different growing conditions to other cacti. Mist the plant regularly, preferably with lime-free water, to maintain humidity.

Flowers are normally freely produced from year to year, but they will probably appear later in the season than when the plant was acquired.

SCINDAPSUS AUREUS **see** *EPIPREMNUM AUREUM*

SEDUM MORGANIANUM
Crassulaceae

DONKEY'S TAIL

The sedum family is vast and includes many hardy outdoor plants as well as subjects suitable for the home. *Sedum morganianum* is one of the most popular of the indoor types. It is easy to grow and makes an excellent plant for a hanging pot. The long, trailing stems are covered with overlapping, fleshy pale green leaves with a grey-white bloom, each about 2.5cm/1in long and pointed-cylindrical in shape. A well-grown plant will completely cover the pot with a dense mound of stems. Small pink flowers are occasionally produced from the stem tips.

Sometimes the closely related *S. burrito* is available. This is a very similar plant, though the stems do not trail quite as pronouncedly and the leaves are rounder and more bean-shaped. It is easier to handle than *S. morganianum*, since the leaves are not so fragile.

FACT FILE

ORIGIN Mexico.

HEIGHT Stems trail to 60cm/2ft.

COMPOST Soil-based, with added coarse sand.

REPOTTING In spring, when the plant fills the pot, move into a shallow pan or half-pot one size larger.

PROPAGATION Take stem tip cuttings in spring and summer; remove the lower leaves to expose the stem and insert it in sandy compost.

KEEPING PLANTS Handle *S. morganianum* carefully so that leaves do not fall off and cause unsightly gaps on the stems.

PLANT CARE

Bright light with some direct sun; shade from strong summer sunshine. ● Keep reasonably cool in winter, with a minimum of 7°C/45°F; normal room temperature at other times. ● Water moderately during the growing season; allow the top 13mm/½in of the compost to dry out between waterings. Water sparingly in winter. ● Feed occasionally with a balanced liquid fertiliser; regular feeding is not necessary.

If leaves are shrivelled, wrinkled and dull looking, check whether the compost is too dry. A large plant may need repotting.

Plants whose stems cover the compost completely may be difficult to water from the top. Be careful not to saturate the compost when watering from below: overwatering will cause the stems to rot at the base.

SELAGINELLA KRAUSSIANA
Selaginellaceae

SPREADING CLUBMOSS

This prostrate, mossy plant has tiny, bright green leaves on creeping, branching stems and quickly forms a dense mat. Since selaginellas like humid conditions, they are most frequently grown in bottle gardens or terraria, but care must be taken that they are kept under control. The variegated and gold varieties grow rather more slowly than the plain-leafed type. Also popular is a rather different selaginella – *Selaginella lepidophylla*, the resurrection plant. This is bought when completely dry and rolled into a ball; it can be 'resurrected' to a fresh green rosette by soaking it in water, and is a favourite with children.

Plants can be grown in pots indoors provided they are not in a draught and are misted frequently with tepid water.

Dry air and draughts will quickly lead to the leaves becoming brown and shrivelled. A terrarium or bottle garden provides the most suitable growing conditions for this plant.

The creeping stems root as they grow to form a spreading mat.

FACT FILE

ORIGIN South Africa.

HEIGHT Prostrate.

COMPOST Peat-based, with added coarse sand.

REPOTTING Repot annually in spring in a shallow pan, until a pot size of 13–15cm/5–6in is reached.

PROPAGATION Take stem tip cuttings in spring.

KEEPING PLANTS Using sharp nail scissors, cut the stems back by up to half in spring when necessary to prevent the plant becoming too large.

PLANT CARE

Moderate light or light shade, with no direct sun. ● Normal room temperature is suitable, but maintain a steady temperature at all times. ● Water thoroughly to keep the compost constantly moist, but do not let the plant stand in water. ● Spray the plant daily with lukewarm water unless it is in a terrarium or bottle garden. ● Apply half-strength standard liquid fertiliser every 4 weeks.

SENECIO × HYBRIDUS (SYN. PERICALLIS × HYBRIDUS)
Compositae

CINERARIA

Colourful, short-term flowering plants, cinerarias are especially popular in midwinter, although the main flowering season lasts until mid-spring. The large, hairy, coarse leaves are light green and roughly heart-shaped. Flowers may be single, semi-double or double and are carried on long stalks above the foliage in dense, rounded heads up to 20cm/8in across. They are daisy-like, with many petals and, usually, yellow centres, but the centres may match the petal colour. The wide colour range includes shades of blue, purple, pink and red. Many varieties have a white band around the central eye; in some this is so pronounced that the petals appear white with coloured tips.

A variety of forms in different sizes is available. The tallest, belonging to the Stellata group, reach a height of 60–76cm/24–30in and have markedly star-shaped flowers that grow in loose clusters. Plants of the Multiflora strain grow to 38–46cm/15–18in and have rounded flower heads, tightly packed with flat, daisy-like flowers. Those of the Multiflora Nana group also have dense rounded flower heads, but the plants are more compact, barely reaching 30cm/12in in height. When buying, look for plants with just a few flowers open and plenty of buds to follow, as in the plant shown here. *Senecio × hybridus* is also known as *S. cruentus* and *Pericallis cruentus* and may be sold as such.

FACT FILE

ORIGIN Hybrid.

HEIGHT To 60cm/2ft depending on variety. Many plants are artificially dwarfed with growth-regulating compounds.

COMPOST Peat-based.

REPOTTING Not necessary.

PROPAGATION Sow seed, usually available in mixed colour ranges, in summer to produce plants to flower the following winter.

KEEPING PLANTS Discard the plant once the flowers have faded.

PLANT CARE

Bright light, with some direct sun. ● Keep the plant cool – preferably at a temperature of around 10°C/50°F – to prolong flowering. ● Water sufficiently to keep the compost just moist at all times. ● Feeding is not necessary.

ALSO RECOMMENDED

There is a lot of choice of different heights, flower size, profusion and season. 'Chloe' is a popular early-flowering strain; 'Brilliant' has restricted leaf growth and large flowers in intense colours; 'Cindy' can be sown in succession for a long flowering season.

The daisy-like flowers are available in a range of bright colours and bicolours.

Cinerarias are particularly prone to attack by aphids. Check young foliage and buds regularly and treat with contact insecticide when necessary.

Plants collapse dramatically if the compost is allowed either to dry out or to become waterlogged. Water carefully to keep the compost just moist.

Flower colours range from deep purple and cerise to pale pink and lavender blue, with many varieties having a white central ring on the petals.

SENECIO ROWLEYANUS
Compositae

*S*TRING-OF-BEADS

This unusual-looking foliage plant is quite different from its close relative, the bright-flowered cineraria. It is a creeping succulent with long slender stems that carry many tiny (5–12mm/^{1}/₅–^{3}/₈in) almost spherical leaves; it is these that give the plant its common name. Small white flower heads that look like shaving brushes are borne in spring.

Several other senecios make good house plants as well. Non-succulent *Senecio mikanioides*, German ivy, (also known as *Delairea odorata*) has mid- to dark green leaves about 8cm/3in long, which are carried alternately on long, trailing or twining stems. Each leaf has about seven lobes, the tips of which end in sharp points. Fragrant yellow groundsel-like flowers are sometimes borne in small clusters.

Senecio macroglossus, the wax vine, is a similar plant, but the leaves have between three and five lobes. The form most commonly seen is 'Variegatus', with irregular creamy yellow markings on a glossy, dark green background. The twining stems become woody with age.

FACT FILE

ORIGIN Namibia.

HEIGHT Trailing stems to 90cm/3ft.

COMPOST Soil-based, with coarse sand added in a ratio of 3:1.

REPOTTING Move into a larger pot in spring, when the plant fills the pot. A hanging pot allows the stems to trail gracefully.

PROPAGATION Take stem tip cuttings during spring and summer.

KEEPING PLANTS Flourishes under warm conditions, but flowers best after a cool early winter rest.

PLANT CARE

Bright light, with some direct sun except in midsummer. ● Warm conditions; a minimum of 10°C/50°F in winter. ● Keep the compost just moist during the growing season; allow the surface to dry out between waterings. Water only enough in winter to prevent the compost drying out completely. ● Apply a balanced liquid fertiliser every 2 weeks during the growing season.

Watch out for aphids, which attack new shoots in summer, and for red spider mites.

Pinch out shoot tips occasionally to keep the plant compact.

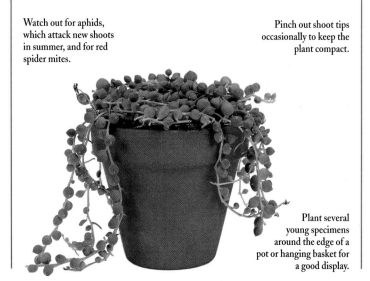

Plant several young specimens around the edge of a pot or hanging basket for a good display.

SETCREASEA PURPUREA
Commelinaceae

*P*URPLE HEART

Also known as *Tradescantia pallida* 'Purple Heart', this is the variety nearly always found, since it is a tolerant, easily grown house plant. The fleshy, succulent, jointed stems and the clasping, lance-shaped leaves are all a rich purple, set off in summer by three-petalled, bright purple-pink flowers that are produced in the leaf axils. Leaves are lance-shaped, about 10cm/4in long and 2.5cm/1in wide, and slightly hairy, the hairs giving them a glistening appearance.

The slender stems are about 40cm/16in long. They start upright but soon arch over the sides of the pot to trail, sometimes turning up slightly at the tips. This is an ideal plant for a hanging basket.

The fleshy, rather brittle foliage is quite delicate and easily damaged. Handle plants carefully, and do not place them where they will be brushed against.

Straggly stems with long gaps between the leaves may be a sign that the plant requires a brighter position, but it is natural for plants to become leggy after a few years.

Bright light, with a fair amount of direct sun, is essential for intense purple colouring in the leaves and stems.

FACT FILE

ORIGIN Mexico.

HEIGHT Stems trail to 60cm/2ft.

COMPOST Soil- or peat-based.

REPOTTING Move to a larger pot as soon as roots show through the drainage holes in the base.

PROPAGATION Stem tip cuttings taken in the spring and early summer root easily.

KEEPING PLANTS Replace plants with newly rooted cuttings when they become straggly, usually after 2 or 3 years.

PLANT CARE

Bright light. Some direct sun but protect the plant from strong midsummer sun. ● 18°–21°C/65°–70°F is the ideal growing temperature, with a minimum of 10°C/50°F or a little lower in winter. ● Keep the compost moist at all times; allow the surface to dry out slightly between waterings. ● Apply a balanced liquid fertiliser every 2 weeks during the growing season.

SINNINGIA SPECIOSA
Gesneriaceae

GLOXINIA

The brilliantly coloured, flaring, trumpet-shaped flowers of this familiar pot plant are extremely showy. Hybrids are more commonly found than the species. The large, 20-cm/8-in-long leaves are more or less oval in shape, and velvety, with short, dense hairs. They grow in opposite pairs on short stems arising from a tuber.

Flower buds emerge from the leaf axils in summer. The flowers, which are about 8cm/3in wide, are velvety and richly coloured. They may be red, pink, purple, blue or white; some are bicoloured or have a picotee edge. The long throats of the flowers are often of a contrasting shade to the flared petals; in some varieties, the petals or throat are densely spotted, giving the blooms the appearance of a foxglove.

'Princess Elizabeth' is blue with a white throat; 'Waterloo' is an intense scarlet. Seed-raised strains include the compact 'Glory' series, with flowers in blue, pink, red, and blue or red with a white edge. 'Brocade' has double flowers in blue, pink, red and red-and-white.

FACT FILE

ORIGIN Brazil; hybrids.

HEIGHT To 25cm/10in.

COMPOST Peat-based.

REPOTTING None.

PROPAGATION Sow seed in spring. Plants can also be grown from leaf cuttings taken in late spring and early summer.

KEEPING PLANTS After flowering, continue to feed the plant but water more sparingly until the leaves die down. Let the compost dry out and overwinter the tuber dry in its pot at about 10°C/50°F. In spring, repot in fresh compost with the dished tuber hollow side up. Water sparingly until new growth begins.

PLANT CARE

Bright light but no direct sun. ● Temperatures of 16°C/60°F or above in a draught-free place. ● Keep the compost moist, but do not overwater or allow water to lie in the hollow-surfaced tuber or the plant will rot. ● Apply a balanced liquid fertiliser every 2 weeks during the growing season.

Plants can be obtained as dormant tubers. Pot them up with the hollow surface upwards and set the tuber level with the surface of the compost.

Fluctuating temperatures and dry air may cause the flower buds to drop before they open.

Stand the pot on a tray of moist gravel to provide extra humidity, but do not mist the hairy foliage or the flowers.

SOLANUM CAPSICASTRUM
Solanaceae

FALSE JERUSALEM CHERRY

Two species of solanum are grown for their colourful winter berries, *Solanum capsicastrum* and *S. pseudocapsicum*. They are very similar and are often confused. *S. capsicastrum* makes a branching, twiggy plant with mid- to dark green, lance-shaped leaves. The leaf surface is slightly hairy and the leaf margins are gently waved. Small, starry white flowers with prominent stamens are carried in summer and are followed by round berries about 13mm/½in in diameter. These are green, turning pale green then white before ripening to orange-red. They are long lasting, remaining on the plant throughout most of the winter. *S. pseudocapsicum*, the winter or Christmas cherry, grows slightly taller, with larger, more brightly coloured berries. Dwarf forms are often offered.

The fruits of both plants may be attractive to young children, but they are poisonous and should not be eaten.

Aphids often infest the young shoots. Spray with a contact insecticide.

Hot, dry conditions will cause the berries to shrivel and fall prematurely.

Plants can be kept for a second year, but berries may fail to form. Ensure good flowering and berrying by placing the plant outside during the summer.

FACT FILE

ORIGIN Brazil.

HEIGHT To 46cm/18in; usually about 30cm/12in.

COMPOST Peat-based.

REPOTTING Move into a pot one size larger in late spring.

PROPAGATION Sow seed in early spring.

KEEPING PLANTS Once the berries have passed their best, reduce watering and cut the stems back by half. Repot the plant and place it in a sheltered, semi-shaded place outdoors when all danger of frost has passed. Bring it indoors in early autumn, before the first frost.

PLANT CARE

A bright position in direct sun. ● Cool conditions for the berries to last well, ideally a maximum of 16°C/60°F. ● Keep the compost moist at all times; reduce watering in spring. ● Stand the pot on a tray of moist gravel and mist the plant frequently while it is flowering. ● Apply a balanced liquid fertiliser every 2 weeks.

SPATHIPHYLLUM WALLISII
Araceae

PEACE LILY

Also sometimes known as white sails, the long-lived peace lily is useful as a dual-purpose plant, with attractive foliage as well as flowers; it also tolerates lower light levels than many plants. The glossy dark green leaves, produced directly from rhizomes, are strongly veined and lance-shaped. They are about 15cm/6in long and are carried on long stalks, which arch outwards elegantly. Arum-like flowers, which are produced during spring and early summer and sometimes into early autumn, rise above the foliage on stiff stems. The white, sail-like spathe surrounds a central spadix of creamy yellow. Flowers remain in good condition for several weeks, but once they are past their best the flower stalks should be cut off as close to the base as possible.

Most of the popular varieties are of hybrid origin. 'Mauna Loa', a vigorous cultivar with long leaves and large flowers, is perhaps the best known, but 'Cupido', 'Illusion', 'Petite' and 'Sensation' are also grown.

The white flower spathes turn pale green as they age and remain attractive for several weeks.

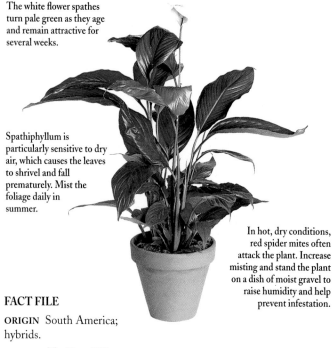

Spathiphyllum is particularly sensitive to dry air, which causes the leaves to shrivel and fall prematurely. Mist the foliage daily in summer.

In hot, dry conditions, red spider mites often attack the plant. Increase misting and stand the plant on a dish of moist gravel to raise humidity and help prevent infestation.

FACT FILE

ORIGIN South America; hybrids.

HEIGHT To 46cm/18in.

COMPOST Peat-based.

REPOTTING Move into a pot one size larger in spring until the maximum convenient pot size is reached; thereafter top-dress annually.

PROPAGATION Divide large clumps in spring; pull the rhizomes apart carefully, and pot up the sections individually.

KEEPING PLANTS Keep out of direct sun, which will scorch the foliage.

PLANT CARE

Bright, filtered light. ● Normal room temperature is suitable, with a minimum of 13°–16°C/55°–60°F. ● Keep the compost moist during the growing season, but allow the surface to dry out before rewatering. Reduce the amount of water in cool conditions. ● Stand the pot on a dish of moist gravel and mist the foliage frequently. ● Feed with a balanced liquid fertiliser every 2 weeks in spring and summer.

STEPHANOTIS FLORIBUNDA
Asclepiadaceae

MADAGASCAR JASMINE

The beautiful, overwhelmingly fragrant flowers of stephanotis make this a much-coveted plant, but it is not among the easiest to grow. It is a strong climber, usually sold twined around a wire hoop.

The slender, light green young stems soon turn woody; they bear glossy, dark green, oval, pointed leaves about 10cm/4in long in opposite pairs. The flowers are carried in clusters from spring through summer; they are waxy, white and tubular, opening into a five-petalled star about 3cm/1¼in across. One cluster of flowers is sufficient to perfume a whole room with a strong, intensely sweet fragrance. Stephanotis is also known as the wax flower.

FACT FILE

ORIGIN Madagascar.

HEIGHT To 4.5m/15ft or more, but usually kept to about 90cm/3ft.

COMPOST Soil-based or a mixture of soil- and peat-based.

REPOTTING Repot in spring, usually every 2 years, until a 20-cm/8-in pot is required.

PROPAGATION Take semi-ripe stem cuttings in summer, but these are not easy to root. Hormone rooting powder and a heated propagator improve the chances of success. Or sow seed in spring.

KEEPING PLANTS Flowers are carried on new growth, so cut out old stems in winter and tie in young shoots as they form.

PLANT CARE

Bright light, but shade from direct midsummer sun. ● Evenly warm, draught-free conditions, ideally 18°–21°C/65°–70°F, with a minimum of 13°C/55°F in winter. ● Keep the compost moist at all times in the growing season, but do not allow the plant to stand in water. In winter, let the top half of the compost dry out between waterings. ● Mist the foliage regularly and stand the pot on a dish of moist gravel. ● Apply dilute high-potash liquid fertiliser every 2 weeks in spring and summer.

The fragrant, waxy, white flowers are popular for bridal bouquets.

Buds will drop before opening in fluctuating temperatures or if the plant is moved to a different position or if the compost is allowed to dry out during the growing season.

Scale insects may be found on the undersides of the leaves. Remove any scales with a fingernail and treat the plant with an appropriate insecticide.

STREPTOCARPUS x *HYBRIDUS*
Gesneriaceae

*C*APE PRIMROSE

The foliage of the popular streptocarpus hybrids forms a rosette, with long, rather ungainly, wrinkled leaves like those of a primrose. Long flower stems arise from the rosette, carrying clusters of trumpet-shaped flowers in shades of red, pink, lavender, purple and white. The flowers have a rather velvety texture, and their throats are often striped or marked with a contrasting colour. Plants can be bought in bloom at virtually any time of the year.

The first popular hybrid, the violet-blue 'Constant Nymph', was introduced some 50 years ago. Since then, hundreds of varieties have been bred, giving improved flower colours and more compact foliage.

FACT FILE

ORIGIN South Africa.

HEIGHT To 25cm/10in.

COMPOST Peat-based.

REPOTTING Repot annually in spring.

PROPAGATION Divide large plants or take leaf cuttings in spring and insert them into a coarse mixture of equal parts of peat moss and perlite. Small plants will grow from the base of the leaf; when they are 5–8cm/2–3in high, pot them up individually.

KEEPING PLANTS In normal room temperature, the plant will grow all year round.

PLANT CARE

Bright light, but no direct sun. ● Average room temperature, with a minimum of 13°C/55°F in winter. ● Water moderately during the growing season to keep the compost just moist. In cooler winter temperatures, allow the top 13mm/½in of the compost to dry out before rewatering. ● Mist the foliage occasionally and stand the pot on a dish of moist gravel, particularly in warm conditions. ● Feed with a high-potash liquid fertiliser every 2 weeks while the plants are growing.

ALSO RECOMMENDED

Streptocarpus 'John Innes' hybrids have flowers and foliage similar to 'Constant Nymph', but the stems are slightly longer (about 20cm/8in). The range of colours includes pink, purple and deep blue. *S.* 'Wiesmoor' hybrids have larger leaves and as many as 5 flower stems on a plant; these are up to 30cm/12in long and carry 3–4 flowers, which can be 7.5cm/3in across. Colours range from dark red through pinks to blue, often with darker markings on the lower lobes of the trumpet.

Not all streptocarpus hybrids are large-flowered. Charming varieties, such as the dainty 'Falling Stars', have now been produced, which bear dozens of tiny flowers on semi-trailing stems.

Flowers are sometimes followed by interesting, long, spirally twisted seed pods, but dead flowers should, ideally, be removed before seed sets to avoid weakening the plant.

If the leaves suddenly become limp and droop, the plant may have been overwatered. Vine weevil grubs attacking the roots may also be responsible.

The plant will benefit from a fine mist spray over the foliage in the morning, but keep moisture off the flowers, since it can cause unsightly brown spots.

The strap-shaped leaves are brittle and easily damaged, so take care when handling the plant.

*S*UCCULENTS

These plants – of which cacti form probably the best-known group – are able to store water very efficiently, so they are well adapted to dry conditions. They usually have fleshy leaves or stems, or both: cacti are those plants that have fleshy stems and small leaves or no leaves. Succulents are generally easy to grow and tolerant of neglect, but they can easily be killed by overwatering. Unlike most house plants, the majority are happy on the brightest of sunny windowsills. They will withstand very hot conditions, and some can survive in a temperature as low as 7°C/45°F. They prefer cool conditions at night, and thrive in widely varying night and daytime temperatures.

There are two types of cacti, desert and jungle, but all are distinguished from other succulents by areoles, bumps or indentations on the stems that bear spines, bristles or hairs, and from which trumpet or bell-shaped flowers arise. Desert cacti have tiny leaves or no leaves. Their thick green stems conserve water and do the job of photosynthesis. Jungle cacti are mostly epiphytes; they grow in niches in trees and rocks that are often dry, hence their need for stems that can store water.

The plants known as succulents are not so easy to define. They do not all belong to a single family. Many families have some more or less succulent members, which store water in their leaves or have no leaves and store water in their stems. Others, such as several of the aloes, have little capacity to store water at all. The plants and their flowers differ widely in habit, shape and size.

Opuntia microdasys, the prickly pear cactus, with oval flattened pads, is a popular house plant. It tends to produce two new pads on the top of an existing one, giving it the appearance of a rabbit's head and the common name bunny ears. Outdoors they can be invasive and they are subject to strict controls in some countries.

Small, round tufts of yellow bristles grow symmetrically all over the pads. If the plant is touched, the bristles can break off and they irritate the skin; handle the plant with a folded newspaper when repotting it.

Opuntias flower and produce prickly fruits outdoors, but plants are unlikely to flower indoors.

ALSO RECOMMENDED

Crassula muscosa is a succulent with woody branches, hidden by a sheath of flat, pointed, grey-green leaves. It bears clusters of yellow-green flowers in summer.

Rhipsalis cereuscula originates in South America. It is a curious epiphytic cactus with two types of stem: long and cylindrical, and short, with branching clusters at the end. These clusters also branch and spread from the apex.

Schlumbergera truncata, crab cactus, is a forest cactus, so it likes shade and high humidity. The segmented stems have two forward-pointing 'claws', and pink and white flowers are borne on the tips in winter.

Black marks at the base of the stem, followed by rotting and the top growth toppling over, are caused by overwatering.

Brown, shrivelled patches on the pads often follow physical damage. Affected parts can be cut out and the exposed tissue treated with fungicidal powder to prevent the problem from spreading.

Mealybugs can be seen as patches of white, waxy wool on the surface of the pads. Remove them carefully with a cotton bud.

Slugs and some caterpillars, which seem impervious to the bristles, eat the stems, causing large holes.

Root mealybugs, a common pest of cacti, are difficult to control. Remove the plant from its pot and check for white, wooly bugs in the roots; if found, drench the roots with a solution of malathion.

Echinocactus grusonii, golden barrel cactus, is a desert plant. The strongly ribbed stem is covered with spines up to 5cm/2in long. In summer it bears yellow flowers.

Gymnocalycium mihanovichii 'Red Cap' is a cultivar. The coloured stem, which can be red, pink or yellow, lacks chlorophyll and cannot survive on its own, so it is grafted onto a green cactus stock.

FACT FILE

ORIGIN **Cacti:** the Americas. **Succulents:** mainly arid regions world-wide.

HEIGHT Varies according to species; *Opuntia microdasys* will grow to about 46cm/18in indoors.

COMPOST **Cacti and succulents:** soil-based with sharp sand or perlite added for good drainage, or special cactus compost.

REPOTTING In spring, when the soil is filled with roots, move the plant to a pot one size larger.

PROPAGATION Some cacti and succulents produce offsets around the base of the plant. In others, single segments can be removed for use as cuttings. Let the base of the cutting dry out for a day or two before inserting it into a sandy compost. Almost all can be raised from seed fairly easily.

KEEPING PLANTS Most cacti and succulents appreciate a spell outdoors in a sheltered but sunny position during summer.

PLANT CARE

Bright light to full sun (except jungle cacti in summer). ● Normal room temperature, with a minimum of 10°C/50°F for succulents and jungle cacti; desert cacti need a cool winter rest. ● Water all types fairly freely in the growing season, allowing the top 13mm/½in of soil to dry out between waterings. In winter give just enough water to prevent plants from shrivelling. ● Feed established plants with a balanced liquid fertiliser (20-20-20) every 2–3 weeks in the growing season.

PESTS & DISEASES

Succulents and cacti do not suffer from many pests. Mealybugs and root mealybugs are the most troublesome, although red spider mites may be a nuisance if the air become too dry. Many species are, however, susceptible to infection by fungi and bacteria – often as a result of overwatering – which causes the stems to rot.

TAKE CARE

Cacti spines and bristles irritate when lodged in the skin. Keep plants out of the reach of children.

SYNGONIUM PODOPHYLLUM
Araceae

ARROWHEAD PLANT

This plant is rather similar to a philodendron and makes a good climbing foliage specimen. The leaves start off more or less heart-shaped when young, gradually becoming arrowhead-shaped (hence the name), then lobed and divided into segments as the plant matures; it is also called the goosefoot plant. Different types of leaves are carried on the plant at one time, adding to its interest. Young plants make a spreading bush, with climbing stems developing later.

The most popular varieties have different patterns of pale green, white or cream marking the leaves. 'Butterfly' has deep green leaves with lighter veins, while 'White Butterfly' has leaves suffused with white or very pale green. 'Pixie' is a compact, small-leafed form.

FACT FILE

ORIGIN South America.

HEIGHT Climbs to 1.2m/4ft or more.

COMPOST Peat-based or soil-based with added peat.

REPOTTING Repot in spring, in a pot one size larger until a 30-cm/12-in pot is required, then top-dress annually.

PROPAGATION Take stem tip cuttings in early summer.

KEEPING PLANTS A moss pole makes an ideal support, since aerial roots are produced and can be encouraged to grow into the moss.

PLANT CARE

Bright light, especially for variegated types, but no direct sun.
● Normal room temperature, with a winter minimum of 16°C/60°F.
● Keep the compost moist in summer, allowing the surface to dry out before rewatering. Water less in winter; letting the top half of the compost dry out. ● Apply a balanced liquid fertiliser every 2 weeks during the growing season.

The leaves are usually variegated and change shape as the plant matures.

A bushy plant with juvenile foliage can be maintained by cutting out the climbing stems as soon as they form.

A hot, dry atmosphere may cause the foliage to shrivel and fall prematurely. Mist it regularly and stand the pot on a dish of damp pebbles.

The stems can be allowed to trail from a hanging basket instead of being trained up a moss pole.

THYMUS VULGARIS
Labiatae

WILD THYME

A strongly aromatic culinary herb, thyme is a useful plant to grow on a kitchen windowsill, especially in winter. *Thymus vulgaris*, common thyme, shown here, makes a small, wiry-stemmed, spreading shrub, with tiny, scented, deep green, pointed leaves carried in opposite pairs. Small, pale lavender flowers are borne near the tips of the stems in summer, but not usually on indoor plants. 'Silver Posie' has attractive silver-variegated leaves.

Creeping thyme, *T. serpyllum*, forms a creeping mat, and has a fragrance and flavour similar to common thyme. 'Aureus' has yellow foliage. There are a number of hybrids, including *T.* x *citriodorus*, lemon-scented thyme, which has a popular golden variegated version, 'Doone Valley'. The low-growing species are probably best for indoor culture. They are hardy plants and should be given a spell outdoors whenever possible. Pinching out the growing tips for use in cooking should help to keep the plants compact.

The low-growing stems of creeping thyme will cascade over the sides of a pot.

Thyme grown indoors tends to have softer leaves and stems and a less pungent flavour than that grown outdoors.

Variegation adds to the interest of the plant, but good light is necessary to maintain the leaf coloration.

FACT FILE

ORIGIN Mediterranean regions.

HEIGHT To 30cm/12in when grown in a pot indoors.

COMPOST Soil-based.

REPOTTING Repot as necessary in spring. Older thyme should be planted out in the garden; young specimens are best indoors.

PROPAGATION Take stem tip cuttings in early summer or sow seed in spring.

KEEPING PLANTS Place the plant outdoors in summer and keep it watered. Bring it inside again in autumn. When it becomes too large and straggly, replace it with a young plant.

PLANT CARE

Bright light, especially for variegated types, with several hours of direct sun. ● Moderately cool room temperature. ● Water well, allowing the plant to dry between waterings. Water sparingly in winter temperatures. ● Apply a balanced liquid fertiliser every 3 weeks during spring and summer.

TILLANDSIA IONANTHA
Bromeliaceae

*A*IR PLANT

These plants have become popular as novelty plants in recent years and are found in a wide range of outlets. *Tillandsia ionantha* is one of the most common. It is a small plant, forming a tight, upright-growing rosette of stiff, silver, pointed leaves. The extremely fine tips usually curl over to give the whole plant the appearance of a small sea anemone. In late spring, the centre of the rosette turns red just before small violet flowers appear. The silver sheen on the leaves comes from the tiny, soft, fur-like scales that cover the leaf surface and absorb moisture and nutrients from the atmosphere.

This tillandsia is an epiphyte, living not in soil but on the limbs of trees in its natural habitat. Like an epiphytic orchid, it can be grown in an open, free-draining compost of shredded bark or osmunda fibre, but it does best when mounted on wood or cork bark. Roots are usually produced to support the plant on its mount.

Mount this tillandsia on wood or bark to simulate the way it grows in its natural habitat. Ordinary potting compost will cause the base of the plant to rot.

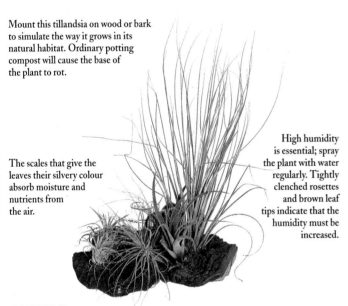

The scales that give the leaves their silvery colour absorb moisture and nutrients from the air.

High humidity is essential; spray the plant with water regularly. Tightly clenched rosettes and brown leaf tips indicate that the humidity must be increased.

FACT FILE

ORIGIN South and Central America.

HEIGHT To 10cm/4in with a similar spread.

COMPOST Wrap the roots or base of a mounted plant in damp sphagnum moss. The plant can also be grown in orchid compost.

REPOTTING Not necessary.

PROPAGATION Detach the offsets that appear around the base of a mature plant with some roots, and establish them separately.

KEEPING PLANTS Tillandsia needs a good circulation of air; plants will benefit from a spell in a sheltered position outdoors during summer.

PLANT CARE

Bright light, but not direct sun. ● Normal room temperature, with a minimum of 10°C/50°F. ● Mist the plant with water twice a week in summer, thoroughly wetting the leaves. In cooler, winter conditions, mist once a week or once every 2 weeks. ● Add a half-strength solution of high-potash liquid fertiliser to the misting water every week in spring and summer.

TOLMIEA MENZIESII
Saxifragaceae

*P*IGGYBACK PLANT

The main decorative feature of *Tolmiea menziesii* is the way in which young plantlets form at the base of the older leaves, giving the plant its common name; it is also sometimes known as mother of thousands and youth-on-age. The plant forms a mound of hairy, bright green, roughly heart-shaped leaves, which are lobed and have toothed margins. They are carried on long leafstalks, and where the leaf joins the stalk, small plantlets arise and eventually weigh the leaf down, inducing it to trail. The plantlets root where they touch the soil.

A yellow-splashed form, 'Variegata', also called 'Taff's Gold', which bears both variegated and plain leaves, is often grown. Tubular, greenish, rather insignificant flowers are occasionally borne in summer.

FACT FILE

ORIGIN Western North America.

HEIGHT To 25cm/10in; 38–50cm/15–20in in bloom.

COMPOST Peat- or soil-based.

REPOTTING Repot at any time, when roots fill the current pot.

PROPAGATION Detach leaves bearing well-developed plantlets and set them in a pot so that their base is in close contact with the compost; roots will soon form. Take off the parent leaf only when it has dried up.

KEEPING PLANTS Tolmieas are good in a hanging pot; put several young plants around the edge, and within 6 months they will cascade downwards gracefully, forming an attractive plant.

PLANT CARE

Bright light with some direct sun, but shade from extremely strong midsummer sun which will scorch the leaves. ● Cool room temperature, with a winter minimum of 7°C/45°F. ● Keep the compost moist throughout the growing season, watering more sparingly in winter. ● Mist the foliage occasionally. ● Feed with a balanced liquid fertiliser every 2 weeks during the growing season.

Brown, crisp, shrivelled leaves indicate that the atmosphere is too hot and dry. The plant needs regular misting in warm conditions.

Leaves become pale and leafstalks elongated when the plant is not receiving enough light. Move it to a brighter position.

TRADESCANTIA FLUMINENSIS 'VARIEGATA'
Commelinaceae

*W*ANDERING JEW

A member of the same family as setcreasea and zebrina, tradescantia is perhaps the best known of the group; it is popular for its rapid growth, colourful foliage and tolerance of poor growing conditions. Most frequently called wandering Jew, it is also called spiderwort and speeding Jenny.

The plant produces long, fleshy stems set with succulent, clasping, alternate leaves about 5cm/2in long. These are light green, striped with cream, and have pale purple undersides. Small, three-petalled white flowers with a fluffy central boss of stamens are sometimes produced on well-grown plants. Another common variety is the fast-growing *Tradescantia fluminensis* 'Quicksilver', which has white-striped leaves.

FACT FILE

ORIGIN South America.

HEIGHT Stems trail to 60cm/2ft.

COMPOST Peat-based.

REPOTTING Repot in spring, when the current pot is filled with roots. Put several rooted cuttings in the same pot for the best effect.

PROPAGATION Take stem tip cuttings, which can be rooted readily at almost any time of year except in midwinter.

KEEPING PLANTS Pinch out the growing tips to create a bushy plant. After a few years, when older leaves fall, leaving bare stems, replace the plant with young rooted cuttings.

PLANT CARE

Bright light with some direct sun for good leaf coloration. ● Average room temperature, with a minimum of 7°C/45°F. ● Water freely during the growing season, keeping the compost moist at all times. In winter, allow the top 2.5cm/1in of compost to dry out before rewatering. ● Mist the foliage occasionally in warm weather. ● Apply a balanced liquid fertiliser every 2 weeks during the growing season.

Pinch out the tips of shoots regularly for a bushy plant.

Remove any all-green shoots from variegated plants. The stronger-growing green shoots will soon take over if they are allowed to do so.

Pinch out growing tips regularly and replace old straggly plants with newly rooted cuttings.

TRADESCANTIA PALLIDA see *SETCREASEA PURPUREA*
TRADESCANTIA SPATHACEA see *RHOEO SPATHACEA*
TRADESCANTIA ZEBRINA see *ZEBRINA PENDULA*

VRIESEA SPLENDENS
Bromeliaceae

*F*LAMING SWORD

Probably one of the easiest bromeliads to grow (see pages 48–49), this vriesea makes a rosette of stiff, arching leaves about 30cm/12in long; these are dark green with purple-brown horizontal bands. A tall flower spike, topped with a series of flattened, bright scarlet bracts, grows from the centre of the rosette. The yellow flowers which emerge from the bracts are short-lived, but the colourful bracts persist for several weeks.

Many vriesea hybrids have been bred to provide colourful flowering indoor plants. Among them are *Vriesea* x *poelmannii* 'White Line', with glossy green leaves which have a broad central yellow stripe; 'Marjan', with yellow bracts flushed red at the base; and 'Margot', with deep green leaves and a branching flower spike.

The brilliantly coloured, sword-like flower spike may be produced at almost any time of year.

It is natural for the main rosette to die back after flowering. Offshoots at the base can be allowed to replace it, but they will not reach flowering size for 2 or 3 years.

When buying plants, look for specimens where the flower spike is only just emerging from the rosette of leaves.

Dull, speckled leaves may have been attacked by red spider mites: look for webbing under the arching tip. Provide high humidity to help prevent infestation.

FACT FILE

ORIGIN Tropical America.

HEIGHT To 60cm/2ft.

COMPOST Peat-based.

REPOTTING Repot in spring, only when the compost is filled with roots; usually every 2–3 years.

PROPAGATION Detach basal offsets carefully with a sharp knife, retaining as much root as possible, and pot them up individually.

KEEPING PLANTS After flowering, the rosette dies back, but offsets are produced around the base of the plant to replace it.

PLANT CARE

Bright light with some direct sun, but protect plants from strong midsummer sun which may scorch the leaves. ● Average room temperature with a winter minimum of 10°C/50°F. ● Keep the compost only just moist at all times and the central 'vase' in the rosette of leaves filled with water. ● Mist the foliage occasionally in warm weather. ● Apply a half-strength solution of balanced liquid fertiliser through the central 'vase' every 4 weeks in the growing season.

YUCCA ELEPHANTIPES
Agavaceae

$\mathcal{S}$*PINELESS YUCCA*

Yuccas are good architectural plants, tolerant of a wide range of conditions. *Yucca elephantipes* is usually available as a stout, woody trunk with one or two rosettes of long, sword-shaped, pointed leaves at the top. The edges of these leaves are toothed but spineless, and the leaves themselves are much softer than other indoor yuccas such as the spiky *Y. aloifolia* (known with good reason as Spanish bayonet), making them safer plants where there are children. The leaves arch downwards and can reach 1.2m/4ft in length. Plants are also available as a stemless or short-stemmed rosette in a pot. The panicles of creamy, bell-shaped flowers are not produced on indoor plants.

Several variegated varieties are available, including 'Silver Star', 'Jewel' and 'Variegata'.

FACT FILE

ORIGIN Mexico.

HEIGHT Varies according to the length of the prepared 'trunk'; usually 1.2–1.8m/4–6ft.

COMPOST Soil-based.

REPOTTING Repot in spring, when the current pot is filled with roots. When maximum convenient pot size is reached, top-dress annually.

PROPAGATION Basal offsets are sometimes produced and can be removed and potted up individually.

KEEPING PLANTS The plant will benefit from standing outdoors in summer in a sheltered, sunny spot.

PLANT CARE

Bright light with plenty of direct sun. ● Normal room temperature, with a winter minimum of 10°C/50°F. ● Keep the compost moist during the growing season. In winter, give just enough water to prevent the compost from drying out. ● Yuccas are fairly tolerant of dry air, but mist the foliage occasionally in warm weather. ● Feed with a balanced liquid fertiliser every 2 weeks in spring and summer.

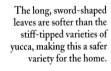

The long, sword-shaped leaves are softer than the stiff-tipped varieties of yucca, making this a safer variety for the home.

Plants may be produced either as a sawn-off trunk with one or two rosettes of leaves near the top, or as a single rosette in a pot.

Tall plants may topple over easily and should be potted in soil-based compost in a clay pot for extra stability.

ZEBRINA PENDULA
Commelinaceae

$\mathcal{S}$*ILVERY INCH PLANT*

A relative of tradescantia, and like tradescantia also sometimes called wandering Jew, *Zebrina pendula* is a fast-growing trailing plant with showy, glistening, colourful foliage.

The lance-shaped leaves are about 5cm/2in long, with the upper surface banded with green and silver (giving rise to its name of zebra plant) and purple undersides. The variety 'Quadricolor' has leaves striped with green, silver, purple and pink, while 'Purpusii', the bronze inch plant, has deep green leaves flushed with purple. Small, purple-pink, three-petalled flowers are carried in spring and summer.

Pinch out the growing tips regularly to prevent stems becoming straggly.

Brown, crisp tips and margins to the leaves indicate a hot, dry atmosphere; this will also encourage attack by red spider mites. Spray to increase humidity and deter the pests.

The glistening leaves and stems are fleshy and break easily if handled carelessly. Pinch out damaged shoots at a leaf node and use the top portion as a cutting.

Leaves may become dull or revert to all-green if they do not receive sufficient light.

FACT FILE

ORIGIN Mexico.

HEIGHT Stems trail to 90cm/3ft.

COMPOST Peat- or soil-based.

REPOTTING In spring, when roots fill the current pot, move to a pot one size larger. Plant several cuttings in a pot for the best effect. This is a good plant for a hanging basket or for training up a small trellis.

PROPAGATION Take stem tip cuttings, which will root readily in spring and summer.

KEEPING PLANTS The plant will last for several years; when it becomes leggy, replace it with newly rooted cuttings.

PLANT CARE

A bright, sunny position to ensure good leaf colour, although the plant is tolerant of shade. ● Normal room temperature, with a minimum temperature of 10°C/50°F in winter. ● Keep the compost moist at all times during the growing season. Reduce watering in winter and allow the surface to dry out before rewatering. ● Mist the foliage occasionally to increase humidity. ● Apply a balanced liquid fertiliser from time to time during spring and summer; the plant does not normally need regular feeding.

ACORUS GRAMINEUS
Araceae

$\mathcal{S}$WEET FLAG

The acorus most frequently grown as an indoor plant is the form with the variegated leaves of a water margin plant from China and Japan. Its fine, grass-like arching leaves grow from a thin rhizome running just below the surface of the compost. They are some 10cm/4in wide and 30cm/12in long, and are narrowly striped with white. An insignificant pale green flower spathe, which is almost indistinguishable from the leaves, is borne in summer.

The plant looks good on its own, but is perhaps better when grown in a bowl with several types of fleshy-leafed plants to provide a contrast.

FACT FILE

ORIGIN India, China, Japan.

HEIGHT To 30cm/12in.

COMPOST Soil-based.

REPOTTING In spring, when the clumps of leaves completely fill the surface of the compost, move into a pot one size larger.

PROPAGATION Divide overcrowded clumps in spring, and pot up individually, ensuring that a piece of rhizome is attached to each portion.

KEEPING PLANTS Plants will last for several years, provided they do not suffer from lack of water or air that is too dry.

Acorus gramineus

PLANT CARE
Bright light with some direct sunlight. ● Normal room temperature with a winter minimum of 4°C/40°F. ● Water daily or sit plant in a water-filled tray. The plant must never be allowed to dry out. ● Apply a standard liquid fertiliser to actively growing plants at 2-weekly intervals.

ADROMISCHUS FESTIVUS
(SYN. *A. COOPERI*)
Crassulaceae

$\mathcal{A}$DROMISCHUS

This is one of 50 species of small succulents that make good indoor plants, since their foliage is attractive all year round. It has thick, fleshy, spoon-shaped leaves, about 2.5cm/1in long and half as wide. The blue-green foliage is splashed with purple-brown blotches, and the edges of the leaves are curiously wavy, which makes them look almost like clam shells; this is particularly noticeable at the tips.

During the summer, the plant sometimes sends up thin, wiry stalks which bear insignificant bell-shaped reddish flowers 6mm/¼in long.

FACT FILE

ORIGIN South Africa (Western Cape).

HEIGHT To 13cm/5in.

COMPOST Soil-based, with added coarse sand for good drainage.

REPOTTING Repot in spring, when the plant has completely filled the current pot.

PROPAGATION Stem cuttings, leaf cuttings or offsets all root easily if taken in spring or summer.

KEEPING PLANTS This small plant will remain attractive for years, and will benefit from a spell outdoors in warm summer weather.

PLANT CARE
Bright, with some direct sunlight. ● Average room temperature from spring to autumn, with a minimum winter temperature of 4°C/40°F. ● Water well during the growing season; allow the compost to dry out between waterings at other times. ● Do not mist the leaves. ● Feeding is not critical; feed plants once or twice in spring and summer with a standard liquid fertiliser. Do not feed newly potted plants for a year. ● Check the plant carefully from time to time for scale insects and mealybugs, which both attack it.

Agapanthus africanus

AGAPANTHUS AFRICANUS
Alliaceae

$\mathcal{A}$FRICAN LILY

This evergreen plant has smooth, lance-shaped leaves, and it produces tall, succulent flowering stems all summer long. The individual flowers are 4cm/1½in long and are borne in a rounded cluster at the top of the stem, giving a large inflorescence. As indoor plants, they are best suited to the conservatory or sunroom.

Agapanthus africanus albus has flower heads of pure white, while the flowers of the Headbourne Hybrids may be blue or white. This is a group of hardy hybrids of garden origin which make excellent large pot plants.

FACT FILE

ORIGIN South Africa.

HEIGHT To 60cm/2ft or more.

COMPOST Soil-based.

REPOTTING Move to a larger pot only when the container is filled with roots or when the plant is divided.

PROPAGATION Divide in spring every 4–5 years. Plants grown from seed may take 2–3 years to flower.

KEEPING PLANTS Agapanthus will benefit from a period outdoors in the summer after flowering.

PLANT CARE
Full sun is essential. ● Average room temperature, with a minimum of 4°C/40°F in winter. ● Keep the compost moist at all times in the growing season; water less in winter. ● Apply a standard liquid fertiliser every 2 weeks in spring and summer.

AGATHAEA COELESTIS **see** *FELICIA AMELLOIDES*

ALBIZIA JULIBRISSIN
Leguminosae

*S*ILK TREE

In mild climates, this plant grows into a large shrub or small tree, with smooth pale greyish brown bark, and produces fluffy, globular heads of tiny pink flowers. When grown in a pot indoors, it is unlikely to flower, and is most often grown for its ferny leaves with oblong 6–13-mm/$\frac{1}{4}$–$\frac{1}{2}$-in-long leaflets. Seeds can be sown in early spring, and the resultant seedlings can be grown on and kept for a year.

FACT FILE

ORIGIN Asia, from Iran to Japan; naturalised in eastern and southern states of the USA.

HEIGHT To 46cm/18in indoors, to 6m/20ft in the garden.

COMPOST Soil-based, with added coarse sand for good drainage.

REPOTTING Every second year, in late winter or early spring, move into a pot one size larger.

PROPAGATION Sow seeds in early spring. Alternatively, take 10-cm/4-in stem cuttings in summer, using hormone rooting powder.

KEEPING PLANTS Prune back to 5 or 6 buds in spring to control the size of the plant and to prevent the lower stems from becoming bare. Albizia is best treated as a fairly short-term indoor plant and discarded after 2 or 3 years.

Albizia julibrissin

Amaryllis belladonna

PLANT CARE
Direct sunlight, with shelter from hot midday sun. ● A minimum winter temperature of 7°–10°C/45°–50°F. ● Water liberally while the plant is in active growth, give less in autumn and water sparingly in winter. ● Feed every 2 weeks during the growing period with a weak liquid fertiliser.

AMARYLLIS BELLADONNA
Amaryllidaceae

*B*ELLADONNA LILY

This is the only species in this genus and it is related to *Hippeastrum*. The bulb is large and produces a hollow, pale green flower stem up to 60cm/2ft long in late summer or early autumn. At the top it carries an umbel 10–13cm/4–5in wide, consisting of 6 to 12 sweetly scented trumpet-shaped flowers on short stalks. The flowers range in colour from pink to cerise and, occasionally, white.

The long strap-shaped leaves appear after the flower stalk and remain on the plant throughout the early summer

following blooming; they should not be removed until they have died back naturally and are completely withered. The plant has a short rest period in midsummer.

FACT FILE

ORIGIN South Africa.

HEIGHT To 60cm/2ft.

COMPOST Soil-based with added leaf mould and sand for good drainage.

REPOTTING Repot when dormant, only if necessary. Amaryllis flowers best when pot-bound.

PROPAGATION Divide established clumps or remove offsets from the base of the plant when dormant and pot them up individually. They will take up to 3 years to flower well.

KEEPING PLANTS This plant is best grown in a large container in which it can remain for 5 or 6 years without disturbance.

PLANT CARE
Bright light with full sun; protect from the sun when in flower. ● Minimum temperature of 4°–7°C/40°–45°F. ● Water plentifully while the plant is in growth; water less as leaves fade; keep quite dry in the rest period. ● Feed once a month with a balanced liquid fertiliser.

ANTHURIUM CRYSTALLINUM
Araceae

CRYSTAL ANTHURIUM

Known also as the strap flower, this plant is grown solely for its decorative foliage: the heart-shaped leaves are attached to 43-cm/ 17-in petioles and can be 38cm/15in long and 30cm/12in wide. When young, they are violet coloured and metallic looking, turning a deep emerald green as they age, with the principal lateral veins and prominent midrib etched in shining silver. Between mid-spring and early autumn, green flower spathes about 9cm/3½in long appear, but they are quite insignificant.

FACT FILE

ORIGIN Colombia, Peru.

HEIGHT To 46cm/18in.

COMPOST Peat-based, with added leaf mould or sphagnum moss; good drainage is essential.

REPOTTING In spring, move into a pot one size larger every third year until maximum desired pot size is reached; top-dress thereafter.

PROPAGATION Divide the plant at repotting time; keep in humid conditions.

KEEPING PLANTS Cover aerial roots, which emerge from the stem, with sphagnum moss or insert them into the damp compost.

PLANT CARE

A light position out of direct sun in winter; shadier in summer. ● Minimum winter temperature of 16°C/60°F; otherwise, normal room temperature. ● Keep the compost moist at all times. ● Mist leaves daily in summer. ● Apply a weak liquid fertiliser every 2 weeks from early spring to late summer.

~

ARISTOLOCHIA ELEGANS
(SYN. *A. LITTORALIS*)
Aristolochiaceae

CALICO FLOWER

A jungle plant originally from Brazil, this vigorous, slender climber is capable of attaining 6m/20ft in a conservatory, but can easily be kept smaller for use in the home. The heart-shaped leaves are smooth green above and grey-green beneath, and are about 8cm/3in wide. The flowers, which appear in summer and autumn and are carried on long stalks, take the form of shallow heart-shaped bowls of deep black-purple with green-yellow marbling.

In nature, aristolochias are pollinated by flies, so the flowers are generally foul-smelling in order to attract their pollinators. Although the flowers of *Aristolochia elegans*

lack the unpleasant smell typical of many other plants of this genus, the leaves when crushed are fetid smelling.

The calico plant is also known as birthwort, although its relative *A. clematis* is the plant that has been used to relieve the pain of women in childbirth.

Aristolochia elegans

FACT FILE

ORIGIN Brazil.

HEIGHT To 6m/20ft.

COMPOST Soil-based with added peat.

REPOTTING Move to a pot one size larger when roots fill the current pot.

PROPAGATION In autumn, sow seed when ripe, or take cuttings in spring and raise them in a warm propagator.

KEEPING PLANTS The plant can become unmanageable, so provide support for the climbing stems and prune it to shape in late winter or early spring.

PLANT CARE

Full sun or partial shade. ● Cool to average room conditions, with a winter minimum of 16°C/60°F. ● Water sparingly in winter, and plentifully at other times. ● Apply a weak liquid fertiliser every 2 weeks when in active growth.

ARUNDINARIA VIRIDISTRIATA
(SYN. *PLEIOBLASTUS AURICOMA*)
Gramineae

BAMBOO

Several of the bamboos make excellent, long-lived specimen plants in a large container. They are especially useful for a sunroom or conservatory, or even a large hallway.

Arundinaria viridistriata is a particularly attractive species, with slender, hollow, purplish green canes, rising from creeping underground rhizomes. The narrow, oblong leaves, 5–15cm/2–6in long, are slightly hairy and are striped along their length in green and brilliant yellow. The thickly growing leafy stems of a mature plant create a feathery effect.

FACT FILE

ORIGIN Japan.

HEIGHT To 1.2m/4ft.

COMPOST Soil-based.

REPOTTING In spring, move into a pot a size larger, until maximum desired size is reached, then top-dress instead.

PROPAGATION Divide in spring; use younger sections from the edge of the clump.

KEEPING PLANTS Cut back old stems in early spring to encourage fresh young growth.

PLANT CARE

Bright light or indirect light. ● Normal room temperature, with a minimum of 7°C/ 45°F. ● Water freely in the period of active growth; keep the compost moist, but not waterlogged. ● Stand the pot on a tray of moist pebbles to maintain humidity. ● Apply a standard liquid fertiliser monthly between spring and autumn.

~

ASCLEPIAS CURASSAVICA
Asclepiadaceae

BLOOD FLOWER

A short-lived small shrub, this asclepias has lance-shaped leaves up to 15cm/6in in length, which are carried in pairs. The flowers, which appear in summer and autumn, are about 2cm/¾in wide and orange-red, with a deep yellow crown carrying the stamens; they are borne in umbels of 5 to 10.

The pod-like fruits contain seeds that are crowned by long silky hairs for wind dispersal. The blood flower can become invasive in gardens in warm climates, so take care when disposing of it.

This is a good plant for the conservatory which will do fairly well in the home.

FACT FILE

ORIGIN Tropical South America.

HEIGHT To 90cm/3ft.

COMPOST Soil-based, with added peat or leaf mould.

REPOTTING Move into a pot one size larger each spring. A better show is achieved if plants are set 3 to a pot.

PROPAGATION Sow seed in spring, or take cuttings of young growth in late spring or summer. **Caution:** Take care when handling cuttings, since the plant bleeds copious amounts of a poisonous latex when cut.

KEEPING PLANTS After flowering, cut back the plant by up to half. Asclepias tends to become straggly and leggy with age, so replace the plant every 2–3 years.

PLANT CARE

Bright light with full sun where possible. ● Cool to warm room conditions. ● Water plentifully when in growth. Reduce watering after flowering and allow a dry rest period for about 2 months during winter. ● Give a dilute liquid feed every 2 weeks from spring to autumn.

~

Asplenium bulbiferum

ASPLENIUM BULBIFERUM
Aspleniaceae

*M*OTHER SPLEENWORT

Also known as the parsley fern and the hen and chickens fern, this plant produces much-divided, mid-green fronds, rather like carrot leaves, in a rosette shape. They grow on wiry black stalks. Tiny brown bulbils are borne near the tips of the fronds, and these develop into miniature replicas of the parent plant. This asplenium grows naturally in rain forests and requires high humidity indoors. The roots are fine and densely packed; a pot-bound plant will develop a deep, spongy layer on the top of the compost.

FACT FILE

ORIGIN Australasia, Malaysia.

HEIGHT To 46cm/18in, with spreading fronds as long as 90cm/3ft.

COMPOST Peat-based with added perlite.

REPOTTING Move into a pot one size larger every second year. Use a shallow pot, or half-pot, for a young plant, since aspleniums are shallow rooting.

PROPAGATION In spring, detach and plant up the bulbils when they have developed 3 or 4 small fronds.

KEEPING PLANTS This easy to grow plant is fairly long-lived in the right conditions.

PLANT CARE

Bright filtered light or indirect light. ● Normal room temperature, with a minimum of 10°C/50°F. ● Water moderately during the period of active growth, but sparingly in winter. ● To increase humidity, stand the pot on a tray of damp pebbles. ● Apply a high-nitrogen liquid fertiliser every month from spring to autumn.

~

ASTROPHYTUM MYRIOSTIGMA
Cactaceae

*B*ISHOP'S CAP CACTUS

The bishop's cap (or mitre, or monk's hood) cactus is a spherical cactus that becomes elongated with age. It is divided into four to eight (usually five) wide, thornless segments, covered with tufts of minute silvery hairs. Bright, shiny yellow daisy-like flowers, each with a reddish centre, emerge from the top of the plant in summer. It is a slow-growing plant best grown in a cactus garden or massed in a shallow bowl with gravel around it.

Astrophytum myriostigma

FACT FILE

ORIGIN Mexico.

HEIGHT To 25cm/10in with a spread of 13cm/5in.

COMPOST Soil-based and coarse sand in a ratio of 2:1.

REPOTTING Repot in spring, when the plant's roots have completely filled the current pot.

PROPAGATION Sow seed in spring.

KEEPING PLANTS The plant is long-lived and blooms only when it is 3 years old or more.

PLANT CARE

Full sunlight. ● A winter minimum of 10°C/50°F; otherwise, normal room temperature. ● Do not let the plant become waterlogged. Allow the top two-thirds of the compost to dry out before rewatering; water more sparingly in the winter rest period. ● Feed with a high-potash fertiliser once a month between spring and autumn.

AUCUBA JAPONICA '*VARIEGATA*'
Aucubaceae

Spotted Laurel

The plain green form of this plant, also known as Japanese laurel, was much used by the English in outdoor shrubberies and large greenhouses in Victorian times. This more frequently seen female variety with yellow-spotted leaves, and other modern hybrids, are considerably more cheerful. Most have leaves strongly marked with cream and yellow. Panicles of purplish flowers are borne in spring, and if male and female plants are grown together, bright red berries may follow. Indoors, plants can be hand-pollinated.

There are several varieties of variegated spotted laurel that make good house plants. *Aucuba japonica* 'Crotonifolia' is a female form with broad leaves mottled with golden yellow. *A.j.* 'Fructu-albo' has leaves spotted with pale green and produces yellowish white berries in fall.

Spotted laurels tolerate a certain amount of neglect, poor light and draughts and can be used in window boxes and in foliage arrangements for cool rooms.

FACT FILE

ORIGIN Cultivar.

HEIGHT To 90cm/3ft in a pot.

COMPOST Soil-based.

REPOTTING Move into a pot one size larger each spring; once plants are in 20-cm/8-in pots, top-dress instead.

PROPAGATION Sow seed in spring, or take 10–15-cm/4–6-in-long stem cuttings in late summer.

KEEPING PLANTS Cut old plants back hard in early spring if they become leggy or too large.

Aucuba japonica

PLANT CARE
Bright light or filtered sunlight. ● A cool room with a temperature of 18°C/65°F is ideal; the plant can withstand considerably colder temperatures, even down to -15°C/5°F. ● Water copiously during the summer; give less water in winter. ● Apply a standard liquid fertiliser once a month from spring to autumn. ● Clean leaves regularly with a damp sponge.

~

BERTOLONIA MARMORATA
Melastomataceae

Bertolonia

The chief ornamental value of this plant is provided by the velvety foliage: short, creeping stems bear green, quilted leaves up to 20cm/8in long, each irregularly streaked with white. The underside of the leaves is reddish purple and lilac-pink flowers are borne in summer.

Bertolonias are best in a group of other plants, where the increased humidity will benefit them, and are good plants for a bottle garden or terrarium. Only young plants are really attractive; older plants can become straggly.

The few named varieties are difficult to find, but they add a different dimension to a plant collection and are worth the search. *Bertolonia marmorata* 'Bruxellensis' has silvery leaves with rows of green spots between the main veins, while those of *B.m.* 'Mosaica' have a broader vein of silver and a pinkish tint.

FACT FILE

ORIGIN Brazil.

HEIGHT To 20cm/8in.

COMPOST Peat-based with added coarse sand.

REPOTTING Repot when the stems cover the surface of the compost and hang over the edge of the container; probably about every 2 years.

PROPAGATION In spring sow seed, which bertolonias produce in quantity, or take stem or leaf cuttings.

KEEPING PLANTS When plants become straggly, replace them with new young plants.

PLANT CARE
Partial shade. ● Normal room temperature, with a minimum of 16°C/60°F. ● Water moderately throughout the year, but do not let water lie on the leaves, since it can cause unattractive brown spots. ● Increase humidity by placing the pot on a dish of damp pebbles. ● Apply a standard liquid fertiliser once a month between spring and autumn.

BOUVARDIA LONGIFLORA
Rubiaceae

Bouvardia

A gloriously scented plant, this bouvardia bears trusses of white or pink star-shaped flowers from summer to midwinter. The plant flowers when it is quite young, and makes an excellent bushy shrub for both the home and greenhouse. But even when it has had the most expert and loving attention, it lasts for only a couple of years,

Bouvardia ternifolia, the scarlet trompetilla, is not scented. But it makes up for this lack with its brilliantly coloured flowers, which form a striking contrast with the plant's whitish grey bark.

Bouvardia longiflora

FACT FILE

ORIGIN Mexico.

HEIGHT To 90cm/3ft.

COMPOST Soil-based.

REPOTTING Move into a pot one size larger in spring.

PROPAGATION Take stem cuttings or root cuttings in spring.

KEEPING PLANTS Prune the plant vigorously in early spring and pinch out growing tips until late summer to make a bushy plant. Keep it fairly dry during the lengthy rest period in late spring and early summer.

PLANT CARE
Bright filtered light. ● A minimum of 7°C/45°F in winter; otherwise, warm room temperature. ● Water an actively growing plant freely; keep it fairly dry during the lengthy rest period in late spring and early summer. ● Apply a weak liquid fertiliser every 2 weeks while the plant is in flower. ● Bouvardia is susceptible to attack by whiteflies; check for these pests and spray with insecticide. Mealybugs may also infest the plant.

~

BOWIEA VOLUBILIS
Liliaceae

CLIMBING ONION

This is more of a curio and a talking point than an attractive plant to enhance a room. Thin stems emerge in late winter from a shiny, light green bulb that can be 15–20cm/6–8in wide; part of the bulb lies above the level of the compost. A few short-lived leaves and greenish white star-shaped flowers appear in late summer and autumn, before the stems die down.

FACT FILE

ORIGIN South Africa.

HEIGHT Stems climb to 1.8m/6ft or more.

COMPOST Peat-based with added coarse sand.

REPOTTING Repot during summer or early autumn, but only when offsets fill the pot.

PROPAGATION Divide offsets from the parent plant in summer or early autumn or sow seed.

KEEPING PLANTS Plants are fairly long-lived in good bright conditions.

PLANT CARE

Bright light, but not direct sunlight. ● Cool room conditions, with a minimum of 10°C/50°F. ● Keep the compost just moist when the stems are actively growing. ● Apply a weak liquid fertiliser once a month from early autumn until late winter. ● The small leaves naturally fall early, but the green stems carry on photosynthesis in their place.

BREYNIA NIVOSA (SYN. *B. DISTICHA*)
Euphorbiaceae

SNOW BUSH

The slender, angular branches of this plant are densely clothed in colourful green leaves marbled with white. The variety 'Rosea-Picta' is more popular than the species; its pink, white and green leaves have a flower-like appearance, hence the plant's other common name of leaf flower. The actual flowers, which are insignificant and greenish, are sometimes produced.

Breynia nivosa, the only member of the genus commonly grown indoors, is slowly becoming more widely available. It is primarily a tropical garden plant, and as such will grow into a shrub. Some years ago it was introduced as an indoor plant, and in the house it tends to remain a small bush. It needs an extremely moist atmosphere.

FACT FILE

ORIGIN Tropical Asia, Pacific Islands, Australia.

HEIGHT To 1.2m/4ft.

COMPOST Soil-based.

REPOTTING Move into a pot a size larger every second spring.

PROPAGATION Take stem cuttings with a heel in summer, or root cuttings.

KEEPING PLANTS When breynia grows too large for the house, transfer it to a tub in the conservatory or outdoors.

Breynia nivosa

PLANT CARE

Bright, filtered light with some sunshine. ● Average room temperature, with a minimum of 16°C/60°F. ● Keep the compost moist at all times. ● Stand the pot on a tray of damp pebbles and mist-spray regularly to maintain humidity. ● Apply a standard liquid feed every 2–3 weeks in the period of active growth.

~

BRODIAEA LAXA (SYN. *TRITELEIA LAXA*)
Liliaceae

GRASS NUT

Also known as Ithuriel's spear, this is equally good as a plant for the sunroom and as a temporary plant for the home, where it will thrive on a sunny windowsill. In any location, it increases and seeds itself freely.

An uncommon plant grown from a corm, the grass nut appeals to those who prefer small, dainty blooms. Plant the corms in late summer or early autumn, in groups of five or six in a 15-cm/6-in pot. The large, loose umbels of deep blue or, rarely, white bell-shaped flowers appear during the following spring and early summer as the foliage dies back. The flowers are carried on stems up to 30cm/12in long and resemble those of alliums. The variety 'Queen Fabiola' has pale violet-blue flowers.

FACT FILE

ORIGIN USA (California, southern Oregon).

HEIGHT To 40cm/16in.

COMPOST Soil-based, leaf mould and coarse sand in equal amounts for good drainage. The corms will rot if conditions are too wet.

REPOTTING Repot in late summer, at the end of the dormant period.

PROPAGATION Remove and pot up offsets at planting time, or sow seeds in spring.

KEEPING PLANTS After flowering, store the pot in a warm, dry place until late summer, when the corms are ready to be repotted. Corms planted outdoors need protection from frost.

PLANT CARE

Full sun. ● Minimum winter temperature of 5°C/41°F. ● Water well once the plants have started to grow; after flowering, reduce watering. Do not water during the dormant period. ● Give 2 or 3 feeds of dilute general fertiliser after the bulbs have started growing and before flowering.

~

BRUGMANSIA x *CANDIDA* see
DATURA x *CANDIDA*

~

Buddleja madagascariensis

BUDDLEJA MADAGASCARIENSIS

(SYN. *NICODEMIA MADAGASCARIENSIS*)

Loganiaceae

ℬUDDLEIA

The name of this plant is now correctly spelt *Buddleja*, but it is still generally known as *Buddleia*. It is a showy evergreen pot plant for a large, bright sunny room or a border plant for a greenhouse. Vigorous, with an upright habit, it can easily reach 1.8–3m/6–10ft or more in height.

It has 13-cm/5-in-long lance-shaped dark green leaves whose undersides are covered with a downy white felt. The small, bright yellow-orange flowers are borne in slender, pyramid-shaped clusters between late autumn and spring. Unlike other buddleias, which have fruits like dry capsules, the flowers are followed by fleshy, berrylike purple-blue fruits.

FACT FILE

ORIGIN Madagascar.

HEIGHT To 3m/10ft.

COMPOST Soil-based.

REPOTTING Move into a pot one size larger only when roots completely fill the current pot.

PROPAGATION Sow seed in spring or take stem cuttings in late summer.

KEEPING PLANTS Stems can be cut back by about half after flowering, to keep the plant in shape or to reduce its size. Flowers are produced on the current year's growth.

PLANT CARE

Full sun or partial shade. ● Minimum temperature of 7°C/45°F in winter. ● Water moderately all year round. Do not allow the plant to wilt, since that can cause serious leaf loss. ● Feed every 2 weeks from spring to late autumn with a dilute standard fertiliser.

~

CALATHEA AMABILIS see STROMANTHE AMABILIS

~

CALLIANDRA HAEMATOCEPHALA

(SYN. *C. INAEQUILATERA*)

Leguminosae

℘OWDERPUFF PLANT

The ball-like flowers of this plant, which blooms in winter, are made up entirely of stamens, and the bright red 8-cm-/3-in-wide 'powder puffs' last for almost two months. The dark green foliage is divided into leaflets, each of which is about 5cm/2in long. In time the plant will develop into a bushy tree, but it will tolerate hard pruning, so can be kept to 60–90cm/2–3ft by cutting it back in spring. It can even be used as a subject for bonsai.

Calliandra needs moist air, bright light and warmth, three conditions generally found in a sunroom rather than in a living room. But if these requirements can be met, it will do well in the house. *Calliandra tweedii* has smaller red flowers and its leaves are feathery.

FACT FILE

ORIGIN Bolivia.

HEIGHT To 1.8m/6ft.

COMPOST Soil-based with some added leaf mould and coarse sand.

REPOTTING In spring move into a pot one size larger, until the plant has reached the desired size, then top-dress annually.

PROPAGATION Take stem cuttings in spring.

KEEPING PLANTS This plant is tough and will last for many years. Set the pot outdoors in summer to ripen the wood and improve flowering the following year.

PLANT CARE

Full sun except for the strongest summer sunlight, or partial shade. ● Warm conditions, with a minimum winter temperature of 16°C/60°F. ● Keep the compost damp at all times. ● Mist regularly to increase humidity. ● Feed every 2 weeks from spring to autumn.

CARICA PAPAYA

Caricaceae

℘AWPAW

Widely grown in tropical countries for its fruit, the pawpaw, or papaya, makes an unusual ornamental foliage plant. The straight stem is usually unbranched and is topped by a cluster of long-stalked, deeply lobed leaves, which may reach 60cm/2ft wide on large plants.

The fragrant trumpet-shaped flowers, borne in summer, are cream or yellow and up to 2.5cm/1in long. Male and female plants in close proximity are required if fruit production is the aim, although bisexual plants that have both male and female flowers, such as *Carica papaya* 'Solo', have been bred. When the pawpaw is grown as an indoor plant, pollination by hand may be necessary.

The 13–30-cm/5–12-in-long melon-like fruits are borne directly on the trunk, in the leaf axils. They are green and turn yellow or orange when ripe. The firm, fragrant flesh is yellow to pinkish orange.

FACT FILE

ORIGIN Tropical America.

HEIGHT To 3m/10ft in a container.

COMPOST Soil-based with good drainage.

REPOTTING Move young plants into a pot one size larger as they fill the container with roots.

PROPAGATION Seeds are frequently available commercially, and can be saved from fruits. Sow in spring, in a temperature not lower than 24°C/75°F. They may not come true to type.

KEEPING PLANTS Replace the plant every 4 years or so.

Calliandra haematocephala

PLANT CARE

Full sun will help to ripen the fruits; as an ornamental, the plant will tolerate partial shade. ● Normal warm conditions, with a minimum winter temperature of 5°C/41°F. A temperature of at least 16°C /60°F is necessary to ripen fruit. ● Water well all year round, but do not overwater. If the compost becomes waterlogged, it will kill the plant within days. ● Apply a weak liquid fertiliser every 2 weeks during the period of active growth.

~

CARLUDOVICA PALMATA
Cyclanthaceae

PANAMA-HAT PLANT

This is one of a small group of short-stemmed palm-like perennials grown mainly for their leaves, although the brightly coloured fruits are also attractive. The bright green, pliable, fan-shaped leaves are up to 90cm/3ft wide, with three to five main segmented divisions. Each lobe has a drooping ragged tip. In tropical regions the bleached leaves provide the material for Panama hats.

FACT FILE

ORIGIN Central America, south to Bolivia.

HEIGHT To 1.8m/6ft or more.

COMPOST Peat-based with added sharp sand.

REPOTTING Repot only young plants as they fill the container with roots.

PROPAGATION Sow seeds at any time of year.

KEEPING PLANTS This is a fairly long-lived plant in a warm sunroom or greenhouse.

PLANT CARE

Full sun. ● Minimum temperature of 13°C/55°F. ● Water plentifully when the plant is in active growth. ● Feed occasionally with dilute liquid general fertiliser.

~

CARYOTA MITIS
Palmae

BURMESE FISHTAIL PALM

Known also as the crested or tufted fishtail palm, this palm is distinguished from all others by its fronds. They are made up of roughly triangular segments, each of which is ragged at the edge, like a fish's tail. With age, the fronds arch over and develop their distinctive double division.

Indoors, *Caryota mitis* is unlikely to grow more than 6 to 10 fronds 90cm/3ft long. The plant may reach a total height of some

Caryota mitis

1.8m/6ft, about a quarter of its potential height in the garden.

FACT FILE

ORIGIN Burma, Malaysia, Java, Philippines.

HEIGHT To 1.8m/6ft indoors.

COMPOST Soil-based.

REPOTTING Every other year, when the plant is starting into growth, move it into a pot one size larger until the maximum desired size is reached; the plant prefers to be slightly pot-bound.

PROPAGATION Sow seed, in heat, during spring or summer; or pot up offset divisions.

KEEPING PLANTS Move the palm outdoors in summer. It cannot be pruned and so should be discarded once it has outgrown its allotted space.

PLANT CARE

Bright indirect sunlight. ● Ideally, warm room temperature between 18°C/65°F at night and 29°C/85°F during the day. ● Water thoroughly, but allow the surface of the compost to dry out before rewatering. ● Increase humidity around the plant by standing the pot on a tray of moist pebbles. ● Apply a weak liquid fertiliser every 2 weeks while growth is active.

~

CEPHALOCEREUS SENILIS
(SYN. *PILOCEREUS SENILIS*)
Cactaceae

OLD MAN CACTUS

The common name for this cactus is derived from the long, fine white hairs that shroud the fleshy columnar body and hide the sharp spines beneath them. The hairs serve to protect the plant from the sun and the brighter the light, the denser they will be. When the hairs become discoloured, they may be washed in a weak solution

of detergent, using a soft brush such as a shaving brush or paint brush. This will remove any dirt, but not the darkening of the hairs due to age.

The flowers, which are red and white, seldom form on potted plants and appear only on older specimens. These cacti are very slow growing, adding perhaps 2.5cm/1in a year.

FACT FILE

ORIGIN Mexico.

HEIGHT To 30cm/12in or more.

COMPOST Soil- or peat-based with added perlite or coarse sand in the ratio of 2:1.

REPOTTING If roots have filled the pot, move the plant into a pot one size larger in spring. Older plants may be top-dressed instead.

PROPAGATION Sow seed in spring.

KEEPING PLANTS These plants look best massed with other cacti in a cactus garden.

PLANT CARE

Direct sunlight. ● A minimum temperature of 4°C/40°F in winter; otherwise, normal room temperature. ● Allow the surface of the compost to dry out completely between waterings; water only enough during the winter rest period to prevent the plant shrivelling. Be careful not to splash the hairs when watering. ● Apply a high-potash liquid fertiliser every 3 weeks between spring and autumn.

Cephalocereus senilis

CEROPEGIA WOODII
(SYN. *CEROPEGIA LINEARIS* SSP. *WOODII*)
Asclepiadaceae

CHAIN OF HEARTS

A long-lived tuberous succulent, this is the only ceropegia commonly grown indoors. It is a good plant for a hanging basket. The grey, woody tuber, which can reach 5cm/2in wide, rests on the surface of the compost, and from it spring several fine purplish flexible stems. Generally, these are about 90cm/3ft long, although they can become much longer.

Every 5–8cm/2–3in along the stem is a pair of 2.5-cm/1-in-long fleshy heart-shaped leaves, that give the plant its common names; it is also known as hearts entangled, hearts on a string and rosary vine.

The dark green leaves are marked with white on the upper surface and are purple underneath. Small tuberous growths are produced at intervals along the stem, and where they form, stems sometimes branch.

Ceropegia woodii

FACT FILE

ORIGIN South Africa (Natal).

HEIGHT Stems trail to 90cm/3ft or more.

COMPOST Soil-based and coarse sand or perlite in equal quantities; good drainage is essential.

REPOTTING In early spring move into a pot one size larger until a 10-cm/4-in pot is reached.

PROPAGATION At any time, remove stem tubers from the plant or take stem cuttings. Set several tubers around the edge of a hanging basket for a good display.

KEEPING PLANTS Keep ceropegia in a bright location; in dim light, leaf colour will be poor and leaves will be widely spaced on the stem.

PLANT CARE

Bright light with at least 4 hours of direct sun daily. ● Normal room temperature, with a minimum of 12°C/54°F. ● Water actively growing plants moderately; water sparingly in the rest period from mid-autumn to early spring. ● Every 4 weeks apply standard liquid fertiliser to mature plants only.

CESTRUM AURANTIACUM
Solanaceae

CESTRUM

An evergreen semi-climbing shrub, cestrum makes a good plant for the greenhouse or sunroom, where it can be trained to a permanent support. It has oval leaves up to 8cm/3in long, which smell unpleasant. Flowers are borne in clusters in summer and they too have an odour that some find unpleasant; it is strongest at night. Each bright yellow-orange bloom has a 2-cm/ ³⁄₄-in-long tubular corolla with five pointed petal lobes at the mouth. The flowers are followed by white berries.

Cestrum elegans 'Smithii' has apricot pink flowers and blooms all year round; *C. nocturnum*, night-blooming jasmine, has white flowers.

FACT FILE

ORIGIN Guatemala.

HEIGHT To 3m/10ft.

COMPOST Soil-based with good drainage.

REPOTTING In spring, when the roots have filled the current pot, move a young plant into a pot one size larger.

PROPAGATION Sow seeds in spring, or take stem cuttings with a heel in late summer

KEEPING PLANTS Pinch off the growing tips of a young plant to encourage bushiness. And cut out a third or so of the oldest wood in autumn to ensure good flowering during the following year.

PLANT CARE

Bright, filtered sunlight. ● A minimum temperature of 10°C/50°F. ● Water well during the growing season and give less water for 4–6 weeks after flowering. ● Apply a weak liquid fertiliser every 2 weeks from spring to autumn.

Cestrum aurantiacum

Clianthus puniceus

CLIANTHUS PUNICEUS
Leguminosae

PARROT'S BEAK

Also known as Kaka beak and lobster claw, *Clianthus puniceus* has flowers with a large showy standard and a long pointed keel, from which it gets its common names. The flowers, which start off red and fade to pink as they age, are borne in clusters from summer to late autumn. The thin stems of *C. puniceus* need support when it is grown as a free-standing shrub, and it is an excellent subject for training against a wall trellis in a cool room or conservatory.

The closely related *C. formosus*, Sturt's desert pea or glory pea, is a relatively low-growing, trailing plant, with feathery leaves some 15cm/6in long. The stems may be pruned or trained in autumn when flowering is over, but the plant often declines at this time and it is best regarded as an annual.

FACT FILE

ORIGIN Australia, New Zealand.

HEIGHT To 1.8m/6ft in a container.

COMPOST Soil-based with added grit.

REPOTTING Repot in spring, but only if the roots fill the current pot.

PROPAGATION Sow seed in spring.

KEEPING PLANTS Prune after flowering. Keep the plant well ventilated at all times.

PLANT CARE

Full sun or dappled shade. ● Cooler room temperatures of 10°–18°C /50°–65°F are best. ● Water well from spring to autumn, but sparingly in winter. ● On hot, dry days, mist the plant with clean water. ● Apply a weak liquid fertiliser every 2 weeks during the period of active growth.

COCCOLOBA UVIFERA
Polygonaceae

SEA GRAPE

In its natural habitat on the coasts of South and Central America, coccoloba grows in almost pure sand. It is a shrubby plant whose leathery, circular to kidney-shaped leaves with red veins turn to ivory with age. The long trusses of white flowers, which are reluctant to form in room conditions, are followed by purple-red fruits 2cm/³⁄₄in long; these resemble grapes and give the plant its common name. In the wild, the leaves become so large that local people use them as picnic plates, and the fruits are used to make a jelly.

Because its leaves are leathery, this plant tolerates dry air fairly well and so is a good plant for heated houses.

FACT FILE

ORIGIN Tropical America, West Indies.

HEIGHT To 1.8m/6ft indoors; 6m/20ft in its natural habitat.

COMPOST Soil-based with added peat.

REPOTTING Move into a pot one size larger each spring. Once a 20-cm/8-in pot has been reached, top-dress instead.

PROPAGATION Take half-ripe tip cuttings in summer; sow seed in spring, or layer at any time of year.

KEEPING PLANTS Cut back just before the plant starts into growth in spring, to encourage branching. Discard after 3 or 4 years; young specimens are more attractive than older ones.

PLANT CARE
Good light but avoid direct sun. ● Minimum winter temperature of 16°C/60°F, with normal room temperature at other times. ● Keep the compost moderately moist at all times. ● Maintain a humid atmosphere by standing the pot on a tray of damp pebbles and misting the plant occasionally. ● Apply a weak liquid fertiliser every 2 weeks from spring to autumn.

~

COFFEA ARABICA
Rubiaceae

ARABIAN COFFEE PLANT

It is not generally known that the coffee tree makes an excellent indoor plant. It is evergreen and may grow to a height of 1.8m/6ft, although there is a compact form, *Coffea arabica* 'Nana', which remains considerably smaller. From its third or fourth year it may even bear flowers and fruit. The uncooked beans can, however, be poisonous, and they must be properly

Coffea arabica

roasted before they can be made into coffee; this important process is best carried out by a professional.

The plant has shiny, dark green elliptical leaves with wavy edges; they can be as much as 15cm/6in long and about 5cm/2in wide. The fragrant, star-shaped white flowers are followed by green fruits 13mm/¹⁄₂in long, which change to bright red and then to almost black as they ripen. The two seeds within the fruits contain caffeine.

FACT FILE

ORIGIN Tropical Africa, Arabia.

HEIGHT To 1.8m/6ft in a pot.

COMPOST Soil-based with added coarse sand; good drainage is essential.

REPOTTING Move into a pot one or two sizes larger each spring.

PROPAGATION Cuttings, taken in summer, do not root easily, but fresh seed can be sown in spring with reasonable success.

KEEPING PLANTS If necessary, prune the plant in spring to control its size and shape.

PLANT CARE
Bright light away from direct sunlight. ● Normal room temperature of 18°–21°C/65°–70°F, but the plant can stand slightly cooler temperatures in the dormant period between mid-autumn and late winter. Young plants up to 2 years old, with tender growth, prefer slightly warmer conditions. ● Water generously in summer, preferably with tepid water and from below; give only enough water in the rest period to prevent the compost drying out completely. ● Apply a weak solution of lime-free fertiliser each week during spring and summer.

CONVALLARIA MAJALIS
Liliaceae

LILY-OF-THE-VALLEY

This familiar plant, with delicate, highly fragrant bell-shaped flowers, is usually seen as a hardy specimen in woodland areas or in a shady spot in the garden. It grows from a creeping rhizome and so spreads quickly.

Convallarias are also easy to force and can be obtained as pot plants or as crowns at almost any time of year. The elliptical leaves grow from the rootstock, usually in pairs, and can be 20cm/8in long. Each flower stalk carries five to eight blooms.

In addition to the type, several good varieties are obtainable, among them *Convallaria majalis* 'Fortin's Giant' with large white flowers, which is most often used for forcing; *C.m.* 'Prolificans' with double flowers; and the less vigorous *C.m.* 'Rosea' with pale pink flowers.

FACT FILE

ORIGIN Europe; naturalised in America.

HEIGHT To 25cm/10in.

COMPOST Soil-based, leaf mould and coarse sand in equal amounts.

REPOTTING Move into a pot one size larger each spring after flowering. Put 6–8 plants in a pot for the best effect.

PROPAGATION Sow seed in spring or divide plants when repotting.

KEEPING PLANTS Overwinter plants in a cold frame or cool greenhouse if possible. As they start into growth, increase watering and increase the temperature to about 21°C/70°F if you want to force them into early blooming.

PLANT CARE
Bright light but not direct sunlight. ● Cool room conditions will prolong the flowering period. ● Keep the compost moist at all times. ● Apply a weak liquid fertiliser once a month during spring and summer.

Convallaria majalis

COSTUS IGNEUS (SYN C. CUSPIDATUS)
Zingiberaceae

SPIRAL GINGER

This plant is unusual in that the leaves spiral around the stem. Each leaf, which can be 15cm/6in in length, is oblong, glossy on the surface and reddish below. The flowers, borne in summer, are 5–8cm/2–3in long, with an orange tube and a deep yellow lip.

Costus speciosus, Malay or crepe ginger, has white flowers; those of C. spiralis are red. C. pulverulentus (C. sanguineus) also has red flowers and decorative 10-cm/4-in-long pointed leaves, which are bluish green and accentuated with silvery central ribs.

FACT FILE

ORIGIN Brazil.

HEIGHT To 60cm/2ft.

COMPOST Soil-based.

REPOTTING Move into a pot one size larger in early spring, when the pot becomes crowded.

PROPAGATION Divide and repot the roots in spring, or take 10-cm/4-in-long stem cuttings at any time of year.

KEEPING PLANTS Cut out old canes at the base when new growth appears.

Costus igneus

PLANT CARE

Bright indirect light. ● Normal room temperature. ● Keep the compost moist at all times. ● Apply a weak liquid fertiliser once a month to actively growing plants.

~

COTYLEDON UNDULATA
Crassulaceae

SILVER CROWN

Cotyledons are shrubby succulents with fleshy, fan-shaped, stalkless leaves arranged in opposite pairs. Each leaf of this plant has an undulating edge and a dense covering of fine, silvery white powder. Although orange-yellow flowers may appear on older plants in summer, the plant is chiefly grown for its characteristic leaves. Mass several

Cotyledon undulata

plants together in a bowl on a low table for maximum effect.

Cotyledon orbiculata is slightly taller and has grey-green leaves edged with red, with just a little white mealy covering. Orange flowers appear in summer.

FACT FILE

ORIGIN South Africa.

HEIGHT To 50cm/20in.

COMPOST Soil-based with coarse sand added in a ratio of 2:1 for good drainage, which is essential for this plant.

REPOTTING Move the plant into a pot one size larger each spring; when a 15-cm/6-in pot is reached, top-dress instead.

PROPAGATION Take 8–10-cm/3–4-in tip cuttings in spring.

KEEPING PLANTS Avoid handling the plant, since the white mealy covering will rub off. When the plant eventually becomes leggy, cut off the leafy top and reroot it. The bare stem may then produce new growth, so it is worth caring for it for a while.

PLANT CARE

Full sunlight. ● Minimum winter temperature of 5°C/41°F, with normal room temperature at other times. ● Water copiously from spring to autumn; give less water in winter. ● Apply a standard liquid fertiliser once a month between spring and autumn.

~

CRASSULA COCCINEA see ROCHEA COCCINEA

~

CRINUM × POWELLII
Amaryllidaceae

SWAMP LILY

An elegant, hardy plant, the swamp, or spider, lily is a hybrid between Crinum bulbispermum and C. moorei, both of which come originally from South Africa. During late summer or early autumn, it bears bright pink trumpet-shaped flowers at the top of a thick, succulent stem up to 90cm/3ft high. The blooms are produced in succession, in clusters of five to eight, over about a month. Each 'trumpet' can be up to 13cm/5in long and 15cm/6in wide. C. × p. 'Album' has pure white flowers.

The spectacular blooms and strap-shaped leaves, of which there are about 20 on a mature plant, arise from large bulbs, often as much as 15cm/6in in diameter. The leaves last for a year, dying only when there are new ones ready to replace them. Because of their relative longevity, they need attention to keep them looking attractive.

FACT FILE

ORIGIN Hybrid.

HEIGHT To 90cm/3ft.

COMPOST Soil-based, with plenty of coarse sand, leaf mould and well-rotted manure added. Put plenty of pebbles or gravel in the bottom of the pot to ensure good drainage.

REPOTTING Crinums flower best when pot-bound, so top-dress annually and repot only every 3–4 years.

PROPAGATION Divide overcrowded clumps in spring by carefully separating the offsets from the parent bulb. For a month after potting up, water the offsets sparingly; thereafter, treat them as adult plants. Otherwise, sow fresh ripe seeds singly in pots.

KEEPING PLANTS Picking off the flowers as they fade will help to prolong the blooming period.

PLANT CARE

Direct sunlight for 3–4 hours daily. ● A minimum temperature of 10°C/50°F during the winter rest period; otherwise, normal room temperature. ● Water daily in summer, but do not let the plant stand in water. Give only enough water in winter to prevent the compost from drying out completely. If necessary, mist the leaves at this time, to prevent them from wilting. ● Apply high-potash fertiliser every 3 weeks in spring and summer.

~

Cyanotis somaliensis

CYANOTIS SOMALIENSIS
Commelinaceae

PUSSY EARS

Unlike the closely related tradescantia, cyanotis bears hairy leaves. The 5-cm/2-in-long shiny green leaves of *Cyanotis somaliensis* are edged with soft white hairs, which gives them an overall pale grey appearance. Three-petalled blue flowers sometimes appear between winter and spring. The plant looks good when growth is compact but unruly when the stems are weak and spindly, which they readily become if light is inadequate. This is a good plant for indoor hanging baskets.

C. kewensis, teddy bear vine, has fine, rust-coloured hairs on its short creeping stems. Its small lance-shaped leaves are green on top and purple underneath. Violet-coloured flowers are produced, but only rarely.

FACT FILE

ORIGIN Tropical Africa.

HEIGHT To 20cm/8in.

COMPOST Soil-based with added coarse sand or perlite in a ratio of 2:1.

REPOTTING A slow-growing plant, cyanotis does best in a shallow pot and rarely needs repotting.

PROPAGATION Take tip cuttings in spring; make sure that each cutting has three pairs of leaves.

KEEPING PLANTS The leaves develop brown tips if the air is too dry; stand the plant on a tray of moist pebbles to increase humidity.

PLANT CARE

Good light with some direct sunlight. ● Normal room temperature. ● Water well year round, but allow the surface of the compost to become dry before rewatering. ● Apply standard liquid fertiliser 4 times between spring and autumn.

CYPERUS PAPYRUS
Cyperaceae

EGYPTIAN PAPER REED

This exotic plant gets its name from the fact that the ancient Egyptians used its stems for making papyrus to write on. It grows in clumps and the smooth triangular stems can reach a height of 3m/10ft. The thin, rich green, grassy leaves are topped by a few bracts and a dense, umbrella-like tuft of pendulous stems that end in tiny brownish flowers.

This is a marsh plant in its natural habitat, so it is almost impossible to give it too much water. It is not always easy to find, but the miniature *Cyperus prolifer* (*C. isocladus*), also known as *C. papyrus* 'Nanus', which grows to 60cm/2ft, is usually easier to come by.

FACT FILE

ORIGIN Tropical Africa.

HEIGHT To 3m/10ft.

COMPOST Soil-based with charcoal added to keep the soil fresh.

REPOTTING Move into a pot one size larger as soon as the roots fill the current container.

PROPAGATION Divide the plant in spring or root stem cuttings in water.

KEEPING PLANTS Do not allow cyperus to dry out, even for a short while, or the bracts will develop brown tips.

Cyperus papyrus

PLANT CARE

Full, bright sunlight or light shade. ● A minimum winter temperature of 13°C/55°F, with warm room temperature at other times. ● Keep the compost moist at all times: stand the pot in a bowl of water and keep it filled. ● Apply a weak liquid fertiliser once a month between spring and autumn, or push fertilising tablets into the soil around the roots.

~

CYRTANTHUS ELATUS see VALLOTA SPECIOSA

~

CYRTOMIUM FALCATUM
Aspidiaceae

HOLLY FERN

This handsome, long-lasting fern produces tufts of dark, scaly frond stalks up to 60cm/2ft in length. These bear shiny, dark green, pointed holly-like leaves, which are often as much as 8–10cm/3–4in long. An easy plant to grow indoors, it even tolerates draughts and the warm dry air of heated homes. Occasional misting should keep the leaves clean, otherwise wipe them with a damp cloth or sponge, but do not use proprietary leaf shine.

Cyrtomium falcatum 'Rochfordianum' is more vigorous than the type. It has shorter but slightly broader fronds, the edges of which are wavy and distinctly toothed.

FACT FILE

ORIGIN South Africa, India, Korea, Japan, Hawaii.

HEIGHT To 60cm/2ft.

COMPOST Soil- or peat-based.

REPOTTING In spring move the plant into a pot one size larger until maximum desired pot size is reached. Thereafter, top-dress instead.

PROPAGATION In spring divide the rhizomes, ensuring each piece has a growing point and at least three fronds.

KEEPING PLANTS This plant is prone to attack by scale insects and mealybugs; keep a close watch for these pests.

PLANT CARE

Bright, indirect light, or semi-shade. ● A temperature of 18°C/65°F is ideal; if the level is much higher than this, it is essential to increase the humidity by spraying the foliage and standing the plant on a tray of moist pebbles. ● Allow the surface of the compost to dry out between waterings. ● Apply a weak liquid fertiliser every 2 weeks to actively growing plants.

Darlingtonia californica

DARLINGTONIA CALIFORNICA
Sarraceniaceae

CALIFORNIA PITCHER PLANT

A carnivorous bog plant, this darlingtonia has 30–50-cm/12–20-in-long tubular emerald green leaves with a conspicuous network of veins. The leaves curve over at the tip, so that the opening of the tube faces downwards, preventing the entrance of rainwater, which would dilute the digestive juices. A two-lobed flap – green, dark brown and purple – hangs near the opening of the tube. The tube, hood and flap together resemble a snake's head, and it is easy to see why this plant is often called the cobra lily. The inside of the tubes is covered in downward-pointing hairs, which prevent insects from escaping. Every year a new rosette of leaves develops at the end of a short rootstock. The flowers have yellow-green sepals and petals, which are heavily veined in purplish red.

FACT FILE

ORIGIN USA (California, Oregon).

HEIGHT To 46cm/18in.

COMPOST Equal parts of peat, sphagnum moss, sharp sand and charcoal.

REPOTTING Repot every 2 years in midsummer.

PROPAGATION Sow seed, or divide, in a bed of sphagnum moss, under glass.

KEEPING PLANTS Do not feed the plant; it contains enough chlorophyll to make its own food when there are no insects around.

PLANT CARE

Bright light but no direct sunlight. ● The plant needs cool room temperature all year round. ● Never allow the compost to become dry. ● Humidity is vital, and the plant will do best as one of a group in a large shallow pan; mist the plant daily.

~

DATURA × CANDIDA
Solanaceae

ANGEL'S TRUMPET

Datura × candida, also known as *Brugmansia × candida*, is a plant that requires attention and plenty of space. It will easily grow to 1.8m/6ft in a container, with a similar spread, and is really best suited to the conservatory, sunroom or garden room.

It bears magnificent trumpet-shaped flowers up to 25cm/10in in length, and has oval, mid-green leaves about 23cm/9in long. The flowers, which are usually white, but can be pink or creamy yellow, have a strong, heady scent that some people find oppressive. D. 'Knightii' (D. × *candida* 'Plena') has white double flowers, one inside the other. After the flowers have faded, the stems can be pruned back, to encourage new growth.

Caution: All parts of the plant are poisonous. Do not grow it if children or pets are present.

FACT FILE

ORIGIN Hybrid between *Datura aurea* and *D. versicolor.*

HEIGHT To 1.8m/6ft in a container.

COMPOST Soil-based with added peat.

REPOTTING Move into a pot one size larger each spring.

PROPAGATION Take stem cuttings in spring; young plants may flower the following autumn.

KEEPING PLANTS Red spider mites can infest this plant; maintain high humidity to help to deter them. In a mild climate the plant will benefit from a spell outdoors in summer.

PLANT CARE

Full sun or light shade. ● Minimum winter temperature of 7°C/45°F, with cool room conditions at other times. ● Water generously between spring and autumn; give less water in winter. ● Apply a weak liquid fertiliser once a week to actively growing plants.

Datura × candida

DICHORISANDRA REGINAE
Commelinaceae

QUEEN'S SPIDERWORT

Although not often seen, queen's spiderwort is worth the search. It is a close relative of the popular tradescantia, but it needs more careful attention if it is to do well.

With its erect stalks, lance-shaped dark green leaves with two silvery lengthwise stripes and a violet mid-rib, this is a most attractive plant. The lavender-coloured flowers, about 2.5cm/1in wide, consist of three sepals, equal in size, and three contrasting petals.

The species *Dichorisandra thyrsiflora* bears clusters of deep blue-violet flowers striped with white in autumn.

FACT FILE

ORIGIN Peru.

HEIGHT To 60cm/2ft.

COMPOST Peat-based, with added loam; good drainage is necessary.

REPOTTING When roots fill the pot, move to a pot one size larger.

PROPAGATION In spring, divide, take cuttings or sow seed.

KEEPING PLANTS A high degree of warmth and humidity is essential.

PLANT CARE

Medium light; no direct sunlight. ● Minimum winter temperature of 16°C/60°F; normal room temperature at other times. ● Water the plant moderately in summer; give less water in winter. ● Apply a balanced liquid fertiliser every 2 weeks from spring to autumn.

Dichorisandra reginae

Dicksonia antarctica

DICKSONIA ANTARCTICA
Dicksoniaceae

SOFT TREE FERN

A sizable fern, this plant is best grown in a greenhouse or sunroom, where it will thrive in a border or large container. Fronds grow from ground level on young plants. As the plant ages it develops a large trunk composed of red-brown matted roots, the surface of which looks like bark.

Fronds form a terminal crown, each frond being 1.2–2.7m/4–9ft long; on mature plants they arch over, giving an elegant lacy effect. The spores are carried at the ends of the veins near the margins of the undersides of the fronds, which reflex to protect them.

FACT FILE

ORIGIN Australia (Tasmania).

HEIGHT To 6m/20ft in the garden.

COMPOST Top soil with added coarse sand, leaf mould and shredded bark in a ratio of 1:2:3:1.

REPOTTING In spring, when roots fill the pot, move into a pot one size larger. When the plant becomes too large, top-dress instead.

PROPAGATION Sow spores in spring, in a temperature of 16°C/60°F.

KEEPING PLANTS Spray the trunk with water regularly in hot weather to prevent the roots drying out.

PLANT CARE

Bright filtered sunlight. ● Average warmth; the plant may suffer in temperatures above 24°C/75°F. The palm can withstand a winter minimum of 7°C/45°F in shelter. ● Do not allow the compost to dry out. ● Apply a high-nitrogen liquid fertiliser every 2 or 3 weeks from spring to autumn.

DROSERA ROTUNDIFOLIA
Droseraceae

COMMON SUNDEW

Although it is a difficult plant to grow, this sundew is an interesting species for a collector of carnivorous plants. It bears a rosette of deciduous, long-stalked leaves that are 13mm/½in wide and open in summer. The leaves are covered with red glandular hairs, or tentacles, which secrete terminal globules of sticky, glistening juice. Small flies and other insects mistake the fluid for nectar and, once in contact with it, stick fast. The insect's struggles cause the surrounding tentacles to bend over, smothering it and pushing it down to the leaf surface. A digestive enzyme then breaks down the animal protein so that it can be absorbed by the plant.

FACT FILE

ORIGIN North America, northern Europe, northern Asia.

HEIGHT To 8cm/3in.

COMPOST Equal parts of peat and washed sharp sand; or pure live sphagnum moss.

REPOTTING Not necessary, since the plant has a remarkably small root system.

PROPAGATION Sow seed at any time of the year, or divide in spring.

KEEPING PLANTS Keep cold in winter, when the plant is resting.

PLANT CARE

Good light but not direct sunlight. ● Cool conditions; frost is tolerated. ● Never allow the compost to dry out; water from below. ● Every 4 weeks, apply weak liquid fertiliser to seedlings only; mature plants will get their nourishment from insects.

DYCKIA FOSTERIANA
Bromeliaceae

DYCKIA

A rosette-forming bromeliad, dyckia – sometimes called miniature agave – has grey-green, elongated, arching leaves equipped with prominent, rather vicious, hooked spines along their margins. In spring, racemes of orange-yellow bell-shaped flowers are carried on tall stems. The rosettes do not die immediately after flowering as is the case with most bromeliads, and a spreading clump of several rosettes soon builds up.

Take care when handling these spiny plants; strong gloves are usually necessary for such tasks as repotting.

FACT FILE

ORIGIN Brazil.

HEIGHT To 15cm/6in; flower stems to 25cm/10in.

COMPOST Soil-based with added coarse sand or grit for good drainage.

REPOTTING In spring, move into a pot one size larger when the rosettes fill the current pot.

PROPAGATION Use a sharp knife to remove offsets when they are about 5cm/2in wide, and pot them up individually in sandy compost.

KEEPING PLANTS Stand the plant outside in a sheltered position in full sun in summer.

PLANT CARE

Full sun. ● A minimum of 7°C/45°F, but will tolerate higher temperatures. ● Water fairly lightly in the growing season; allow the top third of the compost to dry out between waterings. Give just enough water in winter to prevent the compost drying out. ● Apply a balanced liquid fertiliser every 4 weeks in the growing season.

~

ECHEVERIA SECUNDA VAR. *GLAUCA*
Crassulaceae

BLUE ECHEVERIA

Although a succulent, this echeveria comes from cool and fairly moist mountainous regions. It produces decorative rosettes of evergreen, overlapping, fleshy ovate leaves. Each leaf has a small point at the centre and is of an intense blue-green shade.

The rosettes build up to form spreading clumps and may have short stems, although they are usually stemless. The foliage is brittle and easily damaged by careless handling. Arching racemes of red flowers on tall stems appear in spring.

Echeveria secunda var. *glauca*

FACT FILE

ORIGIN Mexico.

HEIGHT To 10cm/4in; flower stems to 30cm/12in.

COMPOST Soil-based with added coarse sand or perlite for drainage.

REPOTTING In spring move a small plant into a pot one size larger annually; move a large plant every 2 years or top-dress instead. Put a layer of gravel in the pot for drainage.

PROPAGATION Remove offsets from around the edge of the plant with a sharp knife and pot them up individually in gritty compost, or take leaf cuttings in spring and early summer.

KEEPING PLANTS The plant will benefit from a spell outdoors in summer.

PLANT CARE

Bright light with direct sunlight. ● Normal room temperature in the growing season; about 13°C/55°F in winter. ● Water growing plants sparingly; give just enough water to prevent the compost drying out completely in winter. ● Apply a balanced liquid fertiliser every 3 weeks during the period of active growth.

~

ECHINOPSIS EYRIESII
Cactaceae

SEA URCHIN CACTUS

The barrel-shaped stems of this cactus, with as many as 18 ribs, become cylindrical as they mature. The ribs bear areoles, each with 14 short, hard, dark brown spines. Large, tubular, fragrant flowers, up to 25cm/ 10in long and 10–13cm/4–5in wide, are freely produced in early summer on three-to

four-year-old plants that have had a winter rest. The flowers, with white petals and yellow stamens, open out flat at night and wilt within 24 hours. This plant is sometimes offered as *Echinocereus eyriesii*.

FACT FILE

ORIGIN South America.

HEIGHT To 25cm/10in.

COMPOST Soil-based and coarse sand or perlite in a ratio of 3:1.

REPOTTING Move into a pot one size larger in spring when the pot becomes overcrowded.

PROPAGATION In spring or summer, remove offsets from around the plant and press them into gritty compost in individual pots.

KEEPING PLANTS In good growing conditions, these cacti will survive for many years.

PLANT CARE

Full, direct sunlight. ● Normal room temperature in summer, but 7°–10°C/ 45°–50°F in winter to ensure good flowering. ● Water moderately in the growing season; give just enough water in winter to prevent the compost from drying out completely. ● Apply a weak solution of high-potash fertiliser every 2 weeks in the growing season to encourage flowering.

~

ERICA x *HIEMALIS*
Ericaceae

FRENCH HEATHER

This winter-flowering heather, which forms a small shrub, has erect stems with whorls of tiny deep green leaves. The 2-cm-/³⁄₄-in long tubular flowers are pink with white tips and are borne in clusters at the ends of the stems. *Erica carnea*, winter heath, is another popular winter-flowering plant. It has more slender stems, which are densely clothed in small, round, rose-pink or purple flowers. Because they need cool conditions, winter heathers are difficult plants to keep in the home, and they should be discarded after they have flowered.

FACT FILE

ORIGIN South Africa (Cape Province); hybrids.

HEIGHT 30–46cm/12–18in.

COMPOST Ericaceous (lime-free) compost.

REPOTTING Plants are usually discarded before repotting is necessary.

PROPAGATION Take semi-ripe stem cuttings in late summer; these are difficult to root successfully in the home.

KEEPING PLANTS Ericas lose their leaves rapidly in a dry atmosphere and tend to be short-lived in heated rooms.

Erica × *hiemalis*

PLANT CARE
Bright light with some direct sun. ● Keep cool, preferably at a maximum of 10°C/50°F. ● Keep the compost moist at all times; never allow it to dry out. Use lime-free water where possible. ● Spray the plant frequently and stand the pot on a tray of moist gravel.

~

ERIOBOTRYA JAPONICA
Rosaceae

ℒOQUAT

Although grown for its edible fruit in warm climates, this plant is unlikely to flower and fruit in the home. It does, however, make an attractive foliage plant, with lance-shaped leaves up to 25cm/10in long and half as wide. Deep-set veins give the leaf surface a textured appearance, and the young foliage is covered with a silvery down. The plant grows into a small tree and is most suitable for a sunroom or large hallway.

FACT FILE

ORIGIN China, Japan.

HEIGHT To 3m/10ft in the home.

COMPOST Soil-based to give extra stability to the plant as it grows.

REPOTTING In spring, move a young plant into a pot 2 sizes bigger; top-dress a large plant.

PROPAGATION Take semi-ripe stem cuttings in late summer; a propagator with bottom heat will increase the chances of success. The plant can also be grown from the stones in ripe fruits.

KEEPING PLANTS As loquats age, they begin to look leggy and ungainly and are best discarded.

PLANT CARE
Bright light with some direct sunlight. ● Normal room temperatures during the growing season. Move to cooler conditions with a temperature of 10°C/50°F for a winter rest. ● Keep the compost moist at all times during the growing season; water sparingly in winter. ● Apply a balanced liquid feed every 2–3 weeks to an actively growing plant.

~

EUCHARIS × *GRANDIFLORA*
Amaryllidaceae

𝒜MAZON LILY

A natural hybrid, this evergreen bulbous plant has broadly oval, deep green, stalked leaves about 30cm/12in long. The pendulous fragrant flowers, which are about 8cm/3in wide, appear in summer and sometimes again in autumn or winter. They are carried in groups of three or more at the top of long slender stems and look somewhat similar to white narcissus, but with a slender greenish tube. The central cup is flushed with green and sometimes has tendril-like outgrowths from the rim. The plant is also known as Eucharist lily and star of Bethlehem.

FACT FILE

ORIGIN Colombia, Peru.

HEIGHT Flower stalks to 60cm/2ft.

COMPOST Soil-based with added leaf mould and coarse sand.

REPOTTING Repot in spring every 3 years or so. Plant the bulb with the nose just covered.

PROPAGATION Detach offsets from around the bulb when the main plant is repotted, and pot them up individually.

KEEPING PLANTS This lily thrives in a pot and will last for several years.

PLANT CARE
A bright position, shaded from direct sun. ● Minimum temperature of 10°C/50°F. ● Water newly potted bulbs sparingly until growth starts, and keep the compost moist at all times during the growing season. Reduce watering in early spring for about 6 weeks to encourage blooming. ● Apply a high-potash liquid fertiliser every 2–3 weeks during the growing season.

Eucharis × *grandiflora*

EURYA JAPONICA
Theaceae

EURYA

An evergreen bushy plant, most suitable for a garden room or conservatory where it can be allowed space to develop fully, eurya belongs to the same family as the camellia. The glossy, deep green, leathery leaves are lance-shaped, with toothed margins, and are about 5cm/2in long.

The small, rather unpleasant-smelling white flowers, tinged with green, are followed by shiny black berries, but this plant is generally grown as a specimen for its beautiful foliage. *Eurya japonica* 'Winter Wine', with leaves that turn deep red in autumn, is smaller and has a more spreading habit of growth.

FACT FILE

ORIGIN China, Japan, South Korea, India.

HEIGHT To 1.2m/4ft.

COMPOST Soil-based.

REPOTTING Move into a pot one size larger in spring, when the plant has outgrown its pot.

PROPAGATION Sow seed from ripe berries or take semi-ripe cuttings in late summer.

KEEPING PLANTS Prune lightly after flowering if necessary, but be careful to retain the plant's characteristic herringbone growth habit.

PLANT CARE

Bright light with some direct sun or light shade. ● Cool conditions, with a winter minimum of 7°C/45°F. ● Water plentifully in the growing period, but allow the surface of the compost to dry out between waterings. Keep just moist in winter. ● Apply a balanced liquid fertiliser every 2–3 weeks when the plant is in active growth.

EUSTOMA GRANDIFLORUM
Gentianaceae

PRAIRIE GENTIAN

Often offered as *Lisianthus russellianus*, this is a relatively new indoor plant. The large flowers, with satiny petals, appear in summer in clusters above grey-green, pointed leaves, and open into a wide poppy shape from spirally scrolled buds.

Eustoma is an annual or biennial grown from seed. Most popular is the 'Yodel' series in purple-blue, pink and white. The 'Echo' series has double flowers in several shades of blue, as well as pink and white, and includes varieties that have a picotee edging to the petals. All eustomas make excellent cut flowers.

FACT FILE

ORIGIN Mexico, southern USA.

HEIGHT To 76cm/30in; compact varieties to about 38cm/15in.

COMPOST Soil-based, leaf mould and coarse sand in a ratio of 2:1:1.

REPOTTING Not usually necessary.

PROPAGATION Sow seed in early spring. Plant seedlings 3 to 20-cm/8-in pot to create a good show.

KEEPING PLANTS Plants are usually discarded after flowering.

PLANT CARE

Bright light with some direct sun. ● Fairly cool conditions with good ventilation. ● Water plentifully, but allow the surface of the compost to dry out between waterings. ● Apply a high-potash liquid fertiliser every 2 weeks from the time the buds start to form.

FELICIA AMELLOIDES
(SYN. *AGATHAEA COELESTIS*)
Asteraceae

BLUE MARGUERITE

This tender perennial makes a bushy plant with rounded, oval leaves. In summer, brilliant blue-mauve, daisy-like flowers with yellow centres are freely produced on long, slender stalks, but they will open only in a bright, sunny location. The plant will not thrive if the atmosphere is too hot and humid, and it will rot if conditions are too cold and damp.

Felicia amelloides

FACT FILE

ORIGIN South Africa.

HEIGHT To 46cm/18in.

COMPOST Peat-based with some added coarse sand.

REPOTTING Repot as necessary in spring.

PROPAGATION Sow seed in late spring, or take stem cuttings in early spring.

KEEPING PLANTS Pinch out growing tips regularly and cut back hard after flowering, to keep the plant compact. Discard the plant when it becomes leggy and untidy.

PLANT CARE

Bright light is essential, with some direct sun. ● Fairly cool room temperature in summer, 7°–10°C/45°–50°F in winter. ● Water moderately in the period of active growth; keep almost dry in winter. ● Apply a high-potash liquid fertiliser every 2–3 weeks during spring and summer.

FEROCACTUS LATISPINUS
Cactaceae

BARREL CACTUS

Also known as the fish-hook cactus and devil's tongue, this is a fiercely spined, slow-growing, globular specimen. The narrow ribs bear red or white radiating spines with clusters of four central spines about 4cm/1½in long. The lowest of these is larger and stouter than the rest and strongly hooked. The red or purple flowers are rarely produced in cultivation.

FACT FILE

ORIGIN Mexico, southern USA.

HEIGHT To 30cm/12in after several years.

COMPOST Soil- or peat-based with grit.

REPOTTING In spring. Allow a 13-mm/¹/₂-in space between the plant and the side of the pot.

PROPAGATION Sow seed in spring.

KEEPING PLANTS This cactus needs maximum light for the spines to develop properly.

Ferocactus latispinus

PLANT CARE

Bright light with plenty of direct sunlight. ● A minimum of 10°C/50°F in winter. ● Water sparingly in the growing season; give just enough water to prevent the compost drying out in winter. ● Apply a high-potassium liquid fertiliser every 4 weeks from spring to fall.

~

GENISTA x *SPACHIANA*
Leguminosae

GENISTA

This broom is grown for its strongly fragrant, bright yellow winter or spring flowers. They are of typical pea-flower shape and are carried in slender racemes at the tips of the branches. The leaves consist of three mid-green leaflets that are covered with silky hairs, particularly underneath. The slender stems give the plant a graceful arching habit. The plant is also known as *Cytisus* x *spachianus* and *C. fragrans*.

FACT FILE

ORIGIN Hybrid.

HEIGHT To 90cm/3ft.

COMPOST Soil-based.

REPOTTING Repot in autumn, only when necessary: the plant resents root disturbance.

PROPAGATION Take stem cuttings in summer.

KEEPING PLANTS Cut back flowering stems once the flowers have faded, then stand the plant in a sheltered, sunny spot outdoors; bring it back indoors in autumn.

Genista x *spachiana*

PLANT CARE

Bright light with 2 or 3 hours of direct sunlight in spring; otherwise, moderate light. ● Cool conditions, with a maximum of 16°C/60°F during flowering. ● Water freely from the time the buds appear to the end of the growing season; do not allow the pot to stand in water. Water more sparingly at other times. ● As soon as buds appear, give a high-potash liquid fertiliser every 3 weeks.

~

GEOGENANTHUS UNDATUS
(SYN. *G. POEPPEGII*)
Commelinaceae

SEERSUCKER PLANT

Related to *dichorisandra*, *tradescantia* and *zebrina*, this foliage plant produces a small number of erect, rather fleshy, unbranched stems, which bear rosettes of tough, oval leaves 8–13cm/3–5in long and 5–10cm/2–4in wide. The dark green leaves are strikingly marked with lengthwise silver stripes and the leaf surface is puckered, giving it the appearance of seersucker. The leaves are purple-red underneath. In summer mature plants may produce small, fringed, purple flowers that last for only a single day.

FACT FILE

ORIGIN Brazil, Peru.

HEIGHT To 25cm/10in.

COMPOST Equal parts of peat moss, leaf mould and perlite.

REPOTTING Move into a pot one size larger in spring, when roots fill the current pot.

PROPAGATION Take stem tip cuttings in spring. Geogenanthus does not root as readily as many other members of the family.

KEEPING PLANTS The plant grows throughout the year, but most actively from spring to late autumn.

PLANT CARE

Bright light but shaded from direct sun. ● The temperature must not drop below 16°C/60°F. ● Keep the compost moist in the growing season; water less in winter. ● Stand the pot on a tray of damp gravel to increase humidity. ● Apply a balanced liquid fertiliser every 2 weeks during the growing season.

Glechoma hederacea
'Variegata'

GLECHOMA HEDERACEA
'VARIEGATA'
Labiatae

GROUND IVY

Although generally regarded as a weed, this trailing plant is very attractive in its variegated form. The rounded, scallop-edged leaves are irregularly margined and splashed with white. They have a downy surface and are aromatic when crushed. In summer, pale lilac – or sometimes white or pink – flowers are produced in the axils of the leaves. Glechoma is a good plant for a hanging basket, easy to grow and hardy.

FACT FILE

ORIGIN Europe.

HEIGHT Prostrate; stems trail to 25cm/10in.

COMPOST Soil- or peat-based.

REPOTTING Repot when the roots fill the pot.

PROPAGATION Stem cuttings root quickly in spring and summer.

KEEPING PLANTS Pinch out growing tips and cut stems back hard in early spring.

PLANT CARE

Bright light but not direct sun. ● Cool room temperature in summer; with a minimum of 10°C/50°F in winter. ● Keep the soil moist in summer; water sparingly in winter. ● Liquid-feed every 2–3 weeks in spring and summer.

GOMPHRENA GLOBOSA
Amaranthacaeae

GLOBE AMARANTH

Often grown in borders in the garden to provide colourful flower heads for drying, this half-hardy annual can be grown on a sunny windowsill.

The rounded flower heads, which give the plant the name of bachelor's button, are composed mainly of brightly coloured papery bracts in shades of red, pink, purple, white, yellow or orange; seed is usually sold in mixed colours.

Some compact forms are available, such as the red-flowered 'Nana', and 'Buddy' with deep purple flowers, which both grow to 15–20cm/6–8in high.

FACT FILE

ORIGIN Old World tropics.

HEIGHT To 60cm/2ft.

COMPOST Soil- or peat-based.

REPOTTING Not usually necessary.

PROPAGATION Sow seed in early spring.

KEEPING PLANTS Discard the plant once it is past its best. The flower heads are good for dried-flower arrangements.

PLANT CARE

Bright light with some direct sunlight. ● Normal to cool room temperature. ● Keep the compost just moist at all times. ● Apply a high-potash liquid fertiliser every 2 weeks.

~

GRAPTOPHYLLUM PICTUM
Acanthaceae

CARICATURE PLANT

Although rarely seen, this evergreen shrub would prosper in the home, especially in a sunroom or conservatory.

The laurel-shaped leaves, arranged opposite each other along the stalk, are up to 15cm/6in long. Each leaf is shiny deep green, marked in the centre with a creamy white or yellow blotch that is sometimes thought to resemble a human face, hence the common name. There is occasionally a pinkish tinge along the central leaf vein. The 4-cm/1½-in-long tubular crimson or purple flowers open wide at the mouth.

FACT FILE

ORIGIN Australasia, Pacific Islands.

HEIGHT To 1.8m/6ft.

COMPOST Soil-based.

REPOTTING In spring, move to a pot one size larger.

PROPAGATION Take stem cuttings in late spring or summer.

KEEPING PLANTS Pinch out the growing tips regularly to encourage bushiness. Replace the plant after 3 or 4 years, when it becomes leggy.

PLANT CARE

Bright filtered light with some direct sun except on the hottest days. ● Average room temperature. ● Water thoroughly, particularly in summer. ● Apply a standard liquid fertiliser once a month between spring and fall.

~

GUZMANIA DISSITIFLORA
Bromeliaceae

GUZMANIA

Like other guzmanias, this unusual-looking plant has a rosette of long, semi-erect strap-shaped leaves that form a central vase. The long flower stalk, rising from the vase, is enclosed in bright red bracts and bears a flower head consisting of 7 to 15 flowers on short stems. These stems are also enclosed in bright red and yellow papery bracts, which are fused into a tube for the greater part of their length. The flowers themselves are small and white.

FACT FILE

ORIGIN Panama, Costa Rica, Colombia.

HEIGHT To 90cm/3ft in flower.

COMPOST Peat-based.

REPOTTING Repot when the pot is overcrowded.

PROPAGATION Offsets can be detached from the base of the plant and potted up separately.

KEEPING PLANTS Warmth, shade and humidity are essential. If they are provided, the plant will last for several years.

PLANT CARE

Bright light but shaded from direct sunlight. ● A minimum of 10°C/50°F; optimum temperature is above 18°C/65°F. ● Keep the compost just moist and top up the central vase occasionally. ● Spray the plant regularly to maintain humidity in the growing season. ● Apply a balanced liquid fertiliser every 2 weeks during the growing season. Foliar feed can be added to the misting water.

Guzmania dissitiflora

HAWORTHIA PUMILA

(SYN. *H. MARGARITIFERA*)
Liliaceae

PEARL PLANT

A succulent plant rather similar to an aloe, this haworthia forms a rosette of fleshy, triangular dark green or purple-green leaves with sharp tips, which tend to curve inwards slightly. Pearly white 'warts' on the back of the leaves make a striking pattern and give the plant its common name. Insignificant flowers may appear. Unlike most succulents, haworthias do not like direct sunlight, which causes the leaves to shrivel.

Haworthia pumila

FACT FILE

ORIGIN South Africa (Western Cape Province).

HEIGHT To 15cm/6in.

COMPOST Soil-based, or peat-based with some added grit.

REPOTTING Repot annually in spring. Use a shallow pot, since the root system is small.

PROPAGATION Remove offsets and pot them up individually in late spring and summer.

KEEPING PLANTS The plant needs a winter rest.

PLANT CARE

Bright indirect light but no direct sunlight. ● Normal room temperature with a rest period at about 10°C/50°F in winter. ● Water freely in the growing season; allow the top one-third to dry out between waterings. Keep the compost almost dry in winter. ● Do not feed haworthias.

HEBE x ANDERSONII

Scrophulariaceae

HEBE

This almost hardy, evergreen shrub makes an attractive short-term indoor plant; it is also suitable for a tub in the conservatory or sunroom. The glossy, oblong leaves are about 10cm/4in long and mid- to deep green. Very small flowers are carried all through the summer in dense, 15-cm/6-in-long, 'bottle brush' racemes; they are pink or mauve, fading to white. The form 'Variegata' has smaller, lighter green leaves margined with cream.

FACT FILE

ORIGIN Hybrid.

HEIGHT To 1.5m/5ft but can be kept much smaller as a pot plant.

COMPOST Soil- or peat-based.

REPOTTING In spring move into a larger pot as necessary.

PROPAGATION Take semi-ripe stem cuttings in late summer.

KEEPING PLANTS The plant will benefit from a spell outdoors during summer. In temperate climates, when it has become too large for a pot plant, it can be hardened off and planted in the garden.

PLANT CARE

Bright light, but protect the plant from strong midsummer sun. ● Keep moderately cool, with a minimum temperature of 4°–7°C/40°–45°F. ● Keep the compost moist at all times in spring and summer; reduce watering during the winter rest period. ● Give a high-potash liquid feed every 2 weeks in spring and summer.

HEDYCHIUM CORONARIUM

Zingiberaceae

BUTTERFLY GINGER

Because of its large size, this plant is best suited for a conservatory or garden room. Hedychium is a perennial that forms a dense clump of lance-shaped, pointed leaves. These rise from the rhizomatous root stock and can grow up to 1.8m/6ft long. The flowers are carried in long spikes of about six strongly fragrant white blooms, which are tubular with a prominent lower lip. The plant is also known as garland flower and white ginger lily. In its natural habitat, this hedychium grows along the banks of streams, and it will tolerate standing in water.

FACT FILE

ORIGIN Tropical Asia.

HEIGHT To 1.2m/4ft or more.

COMPOST Soil- or peat-based.

REPOTTING Move into a larger pot in early spring, when roots fill the current container.

PROPAGATION Divide overcrowded clumps in spring or sow fresh seed.

KEEPING PLANTS Cut out old spikes in winter, when the plant is dormant.

PLANT CARE

Moderately bright light but not direct sunlight. ● Minimum temperature of 16°C/60°F. ● Keep the compost moist in the growing season; water sparingly in winter, allowing the plant to become dormant. ● Give a high-potash liquid feed every 2–3 weeks in spring and summer.

HELICONIA SCHIEDEANA
Heliconiaceae

ℒOBSTER CLAWS

A magnificent perennial for the warm greenhouse or sunroom, heliconia is grown for its stately habit, its superb waxy flowers, and its handsome foliage, rather like that of a banana plant. The flowers resemble those of the exotic strelitzia, the bird-of-paradise plant. Since the tough, oblong leaves grow to 1.4m/4½ft in length, only young, relatively small plants are suitable for bringing into the living room. The upright floral bracts, which can grow to 36cm/14in, are slightly twisted when mature; they are red or orange-red, with yellow or, occasionally, green flowers emerging from them.

FACT FILE

ORIGIN Mexico.

HEIGHT To 3m/10ft.

COMPOST Peat-based, or bark and leaf mould with added dried manure; must be moisture-retentive.

REPOTTING Repot in spring, every 2 years.

PROPAGATION In spring sow seed or separate and pot up offsets, or divide the plant when repotting.

KEEPING PLANTS When stems have flowered, cut them away to encourage new growth. Watch out for red spider mites and scale insects, which can be a problem.

PLANT CARE

Semi-shade. ● A minimum temperature of 16°C/60°F. ● Water moderately at all times. ● Mist the plant daily in warm weather. ● Feed with a high-potash foliar feed every 2 weeks during spring and summer.

Heliconia schiedeana

Hemigraphis colorata

HEMIGRAPHIS COLORATA
(SYN. *H. ALTERNATA*)
Acanthaceae

ℛED IVY

This low-growing, creeping plant, also known as red-flame ivy, gains its common names from the stems and the puckered leaves, which are strongly suffused with red. It needs high humidity and so is well suited to growing in a terrarium or large bottle garden. The upper surface of the oval leaves, which are some 8cm/3in long, is silver grey and quilted; the reverse is purple. In late summer, hemigraphis bears spikes of rather insignificant white flowers, some 2-cm/¾-in long.

Hemigraphis repanda is very similar to *H. colorata*, but the leaves are more slender, purple-green above and deep purple underneath. The hybrid *H.* 'Exotica' has a bushier habit, with smaller white flowers.

FACT FILE

ORIGIN Malaysia; hybrid.

HEIGHT To 30cm/12in.

COMPOST Soil- or peat-based, with added leaf mould. Good drainage is essential.

REPOTTING Move to a pot one size larger every 6–8 weeks during the period of active growth.

PROPAGATION Take tip cuttings at any time.

KEEPING PLANTS Pinch out the growing tips regularly to promote bushy growth.

PLANT CARE

Bright filtered light but no direct sunlight. ● Average room temperature of 18°–24°C/65°–75°F all year round. ● Keep the compost moist at all times; water with tepid soft water or rainwater. ● Feed at 2-week intervals during spring and summer.

HYMENOCALLIS LITTORALIS
Amaryllidaceae

ℐPIDER LILY

This frost-tender, evergreen bulbous plant is best grown in a warm greenhouse and brought indoors for flowering. Its fragrant, beautifully formed flowers have elegantly reflexed, narrow outer segments. These make the whole bloom appear spider-like, and give the plant its common name. They are white, with a greenish tinge to the base, and up to eight blooms may be carried in an umbel on each 76-cm/30-in-long flower stalk.

Hymenocallis littoralis

FACT FILE

ORIGIN Tropical America.

HEIGHT To 90cm/3ft.

COMPOST Equal parts of soil-based compost, leaf mould and coarse sand.

REPOTTING At the end of the winter rest period, repot the bulb in fresh compost in the same pot.

PROPAGATION Separate and divide offsets when repotting, or sow seed in spring or summer.

KEEPING PLANTS Overwatering in winter when the plant is resting will cause the bulb to rot. Keep the compost just moist until new growth starts, then repot.

PLANT CARE

Bright, filtered light but no direct sunlight. ● Average warm greenhouse temperature, with a winter minimum of 16°C/60°F. ● Water plentifully when the plant is in active growth. In the winter rest period, keep the compost just moist. ● Liquid-feed every 2 weeks during the flowering period and for 2 months after the last flower fades.

HYPOCYRTA RADICANS see *NEMETANTHUS GREGARIUS*

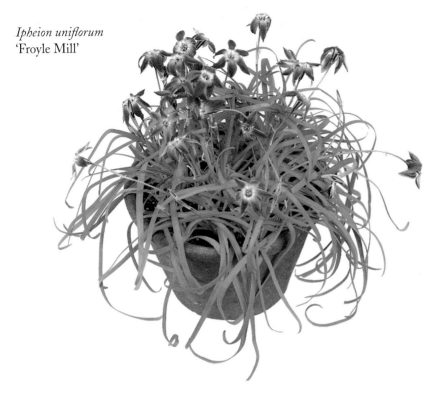

Ipheion uniflorum
'Froyle Mill'

IPHEION UNIFLORUM
Liliaceae

*S*PRING STAR FLOWER

The beautiful star-shaped pale blue or white flowers, carried on slender 15-cm/6-in stems, are the main feature of this bulbous plant. As its name suggests, it blooms early in the season and is tolerant of cold weather, down to -10°C/14°F.

The flower stalks grow through tufts of long, narrow, grass-like leaves, which smell of garlic when crushed, although the flowers themselves have a pleasant smell.

FACT FILE

ORIGIN Argentina, Uruguay.

HEIGHT To 20cm/8in.

COMPOST Soil-based with added grit to aid drainage.

REPOTTING The plant rests from late spring to late summer. Repot in early autumn, after the plant has rested.

PROPAGATION Divide and replant the offsets every 2 or 3 years.

KEEPING PLANTS This is an attractive plant for a deep pot in a well-ventilated cold greenhouse and should be brought into the living room only at flowering time.

PLANT CARE

Full sun, except during the hottest part of the day. ● Cool to average greenhouse conditions; cool room temperature. ● Water moderately during the growing season. ● Apply a standard liquid fertiliser once every 4 weeks during winter and early spring.

IPOMOEA TRICOLOR
Convolvulaceae

*M*ORNING GLORY

Ipomoea is an attractive frost-tender perennial climber that is more usually grown as an annual. It has heart-shaped pale green leaves 15–25cm/6–10in wide and freely produced flowers, which appear from midsummer to mid-autumn. These are purple-blue with a white tube, and open to 13cm/5in wide in the morning, only to fade during the afternoon (hence the common name). 'Heavenly Blue' is a commonly seen cultivar, with sky blue flowers of a particularly vivid colour.

FACT FILE

ORIGIN Tropical America.

HEIGHT Stems climb to 4m/13ft.

COMPOST Soil-based, with added peat.

REPOTTING Not required; the plants are discarded at the end of flowering each year.

PROPAGATION Sow seeds in heat, in spring. Nick the seeds or soak them in tepid water overnight to facilitate germination.

KEEPING PLANTS Deadhead daily to encourage flowering and prolong the flowering season. Discard the plant when flowering is over.

PLANT CARE

Full sun or light shade. ● Average to warm room and greenhouse temperature. ● Water well, but do not waterlog. ● Feed with a high-potash fertiliser every 2 weeks between spring and late summer.

IXORA COCCINEA
Rubiaceae

*F*LAME-OF-THE-WOODS

In its natural habitat, this handsome tropical evergreen shrub enjoys warm, humid conditions, and it will thrive in a well-heated greenhouse. Bring the plant into the home when it is in bloom.

The flat-topped flower heads, which appear from spring onwards, are comprised of many individual tubular flowers, each up to 4cm/1½in long. Cultivars are now freely available with flowers in a range of reds, oranges and pinks. The 10-cm/4-in-long, broadly elliptic leaves are glossy and thick, and are arranged in pairs. New leaves have a bronze tinge, maturing to dark green.

FACT FILE

ORIGIN India, Sri Lanka.

HEIGHT To 1.2m/4ft in 4–5 years.

COMPOST Peat-based, with added leaf mould and coarse sand.

REPOTTING Move into a larger pot every spring until a 46-cm/18-in pot is reached; thereafter top-dress annually.

PROPAGATION Take 8-cm/3-in stem cuttings in spring or summer.

KEEPING PLANTS Protect the plant from draughts and do not water with cold water.

PLANT CARE

Full sun. ● Warm conditions with a minimum temperature of 16°C/60°F. ● When in growth, water freely with soft water or rainwater at room temperature; give less water in winter. ● Stand the pot on a tray of moist pebbles to increase humidity. ● Feed with a standard liquid fertiliser every 2 weeks in summer.

Ixora coccinea

JACARANDA MIMOSIFOLIA
Bignoniaceae

JACARANDA

In the garden, jacaranda grows into a tree up to 12m/40ft high, and in Brazil it is the source of palisander wood. The foliage is doubly pinnate. And the leaves grow opposite along the stem and droop in spring, as some ferns do, so at first sight small specimens may be mistaken for them. Each leaf is composed of numerous tiny oblong pinnae, covered with downy hairs.

Outdoors, dense panicles of hyacinth blue flowers cover the tree in spring. These are reluctant to form on indoor plants until they reach a height of 1.5m/5ft or more. Generally, indoor plants are grown for their fine soft foliage.

FACT FILE

ORIGIN Argentina.

HEIGHT To 1.8m/6ft in a large container.

COMPOST Soil-based.

REPOTTING In spring, move into a pot one size larger, until maximum desired pot size is reached.

PROPAGATION Sow fresh seed in spring, or take stem cuttings with a heel in early summer.

KEEPING PLANTS Prune the plant in spring if it becomes too large. After several years, when it become straggly, discard it.

PLANT CARE

Bright light with at least 3 hours of full sun daily. ● Average room temperature, with a winter minimum of 12°C/54°F, but the plant can tolerate temperatures down to 7°C/45°F. ● Water well from spring to autumn; give less water in the winter rest period. ● Apply standard liquid fertiliser every 2 weeks during the period of active growth.

~

JATROPHA PODAGRICA
Euphorbiaceae

GOUT PLANT

An unusual succulent shrub, also known as tartogo, this is an easy plant to grow. It has a thick, bottle-shaped body, swollen with water-storage tissue, from which it derives its common name. From time to time it produces a few long-stalked shield-shaped leaves with three to five lobes, which can be up to 20cm/8in wide.

Bright red flowers in clusters up to 5cm/ 2in wide, which also have long stalks, are produced both in early spring before the leaves appear and at other times throughout the year.

Jatropha podagrica

FACT FILE

ORIGIN Central America.

HEIGHT To 90cm/3ft.

COMPOST Soil-based with added leaf mould and coarse sand; good drainage is essential.

REPOTTING Every 2–3 years move into a pot one size larger in late winter.

PROPAGATION Sow fresh seed or take cuttings in summer.

KEEPING PLANTS The plant should be kept dry during the winter, when most of the leaves fall.

PLANT CARE

Sunshine or semi-shade. ● Warm room temperature, with a winter minimum of 13°–16°C/55°–60°F. ● Water moderately in summer, hardly at all in winter. The plant must never stand in water. ● Feed twice a year with a half-strength standard liquid fertiliser.

~

JUSTICIA PAUCIFLORA
(SYN J. RIZZINII)
Acanthaceae

JUSTICIA

This is another member of the genus that includes the very different-looking *Justicia carnea*. An attractive, many-branched, shrubby plant, with soft green stems and mid-green leaves in pairs, this justicia forms a small rounded bush. It is a cheerful addition to the list of winter-flowering plants since, from late autumn to early spring, it is covered in clusters of 2.5-cm/ 1-in-long tubular flowers that are scarlet at the base and bright yellow at the tip.

FACT FILE

ORIGIN Brazil.

HEIGHT To 60cm/2ft.

COMPOST Soil-based.

REPOTTING Move the plant into a larger pot whenever roots show through the drainage holes; top-dress instead when the maximum desired pot size is reached.

PROPAGATION In spring take stem tip cuttings.

KEEPING PLANTS Pinch out the growing tips regularly to encourage bushiness. Replace the plant with a rooted cutting when it becomes straggly, usually after about 2 years.

PLANT CARE

Bright filtered light or full sun with protection from the hottest sun. ● Normal room temperature, with a rest period at 13°C/55°F from the end of flowering until new growth appears. ● Keep the compost moist but not waterlogged on the growing season; give less water in the rest period. ● Above 13°C/55°F, stand the pot on a tray of moist pebbles to maintain humidity. ● Apply a standard liquid fertiliser every 2 weeks to an actively growing plant.

Justicia pauciflora

KOHLERIA ERIANTHA AND HYBRIDS
Gesneriaceae

KOHLERIA

All parts of this erect plant are hairy. The elliptic leaves are velvety green and woolly on the underside, with contrasting fine reddish hairs around the margins; the summer flowers are also hairy. They are orange-red, tubular, some 5cm/2in long and are usually carried in clusters of three or four. Cultivars range from shades of orange to red, yellow-orange and orange-red, depending on variety. The inside of the flowers' mouth is marked with yellow spots.

FACT FILE

ORIGIN Colombia; hybrids.

HEIGHT To 1.2m/4ft.

COMPOST Peat-based with added sand or perlite, or equal parts of soil-based compost, peat and perlite.

REPOTTING Move into a pot one size larger each spring.

PROPAGATION In spring divide the rhizomes or sow seed; take root tip cuttings in autumn.

KEEPING PLANTS Be careful not to get water on the leaves; it will be trapped by the hairs and may scorch the leaves or cause botrytis. After flowering, cut the stems back to 2.5–5cm/1–2in.

PLANT CARE

Bright, filtered light. ● Normal room temperature. ● Water moderately during the growing season; give just enough water in winter to prevent the leaves from wilting. ● Feed with half-strength liquid fertiliser every 2 weeks in the growing season.

LACHENALIA ALOIDES
Liliaceae

CAPE COWSLIP

A good plant for a sunny windowsill, lachenalia has two or three arching fleshy leaves 30cm/12in long and about 5cm/2in wide. These spring from a bulb some 4cm/1½in round. The flower stalk is green or purple-brown, and racemes of tubular flowers appear in late winter and early spring. Several varieties are in cultivation: 'Aurea' has flowers of a soft deep yellow; those of 'Pearsonii' are apricot and red. 'Nelsonii' has golden yellow flowers with green tips. Lachenalia is sometimes called soldier boys, from the military look of the plants when grown in rows.

FACT FILE

ORIGIN South Africa (Cape Province).

HEIGHT To 30cm/12in.

COMPOST Soil- or peat-based with added loam.

REPOTTING Repot every year in early autumn.

PROPAGATION Sow seed in spring, or remove offset bulbs when repotting and plant them up separately; they will flower after 2 years.

KEEPING PLANTS As leaves wither, dry off the plant; keep almost dry when dormant.

PLANT CARE

Full sun or light shade. ● Cool temperature in the range of 10°–16°C/50°–60°F. ● Water moderately in the growing period. ● Apply standard liquid fertiliser once a week from the time the flower stalks appear until the last flower dies.

LEEA COCCINEA
Leeaceae

WEST INDIAN HOLLY

This shrub is grown for its velvety wine-coloured, 5–10cm/2–4in-long wavy-edged leaflets, which turn green as the plant matures. When still young, the plant will produce small grape-like flowers, which are red in bud, turning to pink. *Leea coccinea* 'Burgundy' has richer red leaves and needs better light to keep this colouring. *Leea coccinea* 'Green' produces mid-green leaves.

FACT FILE

ORIGIN Burma.

HEIGHT To 1.8m/6ft.

COMPOST Soil-based.

REPOTTING In spring move into a pot one size larger until maximum desired size is reached.

PROPAGATION In spring sow seeds, take stem cuttings or air-layer, all of which are difficult.

KEEPING PLANTS A healthy plant should last 5 or 6 years, but keep it out of draughts.

PLANT CARE

Bright indirect light. ● Minimum temperature of 16°C/60°F. ● Sensitive to both under- and over-watering; keep the compost moist, but not sodden at all times. ● Mist the plant frequently and stand the pot on a dish of moist pebbles to maintain high humidity. ● Feed every 2 weeks in spring and summer with dilute liquid feed.

LILIUM SPP.
Liliaceae

TRUMPET LILIES

Although lilies are usually considered garden flowers, a few types make successful temporary plants for growing indoors. These include the trumpet lilies, the petals of which are fused together for part of the length of the flower to produce a basal tube.

There are dozens of hybrids from which to choose. Some of the most popular are the Mid-Century hybrids, derived from the Asiatic lilies. 'Pixie' is a typical example, with bright orange flowers.

Other good hybrids for growing indoors are 'Chinook', which is also orange, and 'Cinnabar' with maroon-red flowers. 'Connecticut King' has golden yellow flowers, 'Destiny' has lemon yellow flowers, and those of 'Prosperity' are pale yellow.

Autumn is the best time to plant lily bulbs for pot use. Buy plump, firm bulbs with no signs of wrinkling or softness. Plant each bulb in a 15-cm/6-in pot or

larger, with at least 2.5cm/1in of potting mix above its head. Until growth begins, keep it cool, dark and moist; when growth is visible, move it to a brighter position.

FACT FILE

ORIGIN Hybrid.

HEIGHT To 1.2m/4ft.

COMPOST Soil- or peat-based, with good drainage.

REPOTTING Repot annually in autumn. Lily bulbs should be planted in deep pots that are large enough to allow good root development. For example, only 3–4 medium-sized bulbs should be planted in a 30-cm/12-in pot, and there should be at least 2.5cm/1in between the bulbs and between the bulbs and the side of the pot.

PROPAGATION Separate bulblets when repotting; remove and plant bulb scales in winter, or sow stem bulbils (small black bulbs produced on the stem in the axils of the leaves) in late summer.

KEEPING PLANTS Overwatering and bad drainage can cause the bulbs to rot. If the bulbs are not kept for another season's indoor flowering, plant them outdoors. Stake the stems to prevent the plants from toppling over.

PLANT CARE

Bright light but no direct sun. ● Overwinter the bulb in its pot at about 4°C/40°F; move it to a warmer place as growth begins in spring. ● Water well during the growing season. ● Feed with a weak liquid fertiliser once a month in spring and summer.

Lilium 'Pixie'

Liriope muscari

LIRIOPE MUSCARI

(SYN. *L. GRAMINIFOLIA DENSIFLORA*)
Liliaceae

BIG BLUE LILY-TURF

Of the three or four species of liriope available, this is the most suitable for pot culture. When in flower, the plant closely resembles a large grape hyacinth with green foliage. It is an evergreen, stalkless plant with erect, conspicuously veined strap-shaped leaves 30cm/12in long and 13mm/$\frac{1}{2}$in wide. In late summer to autumn, purple to violet flowers are produced in dense racemes, which are almost the same length as the leaves; they are followed by black berries. After flowering, cut off the flower stalks unless you require the berries.

There are several attractive cultivars, including 'Gold-banded', which has wide, arching dark green leaves edged with gold, and the 46-cm/18-in-high 'Silvery Midget', with white markings on the leaves and white flowers.

FACT FILE

ORIGIN China, Japan.

HEIGHT To 30cm/12in.

COMPOST Soil- or peat-based.

REPOTTING Repot every couple of years, in spring.

PROPAGATION Divide in spring or sow seed in summer.

KEEPING PLANTS Keep the plant out of draughts; cold winds can damage the leaves.

PLANT CARE

Bright filtered light. ● Average to warm room temperature; keep at 4°–10°C/40°–50°F in winter. ● Keep the compost fairly moist, but the cooler the temperature, the drier the compost should be. ● Feed actively growing plants every 2 weeks with standard liquid fertiliser.

MIKANIA DENTATA (SYN. *M. TERNATA*)
Compositae

PLUSH VINE

This plant is grown chiefly for its unusual leaf colouring. It is really a jungle weed, with creeping, trailing or slightly climbing red to purple stems. The hairy, compound leaves, up to 4cm/1$\frac{1}{2}$in long, are grey-green, with a violet-purple lustre and violet veining. Small, fairly insignificant, groundsel-like yellow-white flowers appear in summer.

FACT FILE

ORIGIN Brazil.

HEIGHT To 1.8m/6ft.

COMPOST Soil- or peat-based.

REPOTTING Repot in spring, in the same pot.

PROPAGATION Sow seed, take cuttings or divide in spring. Young plants will grow well only if they are raised in warm greenhouse conditions.

KEEPING PLANTS Discard the plant after 2 years or so; older plants become unsightly.

PLANT CARE

Introduce the plant gradually to the light in spring, then set in full sun. ● Normal room conditions, with a minimum of 12°C/54°F. ● Water moderately all year round. ● Stand the pot on a tray of damp pebbles to maintain humidity, but do not spray the hairy leaves, since this may cause them to rot. ● Liquid-feed every 2 weeks during summer.

~

MILTONIA
Orchidaceae

PANSY ORCHID

Although this epiphytic orchid has pseudo-bulbs, it is evergreen and grows all year round. One to three long, narrow, pale green leaves are borne at the tips of the pseudobulbs, and erect flower stems up to 46cm/18in long rise from the base. Each stem may carry as many as 10 flat-faced flowers, up to 10cm/4in wide, which look like pansies and account for the common name. The main flowering season is from late spring through summer, but there is sometimes a second flush of flowers in autumn; each flower lasts four to five weeks.

Miltonia candida produces 8-cm/3-in-wide yellow flowers with chestnut brown patches and a white lip. *M. regnellii* has white flowers 8cm/3in wide, with a pink flush near the base. Numerous hybrids are available, and new forms are constantly being produced.

FACT FILE

ORIGIN Central and South America; hybrid.

HEIGHT To 60cm/2ft.

COMPOST Special orchid compost.

REPOTTING Repot in summer, only when essential; the plant flowers best when it is pot-bound.

PROPAGATION Divide the rhizome in summer; each section must have at least 2 pseudobulbs.

KEEPING PLANTS Remove wilting flowers and leaves at once; they can affect others. Watch out for thrips, which may infest the plant.

PLANT CARE

Medium light; in winter the plant needs bright light and 3 hours of sun. ● Keep within the range of 17°–21°C/63°–70°F at all times. ● Water generously in spring and summer; spray the foliage daily. ● In late spring and early summer give 2 or 3 feeds of standard liquid fertiliser at half strength.

~

MIMOSA PUDICA
Leguminosae

SENSITIVE PLANT

This small shrub, which can grow like a weed in the wild, should not be confused with the yellow-flowered mimosa sold by florists. *Mimosa pudica* bears pale pink pompom flowers from midsummer through to early fall. The feathery leaves are composed of up to 25 pairs of small oblong leaflets; these fold up at night and the entire leaf stalk droops. The leaflets also fold up tightly if they are touched, if the plant is shaken, or if it is subjected to heat from a lighted candle or cigarette, indicating that heat might be the trigger.

The plant is most sensitive at high temperatures – between 24°C/75°F and 29°C/85°F. If left for a while, the leaves will slowly unfold and the stems will straighten.

Mimosa pudica

FACT FILE

ORIGIN Tropical America; naturalised in the tropics worldwide.

HEIGHT To 90cm/3ft.

COMPOST Peat-based, or soil-based with added sand and leaf mould.

REPOTTING Repot throughout the season, whenever roots show through the base of the current pot.

PROPAGATION Sow seed in early spring.

KEEPING PLANTS *Mimosa pudica* is usually treated as an annual and discarded after flowering, since it loses its beauty as it ages.

PLANT CARE

Bright light with some direct sun to promote flowering. ● Normal room temperature. ● Allow the top of the soil to dry out before rewatering. ● Stand the pot on a tray of wet pebbles to increase humidity. ● Feed with a high-potash fertiliser every 2 weeks.

NEMATANTHUS GREGARIUS
Gesneriaceae

*N*EMATANTHUS

Also known as *Nematanthus radicans* and *Hypocyrta radicans*, this plant has trailing stems and is an ideal subject for a hanging basket. The stems are thickly clothed with 3-cm/1¼-in-long oval leaves, which are slightly fleshy and a glossy dark green.

In summer the plant bears waxy orange flowers with yellow lobes, the tubes of which bulge curiously at the base. This nematanthus needs a winter rest period.

FACT FILE

ORIGIN Brazil.

HEIGHT Stems trail to 60cm/2ft.

COMPOST Peat-based.

REPOTTING Move to a pot one size larger either after flowering or after the dormant period.

PROPAGATION Take tip cuttings in summer or divide older plants.

KEEPING PLANTS In summer, after flowering, put the plant outdoors in a warm sheltered spot. Cut back a little each year to ensure flowering.

PLANT CARE

Bright light. ● Temperatures of 10°–13°C/ 50°–55°F during the winter rest period; normal room temperature at other times. ● Water moderately in summer; give less water in winter. ● Apply half-strength standard liquid fertiliser every 2–3 weeks during summer.

NEPENTHES **x** *HOOKERIANA*
Nepenthaceae

*P*ITCHER PLANT

A large plant for the heated, shaded greenhouse, where the atmosphere is humid, this epiphytic carnivorous plant is not very easy to grow, but it is intriguing and worth the effort. The oblong leaves are mid-green, about 30cm/12in long, with a tendril at the tip; this usually develops into a liquid-filled pitcher, topped with a 'lid'. Insects are attracted by the scent produced by nectar glands at the mouth of the pitcher, only to fall into the liquid it contains, where they die and are digested.

The plant produces climbing stems to 3m/10ft or more. The pale yellow-green pitchers, which are broadly oval, some 13cm/5in long and 8cm/3in wide, are heavily marked with purple-brown spots or blotches. Plant nepenthes in lattice or wire baskets to ensure good drainage.

Nepenthes x
hookeriana

FACT FILE

ORIGIN Borneo, Sumatra, Malaysia.

HEIGHT To 3m/10ft.

COMPOST Peat-based with added moss and perlite in the ratio of 1:2:1; or sphagnum moss with charcoal added to prevent it from turning sour.

REPOTTING Repot in spring, but take care, since the delicate roots break easily.

PROPAGATION Air-layer, or take leaf cuttings in spring. Root them in sphagnum moss with bottom heat; rooting may take up to 8 weeks. Spray with fresh water daily.

KEEPING PLANTS Prune old plants heavily in spring to encourage new growth.

PLANT CARE

Avoid bright sunshine at all times; in winter place the plant near a window but out of direct sun. ● A minimum of 18°C/65°F all year round. ● Water well with lime-free water during the period of active growth. ● Spray the plant daily. ● Occasionally during the growing season, drop a few insects into the pitcher if there are none flying around.

NERINE BOWDENII
Amaryllidaceae

*N*ERINE

This frost-tender bulbous plant is grown for its long-lived flowers, which appear in late summer and early autumn. The oval bulb, about 5cm/2in in diameter, produces umbels of 6 to 12 flowers on stalks up to 46cm/18in long. The trumpet-shaped flowers are some 6.5cm/2½in long and vary in colour from bright candy pink to soft rose pink and, rarely, white. The petals have a wavy edge, which gives the umbel a spidery appearance. Arching, deep green strap-shaped leaves some 30cm/12in long emerge after the flowers have bloomed and last throughout the winter and well into the following spring. Nerines are best raised in a greenhouse and brought into the house just before they flower.

Nerine bowdenii 'Fenwick's Variety' is an early-flowering, vigorous form with cyclamen pink flowers. *N.b.* 'Zeal Giant' has large deep pink flowers, and 'Alba' produces white flowers with a hint of pink.

FACT FILE

ORIGIN South Africa.

HEIGHT Flower stems to 46cm/18in.

COMPOST Well-drained, soil-based compost with added leaf mould.

REPOTTING Repot in summer, at the end of the dormant period.

PROPAGATION Sow fresh ripe seed in late winter or early spring, or remove offsets when repotting and plant them up individually.

KEEPING PLANTS Dry bulbs off after flowering is over and store them during the summer when they are dormant. Repot for autumn flowering, or put the bulbs out in the garden.

PLANT CARE

Bright light, with some direct sun. ● Cool greenhouse temperature and cool room conditions; the plant can stand a temperature as low as -15°C/5°F provided conditions are dry. ● Water well during the period of active growth; do not water during the dormant period. ● Liquid-feed every 2 weeks from the time the buds appear until the leaves begin to die down.

Nertera granadensis

NERTERA GRANADENSIS
Rubiaceae

BEAD PLANT

This curious-looking but attractive creeping plant has tiny, fleshy green intertwining leaves, on stems up to 25cm/10in long, that grow into a thick mat. In early summer it bears small greenish white flowers, which are followed by orange-red berries 6mm/¼in in diameter; these can be so numerous that they completely hide the foliage. The plant is also known as coral moss. When it is not covered with berries, the plant's small leaves closely resembles those of *Soleirolia soleirolii*, baby's tears.

Nertera is shallow rooting, so grow it in a shallow pan or half-pot to display the berries well. Keep it well ventilated, since poor ventilation may hamper the formation of berries.

FACT FILE

ORIGIN South America, Australia (Tasmania), New Zealand.

HEIGHT To 8cm/3in.

COMPOST Peat-based with added leaf mould and sand or grit for good drainage.

REPOTTING Move into a larger pot in spring only when necessary.

PROPAGATION When repotting, divide clumps into 3 or more pieces and pot them individually, or put 3 or 4 around the edge of a large shallow pan. Or sow seed or take tip cuttings in spring.

KEEPING PLANTS Stand the plant outdoors in a sheltered spot with some sun in spring. Bring it indoors when berries start to form.

PLANT CARE

Bright light with some sun. ● Cool room temperature with a maximum of 17°C/63°F; in very warm rooms the plant will produce leaves instead of berries. ● Water well, but allow the surface of the compost to dry out before rewatering. ● Stand the plant on a saucer of damp pebbles, and spray it daily from the time the flowers begin to open until the berries have formed. ● Apply a weak liquid fertiliser once a month in summer and autumn, while the berries are forming and are on the plant.

~

NICODEMIA MADAGASCARIENSIS see
BUDDLEJA MADAGASCARIENSIS

~

OLEA EUROPAEA
Oleaceae

OLIVE

The olive tree has become popular as an indoor plant in recent years, since it is very tolerant of a dry atmosphere. In Mediterranean climates this plant forms a tree up to 6m/20ft high; indoors it can be kept far smaller.

The branches are covered with short-stalked, narrow, grey-green leaves 2.5–8cm/1–3in long, the undersides of which are covered with white or rust-coloured hairs. Yellow-white flowers are borne in clusters at the tips of the stems in summer, but the fruits do not ripen until the winter.

Several other higher-yielding varieties are available commercially, but they are no more ornamental for the home than the species.

FACT FILE

ORIGIN Mediterranean region.

HEIGHT To 3m/10ft in a container.

COMPOST Soil-based with added coarse sand; good drainage is essential.

REPOTTING Move to a pot one size larger each spring; once a 46-cm/18-in pot has been reached, top-dress annually instead.

PROPAGATION Sow seeds in spring or summer or take semi-ripe tip cuttings with a heel in summer; however, cuttings do not root easily.

KEEPING PLANTS The plant needs at least 2 months at a temperature below 10°C/50°F to produce flowers, and it will benefit from a spell outdoors in summer. Weighting the branches so that they droop may encourage fruiting. Prune after fruiting, but only if it is necessary to control the plant's size and shape.

PLANT CARE

Full sun or bright light. ● Average to warm temperature, with a winter minimum of 5°C/41°F. ● Water moderately all year round. ● Feed actively growing plants every 2 weeks.

~

OPLISMENUS HIRTELLUS
Gramineae

BASKET GRASS

The wiry, creeping stems make this an attractive plant for a hanging basket, since the stems will trail. It has yellowish green lance-shaped leaves, 5–15cm/2–6in long, with sharply pointed tips and a slightly undulating, or wavy, surface. *Oplismenus hirtellus* 'Variegatus' has white, green and rose-red striped leaves. Pinch out the insignificant flowers as soon as they appear.

FACT FILE

ORIGIN Southern USA, West Indies, Mexico, Argentina.

HEIGHT To 90cm/3ft.

COMPOST Soil- or peat-based.

REPOTTING Move into a pot one size larger in spring, if plants are kept for a second year.

PROPAGATION The long runners root spontaneously; detach and pot up the resulting plantlets. Take tip cuttings in spring.

KEEPING PLANTS As it ages, this plant loses some of its leaves and becomes straggly; cut it back severely or replace it after a year or two.

PLANT CARE

Bright light, but direct sun only in winter. ● Normal room temperature. ● Keep the compost moist at all times; the plant will lose its leaves if it is allowed to dry out. ● Liquid-feed every 4 weeks in summer.

~

OREBEA VARIEGATA see STAPELIA
VARIEGATA

~

OSMANTHUS HETEROPHYLLUS 'VARIEGATUS'

Oleaceae

VARIEGATED FALSE HOLLY

Also known as *Osmanthus ilicifolius* (holly-leafed osmanthus) this dense, woody-stemmed shrub has prickly, glossy leaves that are arranged in pairs. The leaves of 'Variegatus' are about 6.5cm/2½in long and have creamy white markings, sometimes with a tinge of pink at the margins. The shape of the leaves varies, even on the same plant. Some may be almost egg-shaped with smooth edges and a single spine at the tip, while others may be elliptic, with a number of large spiny teeth, including a long spine at the tip. Plants grown indoors only rarely produce small, white, scented flowers in autumn.

FACT FILE

ORIGIN Japan; cultivar.

HEIGHT To 1.8m/6ft in a container.

COMPOST Soil-based.

REPOTTING Move into a pot one size larger each spring.

PROPAGATION Take tip cuttings, with a heel, in spring or summer.

KEEPING PLANTS Pinch out growing tips regularly to prevent the plant becoming lanky.

Osmanthus heterophyllus

PLANT CARE

Full sun. ● Cool temperature, ideally between 13°–18°C/55°–65°F at all times. ● Water moderately throughout the year. ● Feed actively growing plants every 2 weeks.

~

PANDANUS VEITCHII

Pandanaceae

SCREW PINE

The best known of the five or so commonly grown pandanuses, the screw pine is a stately plant, especially when it grows older. It has leaves up to 90cm/3ft long, the lower ones arching, with coarse spines along the margins. A feature of the foliage is the lengthwise creamy white striping. Mature plants develop beautiful stilt-like aerial roots. This pandanus enjoys very humid air and warmer temperatures. It is, therefore, better suited to a greenhouse, but properly looked after it will thrive in the living room.

FACT FILE

ORIGIN Polynesia.

HEIGHT To 2m/7ft.

COMPOST Soil- or peat-based with good drainage.

REPOTTING Young plants may require repotting more than once a year, but after the plant is a year old, repotting each spring will be sufficient.

PROPAGATION Remove suckers from older plants and pot these up individually.

KEEPING PLANTS High humidity is essential for luxuriant leaf growth.

PLANT CARE

A well-lit position; no full sun. ● Minimum temperature of 18°C/65°F. ● Water moderately, using water at room temperature; keep the compost a little drier from mid-autumn until mid-spring. ● Stand the pot on a tray of moist pebbles and spray the plant daily. ● Feed every 2 weeks from spring to autumn.

~

PAPHIOPEDILUM SPP.

Orchidaceae

SLIPPER ORCHIDS

Several species of this orchid, particularly *Paphiopedilum callosum* and *P. sukhakulii*, and some of the smaller hybrids will do well in a living room, preferably near a window that does not receive too much sunlight. Wherever slipper orchids are sited, they require plenty of humidity as well as good ventilation during the hotter months. Paphiopedilums do not require a dormant season, but if the temperature drops in

Paphiopedilum

winter, the water supply must be decreased.

The blooms of these popular orchids have a striking sepal, usually called the flag; the lip of the flower is called the 'slipper' because its pouch-like shape resembles a house slipper. Many hybrids are available from specialist suppliers, and new ones are being added constantly.

FACT FILE

ORIGIN Tropical Asia; hybrids.

HEIGHT To 38cm/15in.

COMPOST Special orchid medium.

REPOTTING Repot annually in late winter. Always provide excellent drainage in the bottom of the pot. *P. callosum* should be kept completely dry for a few weeks after being repotted.

PROPAGATION Divide when repotting.

KEEPING PLANTS High humidity (65–75%) and a daytime temperature some 5°C/9°F above the night temperature are needed.

PLANT CARE

Bright light, but full sun only in winter. ● Normal room temperature, but not below 18°C/65°F at night. ● Water once a week throughout the year. ● Spray the plant daily and stand the pot on a tray of moist gravel to maintain humidity. Never allow water to lie on the leaves or in the centre of the growth; this will encourage botrytis and cause the plant to rot. ● Apply a weak foliar feed once a month from spring to autumn.

PASSIFLORA CAERULEA
Passifloraceae

COMMON PASSION FLOWER

The common, or blue, passion flower grows in tropical conditions, clinging by tendrils to the trunks of jungle trees. Indoors it needs heat, sun and good ventilation in order to do well.

The hand-like leaves are large and glossy dark green. The 8-cm/3-in-wide flowers, give the plant its name. They have five white petals, five white sepals and fine purple-blue filaments surrounding prominent gold anthers. Jesuit missionaries who discovered the plant in Brazil in the 18th century likened its white petals and sepals to the Ten Apostles who witnessed Christ's crucifixion. The anthers were seen as the five wounds, the rays of the corona of filaments as His crown of thorns, and the three stigmas as the nails that pinned Him to the Cross.

Passiflora caerulea

FACT FILE

ORIGIN Brazil to Argentina.

HEIGHT To 5m/16½ft; but as a house plant it is frequently sold trained around a hoop.

COMPOST Soil-based.

REPOTTING Repot in spring for 2 or 3 years, then top-dress instead; the plant flowers best if its roots are restricted.

PROPAGATION Take 18-cm/7-in tip cuttings in summer.

KEEPING PLANTS Pruning does the plant no harm. Each spring, cut the stems of a young plant down to about 23cm/9in. Prune an older plant to keep it within bounds; cut side branches back to 8–10cm/3–4in.

PLANT CARE

Full sun; the plant will not flower if the light is not bright enough. ● A temperature of about 21°C/70°F in summer, 10°C/50°F in winter. ● Water freely in summer; in winter water just enough to prevent the compost drying out. ● Feed with standard liquid fertiliser every 2 weeks in summer.

~

PELLAEA ROTUNDIFOLIA
Sinopteridaceae

BUTTON FERN

A native of the temperate forests of New Zealand, the button fern produces a mass of thin dark stems that, close-up, are seen to be covered with brown scales and hairs. From these stalks arise small, arched fronds of leathery green leaflets, which trail over the edge of the pot, making it ideal for a hanging basket. Unlike most ferns, pellaea tolerates relatively dry conditions.

FACT FILE

ORIGIN New Zealand, Australia.

HEIGHT Fronds trail to 30cm/12in.

COMPOST Soil-based, with added peat and sand.

REPOTTING Use a shallow pot and repot only when roots fill the current container.

PROPAGATION In spring, divide the plant into 2 or 3 sections with roots and top growth.

KEEPING PLANTS Mist when the temperature rises above 21°C/70°F; if the soil becomes waterlogged the plant will die. If conditions are right, it will grow year round, with no rest period.

PLANT CARE

Bright light but not direct sunlight. ● Normal room temperature, as constant as possible. ● Water freely in summer but allow the surface of the compost to dry out before rewatering. ● Feed once a week in summer with a weak solution of standard liquid fertiliser.

Pellaea rotundifolia

PELLIONIA DAVEAUANA (SYN. *P. REPENS*)
Urticaceae

WATERMELON BEGONIA

Although this exotic creeper grows in tropical forests, it adapts well as an indoor plant and looks especially good in a hanging basket. It produces a profusion of succulent stems that carry fleshy, elliptic leaves up to 5cm/2in long. These are bronze to olive green with a pale green band in the centre. This creeper enjoys plenty of light, warmth, high humidity and a protected position.

Pellionia pulchra, satin pellionia, has green stems with a pink tinge and pale grey-green leaves marked with brown-black veins.

FACT FILE

ORIGIN Burma, Vietnam, Malaysia.

HEIGHT To 60cm/2ft.

COMPOST Soil-based.

REPOTTING Move to a pot one size larger each spring until a 13-cm/5-in pot is reached.

PROPAGATION Divide in summer; make sure that each section has some roots. Or take 5-cm/2-in-long stem cuttings at any time.

KEEPING PLANTS The plant should live for several years, but divide it every 2–3 years to prevent it becoming spindly.

PLANT CARE

Bright light or partial shade; no direct sunlight. ● Warm room temperature, up to 28°C/82°F. ● Water well all year. ● Humidity is essential; stand the pot on a dish of moist pebbles and mist the plant daily. ● Apply a weak liquid fertiliser every 2 weeks from spring to autumn.

~

PENTAS LANCEOLATA (SYN. *P. CARNEA*)
Rubiaceae

EGYPTIAN STAR CLUSTER

An upright shrubby plant with pale green, hairy oval leaves 5–10cm/2–4in long and 2.5cm/1in wide, this is the most common species grown as an indoor plant. It thrives best in a heated greenhouse where the air is not too dry. And it should really be regarded as only a temporary plant in the home.

The flowers, which appear in late summer and autumn, grow in terminal clusters on the many branches. They come in shades of pink, lilac and carmine red to mauve and blue, and, occasionally, white. The corona has a narrow, 2-cm/¾-in-long tube, widening slightly towards the top and ending in a five-lobed star.

FACT FILE

ORIGIN Tropical East Africa, Arabian Peninsula.

HEIGHT To 90cm/3ft.

COMPOST Soil- or peat-based.

REPOTTING Move into a pot one size larger in spring.

PROPAGATION In spring or early summer, take 5–8cm/2–3in stem cuttings.

KEEPING PLANTS Pinch out the growing tips from time to time to encourage bushiness.

PLANT CARE

Good light with 4 hours of direct sunlight. ● Normal warm room temperature, but never allow the level to drop below 10°C/50°F. ● Water moderately in the growing period; give less water when flowering is over. Overwatering causes the leaves to turn yellow, and they will not recover. ● Feed every 2 weeks in summer.

~

PHALAENOPSIS SPP.
Orchidaceae

MOTH ORCHID

A free-flowering epiphyte, the moth orchid blooms throughout the year. Its branched spikes bear up to 30 flowers at a time. Individual blooms can be as much as 13cm/5in wide, but in many varieties they are smaller. The flowers vary in colour from white through pinks to red and yellow, often with stripes or spots. Numerous hybrids are available.

FACT FILE

ORIGIN Asia, Australasia; hybrid.

HEIGHT Foliage to 20cm/8in; flowers to 1.2m/4ft.

COMPOST Special orchid compost.

REPOTTING Repot only about every 2 years, when the current pot becomes crowded.

PROPAGATION Not applicable.

KEEPING PLANTS These orchids grow well in wooden or wire baskets lined with sphagnum moss.

PLANT CARE

Bright filtered light or partial shade. ● Normal room temperature, with a minimum of 21°C/70°F. ● Water well all year round. ● Apply an orchid fertiliser once a month; overfeeding will produce leaves at the expense of flowers.

~

PILOCEREUS SENILIS see *CEPHALOCEREUS SENILIS*

~

PIPER NIGRUM
Piperaceae

BLACK PEPPER

This climbing member of the pepper family is suitable for the warm greenhouse; it spreads extensively and needs support. It is an interesting plant to grow and produces fruits some 6mm/¼in round, which ripen to red, then black, and are the source of the culinary spice. The 10-cm/4-in-long heart-shaped leaves are dark green with strongly marked veins.

FACT FILE

ORIGIN South India, Sri Lanka.

HEIGHT To 4m/13ft.

COMPOST Peat-based.

REPOTTING In spring move the plant into a pot one size larger.

PROPAGATION Sow seed in spring or take semi-ripe cuttings in summer.

KEEPING PLANTS Support the plant on a wire or trellis to show it to its best advantage. Prune annually in late winter or early spring, before growth starts, to remove weak, congested stems.

PLANT CARE

Bright indirect light. ● Minimum winter temperature of 10°C/50°F. ● Water moderately when in growth. ● Feed every 2 weeks from spring to autumn.

~

PISONIA UMBELLIFERA 'VARIEGATA'
Nyctaginaceae

BIRD-CATCHER TREE

Although the plain form of pisonia, also known as para-para, grows into a tree in the wild, this attractive form with variegated foliage makes a good indoor plant. The 40-cm/16-in-long leaves, marbled with pale green, have creamy coloured margins that are faintly pink when young. In the cultivated form, small pink or yellow flowers bloom in clusters.

FACT FILE

ORIGIN Australia, New Zealand, Mauritius.

HEIGHT To 3m/10ft in a container.

COMPOST Soil-based.

REPOTTING Repot young plants in late winter or spring; top-dress older plants.

PROPAGATION Take stem cuttings, or air-layer, in summer.

KEEPING PLANTS The plant may quickly outgrow its space, but it can be pruned to maintain size and shape when it is repotted. Set the plant outdoors in summer in mild climates.

PLANT CARE

Full sun or partial shade; the plant loses its colour if the light is not bright enough. ● Warm room or greenhouse conditions, with a winter minimum of 10°C/50°F. ● Water moderately when in growth, sparingly in winter. ● Feed every 2 weeks from spring to autumn.

~

PITTOSPORUM TOBIRA
Pittosporaceae

JAPANESE PITTOSPORUM

Increasingly used by interior decorators, this glossy-leafed small tree, also called Australian laurel, will survive fairly inhospitable indoor conditions. It is a flat-topped plant with dark green leaves up to 10cm/4in long. The leaves of *Pittosporum tobira* 'Variegatum' are a soft grey-green, with a creamy margin. In spring clusters of fragrant, tubular, starry white flowers are carried at the ends of the stems on both varieties, but only on plants that receive good light. Each bloom is 13mm/½in wide. A cool period is required in winter.

Pittosporum tobira

FACT FILE

ORIGIN China, Japan.

HEIGHT To 1.2m/4ft in a container.

COMPOST Soil-based.

REPOTTING Move into a pot one size larger each spring.

PROPAGATION Take tip or stem cuttings in spring; these can be difficult to root, so use hormone rooting powder and bottom heat.

KEEPING PLANTS Prune in spring to restrict size and to remove any straggly growth.

PLANT CARE

Bright light; avoid direct sunlight. ● Although hardy, as an indoor plant it needs normal room temperature, with a winter minimum of 4°C/40°F. ● Water well in the growing period, but sparingly in winter. ● Feed every 2 weeks from spring to autumn with a general fertiliser.

PLEIOBLASTUS AURICOMA see
ARUNDINARIA VIRIDISTRIATA

~

PLUMERIA RUBRA (SYN. *P. ACUMINATA*)
Apocynaceae

Frangipani

Other common names for this popular
shrub include temple tree, nosegay, West
Indian jasmine and pagoda tree. Because
it likes warm conditions and grows quite
large, it is a rarity in the home. The glory
of the plant is the large clusters of heavily
scented flowers carried at the ends of the
branches in summer and autumn. Each
5-cm/2-in-wide flower comprises five thick
overlapping petals, which are often white
but can be pink, yellow, bronze, salmon or
red, invariably with yellow-stained centres.
The pointed oval leaves can be as much
as 30cm/12in long.

FACT FILE

ORIGIN Central America.

HEIGHT To 3m/10ft in a container.

COMPOST Soil- or peat-based.

REPOTTING Repot in spring, every second year.

PROPAGATION Take stem cuttings in late
spring.

KEEPING PLANTS Watch out for infestation by
red spider mites, particularly in dry conditions.

PLANT CARE

Bright light with some direct sun. ● Warm
temperatures, with a winter minimum of
13°C/55°F. ● Water well during the growing
period and sparingly in winter. ● Feed every
2 weeks from spring to autumn with a general
indoor plant fertiliser.

~

PODOCARPUS MACROPHYLLUS
Podocarpaceae

Buddhist Pine

If this slow-growing plant is to live
successfully indoors, it must be kept in an
unheated room; since it will tolerate a
draughty situation, it is ideal for a cool hall
or passageway. The upright stems bear
narrow, strap-like, glossy 8-cm/3-in-long
leaves, but the catkin-like flowers are not
produced indoors.

The plant is also known as Japanese yew
or Kusamaki; indeed, the variety most
frequently seen as a house plant is 'Maki',
whose growth is compact and whose leaves
are only 13mm/¹/₂in long.

Podocarpus macrophyllus

FACT FILE

ORIGIN Japan.

HEIGHT To 1.8m/6ft in a container.

COMPOST Soil- or peat-based.

REPOTTING Repot in spring, when roots have
filled the current container.

PROPAGATION In late spring or summer, take
stem cuttings or sow seeds (the latter is the
more difficult of the two methods).

KEEPING PLANTS The plant's slow-growing
habit means that it requires little attention, but
it can be kept compact by regular pruning.

PLANT CARE

Bright light to partial shade. ● Cool to normal
indoor conditions, with a winter minimum of
4°C/40°F. ● Keep the compost moist at all
times; water sparingly in winter. ● Mist the
plant regularly during hot weather. ● Feed once
a month from spring to autumn with a standard
liquid fertiliser.

~

POLYSCIAS SCUTELLARIA '**BALFOURII**'
Araliaceae

Ming Aralia

Previously known as *Polyscias balfouriana*,
this is an excellent specimen plant when
placed in a decorative container. The dark
green, rounded leathery leaflets, up to
8cm/3in wide, are carried on stems speckled
with a pale green or grey.

It is not an easy plant to grow in normal
room conditions and in a less than ideal

environment will readily drop its leaves.
Large plants are prohibitively expensive, so
it is better to buy a small plant and look
after it well.

FACT FILE

ORIGIN New Caledonia.

HEIGHT To 1.8m/6ft in a container.

COMPOST Soil-based.

REPOTTING Repot every spring in a pot one
size larger until maximum desired pot size is
reached; thereafter, top-dress annually.

PROPAGATION Take stem tip cuttings or pieces
of stem in summer. Cuttings root readily in a
closed environment with bottom heat.

KEEPING PLANTS Humidity is essential, so mist
the plant daily in warm weather and stand the
pot on a tray of damp pebbles.

PLANT CARE

Bright light, but no direct sunlight. ● Normal
to warm room conditions with a minimum of
18°C/65°F. ● Water moderately during the
growing season; give less water in winter.
● Apply a standard liquid fertiliser every
2 weeks when the plant is in active growth.

Polyscias scutellaria
'Balfourii'

PSEUDERANTHEMUM ATROPURPUREUM
Acanthaceae

Pseuderanthemum

Sometimes still sold under the name of *Eranthemum atropurpureum*, this small erect shrub is grown chiefly for its brightly coloured oval leaves. These are dark green marked with purple or wine red, and about 13cm/5in long. The varieties 'Variegatum' and 'Tricolor' have splashes of pink, cream and purple on the leaves. The plant requires warmth and high humidity, and if conditions are right a mature specimen will produce tubular purple-eyed white flowers 2cm/^{3}/$_4$in wide in late spring and summer.

Pseuderanthemum atropurpureum

FACT FILE

ORIGIN Polynesia; naturalised in tropical America.

HEIGHT To 1.2m/4ft.

COMPOST Soil- or peat-based.

REPOTTING Repot in spring, but only when roots fill the container.

PROPAGATION Take tip or stem cuttings in spring or summer.

KEEPING PLANTS Cut the plant back if necessary to maintain its shape and size.

PLANT CARE

Bright light; partial shade. ● Warm room conditions, with a minimum winter temperature of 16°C/60°F. ● Allow the surface of the compost to dry out between waterings. ● Mist the plant daily and stand the pot on a tray of moist pebbles. ● From spring to autumn, feed every 2 weeks with a standard liquid fertiliser.

Pteris cretica

PTERIS CRETICA
Adiantaceae

Table Fern

Also known as Cretan brake and ribbon fern, this long-lived plant should thrive in most indoor situations, provided it is never allowed to dry out. Its main feature is the elegant, compact fronds that die back from time to time; but if they are cut back to the base, new ones will form. Do not use leaf shine.

Two good varieties are *Pteris cretica* 'Albolineata', variegated table fern, with deep green leaf edges and a broad white central stripe, and *P.c.* 'Alexandrae', cristate table fern, which has lighter green pinnae tipped with a cockscomb of leaflets.

FACT FILE

ORIGIN Old World tropics, subtropics.

HEIGHT To 90cm/3ft.

COMPOST Soil-based with low acidity.

REPOTTING Repot in spring only when pots become congested; the plant grows best when pot-bound. Do not bury the crown.

PROPAGATION Divide large plants into two or three pieces in spring.

KEEPING PLANTS Fronds will turn yellow if the air is too warm and dry; mist regularly to maintain high humidity.

PLANT CARE

Bright indirect light. ● Average temperatures, ideally 10°–24°C/50°–75°F. ● Keep the compost moist, but not sodden, at all times. ● Feed every week in spring and summer with a dilute standard liquid fertiliser.

PUNICA GRANATUM 'NANA'
Punicaceae

Dwarf Pomegranate

This compact and shrubby plant, with masses of 2.5-cm/1-in-long evergreen leaves, is not difficult to care for. The tubular scarlet flowers, borne in summer, hang from the plant rather like those of fuchsia, but they are not as plentiful. If the blooms are pollinated with a soft brush, there is a good chance that small orange-red fruits will develop; these are not edible, but are interesting and attractive to look at.

FACT FILE

ORIGIN Eastern Mediterranean to Himalayas.

HEIGHT To 90cm/3ft.

COMPOST Soil-based.

REPOTTING Move into a pot one size larger in spring, but only when roots have filled the pot.

PROPAGATION Take stem cuttings in summer, or sow seed in spring (named varieties do not come true).

KEEPING PLANTS To encourage flowering, shorten outward-growing shoots when the buds are breaking in early spring, and prune out old or weak wood in late spring or summer.

PLANT CARE

Bright light with some direct sun. ● Normal room temperature, with a winter minimum of 10°C/50°F. ● Keep the compost moist at all times. ● Feed every 2 weeks from spring to autumn with a high-potash fertiliser.

Punica granatum 'Nana'

RADERMACHERA SINICA
(SYN. *STEREOSPERMUM SINICUM*)
Bignoniaceae

EMERALD TREE

This tree-like plant succeeds indoors because of its tolerance of the dry atmosphere in most homes. It has shiny, pointed, veined leaves up to 6.5cm/2½in long. In its natural habitat, it has sweetly scented, yellow bell-shaped flowers – hence its other common name, Asian bell tree – but these are not usually produced on young plants grown in the home.

FACT FILE

ORIGIN China.

HEIGHT To 1.2m/4ft.

COMPOST Peat-based.

REPOTTING Repot in spring, but only if roots have filled the pot.

PROPAGATION Take stem cuttings in summer.

KEEPING PLANTS Keep away from open fires and smokers: a smoky atmosphere will make the leaves drop. Prune after flowering to keep the plant compact. Put the plant outdoors in summer in a protected spot.

PLANT CARE
Bright, indirect light. ● Normal room temperature, with a minimum of 10°C/50°F in winter. ● Keep the compost moist at all times. ● Mist frequently to maintain humidity. ● Feed every week in spring and summer.

~

REBUTIA MINUSCULA
Cactaceae

RED CROWN CACTUS

All rebutias are beautiful in the spring flowering period, and this quick-growing species is particularly good. The individual heads of this solitary or clustering cactus are globular, sometimes with a flattened top, and reach a height of only 5cm/2in or so. The short white spines form a neat pattern against the green stem, and in spring each head is surrounded by 4-cm/1½-in-wide crimson-scarlet flowers, which give it its other name, Mexican sunball. In the home, as in its natural habitat, rebutia needs plenty of sunshine, so it will be happiest standing on a sunny windowsill.

Rebutia minuscula

FACT FILE

ORIGIN Northern Argentina.

HEIGHT To 5cm/2in.

COMPOST Soil- or peat-based with added coarse sand or grit for good drainage.

REPOTTING Repot in summer every 2 years in a wide, shallow pot.

PROPAGATION Remove offsets in summer and pot them up individually, or sow seed in spring.

KEEPING PLANTS Watch out for mealybugs, which may be a problem, especially on new growth.

PLANT CARE
Full sun, but protect from hot midsummer sun. ● Normal to warm room temperature, with a winter minimum of 7°C/45°F. ● Water freely during spring and summer, but never overwater. Do not water in winter. ● Feed every 2 weeks with a high-potash fertiliser from the time the buds form and throughout the period of active growth.

~

RHIPSALIS BACCIFERA (SYN. *R. CASSUTHA*)
Cactaceae

MISTLETOE CACTUS

One of the epiphytic forest cacti, this plant hangs from trees in its natural habitat. Indoors, its long, light green, cylindrical branching stems trail over the rim of the pot. Insignificant greenish flowers about 6mm/¼in wide appear in winter and spring, and are followed by slightly smaller, translucent whitish fruits, which look rather like the berries on mistletoe.

Radermachera sinica

FACT FILE

ORIGIN Brazil, Peru, USA (Florida), Africa, Madagascar, Sri Lanka.

HEIGHT Stems trail to 1.8m/6ft indoors.

COMPOST Slightly acid epiphyte-type compost composed of equal parts of organic and inorganic matter.

REPOTTING Repot annually, after the spring blooms have faded, in a small pot.

PROPAGATION Take cuttings in summer, or sow seed in spring.

KEEPING PLANTS The stems are fragile and may break off at the joints if this plant is roughly handled.

PLANT CARE

Bright light, but shade from direct sunlight, which causes stems to shrivel and turn reddish. ● Normal to warm room temperature, with a cool winter rest at a minimum of 10°C/50°F. ● In spring and summer; allow the surface of the compost to dry out before watering; water less in winter. ● Mist frequently: otherwise, the stems will dry out and become soft. ● Apply a high-potash fertiliser every 2 weeks from the time the buds form until the end of flowering; once a month at other times.

ROCHEA COCCINEA (SYN. *CRASSULA COCCINEA*)
Crassulaceae

ROCHEA

A small shrubby bush, rochea carries masses of leathery, oval, pointed leaves 2.5cm/1in long in pairs along the many-branched stems. In summer, showy clusters of scented tubular red flowers, each about 2.5cm/1in long, appear at the ends of the stems. The varieties 'Alba', with white flowers, and 'Bicolor,' with red-and-white flowers, are also popular.

FACT FILE

ORIGIN South Africa (Cape Province).

HEIGHT To 46cm/18in.

COMPOST Soil-based.

REPOTTING Repot in spring only if necessary.

PROPAGATION Take stem cuttings in spring or summer. Allow the cuttings to dry for 2 days before inserting them into fresh compost.

KEEPING PLANTS *Rochea coccinea* needs plenty of ventilation, light and water in summer, and a period outdoors in a sheltered spot. Watch out for mealybugs and scale insects.

PLANT CARE

Bright light with some direct sunshine. ● Cool to normal room temperature. ● Water well during the growing season; give less water in winter. ● Feed every 2 weeks with a standard liquid fertiliser in the period of active growth.

Rosa

ROSA SPP.
Rosaceae

MINIATURE ROSE

These roses are invariably hybrids from *Rosa chinensis* 'Minima' and have all the qualities of a good temporary house plant, yet they are seldom seen indoors. There are dozens of excellent varieties, with flowers in all colours, from white, pink and cream through oranges, reds and yellows. Plants may bloom indoors from early spring to late summer, depending on variety, but they should be treated as outdoor plants.

After the leaves have fallen, give the plant a two-month rest period and in late winter prune it, cutting stems back by about one-third. Then bring it indoors and leave it in an unheated room for a week or two before moving it into the warmth to start it into growth. Put the plant in a brightly lighted location, give it plenty of water when it is flowering and deadhead it to prolong the flowering season.

FACT FILE

ORIGIN Hybrid; cultivars.

HEIGHT To 38cm/15in.

COMPOST Soil-based.

REPOTTING Repot in autumn, in a pot large enough to accommodate the roots. Overwinter in a cool greenhouse or shed or on a balcony, or bury the plant in the pot outdoors.

PROPAGATION Take tip cuttings in spring; they do not, however, always come true to type.

KEEPING PLANTS Miniatures are prey to all the usual rose pests and diseases; deal with them as you would for other rose types.

PLANT CARE

Full sun or bright light while the plant is actively growing. ● Normal room temperature during the period of active growth. Keep below 7°C/45°F for 2 months during the rest period. ● Water well in the growing period; keep the compost just moist at other times. ● Mist the leaves regularly and stand the pot on a tray of damp pebbles, but make sure that ventilation is good, since roses are prone to fungal diseases. ● Feed every 2 weeks from early spring to late autumn with a standard rose fertiliser.

RUELLIA MAKOYANA
Acanthaceae

MONKEY PLANT

A pretty plant, this ruellia has velvety oval leaves up to 8cm/3in long. They are soft olive green, tinged with purple and have prominent silver veins and purple edges; the undersides of the leaves are also purple. In autumn and winter, beautiful 5-cm/2-in-long, trumpet-shaped carmine flowers, which flare out to some 6.5cm/2¹/₂in wide, grow singly from the axils of the leaves.

Ruellia makoyana is an excellent plant for indoor hanging baskets and is sometimes known as trailing velvet plant.

FACT FILE

ORIGIN Brazil.

HEIGHT Stems trail to 46cm/18in.

COMPOST Soil-based and leaf mould in equal quantities, with some added grit or perlite.

REPOTTING In spring, when roots fill the current container, move the plant to one a size larger.

PROPAGATION Take 8–10cm/3–4in-long tip cuttings in spring or summer; alternatively sow seed or divide mature plants in summer.

KEEPING PLANTS Pinch out the growing tips regularly to encourage bushiness. The plant should last for 2 or 3 years. Watch out for aphids, which often infest the plant.

PLANT CARE

Bright indirect sunlight. ● Normal room temperature. ● Water well during the flowering period, but allow the surface of the soil to dry out before rewatering. Water just enough to keep the plant from drying out for 6–8 weeks after flowering. ● Mist the plant frequently to maintain humidity. ● Apply a standard liquid fertiliser every 2 weeks between spring and autumn.

SALPIGLOSSIS SINUATA
Solanaceae

*P*AINTED TONGUE

Salpiglossis is an annual that makes an outstanding pot plant for the conservatory or garden room and, although not often seen in the home, it makes a good temporary indoor plant. The beauty of the individual flowers is often lost when it is grown outdoors, and the five-pointed star-shaped blooms, some 5cm/2in wide, should really be examined closely. They come in a choice of colours, including yellow, orange, red and lilac, with velvety petals heavily veined and overlaid in contrasting colours.

FACT FILE

ORIGIN Chile; hybrids.

HEIGHT To 60cm/2ft.

COMPOST Peat-based.

REPOTTING Move seedlings into larger pots as they grow, until a 13-cm/5-in pot is reached.

PROPAGATION Sow seed in spring for summer flowering, or autumn for early spring blooming.

KEEPING PLANTS Stake stems as they grow, to prevent them from falling over and breaking.

PLANT CARE

Bright light with some full sun. ● Cool to normal room conditions. ● Water well, but allow the top of the compost to dry out before rewatering. ● Feed every 2 weeks until early autumn with a standard liquid fertiliser.

SANCHEZIA SPECIOSA (SYN. *S. NOBILIS*)
Acanthaceae

*S*ANCHEZIA

A striking plant best grown as a small shrub in the sunroom or greenhouse, sanchezia will thrive as an indoor plant if the humidity is high enough. The 30-cm/ 12-in ovate leaves are pointed, with yellow and ivory veins. They provide the main display, although attractive yellow flowers are borne in upright clusters above the foliage in early summer. High humidity is essential.

FACT FILE

ORIGIN Ecuador, Peru.

HEIGHT To 1.5m/5ft.

COMPOST Soil-based, with added grit or perlite.

REPOTTING Repot annually in spring.

PROPAGATION Take stem cuttings in spring or summer.

KEEPING PLANTS Prune the plant in spring to keep it bushy and within bounds; it can easily be kept to half its potential growing height.

PLANT CARE

Bright light, but not direct sunlight in summer. The plant will, however, also tolerate low light. ● Normal room temperature, with a minimum of 13°C/55°F in winter. ● Water liberally when the plant is in active growth, but allow the top 13mm/¹/₂in of the compost to dry out before rewatering. ● Stand the pot on a tray of moist pebbles to increase humidity. ● Feed every 2 weeks from spring to autumn with a standard liquid fertiliser. ● Make sure that there is adequate ventilation.

Sarracenia flava

SARRACENIA FLAVA
Sarraceniaceae

*Y*ELLOW PITCHER PLANT

Known also as the huntsman's horn, this is a carnivorous plant for a cool room or greenhouse. Like *Darlingtonia californica*, the California pitcher plant, the leaves are fused into a pitcher shape, with the top slightly bent over to act as a lid. Insects falling into the liquid contained by the pitcher are unable to escape, and they are then absorbed by the plant's juices.

The leaves are bright yellow-green, often with red veining on the lid, and in summer the plant produces yellow flowers up to 10cm/4in wide.

FACT FILE

ORIGIN USA (Virginia to Florida and Louisiana).

HEIGHT To 60cm/2ft in a container.

COMPOST Sphagnum peat, sand and leaf mould in a ratio of 2:1:1.

REPOTTING Move into a larger pot only when the current pot becomes overcrowded.

PROPAGATION Divide when repotting, or sow seed in spring.

KEEPING PLANTS Remove leaves from the base of the plant as they die off.

PLANT CARE

Bright light with some direct sun. ● Cool room temperature, with a winter minimum of 4°C/ 40°F at night and 10°C/50°F in the daytime. Water copiously with soft water when in active growth. ● Stand the pot on a dish of moist pebbles, but do not let water stagnate around the roots.

SCHIZANTHUS PINNATUS
Solanaceae

*P*OOR MAN'S ORCHID

Usually only hybrids of this plant, also called butterfly flower, are available. Since it is an annual, the plant should be raised from seed or bought in bud in spring and discarded when flowering is over – often in late autumn. The 5-cm/2-in-wide flowers have a resemblance to those of an orchid and come in shades of red, pink, mauve and white with a yellow centre, which is often marked with purple. The foliage is fern-like, and the stems are somewhat sticky.

Schizanthus pinnatus

FACT FILE

ORIGIN Chile; hybrids.

HEIGHT To 90cm/3ft.

COMPOST Peat-based.

REPOTTING Pot seedlings as they grow, ending with a 13-cm/5-in pot for dwarf varieties, and a 18-cm/7-in pot for taller forms.

PROPAGATION Sow seed in spring for summer flowering, or autumn for early spring.

KEEPING PLANTS Pinch out growing tips to encourage bushiness. Stake the stems to prevent them from toppling over and splitting.

PLANT CARE

Full sun. ● Cool or normal room temperature. ● Keep the compost moist at all times. ● Feed every 2 weeks until flowering is over.

Sedum sieboldii

SCILLA SIBERICA
Liliaceae

SIBERIAN SQUILL

A hardy spring-flowering bulb, this scilla makes an attractive pot plant. The strap-shaped shiny leaves are about 15cm/6in long. Pendant, intensely blue bell-shaped flowers appear in late winter or early spring, in clusters of three or more on 10-cm/4-in stalks. The deep blue, early flowering 'Spring Beauty' is commonly offered; 'Alba' is a white-flowered form.

Once the bulbs have been potted up, leave them in a sheltered location outdoors until the shoots are well developed, then bring them into a cool room to flower.

FACT FILE

ORIGIN Turkey, the Caucasus.

HEIGHT To 15cm/6in.

COMPOST Free-draining, peat- or soil-based.

REPOTTING Set the bulbs close together in a shallow pan or half-pot in early autumn, with the noses of the bulbs just covered with soil.

PROPAGATION Take offsets when the foliage dies back.

KEEPING PLANTS Feed and keep moist until the leaves die down, then plant the bulbs outdoors in autumn.

PLANT CARE

Bright light, but not direct sunlight while flowering. ● Keep pots of bulbs in a sheltered spot outdoors until ready to flower. Keep the plants in a temperature of about 10°C/50°F to prolong flowering. ● Keep the compost just moist at all times. ● Apply a balanced liquid fertiliser every 2 weeks after the plants are brought indoors.

SEDUM SIEBOLDII
(SYN. *HYLOTELEPHIUM SIEBOLDII*)
Crassulaceae

STONECROP

The variety of this sedum that is usually grown is the hardy, long-lived 'Medio-variegatum'. It has slender stems, which begin to grow upright but soon arch over. They trail to about 25cm/10in, making this a good plant for a hanging basket.

The fleshy round leaves, with lightly scalloped edges, are carried in whorls of three; they are steely blue-grey tinged with pink and have a cream central splash or stripe. Heads of small pink flowers are borne at the ends of the stems in late summer or early autumn.

FACT FILE

ORIGIN Japan.

HEIGHT To 10cm/4in; stems trail to 25cm/10in.

COMPOST Soil- or peat-based, with added perlite or coarse sand for good drainage.

REPOTTING Move into a pot one size larger in spring.

PROPAGATION Take stem tip cuttings in spring or summer. Remove the leaves to expose about 2.5cm/1in of the stem and allow it to dry for 1–2 days before inserting it into compost.

KEEPING PLANTS Watch out for mealybugs and aphids, which both attack this plant.

PLANT CARE

Bright light with plenty of direct sunshine. ● Cool to moderate temperatures: 10°–16°C/50°–60°F. ● In summer allow the top 13mm/½in of the compost to dry out before rewatering; water more sparingly in winter. ● It is not necessary to feed this plant.

SIDERASIS FUSCATA
Commelinaceae

BROWN SPIDERWORT

Although related to the easy-to-grow tradescantia, this plant needs high humidity and is best grown in a bottle garden. The broad leaves form a low rosette; on the surface they are deep green with a central silvery stripe, and their undersides are deep purplish red. The whole plant is covered with fine rust-coloured hairs. Purple flowers, about 2.5cm/1in wide, emerge from the centre of the rosette in summer, and have the typical three-petalled shape of those of the *Tradescantia* genus.

FACT FILE

ORIGIN Brazil.

HEIGHT Usually less than 20cm/8in.

COMPOST Soil-based and peat-based in equal amounts.

REPOTTING Move into a pot one size larger in spring; this is not usually necessary every year. Put a layer of gravel or crocks in the pot to ensure good drainage.

PROPAGATION Divide the clumps of rosettes as they become crowded.

KEEPING PLANTS If the plant is not being grown in a bottle garden or terrarium, it should stand on a tray of moist pebbles to maintain high humidity, which is essential.

PLANT CARE

Partial shade. ● Warm temperatures of 21°–29°C/70°–85°F are essential. Protect from draughts. ● Water moderately; allow the surface of the compost to dry out between waterings. ● Keep the humidity high at all times. ● Apply liquid fertiliser every 4 weeks.

SINNINGIA CARDINALIS
Gesneriaceae

CARDINAL FLOWER

This plant belongs to the same genus as gloxinia, but the two have little in common except that both grow from fibrous tubers and bear rather coarse, hairy leaves and brightly coloured flowers. The mid-green leaves of sinningia have rather darker veins and are up to 15cm/6in long.

The scarlet flowers open in clusters at the tips of the stems in summer. They are long and tubular, and the top of the corolla juts out over two distinct lower lips. This gives the flowers the appearance of a helmet with an open visor, hence sinningia's other name, helmet flower.

FACT FILE

ORIGIN Brazil.

HEIGHT To 25cm/10in.

COMPOST Peat-based.

REPOTTING Set the dormant tubers level with the surface of the compost in spring. Move into a larger pot only after several years.

PROPAGATION Take cuttings of young shoots in late spring. A heated propagator will improve the success rate.

KEEPING PLANTS Sinningia has a short dormant period after flowering; keep the tuber dry and store the pot on its side.

PLANT CARE

Bright light with no direct sun. ● Keep at about 21°C/70°F during the growing period; 10°C/50°F or less when the tubers are dormant. ● Water sparingly after potting until growth is evident, then keep the compost constantly moist until flowering has finished. Gradually reduce watering as the stems die back, and keep the tubers dry while dormant. ● Apply a high-potash liquid fertiliser every 2 weeks from the time flower buds form until the leaves die down.

SMITHIANTHA HYBRIDS
Gesneriaceae

TEMPLE BELLS

Several species of smithiantha have been crossed to produce a race of free-flowering plants. They have heart-shaped, velvety-textured, deep green leaves topped with panicles of long-stalked, tubular blooms that resemble penstemon flowers. The flowers are carried between late summer and early spring and come in shades of bright orange, yellow or pink. Plants grow from fleshy rhizomes and become dormant once they have flowered.

FACT FILE

ORIGIN Mexico.

HEIGHT To 30cm/12in.

COMPOST Peat-based, with a little added lime to reduce the acidity of the peat.

REPOTTING In late winter, set 2 or 3 rhizomes in a pot; barely cover them with compost.

PROPAGATION Divide when repotting.

KEEPING PLANTS Store dormant tubers in cool conditions in the pot or in dry peat.

PLANT CARE

Light shade. ● In the growing season, about 21°C/70°F; cooler in the dormant period. ● Allow the top 13mm/$\frac{1}{2}$in of the compost to dry out before rewatering in the growing season. Reduce watering after flowering; keep dormant tubers dry. ● High humidity is necessary; stand the pot on a tray of moist pebbles, but do not spray the hairy leaves. ● Feed with high-potash liquid fertiliser every week during the growing season.

SOLEIROLIA SOLEIROLII
Urticaceae

MIND-YOUR-OWN-BUSINESS

The common name of this evergreen creeping plant derives from its fast-growing, mat-forming habit: it can become a weed in gardens in mild areas or in terraria indoors. The tiny round leaves, which give it another of its names, baby's tears, are carried alternately on slender, fragile stems. The leaves are silvery green in the variety 'Argentea', while 'Aurea' has pale yellow foliage. It was formerly known as *Helxine soleirolii* and is still sold under that name.

FACT FILE

ORIGIN Corsica, Sardinia.

HEIGHT To 5cm/2in; prostrate.

COMPOST Soil-based, with added leaf mould and grit for good drainage.

REPOTTING Repot in spring, in a wide shallow pot.

PROPAGATION Divide plants into smaller clumps by pulling them apart carefully.

KEEPING PLANTS Soleirolia makes an attractive groundcover under taller pot plants.

PLANT CARE

Bright filtered light; direct sun will scorch the foliage. ● Normal to cool room temperature. ● Keep the compost moist at all times. ● Feed occasionally with dilute liquid fertiliser.

SONERILA MARGARITACEA
Melastomataceae

PEARL PLANT

This plant is not easy to grow: it demands even warmth and a humid atmosphere. It is a good candidate for a terrarium, where these conditions can be easily provided. The upper surface of the highly decorative lance-shaped leaves is puckered, and they are heavily marked with silver, which gives the plant a frosted or metallic appearance. Small, rosy pink, three-petalled flowers appear in summer.

FACT FILE

ORIGIN Java to Burma.

HEIGHT To 25cm/10in.

COMPOST Peat-based, with added leaf mould and coarse sand for good drainage.

REPOTTING Move into a pot one size larger each spring; a shallow pot is most suitable.

PROPAGATION Take stem cuttings in spring and summer. A heated propagator will aid rooting.

KEEPING PLANTS Older, larger plants tend to lose their bottom leaves and are best replaced with cuttings when they begin to get leggy.

PLANT CARE

Bright, filtered light all year-round; no direct sun. ● A minimum of 18°C/65°F in winter; 21°C/70°F and more in the growing season. ● Keep the compost just moist while the plant is in active growth; water more sparingly in winter. ● Mist the foliage frequently and stand the pot on a tray of moist gravel. ● Apply a balanced liquid fertiliser every 2 weeks during spring and summer.

Soleirolia soleirolii

Sparmannia africana

SPARMANNIA AFRICANA
Tiliaceae

$\mathcal{A}$FRICAN HEMP

Also known as the indoor lime, or linden tree, this plant quickly forms a tree shape when grown in a large container. It has 13–15-cm/5–6-in-long, downy, pale green heart-shaped leaves with toothed edges. In late winter and early spring umbels of white-petalled flowers, with a central boss of purple-tipped golden stamens, are borne at the ends of the stems.

FACT FILE
ORIGIN South Africa.

HEIGHT To 90cm/3ft in a container.

COMPOST Soil-based.

REPOTTING Move into a larger pot whenever the roots fill the current pot.

PROPAGATION Take stem cuttings of young shoots in spring.

KEEPING PLANTS Replace large, untidy plants by cuttings. Cut stems back after flowering and pinch out growing tips to encourage bushiness.

PLANT CARE
Bright light; protect from direct sun in summer. ● Best at about 16°C/60°F. ● Water freely in spring and summer; give less water in winter. ● Give high-potash liquid fertiliser every 3 weeks from the time flower buds appear until autumn.

STAPELIA VARIEGATA
Asclepiadaceae

$\mathcal{C}$ARRION FLOWER

Although striking in appearance, as the name suggests the flowers of this plant smell unpleasantly of rotting meat to attract pollinating flies. The upright stems are thick and fleshy. They tend to sprawl as the plant ages, and the leaves are then reduced to spine-like protuberances. In summer, flowers may be produced singly or in small groups at the base of the stems. The star-shaped flowers are pale yellow with purplish brown blotches and are up to 8cm/3in wide.

Stapelia variegata

FACT FILE
ORIGIN South Africa.

HEIGHT To 20cm/8in.

COMPOST Soil-based with added coarse sand.

REPOTTING Move into a pot one size larger in spring or whenever the stems appear crowded.

PROPAGATION Sow seed or take stem cuttings in spring and summer. Allow the base of the cuttings to dry before inserting them into a sandy compost.

KEEPING PLANTS Warm, dry air is essential.

PLANT CARE
Direct sunlight. ● A minimum of 13°C/55°F in winter. ● Water from below to moisten the compost thoroughly, then let the top half of the compost dry out before watering again. ● Apply a high-potash liquid fertiliser every 4 weeks in the growing season only.

STENOTAPHRUM SECUNDATUM 'VARIEGATUM'
Graminae

$\mathcal{B}$UFFALO GRASS

Also known as St. Augustine grass, this plant looks a little like chlorophytum. The pale green leaves are long and strap-like, blunt tipped, with a broad cream band down the centre. The creeping stems produce clumps of leaves from the nodes and will root easily wherever they touch the soil. The flowers are inconspicuous and are not often produced on plants grown in containers.

This is a good plant for a hanging basket that allows the stems to trail.

FACT FILE
ORIGIN Southern USA, tropical America.

HEIGHT To 20cm/8in.

COMPOST Soil-based.

REPOTTING Move into a larger pot whenever the roots appear crowded; use a half-pot or other shallow container.

PROPAGATION Separate rooted clumps from the parent plant and pot them up individually.

KEEPING PLANTS When leaves lose their colour and die back, gently pull them off the plant. This will not damage the plant at all.

PLANT CARE
Bright light with 3 or 4 hours of direct sun daily to help keep the variegation of the leaves. ● Normal room temperature, with a winter minimum of 10°C/50°F. ● Water freely in spring and summer; more sparingly in winter. Never let the plant stand in water. ● Apply a balanced liquid fertiliser once a month during the period of active growth.

Strelitzia reginae

PLANT CARE

Bright light with 3–4 hours of direct sun daily.
● Normal room temperature in the growing
season; about 13°C/55°F in the winter rest
period. ● Let the surface of the compost dry
out between waterings in spring and summer;
water sparingly in winter. ● Give a high-potash
liquid feed every 3 weeks when in active growth.

STREPTOSOLEN JAMESONII
Solanaceae

MARMALADE BUSH

In summer, at the tips of the branches,
streptosolen produces plentiful clusters of
bright orange and yellow, tubular, flared
flowers, which give it its other common
name of fire bush. A scrambling shrub, with
ovate, deep green, rather wrinkled leaves, it
can be grown as a trailer, but is probably
best in a garden room or conservatory
where it can be trained against a wall.

Streptosolen jamesonii

FACT FILE

ORIGIN Colombia, Ecuador, Peru.

HEIGHT To 1.8m/6ft.

COMPOST Soil-based.

REPOTTING Repot after flowering, or top-dress
a large plant.

PROPAGATION Take stem cuttings in late spring
or early summer.

KEEPING PLANTS Cut back the stems of old
plants by half in late winter. Pinch out growing
tips to promote bushiness.

PLANT CARE

Bright light with some direct sun, but shade
from hot midsummer sun. ● A minimum of
10°C/50°F in winter. ● Keep the compost moist
in the growing season; give less water in winter.
● Apply a high-potash liquid fertiliser every
3 weeks while the plant is actively growing.

STRELITZIA NICOLAI
Strelitziaceae

WHITE BIRD-OF-PARADISE

This is a tall-growing species with woody
stems carrying glossy, deep green, ovate leaf
blades up to 1.2m/4ft long. The white or
pale blue flowers are held in a long, brown,
boat-shaped bract.

FACT FILE

ORIGIN South Africa.

HEIGHT To 1.8m/6ft in a container.

COMPOST Soil-based.

REPOTTING Repot in spring until the largest
desired pot size is reached; thereafter top-dress.

PROPAGATION In spring, divide the clumps of
rooted suckers.

KEEPING PLANTS Patience is required when
growing strelitzias, since they do not flower
until they are about 6 years old.

PLANT CARE

Bright light, with some direct sun. Shade from
midsummer sun. ● Normal room temperature
in the growing period, about 13°C/55°F in the
winter rest period. ● Allow the surface of the
compost to dry out before rewatering in the
growing season. Water sparingly in winter.
● Give a high-potash liquid feed every 3 weeks
in the period of active growth.

STRELITZIA REGINAE
Strelitziaceae

BIRD-OF-PARADISE

Also known as crane flower, this spectacular
plant has flowers that look like the head of
the exotic crested crane. The slender green
bracts, some 20cm/8in long, are sharply
pointed and held horizontally, giving the
appearance of a beak. Bright orange-and-
blue-petalled flowers emerge from the
bracts to form a colourful 'crest'. Flowers
are borne on plants 5–6 years old in early
spring and summer and sometimes to late
summer. Individual flowers last for about a
week, but each spathe produces several,
which open in succession.

The oblong, leathery leaves up to
46cm/18in long, on stalks almost twice as
long, rise directly from the base of the plant.

FACT FILE

ORIGIN South Africa.

HEIGHT To 90cm/3ft.

COMPOST Fertile, well-drained, soil-based.

REPOTTING Every year in spring, move into a
larger pot until a 25-cm/10-in pot is reached;
thereafter top-dress annually.

PROPAGATION In spring, sow seed or divide.

KEEPING PLANTS Strelitzias need sunlight; they
will not flower if the light is not bright enough.

Strobilanthes dyeranus

STROBILANTHES DYERANUS
Acanthaceae

PERSIAN SHIELD

This is an attractive, erect, evergreen foliage plant with lance-shaped leaves. The pointed oval leaves, about 15cm/6in long, have a metallic, silvery purple surface with green margins and deep purple undersides; the colour becomes lighter as the leaves age.

FACT FILE
ORIGIN Burma.

HEIGHT To 60cm/2ft.

COMPOST Soil-based with added leaf mould.

REPOTTING Repot whenever roots fill the pot.

PROPAGATION Take stem cuttings in spring; root them in a propagator with bottom heat.

KEEPING PLANTS Replace the plant by a cutting when it becomes straggly, usually after a year.

PLANT CARE
Bright, filtered light. ● A minimum of 16°C/60°F. ● Let the surface of the compost dry out between waterings. ● Apply a balanced liquid fertiliser every 2 weeks to a plant that is in active growth.

STROMANTHE AMABILIS
Marantaceae

STROMANTHE

This plant is also known as *Ctenanthe amabilis* and is a member of the same family as maranta and calathea. It was formerly included in those genera and may be offered under those names. It has typical feathered herringbone markings on oblong, grey-green leaves and forms a compact clump.

FACT FILE
ORIGIN Brazil.

HEIGHT To 25cm/10in.

COMPOST Peat-based.

REPOTTING Move into a larger pot in spring, when the current one is crowded with foliage.

PROPAGATION Divide clumps in spring.

KEEPING PLANTS Stromanthe does not like to stand in a draught, so be careful where you site it.

PLANT CARE
Moderately bright light out of direct sun. ● Normal to warm room temperature with a winter minimum of 18°C/65°F. ● Water moderately; allow the top 2.5cm/1in of the soil to dry out between waterings. ● Apply a balanced liquid fertiliser every 3 weeks during the growing season.

SYAGRUS WEDDELLIANA
Palmae

WEDDEL PALM

Rather similar to *Chamaedorea elegans*, the parlour palm, this is a slow-growing, graceful plant with feathery fronds on arching stems. It is not as robust as the parlour palm and is more difficult to grow successfully, requiring higher temperature and humidity. The tips of the fronds will quickly turn brown and crisp in dry conditions. It is also known as *Microcoelium weddellianum* and *Cocos weddelliana*.

Syagrus weddelliana

FACT FILE
ORIGIN Brazil.

HEIGHT To 1.2m/4ft in a container.

COMPOST Soil-based.

REPOTTING Repot in spring when essential; usually not more than every 3 years.

PROPAGATION Plants are raised from seed, but this is not practicable in the home.

KEEPING PLANTS This palm will remain small for many years, so is a very suitable house plant.

PLANT CARE
Bright light, but shaded from direct sun. ● Does best at 21°–24°C/70°–75°F, with a minimum of 13°C/55°F in winter. ● Water moderately; allow the top 13mm/1/2in of compost to dry out before rewatering. Water more sparingly in cooler conditions. ● Stand the pot on a tray of moist gravel and mist the foliage frequently to increase humidity. ● Apply a balanced liquid fertiliser every 4 weeks in the growing season.

TETRASTIGMA VOINIERANUM
Vitaceae

CHESTNUT VINE

Related to the more popular grape ivy and kangaroo vine (*Cissus* genus), tetrastigma is a large and vigorous climber that needs plenty of space. The deep green leaves, composed of five leaflets, are shaped rather like a horse chestnut leaf and can be more than 30cm/12in wide. The leaf edges are toothed, and the undersides are covered with reddish brown hairs. Strong, wiry tendrils cling firmly to any support, and the stems will rapidly cover a wall or trellis.

FACT FILE
ORIGIN Southeast Asia.

HEIGHT Climbs to more than 1.8m/6ft.

COMPOST Soil-based with good drainage.

REPOTTING Move into a pot 2 sizes larger in spring; when maximum desired pot size is reached, top-dress annually instead.

PROPAGATION Take stem tip cuttings in late spring and summer.

KEEPING PLANTS This vigorous, large-leafed plant needs a sturdy trellis or similar support. Prune in spring, removing overcrowded stems.

PLANT CARE
Bright light, shaded from direct sun; will tolerate partial shade. ● Ideally, an even temperature of 16°–18°C/60°–65°F, with a winter minimum of 13°C/55°F. ● Keep the compost moist in the growing season; give less water in winter. ● Liquid-feed every 4 weeks in spring and summer.

THUNBERGIA ALATA
Thunbergiaceae

BLACK-EYED SUSAN

Generally grown as an annual, this fast-growing climber is easily raised from seed. The slender, twining stems bear light green, arrowhead-shaped leaves with indented margins. In summer, daisy-like flowers with a tubular throat appear; the species has orange petals, but there are varieties with yellow or white petals, and all have a deep chocolate brown centre. Provide stakes around the edges of the pot for the plant to twine around, or train it over a trellis or similar support; it also makes a good candidate for a hanging basket.

FACT FILE

ORIGIN Tropical Africa.

HEIGHT To 1.8m/6ft.

COMPOST Soil-based.

REPOTTING Move the plant into a larger pot when roots can be seen through the drainage holes in the bottom.

PROPAGATION Sow seed in early spring.

KEEPING PLANTS Discard after flowering.

PLANT CARE

Bright light with some direct sun. ● Normal room temperature. ● Keep the compost moist at all times. ● Apply a high-potash liquid fertiliser every 2 weeks from the time the flower buds start to form.

~

TRACHYCARPUS FORTUNEI
Palmae

WINDMILL PALM

When they first appear, the leaves of this hardy palm are attractively pleated and covered with fine hairs, but these fibres curl away from the edges as the leaves gradually open out into wide, deeply segmented fans. As the plant ages, a stout stem develops, covered with coarse brown fibres from decomposing leaf sheaths.

FACT FILE

ORIGIN Southeast Asia.

HEIGHT To 2.4m/8ft in a container.

COMPOST Soil-based.

REPOTTING In spring, move into a pot one size larger.

PROPAGATION Sow seed, but seedlings are so slow-growing, this is not practical for an amateur.

KEEPING PLANTS This palm will benefit from a spell outdoors in summer, but keep it out of heavy winds, which can shred the leaves.

Trachycarpus fortunei

PLANT CARE

Bright light with plenty of direct sun. ● Normal room temperature, with a winter minimum of 4°C/40°F in winter. ● Water moderately throughout the growing season, but sparingly in cooler temperatures. ● Apply a balanced liquid fertiliser every 2–3 weeks in spring and summer.

~

TRITELEIA LAXA **see** *BRODIAEA LAXA*

~

TULIPA HYBRIDS
Liliaceae

TULIPS

Early-flowering single and double tulips make good short-term pot plants. Singles include scented yellow 'Bellona'; red 'Christmas Marvel' and 'Flair', which is golden yellow with red feathering. Good doubles include orange-yellow 'Maréchal Niel'; rose pink 'Peach Blossom', and white 'Schoonoord'. Also attractive are varieties of the low-growing *Tulipa greigii*, with mottled foliage, and *T. kaufmanniana*, the water-lily tulip, with wide, open blooms.

Treat tulip bulbs like those of hyacinth and narcissus and give them a cool, dark period after planting so they will develop an adequate rooting system. Plunge the pot into the ground outdoors under a covering of peat or enclose it in a black plastic bag and stand it in a cool place.

FACT FILE

ORIGIN Turkey, East Asia; hybrid.

HEIGHT To 60cm/2ft, depending on variety.

COMPOST Peat-based or bulb medium.

REPOTTING Set bulbs close together in a pot in autumn, with their noses just covered.

PROPAGATION Not practical for the amateur. Seedlings take 5–7 years to flower. Mature bulbs increase slowly by offsets.

KEEPING PLANTS Plant bulbs outdoors once flowering is over; it is not worth growing them for indoor use again.

PLANT CARE

Give bulbs a cool, dark period of about 10 weeks after planting; bring them into the light when they have about 5cm/2in of top growth. Keep in a bright position during flowering. ● About 4°C/40°F for 10 weeks after planting; increasing gradually to about 13°C/55°F for flowering. ● Keep the compost just moist at all times. ● Give a balanced liquid feed every 2 weeks.

~

VALLOTA SPECIOSA
(SYN. *CYRTANTHUS ELATUS*)
Amaryllidaceae

SCARBOROUGH LILY

This evergreen plant produces tall stems topped by clusters of brightly coloured, trumpet-shaped flowers from summer to autumn. Although the flowers are not as large as those of hippeastrum, to which the plant is related, they are showy. The leaves are strap-shaped and about 30cm/12in long. The flower stems rise above the foliage and bear groups of four to eight scarlet, white or salmon pink flowers.

FACT FILE

ORIGIN South Africa.

HEIGHT To 60cm/2ft.

COMPOST Soil-based.

REPOTTING In spring set the bulb in a 13-cm/5-in pot, half burying it in the soil. Plants flower best when undisturbed, so top-dress annually and repot only every 3 to 4 years.

PROPAGATION Remove offsets in spring or early summer and pot up individually.

KEEPING PLANTS The plant needs a rest period in cool conditions in the winter.

PLANT CARE

Bright light with some direct sun. ● Normal room temperature in summer, but a cooler period in winter at about 10°C/50°F. ● Water sparingly until growth starts in spring; keep the compost just moist during the growing season. ● Apply a high-potash liquid fertiliser every 2 weeks from spring until flowering ceases.

Washingtonia filifera

WASHINGTONIA FILIFERA
Palmae

Desert Fan Palm

One of only two species of washingtonia, this palm is a tall, handsome plant with spiny leafstalks some 46cm/18in long supporting greyish green fan-shaped leaves up to 60cm/2ft wide. The leaves are split about halfway down into many narrow segments, from the tips of which hang fine, dry, brown fibres.

In the wild, the tapered red-brown trunk is densely clothed in dead foliage, which is generally cut away on cultivated plants. This fringe of dead leaves gives the plant its name of petticoat palm.

In their arid natural habitat, these palms are a sure sign of subterranean water, into which they send down long, deep roots. Since they thrive in hot, dry regions, the palms do well in heated homes.

FACT FILE

ORIGIN USA (California, Arizona).

HEIGHT To 3m/10ft; to 24m/80ft in the wild.

COMPOST Soil-based with added peat or leaf mould in a ratio of 2:1.

REPOTTING Move into a pot one size larger when roots appear on the surface of the soil – every 2 or 3 years – and then only when the plant is in active growth. Plant the palm firmly, but be very careful not to damage the brittle roots, especially the larger, thicker ones.

PROPAGATION Sow seed in considerable heat; but this is generally not practicable for the home gardener.

KEEPING PLANTS The palm will benefit from a spell outdoors in a sheltered spot during the summer. Bring it indoors again in autumn before the first frost.

PLANT CARE

Bright light with plenty of direct sun. ● Warm or hot rooms, with a minimum of 10°C/50°F. ● Water plentifully in the growing period, more sparingly in winter. ● Stand the pot on a tray of damp pebbles in very dry conditions. ● Apply a standard liquid fertiliser every 2 weeks in the growing period.

~

ZANTEDESCHIA AETHIOPICA
(SYN. *Z. AFRICANA*)
Araceae

Calla Lily

In late spring the stately calla, or arum, lily produces its golden, club-shaped spadix surrounded by a pure white spathe. The tall stem stands above the large, shiny, dark green arrowhead-shaped leaves, which are strongly veined and rise on long leafstalks directly from the rhizome.

Many varieties have been developed that are more compact and free-flowering than the species. 'Childsiana' is a compact form. 'Green Goddess' has white spathes tipped and streaked with green; those of 'Little Suzie' are tinged with pink. *Zantedeschia rehmannii* has slender pink spathes and long leaves, and *Z. elliotiana* has extremely large, lush, dark green leaves spotted with white, and golden yellow spathes.

FACT FILE

ORIGIN South Africa (Cape Province, Natal, Transvaal), Lesotho.

HEIGHT To 90cm/3ft.

COMPOST Soil-based.

REPOTTING Move into a pot one size larger in early spring, when roots fill the current pot.

PROPAGATION Divide clumps when repotting.

KEEPING PLANTS The plant usually has a short rest period after flowering. Set the pot in a sheltered place outdoors in summer.

PLANT CARE

Bright light with some direct sun. ● Cool to average room temperature to prolong the life of the blooms. ● Water sparingly until growth starts, then plentifully throughout the flowering season; do not let the compost dry out. Reduce watering as the leaves begin to die back, and water sparingly from midsummer. ● Apply a balanced liquid fertiliser every 2 weeks in the growing season.

Zantedeschia aethiopica
'Little Suzie'

CARING FOR PLANTS

ALL PLANTS REQUIRE CERTAIN conditions for healthy growth, and a good understanding of a plant's basic needs will set you on the right road to correct cultivation.

Every plant needs light in order to photosynthesize (manufacture food from sunlight), but the quality of light each plant demands varies from species to species. Ideal temperature ranges vary too, as does the quantity of water required. The Plant Directory gives you details of the requirements of individual plants, and this chapter aims to help you understand the role played by these variables in the existence of all plants. Most indoor plants are grown in conditions very different from those of their natural habitat, but with a little help, the majority of them can adjust to the environment in our homes.

There is no substitute for experience and observation. Trying out different types of plants, and learning to observe them closely, will do more than anything else to help you acquire those coveted green fingers. People who complain that they just can't get plants to grow often simply fail to pay enough attention to them. Learn to look at your plants carefully, checking for healthy young growth, noticing yellowing foliage or the early signs of pests or disease. Turn the leaves over to look at the undersides; that's where many pests hide.

To help you to decide whether the plant needs water, prod the surface of the compost with a finger and try the weight of the pot to judge the moisture content. Check the colour and size of the leaves to estimate whether a plant is running short of nutrients. It takes only a few minutes every few days, and you will soon find that your plants begin to speak to you.

When buying a plant you have not grown before (or have tried and failed with), seek advice from the seller. At any reliable garden centre or nursery, there should be qualified people who can help you with queries.

Give a new plant time to adjust to the conditions in your home. Don't keep moving it from room to room because it doesn't look happy. Find out a suitable care regime and stick to it. Resist the temptation to overwater and overfeed an ailing plant for the sake of doing something to help, when all it really needs is to be left alone for a while to get over the move.

Finally, do not expect miracles. Some plants were never intended to do more than provide a little colour and cheer for a few weeks; others are notoriously difficult to grow well, and you should not be too disappointed if you fail.

The golden rule is never to spend more on buying a plant than you feel happy about, unless you are certain you can keep it alive long enough to get your money's worth from it.

Any corner of a garden shed or utility room (left) *can be equipped to provide a place where you can deal with your house plants. All you need is good light, a bench, some shelves to store your equipment on and easy access to water.*

COMPARING PLANTS: HEALTHY VS. UNHEALTHY

Plentiful flowers and new buds

Drooping, brown leaves and no flowers

This healthy, well-fed begonia is full of leaves and flowers and is obviously grown in conditions it enjoys. Care for your plants and they will reward you with vigorous growth and profuse flowers.

This begonia shows signs of neglect. Given little water and no food, it is sickly and prey to pests.

Healthy, shiny leaves

Compost has been allowed to dry out

PLANT ANATOMY

THE FORM OF PLANTS VARIES GREATLY but, as the simplified diagram below shows, the major parts of a typical specimen can be observed on almost every kind of plant.

APICAL BUDS
These are the growth buds at the tips of the shoots.

AXILLARY BUDS
Buds in the leaf axils (the upper point where the leaves join the stem) may develop into either shoots or flowers.

FLOWERS
The reproductive organs of the plant are carried in the flowers. Their form differs tremendously, but a typical flower has brightly coloured petals, which serve to attract pollinating insects, and sepals, which cover the bud; these may also be coloured, but are often green. Both petals and sepals are modified leaves.

The female reproductive organs are the ovary, usually hidden by the petals, from which emerges the style (stalk) topped by a stigma, which receives pollen grains from another flower. The three parts are known collectively as the pistil. The male organs are the filament, which is topped by pollen-bearing anthers; together they make up the stamen.

LEAVES
The plant's food manufacturing process normally takes place in the leaves, which may or may not have stalks. Again, the leaves are extremely variable in form, but they tend to be thin, with a

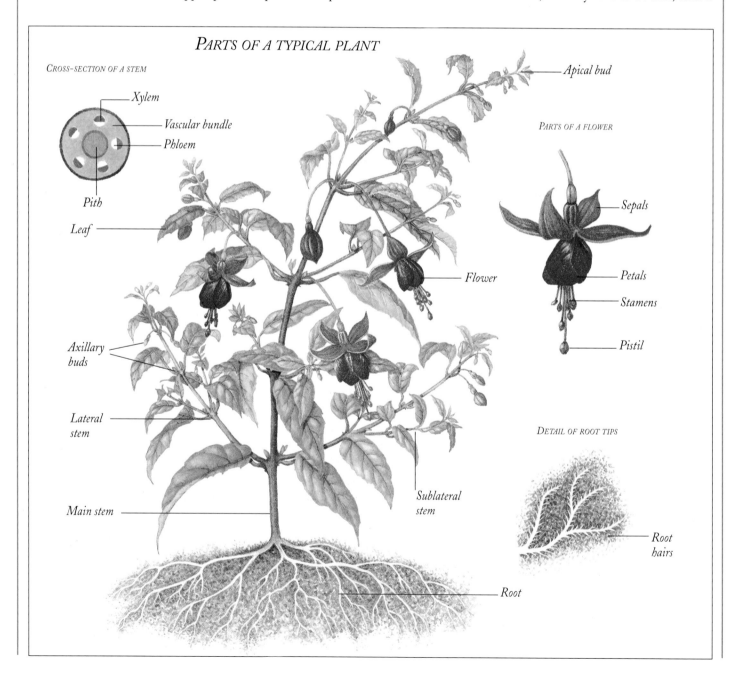

PARTS OF A TYPICAL PLANT

CROSS-SECTION OF A STEM

Xylem

Vascular bundle

Phloem

Pith

Leaf

Apical bud

PARTS OF A FLOWER

Sepals

Petals

Stamens

Pistil

Flower

Axillary buds

Lateral stem

Main stem

Sublateral stem

DETAIL OF ROOT TIPS

Root hairs

Root

large surface area to absorb maximum sunlight. In some plants green stems take on this role.

STEMS

While the stems of many plants grow upright, others are prostrate, trailing or climbing. There may be one main stem with laterals (side stems) branching off it and sublaterals branching off those, or there may be several stems arising from soil level. Throughout the stems, shoots and roots are vascular bundles, which act rather like a system of veins and arteries, transporting food and water to all parts of the plant. Xylem carries water from the roots, while phloem transports nutrients from the site of manufacture, which is generally in the leaves and stems. The centre of the stem is woody pith, which provides support.

ROOTS

Water and dissolved nutrients from the soil are absorbed largely through very fine root hairs found towards the tips of the rootlets. A plant may have a fibrous root system with a mass of equal-sized roots, or a taproot that branches in much the same way that stems do. It may have tuberous roots or aerial roots that grow above the soil. In addition to absorbing food and water, roots anchor and support the plant.

TYPES OF PLANT

The plant kingdom contains an astounding range of plants, from single-celled algae found in pond water to ancient, towering trees. Along the way are plants of all shapes and sizes, some wonderfully adapted to their natural habitats. Among the many species we grow as house plants can be found a good selection of different types.

Annuals grow from seed, flower and die in one season, persisting only as seeds for future years. Perennials persist from year to year (although many are short-lived and will die after only a few years). Most indoor plants are perennials, but exacum, schizanthus and ipomoea are among the annuals grown in the home.

Perennial plants may be deciduous, losing their leaves during the autumn and winter, or evergreen, keeping their leaves all year round. The distinction between evergreen and deciduous plants is somewhat blurred when it comes to house plants, since the artificially warm conditions indoors can make evergreens of plants that would normally shed their leaves in a more natural environment.

The majority of foliage house plants are evergreen – monsteras, peperomias, ficuses, dieffenbachias and many others.

Caladiums are among the few deciduous foliage plants; they die right back below soil level in winter.

Plants are split into further categories according to their habit of growth. Herbaceous plants produce soft, non-hardy stems and foliage, whereas shrubby plants produce woody stems that tend to persist from one year to another. Ficuses, camellias and fuchsias are among the shrubs or sub-shrubs grown indoors. Several of the plants we grow would become trees if given sufficient room for both roots and top growth to expand naturally, but by confining them in containers, we can keep their size to more manageable proportions. Some plants, such as one or two of the palms, are slow-growing and would take many years to achieve the height and spread of trees; others, such as eucalyptus, will reach 6m/20ft or more in a very short time when planted outdoors.

Bulbs, corms and tubers are plant storage organs that hold food reserves for the following year's growth: cyclamens, hyacinths, narcissi, hippeastrums and freesias are popular examples. All these plants have a dormant period after the flowers and foliage have died down.

Some plants have highly specialised systems to help them overcome problems encountered in their natural environment. Epiphytes, such as several orchids and bromeliads, cope with the lack of light beneath the tree canopy in dense tropical and temperate rain forests by growing high on the branches of trees where the light is better. They absorb moisture and nutrients from the humid atmosphere through their leaves.

Cacti and succulents from hot, arid regions store water in fleshy stems and are often covered with dense hair to protect them from scorching by the sun. Carnivorous plants obtain nutrients by trapping passing animal life, rather than relying on the impoverished soil in which they grow. A number of ingenious traps allow the plants to lure and capture insects, which they then digest, making them fascinating, if rather gruesome, plants to cultivate in the home.

The term 'bulbs' is commonly used to cover all plants that grow from bulbs, corms, rhizomes and tubers. Although these are botanically quite different, they are all organs for storing food for the plant, and many common indoor plants grow from one or another of these organs.

Tubers are large, often branching, storage organs; some begonias grow from tubers.

Bulbs are specialised shoots in which the swollen leaves, or scales, are folded over each other – tightly in narcissi (below) and loosely in some lilies.

Corms are solid, swollen stems with a bud at the top. Crocuses and cyclamens have corms.

THE IMPORTANCE OF LIGHT

PLANTS NEED GOOD-QUALITY LIGHT in order to manufacture food through photosynthesis. The amount of light in a typical room (*below right*) is extremely variable: it depends not only on the size and position of windows, but also the season, weather and trees or buildings outside, which may block the light.

The conditions that apply to the south-facing wall in the northern hemisphere (NH) apply to the north-facing wall in the southern hemisphere (SH).

EAST WALL

An east-facing window receives direct sun in the morning and moderately bright light for the rest of the day. It is a suitable position for plants that like only a few hours of direct sunlight.

The area on each side of the fireplace in the illustration, particularly to the left, receives little direct light, and could be a difficult place for plants. White or light-coloured walls or mirrors will help to reflect what light there is.

SOUTH WALL(NH)/ NORTH WALL(SH)

Patio doors or French windows take full advantage of the sun falling on this wall. The area directly in front of the window receives good light all day, but the intensity of the light falls off quickly the farther away from the window you are; each side of the window is relatively dark.

This is a good place for a floor-standing group of sun-loving plants; it is especially suitable for taller subjects, which can make maximum use of the floor-to-ceiling brightness.

WEST WALL

The windows on this wall receive good light all day, with direct afternoon sun. Here you can grow plants similar to those on the east wall. (The amount of direct sun east and west windows get varies according to the time of year and the height of the sun in the sky; no sun may fall through the windows for some weeks at the height of summer.)

Plants that need bright but diffuse light can be protected by a sheer curtain or translucent blind that will filter the sun falling on the foliage.

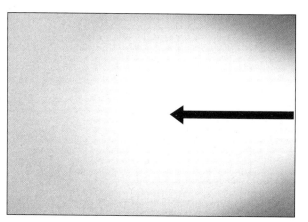

Where direct sunlight enters a room, the level of the light is almost constant. As you go farther from the source of the light, the brightness decreases until, at the opposite end of a large room, light levels are low. There are also unexpected darker corners at each side of the window. You should bear these facts about light levels in mind when deciding where to site your plants.

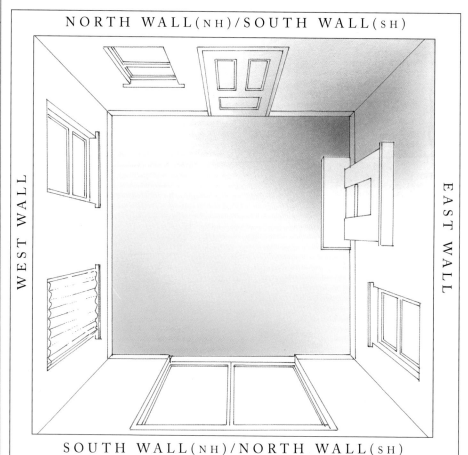

NORTH WALL (NH)/ SOUTH WALL (SH)

Although this area may appear fairly bright because it faces the large window area in the opposite wall, the quality of light is much reduced. The small, high window receives no direct sunlight, but does give an even level of light during the day, which is suitable for plants that like moderately bright conditions without direct sun. To the right of the door is one of the darkest areas in the room, a corner with no immediately adjacent windows. Even the most shade-tolerant plants would struggle to thrive here. To widen the selection of plants that can be grown, you can add artificial light. A special plant table, with a fluorescent tube suspended above the plants, makes an interesting and attractive feature.

NORTH WALL(NH)/SOUTH WALL(SH)

The dark area on the right of the doorway is an excellent place for growing plants under artificial light.

Incandescent bulbs give off too much heat to be suitable, but twin 40-watt fluorescent tubes about 25–60cm/10–24in above the tops of the plants are excellent.

Plants raised under artificial light will grow continuously. This is acceptable for most tropical foliage plants, and flowering plants will bloom more regularly and for longer periods.

EAST WALL

The area on each side of the fireplace receives little or no direct light. Pale-coloured walls and mirrors help to reflect what light there is.

The east-facing window receives morning sun and provides suitable light for plants that like just a few hours of direct sunlight.

Saintpaulias, fuchsias and tradescantias will thrive on the windowsill, and sansevieria will do well on the floor on the right of fireplace. *Philodendron scandens* would be suitable in a wall-mounted pot close to the window.

WEST WALL

The windows on this wall receive good light all day, with direct sun in the afternoon.

Clivias, chrysanthemums, codiaeums, cacti and succulents will all thrive in the warmth and bright, direct light on the windowsill.

Plants such as nephrolepis, pachystachys, *Piper ornatum*, aphelandras, columneas and cyclamens, which need bright diffuse light, can be protected by a sheer curtain or blind.

SOUTH WALL(NH)/NORTH WALL(SH)

Although the area directly in front of the doors receives some direct sun and good light all day, it is an impractical place for plants. The area needs to be clear so that people can move in and out.

This is a good place for a floor-standing group of plants that revel in plenty of light, such as pelargoniums, jasmines, hibiscuses and cordylines.

A tall specimen plant – a fatsia, gardenia or *Aucuba japonica*, for instance – would be quite at home in the corner near the doors.

TEMPERATURE AND HUMIDITY

TO DISCOVER THE TYPE OF GROWING conditions a particular indoor plant requires, it is useful to know where in the world it originated. That will give you a good idea of the conditions under which it grows naturally and which you should try to imitate to make it feel at home. But you should also remember that in many instances a great deal of selective breeding of plants has taken place to produce varieties that are suited to growing in conditions rather different from those of their natural habitat.

Most houses are heated and ventilated to suit their human occupants, and few people are going to make drastic alterations just for the sake of their indoor plants. But while plants, by and large, have to fit in with people, you can still make sure that they have the most congenial environment possible.

Most house plants probably originated in tropical regions, particularly evergreen foliage plants such as philodendrons and monsteras. In tropical forests the atmosphere is hot and very humid; dense tree canopies mean that, at best, only dappled sunlight penetrates to the places where these plant species grow. In the home, the ideal conditions for these plants are even warmth, with no draughts or sudden temperature fluctuations, and frequent spraying or moist pebble trays to increase humidity. As a rule, plants should also be kept out of direct sunlight, which will scorch the leaves.

Cacti, most of which originate in extremely hot and dry desert regions, are well adapted to arid conditions, and frequent watering and regular misting would soon cause them to rot and die.

Plants from more temperate regions, like cyclamens, and bulbs such as narcissi and crocuses, prefer cooler conditions than the average home can easily provide. Too much heat leads to pale, drawn stems and foliage, weak, spindly growth and short-lived flowers.

Indoor plants come from virtually every continent. The temperate regions of Asia have provided us with chrysanthemums, camellias and aspidistras, which thrive in cool rooms. Warm, damp areas of India have given us several species of ficuses, which are common plants in many tropical and subtropical regions of the world. From parts of Australia that have warm summers and fairly good summer or winter rainfall, come eucalyptuses, callistemons and grevilleas.

The hot arid regions of Africa are home to many species of succulents, such as lithops and haworthia, as well as most of the aloes; and these plants need dry conditions and well-drained soil to do well in the home. A wide variety of foliage plants, such as dracaenas, peperomias and begonias, which all need humidity in the home, come from the tropical areas, as do the popular African violets. From the Cape mountains of South Africa, which have wet winters, hot dry summers and well-drained soil, come streptocarpus and bulbs such as ixias and hippeastrums.

The Americas supply a great wealth of indoor plants. Some of the most popular species of cacti come from arid areas of the southern US and Mexico, which also produces *Euphorbia pulcherrima*, poinsettia, achimenes and dozens of other plants. Many species of bromeliads

In the mountainous regions of the Eastern Transvaal in South Africa (left), with its well-drained soil, lilies bloom along the roadside in early autumn. Summers are warm and rainy, winters are cool and dry, and there is plenty of sunshine to bake the bulbs and ripen them for good flowering the following season.

Hot, humid rain forests, such as those of Costa Rica (right), are home to a wide variety of large-leafed foliage plants, bromeliads and ferns that have become common plants in the home. It is often a challenge to provide the growing conditions these plants enjoy in their natural habitat and still demand when you grow them indoors.

grown as house plants are from the hot, humid rain forests of Central and South America.

Europe has provided relatively few plants for indoors. *Campanula isophylla*, the bellflower, comes from Italy; *Chamaerops humilis*, the European fan palm, and oleander are from Mediterranean regions with hot dry summers and wet winters; *Hedera helix*, common ivy, is widespread across Europe.

MINIMUM AND MAXIMUM TEMPERATURES

The temperatures that are comfortable for people, 18°–24°C/65°–75°F, are also, fortunately, comfortable for most indoor plants. Within their preferred temperature range, plants will grow and develop steadily, provided they have enough light. If temperatures drop below the preferred range, growth slows down and at a certain point it will stop altogether. If the temperature drops too low, plants will die.

Most indoor plants, even the hardy species, will be killed by frost because their growth will be soft and susceptible since they have been grown in warm, indoor conditions. Such extremely low temperature damage is not common in most homes, but in cold areas plants in unheated rooms are at risk, as are plants on windowsills. When curtains are closed at night, these plants may be cut off from the warmth of the room and in cold spells the temperature on the windowsill can drop to freezing. Either move the

plants off the windowsill in the evening or open the curtains before going to bed.

Most low-temperature damage is not as dramatic as this. There may be localised damage to leaves and growing points after an unexpected cold snap or when the heating system fails. And if conditions are consistently too cool for a particular species, the plant may simply fail to thrive and gradually fade away.

Widely fluctuating temperatures should be avoided, although many plants will cope with a temperature a few degrees outside their preferred range as long as it is steady. A fall in temperature at night is, however, normal and acceptable as long as it is not too pronounced.

Temperatures that rise above the plant's preferred range pose different problems. Warm air is capable of containing a lot more moisture vapour than cool air: as the temperature rises, moisture is drawn

Desert areas of the western United States and Mexico are home to a huge variety of cacti. A miniature version of the fishhook cactus shown here (above) *is a common house plant.*

A native of the meadows and woodlands of western and southern European countries, the pale yellow common primrose, Primula vulgaris (left), *is the source of the brightly coloured spring-flowering plants often seen indoors.*

into the air from any available surface, including plant foliage. As long as the atmosphere is humid enough, the compost is kept sufficiently moist and ventilation is good, most plants can tolerate temperatures a bit above their ideal. To be comfortable, plants generally need 50–60 percent relative humidity; in most modern homes, the humidity is nearer 15–20 percent. Placing dishes of water near radiators can help, but increasing the humidity directly around the plants is preferable. Misting and setting pots on wide dishes of moist pebbles or gravel are the easiest ways to increase humidity. Grouping plants helps to create a humid microclimate in which they can flourish.

If the temperature is markedly above a plant's preferred range, growth will be soft and drawn, making the plant leggy, and any flowers will have a very short life.

WATERING

ALL PLANTS NEED WATER TO GROW and develop, but the amount of water they require varies considerably from species to species.

In addition to providing the necessary turgor (stiffness) to keep the plant upright, water is essential for many chemical processes within the plant. It is generally taken up from the compost through the roots, although epiphytic plants (such as some orchids and bromeliads) absorb water through their leaves rather than their roots. Water is distributed throughout the plant by a network of water-conducting tissues.

Water vapour is given off into the atmosphere, in a process known as transpiration, from all the above-ground surfaces of the plant, but mainly from the leaves. This sets up a suction effect, whereby water is constantly being pulled up through the plant from the soil.

The most practical piece of equipment for watering plants is a watering can with a long spout, but many ingenious devices have been produced both to detect when plants need watering and to water them when you are unable to do so yourself.

The drier and warmer the atmosphere, the more water is lost from the leaves, and the more water is required at the roots to replace it. The compost must, therefore, always contain adequate reserves of water to supply the needs of the plant.

But roots also need air, which should be present in the gaps between the particles of compost. If these gaps are kept constantly filled with water – in other words, if the soil is saturated – the roots will be killed and will rot away. So watering any plant necessitates maintaining a delicate balance, which is even more pronounced with house plants in pots. They have only a small volume of soil around the roots, which allows little room for mistakes to be rectified.

Capillary matting is useful for watering plants when you go away. Fill the sink with water and put the matting on the draining board, with about half of it in the water. The mat is made of thick felt or felt rubber that absorbs water, and plants standing on it take up the water they need by capillary action. It works best with plastic pots; with clay pots, too much of the water is absorbed by the pot itself.

Use a hand sprayer to mist the leaves of plants in order to increase humidity.

A watering can with a long spout is the easiest vessel to use when watering plants. If you put a sprinkler on the spout, you can wash dust off the leaves as well. Use soft water – hard water leaves lime spots on the leaves.

An irrigator (left) is another way to water a plant when you are away. Fill the plastic bag with water, insert the green paper strip into the soil, then attach the bag to the pot by pushing the plastic pin through the tab and into the soil. Water seeping through the paper strip keeps the soil evenly moist.

These tabs help to prevent over- or underwatering. Push one into the pot so that the bottom of the green area is just below the soil surface. Water the plant from the bottom until the yellow can and water drops turn green; give more water when they begin to revert to yellow. The spot at the top right remains yellow for comparison.

HOW TO WATER

For the majority of plants, the compost should be kept just moist throughout the growing season. Apply water until it starts to seep through the drainage holes of the pot, let it stand for 10–30 minutes, then throw away any water that remains in the saucer. Do not water again until the surface of the compost is dry to the touch: since the surface will dry out first, the compost will still be slightly moist below. More frequent watering will be necessary in warm conditions. In winter, watering should be reduced for most plants. They will be growing more slowly, if at all, so less water is required and roots are more liable to rot in cool conditions.

Some species need frequent watering and should never be allowed to dry out; indeed, some such as cyperus are adapted to growing with their roots standing in water at all times. Other plants, like cacti, are adapted to dry conditions and need watering only sparingly. Such exceptions are noted in The Plant Directory.

The simplest way to water pot plants is to apply water directly to the surface of the compost with a long-spouted can.

But, like cyclamens, many plants do not like water being splashed on to the crown, where it can cause rotting.

If the plant is difficult to water from above, pour water into the saucer and let the plant stand in it for not more than 30 minutes before emptying away any remaining water. If the compost is very dry, immerse the plant in a bucket of water up to the rim of the pot until the compost has been completely moistened, but do not let the water flow into the pot. Allow the plant to drain well before replacing it on its saucer.

WATERING SPARINGLY

1 Let the top half to two-thirds of the compost dry out before watering a plant that needs little water. Test with a stick.

2 Pour water on the surface so that it seeps down through the compost but does not run into the saucer.

3 Test it again with the stick. Make sure the compost is just damp throughout; add a little more water if necessary.

WATERING MODERATELY

1 Water a plant that needs a moderate amount of water when the top 13mm/½in of the compost feels dry to the touch.

2 Pour water on the surface of the compost until the entire mixture is thoroughtly wet but not sodden.

3 If water percolates through into the saucer, stop watering and drain the saucer. Do not let the plant stand in water.

WATERING LIBERALLY

1 Water a plant that needs plenty of water when the surface of the compost feels dry to the touch and the pot feels light.

2 Pour plenty of water on the surface of the compost and let it flood out through the drainage holes in the bottom of the pot.

3 When water ceases to flow out through the drainage holes, empty the saucer before replacing the plant on it.

FEEDING

ALTHOUGH PLANTS MANUFACTURE their own food from sunlight, they need various minerals to start this manufacturing process working. The minerals occur naturally in the soil but, because pot plants have only a limited volume of soil to draw on, we generally have to supply some extra nutrients in the form of fertilisers.

PLANT NUTRIENTS

The elements required by plants in the largest quantities are nitrogen, phosphorus and potassium (often referred to by their chemical symbols N, P and K). These are known as the macronutrients. Very small amounts of other minerals, called micronutrients or trace elements,

are also needed. Among the most important of these are iron, zinc, magnesium and manganese.

The nutrients are required for a range of different processes within the plant. But, to simplify, we can say that nitrogen is needed for leafy growth, phosphorus for healthy root development and potassium for general hardiness and the production of flowers and fruits.

Most fertilisers contain a mixture of nutrients in varying proportions. House-plant fertilisers are generally formulated either as fertilisers for foliage plants (high in nitrogen) or as fertilisers for flowering plants (high in potassium).

Fertilisers that are rich in trace elements may be formulated as fast-acting foliar

feeds. A deficiency of trace elements is often shown by yellowing of the leaf veins or of the area between the veins, while the rest of the leaf stays green.

TYPES OF FERTILISER

Food of all types is always taken up by the plant in solution, but it does not need to be applied in that way: dry fertilisers, for instance, will dissolve in the moisture in the soil and so become available to plants. Fertilisers for house plants can be obtained in a wide variety of forms.

Most pot plants need only a standard fertiliser, whether in liquid or solid slow-release form, but special fertilisers are available for all types of plant from cacti to orchids.

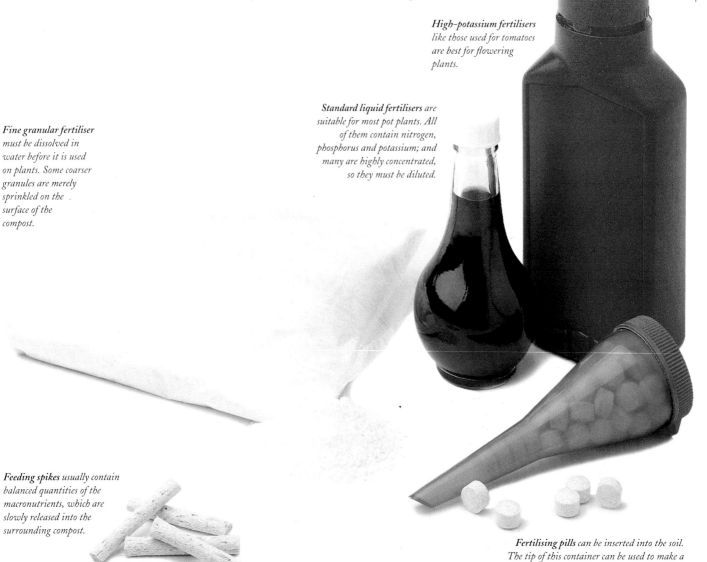

High-potassium fertilisers like those used for tomatoes are best for flowering plants.

Standard liquid fertilisers are suitable for most pot plants. All of them contain nitrogen, phosphorus and potassium; and many are highly concentrated, so they must be diluted.

Fine granular fertiliser must be dissolved in water before it is used on plants. Some coarser granules are merely sprinkled on the surface of the compost.

Feeding spikes usually contain balanced quantities of the macronutrients, which are slowly released into the surrounding compost.

Fertilising pills can be inserted into the soil. The tip of this container can be used to make a hole in the compost in which to insert the tablet.

Liquids
These fertilisers may be ready to use but are more usually found as concentrates, which require dilution before they are applied to the soil. Because the nutrients are already dissolved, the fertilisers are fast-acting. Liquids are probably the most popular types of fertilisers for use with indoor plants.

Powders
This type of fertiliser generally needs to be dissolved in water before use. It is sometimes recommended that pinches of dry fertiliser should be applied directly to the soil in the pot, but there is a risk of scorching the roots with an over-concentration of fertiliser in this way. Powders are often good value for money.

Granules
These are usually mixed with the compost when plants are potted, or they are scattered on the surface of the soil around established plants. Because the granular formulation is slow to break down, there is less risk of scorching the roots than with powdered fertilisers.

Some granular fertilisers are formulated as slow-release. This means that they are manufactured to break down slowly and release small amounts of fertiliser gradually over a long season so that only one application is necessary. The breakdown rate is faster in warm, moist conditions, so the rate of nutrient release is highest when the plants are growing most strongly.

Fertiliser pills and sticks
This is another way of making a single fertiliser application last a long time. Powdered fertilisers are compressed into tablet or stick form and are pushed down into the soil in the pot. The stick or tablet dissolves gradually, releasing fertiliser to the plant as it does so. These types are useful for people who are busy and so likely to forget to feed their plants on a regular basis, and for those who find it difficult to do so.

Foliar feeds
Although the roots are mainly responsible for taking up nutrients, the leaves can also absorb them, and this is an extremely quick way of getting food to work in the plant. The majority of fertiliser formulations would scorch the foliage if they were applied to the leaves, but some fertilisers are specifically made to be applied in this way. Most foliar feeds contain trace elements.

WHEN TO FEED
Overfeeding a plant is potentially more damaging than not feeding it, and an excess of fertiliser can quite easily kill it. Plants need feeding only when they are growing actively, and for most this means between spring and autumn. In winter, when temperatures and light levels are lower, plants generally need less water and fewer nutrients than in spring, summer and autumn. Plants that bloom in winter should, however, be fed during the flowering period.

All soil contains some plant nutrients, and a newly potted plant does not usually need any additional fertiliser for several weeks. Peat-based (or peat substitute) compost contains a much lower level of nutrients than soil-based composts. Consequently plants set in a peat-based compost will need feeding sooner and more frequently than plants potted up in a soil-based compost.

As a general rule, the faster-growing the plant, the more frequently it will need feeding. Every 2–3 weeks is a good rule of thumb for the majority of plants, but always check the pack recommendations for the particular fertiliser you are using. The Plant Directory gives feeding guidelines for all the plants featured in this book.

METHODS OF FEEDING PLANTS

Sticks of concentrated powdered fertiliser should be pushed fairly deeply into the soil near the edge of the pot. Watering the plant will dissolve them over time.

Push pills containing slow-release fertiliser almost to the bottom of the pot, using a pencil or stick. Be careful not to damage the roots of the plant as you do so.

Liquid fertilisers in solution are the most common type of fertiliser, and may be applied either from on top or from below. Do not make the solution too strong or you may kill rather than feed the plant.

Spraying with foliar feed is a good way to feed plants such as bromeliads, which have a small rooting system, and large-leafed plants like philodendrons. This will also quickly revive a plant that has been starved of nutrients.

REPOTTING

THE CULTIVATION AND GROWTH OF a plant in a pot are markedly different from those of a plant growing outdoors. The container restricts the spread of the roots, which in turn restricts the size of the top growth. Thus many indoor plants, while perfectly healthy, are in effect stunted by their containers.

A pot of any size holds only a small volume of compost compared with a garden situation, and this affects the plant in a number of ways. First, the supply of nutrients available to the plant is limited and may quite quickly be exhausted. The supply of water is also limited. But, paradoxically, because the drainage is not as efficient as in an outdoor situation, plants in containers are frequently damaged by waterlogging.

The composts for pot plants are sterile. This eliminates competition from weed seedlings and potential damage by harmful organisms and pests in the soil, but the many beneficial effects of a natural soil flora and fauna are also absent. As a consequence, the indoor gardener must exercise caution when caring for container-grown plants.

REMOVING A PLANT FROM A SMALL POT

1 Place your hand over the surface of the compost with the main stem or stems of the plant between your fingers.

2 Turn the pot upside down and gently but firmly knock it against the edge of a bench or table to loosen the plant.

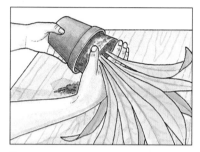

3 Remove the plant from the old pot with the rootball intact. Tease out the old compost from around the roots and repot.

REMOVING A PLANT FROM A LARGE POT

1 To remove a plant from a large pot, first ease it away from the edge of the pot with a large knife or spatula.

2 Lay the pot on its side. Turn it as you tap it with a piece of wood to loosen the compost. Hold the plant with one hand.

3 Make sure the plant is loose before trying to remove it from the pot. If the plant is large, you may need some help.

REMOVING A CACTUS FROM A POT

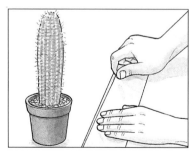

1 The best way to remove a cactus or other prickly plant from a pot is to protect your hands with thickly folded newspaper.

2 Wrap the paper around the plant, making sure that it is long enough to give you something to hold on to.

3 Grip the paper firmly in one hand and then gently ease the pot away from the soil with the other hand.

TYPES OF COMPOST

There are many different brands of house plant compost, each with its own devotees, but the main choice you need to make is between peat-based and soil-based compost. Although some plants are said to do better in loam-based (soil-based) compost and some in loamless (peat-based) compost, which of these is used is generally determined by what the gardener feels happier with. Nearly all plants adapt quite well to either.

Different brands of compost have different formulations, however slightly they may vary, and it will be a matter of trial and error to find one that suits you and your plants.

Seeds and cuttings compost contains only small amounts of nutrients and is suitable mainly for propagation. Potting compost contains more fertiliser and is suitable for growing and mature plants.

LOAM-BASED COMPOST

This type of compost was originally based on rotted-down meadow turf with specified quantities of added fertiliser. Forest and farm by-products are also sometimes used. It looks, feels and handles like good garden soil. Firm plants moderately when potting, but take care not to damage the roots by over-firming.

ADVANTAGES

Provides a long-lasting nutrient supply. ● Creates a stable base for large plants and pots. ● Available in different strengths for different types and sizes of plant.

DISADVANTAGES

Heavy to transport, both in pots and in the bag. ● Messier to use than loamless compost. ● Quality is variable.

LOAMLESS COMPOST

These mixes were formerly based on peat, but with the growing controversy over the ecological damage said to be caused by harvesting, several substitutes are now available. These include coir, made from coconut husks. It is still too early to assess exactly how successful these substitutes may prove to be. Meanwhile, peat-based compost is still widely available and popular. Plants need to be firmed in only lightly when they are potted in loamless compost.

ADVANTAGES

Lightweight. ● Clean to handle. ● Standard quality, with only fairly minor differences between brands.

DISADVANTAGES

Soon runs out of nutrients, so supplementary feeding is necessary from an early stage. ● Large plants can become top-heavy and topple over. ● Can be difficult to rewet if allowed to dry out.

SPECIAL COMPOSTS

Some plants do best in a more specialised medium. The most commonly found is orchid compost, which is suitable for epiphytic plants such as orchids and some bromeliads. This is an open, free-draining mixture usually consisting of pieces of bark, osmunda fibre, sphagnum moss or polystyrene chips.

Ericaceous composts, which are suitable for lime-hating plants such as ericas and azaleas, are acidic and contain no free lime.

It is also possible to buy cactus composts, which are particularly free-draining.

Loamless, or peat-based, compost consists of peat or peat substitutes such as coir with added nutrients.

This loam- or soil-based compost has a base of superphosphate, blood and bone meal, and sulphate of potash in a ratio of 2:2:1, added to varying amounts of loam, peat and sand.

This orchid compost consists of sphagnum moss, bark chips or osmunda fibre, and coarse peat in a ratio of 2:2:1 by volume.

This cactus compost consists of two-thirds of any general commercial potting compost and one-third of grit or coarse sand by volume.

REPOTTING (continued)

POTTING ON

Plants are usually bought or obtained at an immature stage of growth because they are less expensive and easier to transport and market while they are relatively small. As they develop in the home, most will need moving on into progressively larger pots, a process known as repotting, or potting on.

While it might seem sensible to pot the plant immediately into the largest size pot it is likely to need and skip the intervening stages, this does not lead to healthy growth. Plants should generally be moved into a pot just one size larger than the one they are in (quick-growing species can be moved into pots two sizes larger). This means that the fresh compost around the existing rootball will soon be penetrated by new roots. If there is a large expanse of compost that does not contain roots, it is likely to become waterlogged and stale.

Plants that resent root disturbance or are in pots of the biggest practical size should be top-dressed, not repotted.

GETTING THE TIMING RIGHT

With experience it becomes quite easy to tell when a plant needs repotting. The most obvious sign is when roots cover the surface of the compost or emerge from the drainage holes in the base of the pot. When the latter is very evident, turn the plant out of its pot to check the state of the rootball.

If the rootball holds together and the compost appears full of roots, the plant is ready for potting on, but if the compost falls away, place the plant carefully back in the same container, lightly firm the compost around it and leave it for a little while longer.

The best time for repotting is at the beginning of the period of active growth, which is generally spring, although plants that bloom in winter will need to be repotted in early autumn, after their dormant period.

TWO WAYS TO REPOT A PLANT

1 **Put a layer of pebbles** or broken crocks on the bottom of a clean pot one size larger than the old one. Cover it with compost and set the plant in the pot.

2 **Fill the gap** between the plant and the side of the pot with compost. Dribble it in carefully by hand to avoid damaging the plant and press it down quite firmly.

3 Finally, water the plant thoroughly, using a rose on the watering can, or plunge the pot into a bucket of water to soak the compost. Then drain the pot.

4 **Alternatively,** use the old pot as a mould. Add drainage layer as instructed in Step 1. Set the plant in the pot and check that it will sit at the same level in the new pot.

5 **Remove the plant.** Put the old pot inside the new one and make a mould in which to set the plant by filling the space between the two pots with compost.

6 **Insert the plant** and fill any gaps with compost, firming it down to make sure that the plant is well supported. Water the plant as described in Step 3 above.

REPOTTING A PLANT IN THE SAME-SIZED POT

1 Repot plants that prefer to be slightly pot-bound in the same-sized pot. Crumble away some of the old compost and, if necessary, cut off part of the rootball.

2 Put layers of gravel and compost in the bottom of the pot and set the plant in it. Fill in around the edges of the rootball with new compost. Water thoroughly.

MAKING A BROMELIAD TREE

Epiphytic plants, such as some bromeliads, which have few or no roots, will grow readily on a tree branch as they do in nature, provided they are kept thoroughly moist. Choose a forked branch with attractive bark.

TOP-DRESSING

1 With an old kitchen fork or similar instrument, gently scrape away the top 5–8cm/2–3in of compost, taking care not to damage the roots.

2 Fill the pot to the old level with the right type of new compost, to which slow-release fertiliser has been added. Firm the compost down and water the plant.

PREPARING A PLANT FOR A BROMELIAD TREE

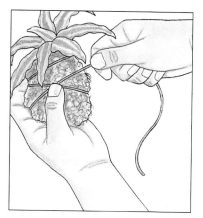

1 Turn an epiphyte out of its pot and wrap a mixture of potting compost and sphagnum moss around the rootball, attaching it with fine plastic-coated wire.

2 Put the plant in a tree fork or remove a piece of bark to provide a niche for it. Wire the plant to the branch and mist the moss frequently until the roots have taken hold.

TRAINING

A NUMBER OF INDOOR PLANTS WITH lax stems or with large, heavy flowers benefit from the unobtrusive support of slender canes. But the climbing and scrambling plants need serious attention paid to their training. A well-trained plant is not only neater and easier to care for, it is usually more attractive, since it permits you to show off its flowers or foliage to advantage.

Some plants are true climbers with clinging tendrils and they will rapidly attach themselves to a support. Many others are scramblers in their natural habitat. They make their way over and through the mass of vegetation that surrounds them, using it to hold themselves up. In the home, they need to be encouraged to use a support and to be tied into it at intervals. (See page 27 for more detail on supports.)

Climbing plants all produce long, lax stems. They may also have tendrils that arise either from the stems or from the tips of the leaves and that coil tightly around any object they come into contact with. Or they may have aerial roots, which need a damp surface to which they can attach themselves.

TENDRILS

Plants with tendrils, such as *Cissus antarctica* and *Gloriosa superba*, do not need much help to climb. A simple trellis will provide ample support. And the only training necessary will be to keep the shoots within the bounds of the support by pinching, and occasionally to thread in the tips of the shoots so that all parts of the trellis are evenly covered.

AERIAL ROOTS

Aerial roots can be a problem. Plants such as monsteras and philodendrons, which produce thick, fleshy roots, need a moss pole – a sturdy stake covered with moss that is kept constantly moist – into which the roots can be trained. The lower roots on these plants can be trained down into the compost.

Roots of this type can be brittle, and they need careful handling. Anchor them in the required position with pieces of fine wire bent into a hairpin shape and pushed firmly through the moss.

The aerial roots will not support the upper stems of the plant, which are generally wound loosely around the pole and kept in place with similar loops of bent wire.

Hedera, ivy, produces a quite different type of aerial root: small pads of fringe-like roots are formed at intervals along the stems. These are very effective at supporting the plant on brick walls or tree trunks, but they cling extremely tightly and are not usually welcome in the home because they can damage walls, furniture and fixtures. Ivies are, therefore, usually treated as plants that need to be provided with supports.

SCRAMBLERS AND TRAILERS

These plants, which include hoya, jasmine, passion flower and stephanotis, do not have the means of attaching themselves to a support. They can be grown up trelliswork and tied in at intervals with soft twine in a figure-of-eight loop, but they are often trained around hoops made from wire or cane.

The hoop is inserted firmly into the compost (see page 27), and the stems are

PINNING DOWN AERIAL ROOTS

1 To pin the aerial roots of large plants such as *Monstera deliciosa* into a moss pole, first make sure that the moss is thoroughly moist by spraying it with water. Then secure the roots with hoops of fine wire.

2 Wind the long, heavy stems around the moss pole, tying them in at intervals, or pin them to the pole with wire hoops in the same way as the roots. Always keep the moss on the pole damp.

COILING SHOOTS AROUND A SUPPORT

1 To train an ivy plant around a hoop, first push the 'legs' of the support firmly into the mix over the top of the plant. Then twist the stems around the hoop or use soft twine to tie them firmly in place.

2 As the plant grows, gently weave the new stems around the hoop. When a stem reaches the end of the hoop, turn it back on itself. That way, the plant will form an attractive bushy shape.

simply twisted gently around the wire while they are still young and supple. They may need tying into place at first, but as a framework of stems builds up, they will stay in position more easily. When the tip of the stem reaches the surface of the compost on the other side of the hoop it can be turned back gently.

PINCHING AND PRUNING

Most house plants do not need regular pruning, but many require some form of pinching out, or stopping, to keep them shapely. Removing the growing tip from a stem stimulates several buds in the leaf axils below it into growth. In this way, not only is the stem kept short, but it branches outwards as well.

The process is highly beneficial since it results in healthy-looking, bushy compact plants that are generally more desirable in the home. As well as having a more pleasing shape, such plants will often bear more flowers than plants that have not been stopped.

Because it is generally the soft tips of stems that are removed, this job is normally easily carried out with finger and thumb. But if the stems are too tough for this to be done cleanly, use a very sharp knife or a single-edged razor blade. Pinch the stem just above the first or second node, the point at which the leaves join the stem.

For some plants, regular pinching out is required all through the growing season; others are stopped once or twice at the beginning of the season only. Care must be taken with plants that carry their flowers at the ends of the stems, since too-frequent pinching out could prevent flowering altogether.

Plants that are more drastically pruned back at the end of the season or after flowering should also be cut just above a node where possible, using a sharp pair of secateurs. Details of pruning and pinching, where applicable, are given for individual plants in The Plant Directory.

DEADHEADING

It is nearly always recommended to remove dead flowers, a process known as deadheading. Dead and fading flowers look unattractive and they can encourage attack by the fungus disease botrytis. If flowers are allowed to set seed, the plant's energy is wasted. And setting seed signals to the plant that the flowering season is over, preventing further flushes of bloom that might otherwise have occurred. Once again, try to remove stems just above a node.

PINCHING OUT GROWING TIPS

1 **Many plants produce** trailing stems that can become lank and unattractive, with long gaps between the leaves. Shorten such stems by pinching out the growing tips with your finger and thumb.

2 **Pinching out the tips of soft stems** encourages the plant to put on new growth, and the new leaves will grow closer together. It is also a good way to keep a plant looking shapely.

PRUNING TO ENCOURAGE BUSHINESS

1 **At the end of the growing season,** cut back woody plants and fast-growing plants that have become too large for the space. Stems can usually be reduced by up to two-thirds without damaging the plant.

2 **Pruning plants in this way** reinvigorates them and encourages them to put on plenty of strong new growth. To keep the plant's bushy shape, pinch out the growing tips as described above.

Flowering plants like chrysanthemums will produce more blooms and continue to flower for far longer if they are regularly deadheaded. Pick off any dead or fading flowers with your finger and thumb.

Obviously, flowers should not be removed from plants that are grown for their fruits, such as capsicums and solanums, and care should be taken with hoyas, since the following season's flowers will arise from the same spurs.

PROPAGATION METHODS

MOST INDOOR PLANTS ARE BOUGHT as young or established plants from garden centres and nurseries. Even so it is advisable to have a supply of young plants ready to replace the older ones that are past their prime. You may also wish to have several specimens of a particular plant around the house, or to have spare plants to give to friends. If this is so, you do not need to buy more plants – it is quite easy to increase your stock of many specimens by a variety of means.

No specialised equipment is needed for propagating the easier species, although a seed tray with a clear plastic lid is cheap to buy and always worth having. A propagator with bottom heat will certainly help you to increase your stock of some of the more difficult subjects.

CUTTINGS

Probably the method most often used to increase pot plants is to take cuttings. A cutting is a portion taken from the parent plant and encouraged to make its own roots (or sometimes shoots). Two types are used to propagate house plants: stem cuttings and leaf cuttings.

Stem cuttings

These are generally taken in spring or early summer. Snap a healthy young shoot, preferably without flower buds, from the parent plant. If it will not snap cleanly, use a sharp knife and cut just above a node.

The length of the cutting will vary, but it should have three or four pairs of leaves or leaf nodes (joints) between the tip and the base.

Trim the base of the cutting to just below a node and remove the bottom leaves to give a clear portion of stem. Hormone rooting powder is recommended for some species, although most do just as well without it. If it is used, a light dusting of powder on the base of the stem is all that is needed.

Fill a shallow pot or seed tray with moist seed and cuttings compost and press it until it is firm. Scatter a thin layer of sharp sand on top. With a pencil or dibber, make holes in the compost and insert the cuttings into them, making sure the base of the cutting is in good contact with the compost. Firm the compost lightly.

Space the cuttings so their leaves do not touch and water the completed tray or pot, using a fine rose on the can. Put a plastic cover over the tray and place it in a warm (20°C/68°F), bright position out of direct sun.

The time the cuttings take to root will vary, but eventually they will start to look fresh and to grow from the centre. They can then be potted up individually.

Leaf cuttings

Some fleshy-leafed plants can be propagated from their leaves. New plants are produced from either the plant's leaf-stalks or from the veins.

Saintpaulias, the African violets, for instance, are generally increased from leaf stem cuttings. With a sharp knife or razor blade, cut off a fully opened, healthy leaf at the base of the leafstalk.

Trim the stalk to 2.5–4cm/1–1½in long, dip the base in hormone rooting powder and insert it, at an angle, into moist seed and cuttings compost close to the edge of a small pot; bury about two-thirds of the stalk. Firm the compost gently and then place the pot in a warm position in light shade.

Keep the compost just moist, and plantlets will appear within about eight weeks. Once they have grown into strong young plants that can be handled easily, remove them from the pot, tease them apart carefully, and pot them individually. Saintpaulias will also root in water.

Some plants – streptocarpus and begonias, for example – can be propagated by leaf vein cuttings, which are taken in one of two ways.

Again, remove a healthy, fully formed leaf cleanly from the parent plant. Cut the leaf horizontally into three or four

TAKING SOFT STEM CUTTINGS

1 Plants with soft stems, such as pelargoniums, can be rooted from the tip of a healthy stem. Cut a stem with 3 or 4 leaf nodes between the tip and the base.

2 Remove the lower leaves from the stem and with a sharp knife, trim it cleanly to just above a leaf node.

3 Dip the end of the cutting into hormone rooting powder and shake off any excess. (It is not essential to use rooting powder.)

4 Fill a small pot with seed and cuttings compost and make a hole in it with a pencil or dibber. Insert the cutting and gently firm the compost around it.

TAKING LEAF STEM CUTTINGS

1 Choose a strong, healthy leaf and, with a sharp knife, cut it away from the plant at the base of the stalk. Trim the stalk to about 4cm/1½in long.

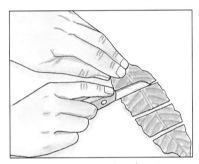

2 Holding the leaf gently between your fingers, dip the cut end into hormone rooting powder. Several cuttings can be taken at one time.

3 Insert the leafstalks into seed and cuttings compost near the rim of the pot. If you push the stems in at an angle of 45°, they will have underground support.

TAKING CUTTINGS FROM LEAF SEGMENTS

1 Plants like streptocarpus can be rooted from small pieces of the leaf. To take a cutting from a leaf, first cut off a good healthy mature leaf at the base.

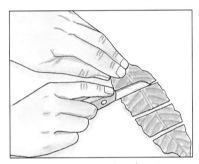

2 Cut the whole leaf horizontally into strips about 2.5cm/1in wide. Dip the base of each cutting (the end nearest the stalk) in hormone rooting powder.

3 Insert the base of each piece of leaf into a tray of seed and cuttings compost, and gently firm the compost around the cuttings with your fingers.

sections, or split it lengthwise straight up the centre of the midrib. Use a razor blade or sharp knife to make the cuts. If you cut the leaf into horizontal sections, make sure you know which is the top and the base (the part nearest the leafstalk) of each section.

Dust the bases or the split midrib with hormone rooting powder and insert them to about one-third of their depth in moist seed and cuttings compost in a pot or seed tray. Plantlets will be produced in the same way as with leaf stem cuttings.

OFFSETS
Several plants naturally produce small plantlets around the outer edge, which can be carefully removed and potted up. This is an easy way to propagate succulents such as echeverias, bromeliads, some cacti and bulbous plants.

Wait until the offsets are a reasonable size and can be handled easily, then carefully separate them from the parent plant; you may need to use a sharp knife to cut through the rootstock. Keep as many roots on the offset as possible. If there are none, keep the newly potted offset in a warm, humid atmosphere and treat it like a cutting. Roots should form within a few weeks. (*Continued on p. 208*)

PROPAGATING BY OFFSETS

1 Many plants produce offsets around the base. Remove the plant from its pot and detach a good-sized offset, preferably with roots, from the parent.

2 Pot up the offset in rooting medium to the same depth as it was on the parent. When the root system is established, treat it as a mature plant.

DIVISION

Plants such as saintpaulias, sansevierias, many ferns, spathiphyllums, calatheas and several others are suitable for division. This is usually done when the plant has outgrown its pot.

Turn the plant out of its pot and carefully crumble away the compost until you can see the best way to split the plant. Every portion should have a healthy growing point and plenty of roots. Tease the portions apart carefully with as little damage to the root system as possible. Pot up the portions individually in moist compost and keep the pots just damp and out of direct sun until the plants have become established.

LAYERING

The technique whereby a new plant is induced to form roots while still attached to the parent is known as layering. One of the most common examples is chlorophytum, which produces young plantlets on long stems in great abundance. When the base of a plantlet comes into contact with the compost, it will rapidly produce roots and can soon be separated from the parent. A piece of wire bent into a hairpin shape is useful for pinning the plantlet down to keep it in close contact with the compost while roots form.

Many climbing and trailing plants, such as the ivies, increase naturally by layering, and as indoor plants they can be layered simply by pinning a section of stem firmly into a pot of compost. If the stem is woody, first scrape off a little bark from the underside with a sharp knife; roots will form at this point.

PROPAGATING BY DIVISION

1 Tip the plant out of its pot, crumble or wash away some of the compost, and lever or cut the sections apart. Be sure that each part has plenty of roots and a growing tip.

2 Pot up the divisions, at the same level as they were, in moist compost in a pot a little larger than the rootball. Water sparingly until new growth can be seen.

Air-layering is slightly different. Here the stems cannot be brought down to soil level, so the compost is brought up to them. Plants that have stiff, woody stems or that have grown too tall and leggy are often treated in this way; *Ficus elastica* is a common candidate.

A ring of bark is carefully removed from the stem just below the lowest leaf. Alternatively, a sloping cut is made about one-third of the way through the stem. It is dusted with hormone rooting powder and wedged open with a matchstick or wad of sphagnum moss.

Moist sphagnum moss is then packed around the wounded area, and a piece of plastic is wrapped firmly around it and taped top and bottom. (Peat-based potting mix can be used instead of the moss, but it is not so easy to handle.)

Care for the plant being layered in the normal way while roots slowly form

within the moss: if clear plastic is used, they can be seen developing. Once they are well grown, cut off the rooted portion with a sharp knife or secateurs and pot it. Cut back the stump of the original plant and water it sparingly until new growth has appeared.

SEEDS

Only a relatively small number of house plants are raised from seed, but cyclamens, cinerarias, capsicums, primulas, coleuses, fuchsias and many cacti, among others, are not difficult to grow this way. A heated propagator and a greenhouse will make it easier to raise some species, but others will germinate quite easily in an airing cupboard or similar warm place.

Seeds can be obtained from most major seed merchants, as well as a number of smaller, specialist companies. If you save seeds from your own plants, remember

PROPAGATING BY LAYERING

1 Some plants, such as ivy, are very easy to layer. Scrape the underside of the stem, or make a nick in it, to check the flow of sap and stimulate rooting.

2 Fill a small pot with compost and anchor the stem firmly by pegging it down with small hoops of fine wire; otherwise, cover the stem with compost.

3 Cut the layered plant away from the parent when new growth is evident. Be careful to preserve the shape of the original plant.

that the chances are they will not produce plants of the same variety as the parent. Many seeds from seed merchants are also 'pot luck' mixtures that produce unpredictable colours and forms.

Fill a shallow pan or seed tray with seed and cuttings compost and firm it with a small flat piece of wood. Water the compost with a fine rose on the can or a sprayer and let it drain.

Sow the seeds thinly and evenly on the surface of the compost; very small seeds can be mixed with fine sand as a carrier to aid even sowing. Cover the seeds to their own depth with compost (such as a mixture of sharp sand and peat or perlite); take care not to bury them too deeply. Some fine seeds, such as those of orchids, are best left uncovered.

Place a clear plastic propagator cover on the tray (a plastic bag supported by split canes can be used instead) and leave it in a warm place at a temperature between 20°C and 27°C/68°F and 80°F,

depending on the species. Bring the tray into diffuse light when most of the seedlings are visible. Keep the plastic cover on the tray for the time being, but open the vents to allow fresh air to circulate around the plants. Once the plants are growing strongly, remove the cover. Keep the compost just moist.

When the seedlings can be handled easily, prick them out into another container to give them extra space. Handle them by the seed leaves (the first pair of leaves they produce), never by the stems. Keep them in good, bright, but diffuse light. As the young plants develop, prick them out into other trays and finally into individual pots.

Fern spores
Ferns produce spores instead of seeds, and they are challenging plants to raise. Spores are sown on the surface of the compost in a similar way to seeds, but the compost is kept more thoroughly moist. Cover the tray or pan with a propagator

top and keep it in a warm, light position. After several weeks, a green mossy growth will gradually cover the compost surface; this contains the plant's male and female organs and fertilisation takes place at this stage. Eventually tiny ferns will develop and can be potted up, first in groups, then separately as they develop. But you will have to be patient: the process is very slow.

LEAF EMBRYOS
A small number of plants produce tiny, complete plantlets on their leaves and are very easy to propagate. Some such as *Kalanchoe daigremontiana* can be a real nuisance, since large numbers of plantlets can take root among other plants, wherever they happen to fall. *Tolmiea menziesii* and *Asplenium bulbiferum* also produce plantlets on their leaves. All that is necessary for propagation is to make sure that the base of the plantlet comes into contact with moist compost.

PROPAGATING BY SOWING SEEDS

1 Put a thin layer of gravel on the bottom of a seed tray to provide good drainage and cover it with seed and cuttings compost. Press it down gently to firm it.

2 Scatter larger seeds thinly on the surface of the compost. If you mix small seeds with sand, they will be much easier to handle.

3 Cover the seeds with a thin layer of compost and spray it with water until it is thoroughly moist. Remember that some seeds should not be covered.

4 Put a specially made plastic top on the seed tray, or cover it with glass or a plastic tent. This will create a humid atmosphere and induce the seeds to germinate.

5 Thin out the seedlings so that the space between them is about the same as their height. When they are well grown, prick them out into another tray.

6 When the seedlings have at least two true leaves in addition to the first pair of seed leaves, lift them carefully from the tray and transfer them to individual pots.

SPECIALIST GROWING METHODS

HYDROPONICS

Plants do not need soil or compost in order to grow, they require merely a source of nutrients and water. House plants can be grown by a method of soil-less culture known as hydroponics, or hydroculture. Its advantages are that it is clean and convenient and takes away the worry of over- or underwatering (both common causes of indoor plant death).

The simplest method of hydroculture is a bulb glass containing a fertiliser solution; this is suitable for such bulbs as hyacinths. In a single container (right), the plant roots are anchored in aggregate, some of which is covered by water. In a double container (centre), the roots grow through a small pot filled with aggregate into the fertiliser solution in the large outer pot.

A gauge is often used to indicate the depth of the fertiliser solution. It is inserted into the pot and, as the cross-section on the right shows, a marker moved by a float drops as the level falls.

The substrate used to support the plant's roots can be pebbles, glass beads, vermiculite or several other substances, although the most common is light-weight expanded clay aggregate (Leca). This is a by-product of the building trade and consists of extremely light, porous, round granules. Hydroculture plants are usually grown in a mesh pot full of Leca, which is set in an outer container filled with nutrient solution. Water and fertiliser are added through a tube that contains a gauge to show exactly how much water is needed.

While ready-potted hydroculture plants can be bought, plants can be converted to

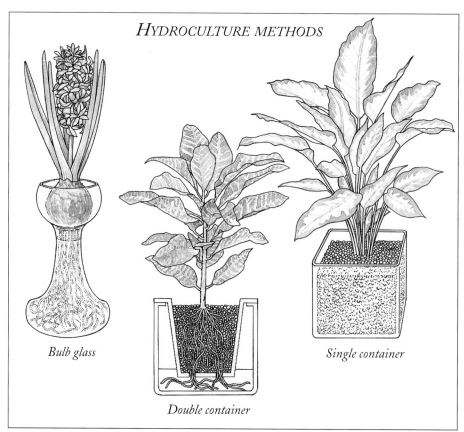

HYDROCULTURE METHODS

Bulb glass

Double container

Single container

TRANSFERRING A PLANT FROM COMPOST TO HYDROCULTURE

1 Remove the plant from its pot carefully so that the rootball does not suffer any damage. Soak the plant in a bucket of water for half an hour.

2 Hold the plant firmly in one hand and gently tease apart the rootball. Remove as much of the compost as you can without harming the roots.

3 Wash the roots under tepid running water to get them clean. Put the plant into a pot of aggregate and give it warmth and high humidity while the roots adapt to hydroculture.

the method in the home. The best way is to take cuttings and root them in water, but healthy young plants growing in compost can often be successfully transferred to the hydroculture system.

Remove the plant from its pot and place the rootball in a bucket of water to soak for half an hour, then gently wash the soil off the roots under a tap. Pot the plant in soaked Leca granules (or similar material) in much the same way as if it were being repotted conventionally. A plastic cover or inflated plastic bag placed over the top of the plant will help to keep the atmosphere humid and prevent the plant wilting while new roots form.

ARTIFICIAL LIGHT

Although a heated room may provide summer-time warmth in midwinter, plants will not grow as well as they do in summer because of the difference in light levels. Not only are the days shorter, but the intensity of the light is less. Even in midsummer, the light intensity in a room is a small fraction of that outside: on overcast winter days it is hardly surprising that many plants indoors merely 'tick over'.

Artificial lighting can supplement natural daylight or replace it altogether, keeping plants growing and sometimes flowering throughout the winter months. Special lamps, such as high-pressure mercury-vapour lamps, can be used to stimulate plant growth. These lamps provide the correct wavelengths of light (the blue and red parts of the spectrum are most important for photosynthesis). However, ordinary fluorescent tubes, including the compact types, are quite satisfactory for most indoor plants. The normal incandescent light bulb is not suitable, since it gives off too much heat in relation to the intensity of light.

The source of light must be quite close to the plants: generally a maximum of 60cm/2ft above the top of the foliage. Some flowering plants, such as saintpaulias, should be as close as 23cm/9in for the best results. If the lamp cannot easily be moved (a 'rise and fall' light fitting is particularly useful), the plants themselves can be raised and lowered.

Artificial lighting is generally used for between 8 and 12 hours a day, but flowering plants may need up to 18 hours for the initiation of buds and for their development.

The fluorescent lights commonly found in the kitchen will keep plants in good condition, and even in flower, during the short days of winter. Fluorescent tubes provide a high level of light without the heat that is generated by ordinary incandescent light bulbs.

DAY LENGTH AND FLOWERING

For some plants the time of flowering is controlled by day length: this response is known as photoperiodism. While many plants flower when days are long, for some the signal to initiate their buds is the shortening of the days: kalanchoes, poinsettias and chrysanthemums are common examples. Each species has its own critical day length, and these have been used by commercial growers to manipulate flowering times to suit specific markets.

As far as the indoor gardener is concerned, the importance of this response is that plants may fail to flower if subjected to artificial light in autumn and winter. For although ordinary lightbulbs may not provide enough light to promote plant growth, it can easily be enough to interfere with bud initiation. Exposure to sodium street lighting can have the same effect on plants.

So-called short-day plants, such as *Euphorbia pulcherrima*, poinsettia, can be brought into flower as required by blacking them out for certain periods each day, but this is difficult to carry out satisfactorily in the home. A better method is to keep the plants in a room that is not used at night – perhaps a spare bedroom – so that they receive only natural daylight. Remember that accidentally switching on the light for even a short period can break the cycle and delay or prevent flowering.

REST PERIODS

In their natural environment, most indoor plants from tropical regions will continue to grow vigorously all year. Others, from temperate zones, will have a marked seasonal response: growth stops in late autumn, the plant becomes more or less dormant during the winter and then starts into growth again in spring.

Most homes are heated to a comfortable level throughout the year so that there is little, if any, seasonal temperature change for the plants. The amount and intensity of light does, however, change in winter, as we have seen. This presents the plant with a confusing set of conditions, since the warmth stimulates growth, which then becomes leggy and drawn because of poor light.

When days shorten, it is a good idea to give many plants a rest period. Move them into a room with cooler conditions, if necessary, stop feeding them and cut down on the watering. Growth will slow down or stop and the plants will become dormant or continue to tick over slowly until spring. The Plant Directory gives more detail on the winter requirements of individual plants.

The plants' rest period does not, however, always coincide with winter. Some winter-flowering plants, such as cyclamens and spring-flowering bulbs like narcissus and crocus, have their rest period during the late spring and early summer or even through to autumn.

PESTS AND DISEASES

INDOOR PLANTS ARE SUBJECT TO attack by a surprisingly large number of pests and diseases; not quite as many as outdoor plants perhaps, but more than enough for most plant owners. Constant vigilance is the answer.

PREVENTING PROBLEMS
Most pests and diseases arrive with new plants, so always inspect these carefully before putting them with your existing house plants. When buying plants, reject those with obvious signs of disease or infestation, and keep new plants apart from your others until you are sure that they are free from pests or diseases.

The correct cultivation techniques will keep your plants strong and robust. It will not make them immune to attack, but it will increase their ability to cope with it. Inspect all your plants regularly and deal promptly with any pest or outbreak of disease. They are much easier to control at an early stage.

PEST AND DISEASE CONTROL
While garden centres have an impressive array of pesticides, it is not always necessary to use them. Indeed, there are several ways of dealing with problems.
Physical
A localised outbreak can often be literally nipped in the bud by removing and destroying the affected part of the plant. Pinch out a shoot tip infested by aphids or pick off a single caterpillar on a leaf, and that may be the end of the problem.
Cultural
Several pests and diseases are encouraged by specific conditions. Red spider mites

Pinch out the affected part of the plant.

(two-spotted mites), for instance, thrive in hot, dry air; lowering the temperature and misting the plant regularly with plain water will help to prevent attacks.

Basal rot on succulent plants is usually a sign of overwatering, and grey mould (botrytis) is prevalent in excessively cool, damp conditions.
Biological
The use of natural parasites and predators to control pest species is more feasible in the controlled atmosphere of a greenhouse than in the home. Whiteflies, red spider mites, mealybugs and aphids all have natural enemies, which may be available from specialist suppliers. If an affected plant can be moved to a greenhouse for treatment, it will have a better chance of success.
Chemical
Modern pesticides are usually effective, and when used correctly, they are harmless. However, they often contain potentially damaging substances, so use the least persistent form available.

Check that where you live you are permitted to use the products recommended here on indoor plants.
- Choose the right product for the problem.
- Read the label and follow the instructions.
- Use the correct dose.
- Spray outside, if possible, in a sheltered position.
- Spray plants inside a large plastic bag when using aerosol sprays, and leave them for 20 minutes.
- Remove pets (especially fish) from the room where treatment is taking place.
- Keep pesticides away from children and animals.
Alternative remedies
Various home remedies, using homemade brews or household products such as washing-up liquid, are often recommended for the control of pests and diseases on plants.

Sometimes considered preferable to commercial insecticides, they may be ineffective and even dangerous. In some countries their use is discouraged because they have not been officially tested for safety or efficacy.

INDOOR PLANT PESTS

APHIDS

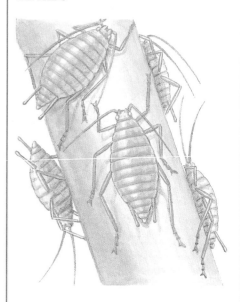

Also known as greenflies (or blackflies, depending on their colour) there are in fact many different species of aphids, but all are treated in the same way. Females give birth to live female young, which can mature within one week. Since they reproduce without the need for fertilisation by a male, colonies increase at an amazingly rapid rate.

Aphids feed by sucking sap from the plant, weakening it and sometimes spreading virus diseases. They excrete a sticky honeydew which is a nuisance when it drops on furniture. In severe attacks, it also encourages the growth of powdery black sooty mould on the leaves of the plant.

Infestations are usually concentrated on soft young growing shoots and around flower buds, and aphids may be present in such numbers that they cause distorted growth. They cast off their skins as they grow, and the presence of the white shed skins is sometimes more noticeable than the creatures themselves.
Non-chemical control
Caught at an early stage, colonies can be removed by pinching out affected shoots or gently washing off the aphids with tepid water. Alternatively use oil sprays.
Suitable insecticides
Pirimicarb is specific to aphids; most other insecticides such as permethrin, resmethirn, derris and fatty acids are also effective.

CATERPILLARS

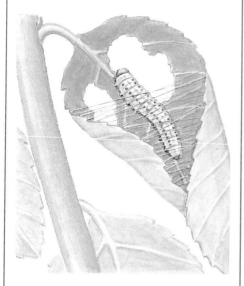

Caterpillars are the larval stage of various insects and they have voracious appetites. One of the more common ones found on house plants is that of the household moth. While they feed, these small grubs climb the plant chewing the young buds and leaves. The grub of the carnation tortrix moth, shown above, while it feeds forms a web at the tip of the shoot, pulling the edges of the leaves together.

Non-chemical control
Pick off caterpillars or any infested shoots or spray with *Bacillus thuringiensis*.

Suitable insecticides
Pirimiphos-methyl and derris are the best insecticides to use.

CYCLAMEN MITES

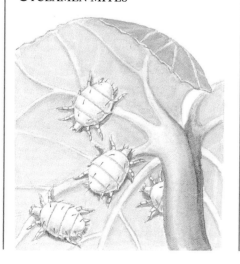

Also called strawberry mites, cyclamen mites belong to a group known as tarsonemid mites. They can attack a wide range of indoor plants besides cyclamens, as well as some outdoor plants.

The mites, which usually congregate in buds and at the tips of shoots, are too tiny to be seen with the naked eye. But if affected plants are studied with a magnifying glass, mites and their eggs can sometimes be seen as a dust-like layer. They feed on plant tissue, causing distorted, puckered growth, often with light brown scabs. The plant's development is generally stunted, shoots and flower buds may wither and die, and flowers that do open are discoloured.

In the warm conditions of homes and greenhouses, the mites breed extremely rapidly, and populations continue to increase during the winter. Insecticides have relatively little effect on them, and infested plants are best destroyed as soon as the mites or their eggs are seen. This will help to prevent the spread of the mites to neighbouring plants.

LEAFMINERS

These larvae eat their way between the two outer layers of a leaf, leaving a characteristic winding, silvery-beige trail. Chrysanthemums and cinerarias are the most commonly affected house plants. Affected leaves are unsightly, but the plant seldom suffers greatly from an attack. Since these are both short-term,

disposable plants, it is not generally necessary to take any action.

Non-chemical control
Remove and destroy affected leaves.

Suitable insecticides
Pirimiphos-methyl and derris are most effective.

MEALYBUGS

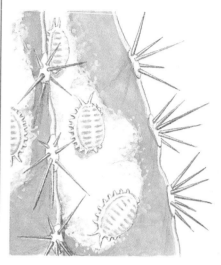

These sap-sucking pests are rather like wood lice in appearance, but mealybugs have a white, waxy, fluffy-looking coating that helps to protect them from insecticidal sprays. They can move around the plant but tend to remain immobile, and are often found clustered in the leaf axils. Cacti are particularly prone to attack by mealybugs.

Root mealybugs present a greater problem, since they are not normally visible, although they may be suspected where a plant fails to grow properly. White woolly masses can be found among the roots when a plant is turned out of its pot. Again, cacti and succulents are particularly at risk.

Non-chemical control
Remove these pests by lifting them off with a moist cotton bud. Or spray plants with a mixture of equal parts of methylated spirits and water. If the plant is infested with root mealybugs, wash the soil and pests from the roots and cut away damaged parts before repotting the plant in fresh potting mix.

Suitable insecticides
It is usually necessary to use systemic insecticides like dimethoate (omethoate) to overcome the water-repellent effect of the pests' waxy coating.

RED SPIDER MITES

Almost invisible to the naked eye, red spider mites (also known as two-spotted mites) form colonies, usually at the tips of shoots. Fine webbing may be seen on the undersides of leaves and under a magnifying glass the reddish mites can be seen scurrying back and forth within it. These sap-sucking pests cause fine yellow speckling on the leaves, which take on a dried-up appearance and eventually fall.

Red spider mites overwinter in woodwork and in other nooks and crannies away from the plants, so infestations may be troublesome from year to year. A hot dry environment provides ideal conditions for them.

Non-chemical control
Remove infested shoots and increase humidity by misting with plain water.

Suitable insecticides
Derris, pyrethrum, permethrin, and malathion (maldison).

SCALE INSECTS

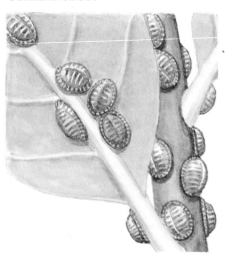

In infestations by these pests, smooth, brown, oval, limpet-like scales can be found attached to the undersides of leaves, usually along the midrib. Thick leathery leaves are most commonly attacked. There are several different stages in the life cycle of the scale, but this immobile, unlife-like stage is the most noticeable. Honeydew, produced as they feed, often attracts sooty mould.

Non-chemical control
Scrape off scales with a fingernail or wipe them off firmly with a damp cloth.

Suitable insecticides
Insecticidal soap, malathion (maldison), pyrethrum and permethrin.

SCIARID FLIES

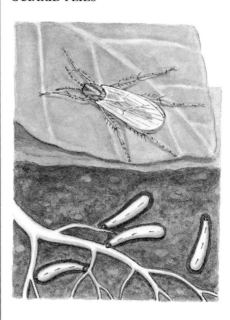

Also known as fungus gnats, these tiny greyish black insects are a nuisance rather than a serious problem on indoor plants.

They live in the soil, and when the plant is disturbed or watered can be seen flying up a short distance, sometimes in considerable numbers. The larvae feed on organic matter in the soil and may sometimes damage young roots.

Non-chemical control
Sciarid fly infestation is usually a sign of overwatering and sodden soil. Let the surface of the soil dry out between waterings.

Suitable insecticides
Drench the soil with permethrin or malathion (maldison) to rid the plant of this pest.

THRIPS

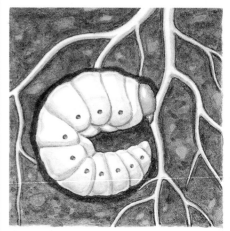

These small, long-bodied creatures with fringed wings are abundant in homes and outdoors in spells of hot weather. They feed on plant tissues and cause a characteristic silvering and mottling of stems, foliage and flowers. They are usually present in large numbers and can often be seen hopping around the plant. A large number of house plants may be affected.

Damage on plants is worst in hot, dry atmospheres.

Non-chemical control
Make sure that plants are being given adequate water and increase humidity.

Suitable insecticides
Thrips can be controlled by spraying with most contact insecticides.

VINE WEEVILS

The larvae of the vine beetle, these relatively large, creamy white grubs live in the soil and eat plant roots. Often the total collapse of the plant is the first sign that anything is amiss. The 2.5-cm/1-in-

long grey-black adult beetles are active at night and can sometimes be seen crawling over the soil surface or biting notches out of leaf margins.

Cyclamens are particularly prone to attack. By the time damage is noticed, it is usually too late to save the plants.
Non-chemical control
Pick off and destroy adults whenever they are seen. Destroy grubs found in the roots of affected plants to prevent the pests from spreading. Biological control may be available in the form of parasitic nematodes, which can be used as a preventive and a treatment.
Suitable insecticides
Drench the soil of plants at risk with gamma-HCH. A dust formulation of this chemical can be mixed with the soil when potting susceptible plants.

WHITEFLIES

These small white moth-like creatures can occur in large numbers, rising up from affected plants in a cloud when they are disturbed. They suck sap, debilitating the plant, secreting honeydew and attracting sooty mould. They are usually more of a problem in greenhouses than in the home.

Whiteflies have a complex life cycle in which only the adult stage is susceptible to insecticides. So spraying must be repeated regularly (at 10-day intervals) to catch each generation as it matures.
Non-chemical control
Yellow sticky cards can be hung near the plants to trap the adults as they fly.
Suitable insecticides
Pirimiphos-methyl, permethrin, resmethrin and pyrethrum are effective. Or use insecticidal soap.

HOUSE PLANT DISEASES

BOTRYTIS

Usually known as grey mould, this fungus prevails in damp, cool conditions and is less common in the home than in greenhouses. It starts on dead tissue and may spread to the rest of the plant. Affected parts become covered in fluffy grey mould.
Non-chemical control
Remove dead and damaged parts of a plant promptly. Keep the atmosphere warmer and drier.
Suitable fungicides
Most are effective.

POWDERY MILDEW

This disease, in which powdery white patches form on foliage, is encouraged by hot dry conditions.
Non-chemical control
Adjust the temperature and humidity.
Suitable fungicides
Most are effective, or use a sulphur-based spray in temperatures below 27°C/80°F.

RUST

Pelargoniums and chrysanthemums are often affected. Pale spots form on leaf surfaces and brown concentric rings of spores appear on their undersides.
Non-chemical control
Burn affected leaves; increase ventilation.
Suitable fungicides
Propoconazole is most effective, or use copper-based or sulphur-based sprays.

SOOTY MOULD

Although this fungal disorder is not a disease in itself, it develops on the honeydew excreted by various sap-sucking pests such as scale insects, whiteflies and aphids. Leaves become coated in a thick black deposit, which is unsightly and interferes with photosynthesis, checking plant growth.
Non-chemical control
Wipe the black deposit from foliage with a damp cloth.
Suitable insecticides
Control each pest with an appropriate insecticide to get rid of the mould.

BUYER'S GUIDE

PLANT	COMMON NAMES	FEATURES	SHAPE	WATERING	LIGHT	IDEAL INDOOR TEMPERATURE	SPECIAL POINTS
A							
Abutilon pictum 'Thompsonii'	Spotted flowering maple	Flowers and foliage	Upright/ bushy	Moderate; sparingly in winter	Bright; direct sun	16°–21°C/60°–70°F	Prune to shape in early spring
Acalypha hispida	Red-hot cat's-tail, chenille plant	Tassel-like flowers	Upright	Plentiful; sparingly in winter	Bright, filtered	21°–24°C/70°–75°F	High humidity required
Acalypha wilkesiana	Copper leaf	Coloured foliage	Upright	Plentiful; more sparingly in winter	Bright, filtered	21°–24°C/70°–75°F	Bright light is essential for well-coloured foliage
Achimenes hybrids	Cupid's bower, hot-water plant	Flowers	Bushy/ trailing	Plentifully in growth; keep dry when dormant	Bright	18°C/65°F	Dormant rhizomes are started into growth in spring
Acorus gramineus	Sweet flag	Foliage	Grassy	Plentiful	Medium; some direct sun	13°–18°C/55°–65°F	Never allow the compost to become dry
Adiantum raddianum	Delta maidenhair fern	Foliage	Arching	Moderate	Bright light or light shade; no direct sun	18°–21°C /65°–70°F	High humidity required
Adromischus festivus (*A. cooperi*)	Adromischus	Foliage	Rosette-forming	Moderate; sparingly in winter	Bright; some direct sun	16°–21°C/60°–70°F	Pot in free-draining compost
Aechmea fasciata (*Billbergia rhodocyanea*)	Urn plant, silver vase plant	Flowers and foliage	Upright/ arching	Moderate; keep the central 'vase' filled with water	Bright filtered light or direct sun	24°–27°C/75°–80°F	The rosette dies after flowering, but is replaced by offsets
Aeonium arboreum 'Atropurpureum'	Purple tree aeonium	Foliage	Rosette-forming	Moderate; very sparingly in winter	Direct sun	18°–24°C/65°–75°F	Direct sun required for good foliage colour. Individual rosettes die after flowering
Aeschynanthus lobbianus	Lipstick vine	Flowers	Trailing	Plentiful while flowering; moderate at other times	Bright light with a small amount of direct sun	16°–24°C/60°–75°F	High humidity required
Agapanthus africanus	African lily	Flowers	Upright	Moderate to plentiful	Full sun	16°–21°C/60°–70°F	Best in a conservatory
Agave americana	Century plant	Foliage	Rosette-forming	Sparing to moderate	Direct sun	16°–24°C/60°–75°F	Beware of the very sharply tipped leaves
Aglaonema 'Silver Queen'	Painted drop tongue, Chinese evergreen	Variegated evergreen	Bushy foliage	Moderate	Moderately bright; no direct sun	16°–24°C/60°–75°F	Plain green varieties are tolerant of subdued light
Albizia julibrissin	Silk tree	Foliage	Bushy	Moderate; sparingly in winter	Bright; some direct sun	13°–18°C/55°–65°F	Best discarded at the end of the season
Allamanda cathartica	Golden trumpet	Flowers	Scrambling	Moderate	Bright; some direct sun	21°–24°C/70°–75°F	Provide support for climbing stems
Alocasia sanderiana	Kris plant	Foliage	Upright/ bushy	Moderate; sparingly in winter	Bright; no direct summer sun	21°C/70°F	High humidity required
Aloe barbadensis (*A. vera*)	Medicine aloe	Flowers and foliage	Rosette-forming	Moderate; sparingly in winter	Bright; some direct sun	18°–24°C/65°–75°F	Sap has been used for healing burns
Aloe variegata	Partridge-breast aloe, tiger aloe	Flowers and foliage	Rosette-forming	Moderate; sparingly in winter	Bright, filtered	18°–24°C/65°–75°F	Tolerant of dry air
Amaryllis belladonna	Belladonna lily	Flowers	Upright	Plentiful in growing season; reduce as leaves fade; keep dry in rest period	Bright; direct sun except when in flower	16°–21°C/60°–70°F	Provide a short rest period in midsummer
Ananas bracteatus var. 'tricolor'	Red pineapple	Foliage	Rosette-forming	Moderate; sparingly in winter	Direct sun	18°–24°C/65°–75°F	Leaves have sharply saw-toothed edges
Anthurium andreanum	Tailflower	Flowers	Bushy	Moderate; more sparingly in winter	Medium to bright	16°–21°C/60°–70°F	High humidity essential

PLANT	COMMON NAMES	FEATURES	SHAPE	WATERING	LIGHT	IDEAL INDOOR TEMPERATURE	SPECIAL POINTS
Anthurium crystallinum	Crystal anthurium	Foliage	Upright	Plentiful while in growth; sparingly at other times	Moderate, filtered light or light shade	21°C/70°F	Very high humidity required
Anthurium scherzerianum	Flamingo flower	Flowers and foliage	Bushy	Plentiful while in growth; sparingly in winter	Moderate, filtered	21°C/70°F	Even temperatures required; keep free from draughts
Aphelandra squarrosa 'Louisae'	Zebra plant, saffron spike	Flowers and foliage	Bushy	Plentiful while in growth; more sparingly at other times	Bright; no direct sun	18°–21°C/65°–70°F	Remove flower stems after flowering
Aporocactus flagelliformis	Rat's tail cactus	Flowers and foliage	Trailing	Plentiful while in growth; moderate to sparingly at other times	Direct sun	18°–21°C/65°–70°F; 7°–10°C/45°–50°F during rest period after flowering	Good drainage is essential
Araucaria heterophylla (*A. excelsa*)	Norfolk Island pine	Foliage	Tree-like	Plentiful; moderate in winter	Moderate to bright	16°–24°C/60°–75°F	Hot dry air causes needles to fall
Ardisia crenata	Coral berry	Berries, flowers, foliage	Upright/ bushy	Plentiful; moderate in winter	Bright; some direct sun	13°–18°C/55°–65°F	Berries will fall prematurely in hot, dry air
Aristolochia elegans (*A. littoralis*)	Calico flower, birthwort	Flowers	Climbing	Plentiful in growing season; sparingly in winter	Bright to moderate	13°–18°C/55°–65°F	Provide support for the climbing stems
Arundinaria viridistriata (*Pleioblastus auricoma*)	Bamboo	Foliage	Upright	Moderate; plentiful during growth	Bright or indirect	16°–24°C/60°–75°F	Needs humidity
Asclepias curassavica	Blood flower	Flowers	Shrubby	Plentiful in growing season; sparingly in winter	Full sun	13°–21°C/55°–70°F	Provide a cool, dry rest period in winter
Asparagus densiflorus 'Sprengeri'/ 'Myers'	Asparagus fern / Foxtail fern	Foliage	Spreading 'Sprengeri', upright 'Myers'	Plentiful during active growth; moderate at other times	Bright; no direct sun	16°–21°C/60°–70°F	Leaves will fall if the compost is allowed to dry out
Aspidistra elatior	Cast-iron plant	Foliage	Upright	Sparing to moderate	Medium; no direct sun	10°–21°C/50°–70°F	Very tolerant
Asplenium bulbiferum	Mother spleenwort, hen and chickens fern, parsley fern	Foliage and baby plants	Rosette-forming	Moderate; more sparingly in winter	Medium; no direct sun	16°–21°C/60°–70°F	High humidity required
Asplenium nidus	Bird's nest fern	Foliage	Rosette-forming	Plentiful during active growth; moderate at other times	Moderate; no direct sun	18°–24°C/65°–75°F	Foliage easily damaged by handling; needs humidity
Astrophytum myriostigma	Bishop's cap cactus, monk's hood cactus	Flowers, succulent stems	Globular	Sparing	Full sun	16°–21°C/60°–70°F	Free-draining compost required
Aucuba japonica 'Variegata'	Spotted laurel, Japanese laurel	Foliage	Shrubby	Plentiful in growing season; moderately in winter	Bright	10°–18°C/50°–65°F	Tolerant of shade

B

PLANT	COMMON NAMES	FEATURES	SHAPE	WATERING	LIGHT	IDEAL INDOOR TEMPERATURE	SPECIAL POINTS
Beaucarnea recurvata (*Nolina recurvata*)	Pony tail plant, bottle palm, elephant foot	Foliage and swollen stem base	Arching	Moderate	Bright; some preferably full sun	16°–21°C/60°–70°F	Do not overwater
Begonia: fibrous rooted e.g. *B.* 'Corallina de Lucerna'	Begonia	Flowers and foliage	Upright/ bushy	Moderate; sparingly in winter	Bright; some direct sun	16°–18°C/60°–65°F	Provide stakes for the tall stems

PLANT	COMMON NAMES	FEATURES	SHAPE	WATERING	LIGHT	IDEAL INDOOR TEMPERATURE	SPECIAL POINTS
Begonia: foliage types e.g. *B. rex*, *B. masoniana*	Painted leaf begonia	Foliage	Spreading/ bushy	Moderate; sparingly in winter	Bright or light shade; little or no direct sun	16°–18°C/60°–65°F	High humidity required
Begonia: tuberous e.g. *B. x biemalis*, *B. x tuberhybrida*	Winter-flowering begonia	Flowers	Bushy	Moderate; no water in dormant period	Bright, filtered	16°–18°C/60°–65°F	Store dormant tubers in dry peat
Beloperone guttata (*Justicia brandegeana*)	Shrimp plant	Flowers	Bushy	Moderate; sparingly in winter	Bright; some direct sun	21°C/70°F	Pinch out growing tips to encourage bushiness
Bertolonia marmorata	Bertolonia	Foliage	Low growing	Moderate	Bright; no direct sun	16°–21°C/60°–70°F	High humidity essential; good subject for a terrarium
Billbergia nutans	Queen's tears, friendship plant	Flowers and foliage	Arching	Moderate	Bright	10°–21°C/50°–70°F	Very tolerant
Bougainvillea glabra	Paper flower	Flowers (bracts)	Climbing	Moderate; very sparingly in winter	Bright light; some direct sun	18°–24°F/65°–75°C; below 16°C/60°F for winter rest	Bright light is necessary for flowers to be produced
Bouvardia longiflora	Bouvardia	Scented flowers	Bushy	Plentiful during active growth; sparingly during rest period	Bright; no direct sun	16°–21°C/60°–70°F	Tends to be short-lived
Bowiea volubilis	Climbing onion	Flowers, stems	Climbing stems from large bulb	Moderate in growing season; keep dry in summer	Bright; no direct sun	10°–16°C/50°–60°F	Grown as a curiosity rather than for its beauty
Breynia nivosa (*B. disticha*)	Snow bush, leaf flower	Foliage	Shrubby	Moderate	Bright; no direct sun	16°–21°C/60°–70°F	High humidity essential
Brodiaea laxa (*Triteleia laxa*)	Grass nut, Ithuriel's sprear	Flowers	Bushy	Moderate; reduce after flowering allowing corm to dry out when leaves yellow	Full sun	10°–16°C/50°–60°F	Plant corms in late summer or early autumn for spring flowers
Browallia speciosa 'Major'	Sapphire flower, bush violet	Flowers	Bushy/ trailing	Moderate	Bright; some direct sun	10°–16°C/50°–60°F	Discard once flowering is over
Brunfelsia pauciflora (*B. calycina*)	Yesterday-today-and-tomorrow	Flowers	Bushy	Moderate; sparingly in winter	Bright; some direct sun	16°–18°C/60°–65°F	Pinch out growing tips to keep plant bushy; mist regularly
Buddleja madagascariensis (*Nicodemia madagascariensis*)	Buddleia	Flowers	Shrubby	Moderate	Full sun or partial shade	13°–21°C/55°–70°F	Best suited to a conservatory

C

PLANT	COMMON NAMES	FEATURES	SHAPE	WATERING	LIGHT	IDEAL INDOOR TEMPERATURE	SPECIAL POINTS
Caladium hortulanum	Angel-wings, elephant's-ears	Coloured foliage; deciduous	Bushy	Moderate; keep tubers virtually dry over winter	Bright, diffused; no direct sun in rest period	18°–24°C/65°–75°F; 16°C/60°F during rest periods	High temperature and humidity essential
Calathea makoyana	Peacock plant	Variegated foliage	Bushy/ upright	Moderate; more sparingly in winter	Bright; no direct sun	18°–24°C/65°–75°F	High humidity essential; mist foliage regularly
Calceolaria x herbeohybrida	Slipper flower	Flowers	Bushy	Plentiful	Bright; no direct sun	10°C/50°F	Needs high humidity; discard after flowering
Calliandra haematocephela (*C. inaequilatera*)	Powderpuff plant	Flowers and foliage	Bushy/ tree-like	Plentiful to moderate	Bright; some direct sun	18°–24°C/65°–75°F	Prune to restrict size in spring
Callisia repens	Callisia	Foliage	Trailing	Moderate; more sparingly in winter	Bright; some direct sun	18°–21°C/65°–70°F	Replace straggly plants with fresh cuttings after two or three years
Callistemon citrinus	Crimson bottle brush	Flowers	Shrubby	Plentiful in summer; sparingly in winter	Bright; some direct sun	18°–21°C/65°–70°F	Stand plants outside during summer
Camellia japonica	Camellia	Flowers	Shrubby	Moderate to plentiful while flowering; more sparingly afterwards	Bright; no direct sun	7°–16°C/45°–60°F	Mist regularly while buds are forming

PLANT	COMMON NAMES	FEATURES	SHAPE	WATERING	LIGHT	IDEAL INDOOR TEMPERATURE	SPECIAL POINTS
Campanula isophylla	Star of Bethlehem, bellflower	Flowers	Trailing	Moderate	Bright; no direct sun	10°–16°C/50°–60°F	Keep cool in winter
Capsicum annuum	Ornamental or Christmas pepper	Fruits	Bushy	Moderate to plentiful	Bright; some direct sun	13°–16°C/55°–60°F	Discard when berries shrivel
Carex morrowii 'Variegata'	Japanese sedge grass	Foliage	Grassy	Moderate	Bright; some direct sun	16°–18°C/60°–65°F	Mist regularly to increase humidity
Carica papaya	Pawpaw, papaya	Foliage	Tree-like	Moderate	Bright, some direct sun; will tolerate light shade	18°–24°C/65°–75°F	Never allow the compost to become waterlogged
Carludovica palmata	Panama-hat plant	Foliage	Bushy	Plentiful when in active growth	Full sun	18°–24°C/65°–75°F	Best suited to a greenhouse or conservatory
Caryota mitis	Burmese, crested, or tufted fishtail palm	Foliage	Bushy	Moderate	Bright; no direct sun	24°–29°C /75°–85°F by day; 18°–21°C /65°–70°F at night	Discard plants when they outgrow their space
Catharanthus roseus	Rose periwinkle	Flowers	Bushy	Moderate	Bright; some direct sun	16°–18°C/60°–65°F	Discard after flowering
Cattleya spp.	Cattleya	Flowers	Upright	Moderate to plentiful in growing period; sparingly after flowering	Bright; no direct sun	18°–24°C/65°–75°F	Use specialist orchid fibre growing medium
Cephalocereus senilis (*Pilocereus senilis*)	Old man cactus	Succulent stems	Upright, columnar	Sparing	Full sun	16°–21°C/60°–70°F	Spines are sharp: take care when handling
Ceropegia woodii (*C. linearis* ssp. *woodii*)	Chain of hearts, rosary vine, hearts-on-a-string	Foliage	Trailing	Sparing	Bright; some sun	16°–21°C/60°–70°F	Produces round stem tubers amongst the leaves
Cestrum aurantiacum	Cestrum	Flowers	Semi-climbing	Plentiful	Bright; no direct sun	16°–21°C/60°–70°F	Cut out some of the oldest stems in autumn
Chamaedorea elegans	Parlour palm	Foliage	Bushy/upright	Moderate; more sparingly in winter	Moderately bright or light shade	18°–24°C/65°–75°F	Humid atmosphere required
Chamaerops humilis	European fan palm	Foliage	Shrubby	Moderate	Bright; some direct sun	18°–21°C/65°–70°F	Tolerant of light shade
Chlorophytum comosum 'Vittatum'	Spider plant	Foliage	Grassy, arching with trailing plantlets	Plentiful; more sparingly in winter	Bright; occasional direct sun	16°–21°C/60°–70°F	Bright light is necessary for well-variegated leaves
Chrysalidocarpus lutescens	Butterfly palm	Foliage	Upright	Moderate; sparingly in winter	Bright, filtered	18°–24°C/65°–75°F	High humidity required
Chrysanthemum x *morifolium*	Florists' chrysanthemum	Flowers	Bushy	Moderate	Bright; no direct sun	13°–16°C/55°–60°F	Discard after flowering
Cissus antarctica	Kangaroo vine	Foliage	Climbing	Moderate	Bright; no direct sun	13°–16°C/55°–60°F	Provide sturdy supports
x *Citrofortunella microcarpus*	Calamondin	Foliage, flowers, fruits	Tree-like	Moderate	Bright; some direct sun	18°–21°C/65°–70°F	Stand plant outside in summer
Clerodendrum thomsoniae	Bleeding heart vine	Flowers	Climbing/trailing	Moderate; sparingly in winter	Bright light; no direct sun	18°–21°C/65°–70°F	Prune back stems by half in spring
Clianthus puniceus	Parrot's beak, Kaka beak, lobster claw	Flowers	Lax, bushy	Moderate; sparingly in winter	Full sun or dappled shade	13°–18°C/55°–65°F	Best discarded after flowering
Clivia miniata	Kaffir lily	Flowers	Upright, arching	Moderate; very sparingly in winter	Bright light; some direct sun	18°–21°C/65°–70°F	Provide a cool, dry winter rest period
Coccoloba uvifera	Sea grape	Foliage	Bushy	Moderate	Bright; no direct sun	16°–21°C/60°–70°F	Tolerant of dry air
Codiaeum variegatum pictum	Croton, Joseph's coat	Coloured foliage	Upright	Moderate; sparingly in winter	Bright light; some direct sun	18°–24°C/65°–75°F	Many varieties available with differently shaped and coloured leaves

PLANT	COMMON NAMES	FEATURES	SHAPE	WATERING	LIGHT	IDEAL INDOOR TEMPERATURE	SPECIAL POINTS
Coelogyne cristata	Coelogyne	Flowers	Upright/bushy	Moderate to plentiful; very sparingly during rest period	Bright, filtered	18°–21°C/65°–70°F in day; lower at night	Provide a winter rest period of about six weeks
Coffea arabica	Arabian coffee plant	Foliage	Tree-like/bushy	Plentiful in summer; more sparingly in winter	Bright; no direct sun	16°–21°C/60°–70°F	Flowers and fruit may form on older plants
Coleus blumei	Flame nettle	Coloured foliage	Bushy	Moderate to plentiful	Bright; direct sun except very strong summer sun	16°–21°C/60°–70°F	Discard when leggy and replace with cuttings
Columnea x banksii	Goldfish plant	Flowers	Trailing	Moderate to sparingly, especially in winter	Bright; no direct sun	18°–24°C/65°–75°F	High humidity required
Convallaria majalis	Lily-of-the-valley	Scented flowers	Bushy	Moderate to plentiful	Bright; no direct sun	10°–16°C/50°–60°F	Cool conditions will prolong flowering
Cordyline australis	Cabbage tree, palm lily, grass palm	Foliage	Upright/bushy	Moderate; more sparingly in winter	Bright; no direct sun	16°–21°C/60°–70°F	Will tolerate light shade
Cordyline terminalis	Good luck plant, ti tree	Foliage	Upright/bushy	Moderate; more sparingly in winter	Bright; no direct sun	16°–21°C/60°–70°F	Bright light is required for well-coloured foliage
Costus igneus (*C. cuspidatus*)	Spiral ginger	Flowers	Upright	Moderate	Bright; no direct sun	16°–21°C/60°–70°F	Best suited to a conservatory
Cotyledon undulata	Silver crown	Foliage	Upright	Plentiful in growing season; more sparingly in winter	Full sun	16°–21°C/60°–70°F	The attractive mealy leaf covering is damaged by handling
Crassula arborescens (*C. cotyledon*)	Chinese, or silver jade plant	Foliage	Tree-like	Plentiful in spring and summer; more sparingly in winter	Bright; some direct sun	16°–21°C/60°–70°F	Benefits from a spell outdoors in summer
Crassula muscosa	Crassula	Succulent stems and leaves; flowers	Upright, then scrambling	Moderate to plentiful in growing season; sparingly in winter	Bright; some direct sun	16°–21°C/60°–70°F	Prone to mealybugs and scale insects
Crassula ovata (*C. portulacea*)	Jade tree, money tree	Foliage	Tree-like	Moderate to plentiful in growing season; sparingly in winter	Bright; some direct sun	16°–21°C/60°–70°F	Mature plants produce white flowers in spring
Crinum x powelii	Swamp lily, spider lily	Flowers	Bushy/grassy	Plentiful in summer; very sparingly in winter	Bright; some direct sun	16°–21°C/60°–70°F	Repot only when essential
Crocus hybrids	Dutch crocus	Flowers	Grassy	Moderate	Bright; no direct sun	10°–16°C/50°–60°F	Corms need a cold, dark period after planting
Crossandra infundibuliformis	Firecracker flower	Flowers	Bushy	Moderate to sparingly	Bright, filtered	21°C/70°F	Replace plants when they deteriorate after two years or so
Cryptanthus acaulis	Green earth star, starfish plant	Foliage	Rosette	Moderate, preferably with rainwater	Bright	24°C/75°F	High humidity and good drainage are required
Cryptanthus bivittatus	Cryptanthus	Foliage	Rosette	Moderate in growing season; sparingly in winter	Bright	24°C/75°F	High humidity; good for a terrarium
Ctenanthe oppenheimiana 'Tricolor'	Never-never plant	Foliage	Bushy	Plentiful in spring and summer; moderate in winter	Bright filtered, or light shade	18°–24°C/65°–75°F	High humidity required
Cuphea ignea (*C. platycentra*)	Cigar flower	Flowers	Bushy	Moderate; sparingly in winter	Bright; some direct sun	16°–21°C/60°–70°F	Replace plants when they become straggly and deteriorate
Cyanotis somaliensis	Pussy ears	Foliage	Trailing	Moderate	Bright; some direct sun	16°–21°C/60°–70°F	Good light required to keep stems compact
Cycas revoluta	Japanese sago palm	Foliage	Rosette-forming	Moderate	Bright; no direct sun	16°–21°C/60°–70°F	Tolerates dry atmosphere
Cyclamen persicum	Cyclamen	Flowers	Bushy	Moderate; keep dry in rest period	Bright	13°–18°C/55°–65°F	Do not splash the tuber when watering
Cymbidium hybrids	Cymbidium	Flowers	Upright	Plentiful in summer; sparingly at other times	Bright, filtered	13°–18°C/55°–65°F	Provide a rest period for 4–6 weeks in autumn

PLANT	COMMON NAMES	FEATURES	SHAPE	WATERING	LIGHT	IDEAL INDOOR TEMPERATURE	SPECIAL POINTS
Cyperus alternifolius	Umbrella plant	Foliage	Grassy	Plentiful	Adaptable; direct sun or light shade	16°–21°C/60°–70°F	Stand pot in a saucer of water
Cyperus papyrus	Egyptian paper reed	Foliage and flowers	Grassy	Plentiful	Adaptable; direct sun or light shade	18°–24°C/65°–75°F	Stand pot in a saucer of water
Cyrtomium falcatum	Holly fern	Foliage	Upright	Moderate	Bright light or semi-shade	18°C/65°F	Tolerant of dry air

D

PLANT	COMMON NAMES	FEATURES	SHAPE	WATERING	LIGHT	IDEAL INDOOR TEMPERATURE	SPECIAL POINTS
Darlingtonia californica	California pitcher plant, cobra lily	Insect-catching pitchers	Upright	Moderate to plentiful	Bright; no strong direct sun	16°–21°C/60°–70°F	High humidity essential
Datura x *candida* (*Brugmansia* x *candida*)	Angel's trumpet	Scented flowers	Bushy	Plentiful in the growing season; more sparingly in winter	Full sun or light shade	10°–16°C/50°–60°F	All parts are poisonous
Davallia fejeensis	Rabbit's foot fern	Foliage, furry rhizomes	Upright/ bushy	Moderate; more sparingly in winter	Bright; no direct sun	16°–21°C/60°–70°F	Creeping, furry rhizomes growing over the edge of the pot are a distinctive feature
Dendrobium spp.	Dendrobium	Flowers	Upright	Moderate in the growing season; keep almost dry in winter	Bright, filtered	16°–21°C/60°–70°F; lower during winter rest period	Mist-spray daily
Dichorisandra reginae	Queen's spiderwort	Foliage	Trailing	Moderate; more sparingly in winter	Medium; no direct sun	16°–21°C/60°–70°F	High humidity essential
Dicksonia antarctica	Soft tree fern	Foliage	Bushy	Moderate	Bright; little or no direct sun	16°–21°C/60°–70°F	High humidity required; best in a conservatory or greenhouse
Dieffenbachia maculata (*D. picta*)	Dumb cane, leopard lily	Foliage	Bushy	Plentiful in spring and summer; more sparingly in winter	Bright; no direct sun	18°–24°C/65°–75°F	Sap is poisonous; take care when handling
Dimorphotheca sinuata (*D. aurantiaca*)	Star of the veld	Flowers	Rosette-forming	Sparing	Full sun	18°–24°C/65°–75°F	Best discarded after flowering
Dionaea muscipula	Venus's fly trap	Foliage; insect-catching traps	Rosette-forming	Plentiful to moderate	Bright; no direct sun	16°–21°C/60°–70°F	Feed with dead insects or meat over winter
Dizygotheca elegantissima	False aralia, finger aralia	Foliage	Upright/ tree-like	Moderate	Bright; no direct sun	18°–24°C/65°–75°F	High humidity required
Dracaena fragrans 'Massangeana'	Corn plant	Foliage	Upright/ tree-like	Moderate; sparingly in winter	Bright; some direct sun	16°–24°C/60°–75°F	Protect from draughts
Dracaena marginata	Madagascar dragon tree	Foliage	Upright/ tree-like	Moderate; sparingly in winter	Bright; no direct summer sun	16°–21°C/60°–70°F	Bright light is necessary for good leaf colour
Dracaena sanderiana	Belgian evergreen, ribbon plant	Foliage	Upright	Plentiful in summer; more sparingly in winter	Bright; no direct sun	16°–21°C/60°–70°F	Repot only when essential
Drosera rotundifolia	Common sundew	Insect-catching traps	Rosette-forming	Plentiful to moderate	Bright; no direct sun	10°–16°C/50°–60°F	Do not overpot; the root system is very small
Dyckia fosteriana	Dyckia, miniature agave	Flowers and foliage	Rosette-forming	Moderate to sparingly	Full sun	10°–24°C/50°–75°F	Sharp spines: take care when handling the plant

E

PLANT	COMMON NAMES	FEATURES	SHAPE	WATERING	LIGHT	IDEAL INDOOR TEMPERATURE	SPECIAL POINTS
Echeveria secunda var. *glauca*	Blue echeveria	Succulent foliage and flowers	Rosette-forming	Sparing	Full sun	16°–21°C/60°–70°F; cooler in winter	Delicate foliage is easily damaged by handling
Echinocactus grusonii	Golden barrel cactus	Spines and flowers	Globular	Moderate in growth; sparingly in winter	Full sun	16°–21°C/60°–70°F; 10°C/50° in winter	Very slow-growing
Echinocereus pectinatus	Hedgehog cactus	Flowers/stems	Columnar	Sparing	Direct sun all year	16°–21°C/60°–70°F; cooler in winter	Full sun is required for reliable flowering

PLANT	COMMON NAMES	FEATURES	SHAPE	WATERING	LIGHT	IDEAL INDOOR TEMPERATURE	SPECIAL POINTS
Echinopsis eyriesii	Sea urchin cactus	Flowers/stems	Cylindrical	Moderate to sparing; very sparingly in rest period	Full sun	16°–21°C/60°–70°F; cooler in winter	Cool winter rest period is necessary for flowering
Epiphyllum ackermannii	Orchid cactus	Flowers	Trailing	Plentiful during active growth; sparingly otherwise	Bright; no direct summer sun	16°–21°C/60°–70°F; cooler in winter	Flowers best if slightly pot-bound
Epipremnum aureum	Devil's ivy, golden pothos, taro vine	Foliage	Climbing	Moderate	Bright; no direct sun	16°–21°C/60°–70°F	Provide a moss pole or similar support
Episcia cupreata	Flame violet	Foliage and flowers	Low, creeping	Plentiful; more sparingly in winter	Bright; no direct sun	16°–21°C/60°–70°F	Free-draining compost is required
Erica x hiemalis	French heather	Flowers	Bushy	Plentiful	Bright; some direct sun	7°–10°C/45°–50°F	Discard after flowering
Eriobotrya japonica	Loquat	Foliage	Tree-like	Moderate; more sparingly in winter	Bright; some direct sun	16°–21°C/60°–70°F; 10°C/50°F in winter	Discard plants when they become leggy
Eucharis x grandiflora	Amazon lily, Eucharist lily, star of Bethlehem	Scented flowers	Grassy	Plentiful while growing; keep bulb virtually dry when leaves die	Bright; no direct sun	18°–24°C/65°–75°F	Water newly potted bulb sparingly until growth starts
Euphorbia milii var. splendens	Crown of thorns	Flowers	Upright/ bushy	Moderate to sparing	Bright; some direct sun	16°–21°C/60°–70°F	Stems produce milky latex when damaged; this can be an irritant
Euphorbia pulcherrima	Poinsettia, Christmas star, Mexican flame leaf	Flowers (bracts)	Bushy	Moderate	Bright; some direct sun	16°–21°C/60°–70°F	Short days are necessary for the production of flower heads
Eurya japonica	Eurya	Foliage	Bushy	Moderate	Bright; some direct sun	10°–16°C/50°–60°F	Will tolerate light shade
Eustoma grandiflorum	Prairie gentian, lisianthus	Flowers	Bushy	Moderate	Bright; some direct sun	13°–18°C/55°–65°F	Discard after flowering
Exacum affine	German violet, Arabian violet, Persian violet	Scented flowers	Low, bushy	Plentiful to moderate	Bright; no strong, direct sun	16°–21°C/60°–70°F	Deadhead to prolong flowering

F

PLANT	COMMON NAMES	FEATURES	SHAPE	WATERING	LIGHT	IDEAL INDOOR TEMPERATURE	SPECIAL POINTS
x Fatshedera lizei	Tree ivy	Foliage	Upright	Plentiful during growing season; otherwise moderate to sparingly	Medium to bright	13°–16°C/55°–60°F	Provide a moss pole or similar support
Fatsia japonica	Japanese fatsia, Japanese aralia, false castor-oil plant	Foliage	Upright	Plentiful to moderate	Medium to bright	13°–16°C/55°–60°F	Prune hard to reduce the plant's size
Faucaria tigrina	Tiger jaws	Flowers and succulent foliage	Rosette-forming	Plentiful in spring and summer; sparingly in autumn and winter	Full sun	16°–21°C/60°–70°F	Repot only when essential
Felicia amelloides (Agathaea coelestis)	Blue marguerite	Flowers	Bushy, rosette-forming	Moderate in active growth period; keep almost dry in winter	Bright; some direct sun	16°–21°C/60°–70°F	Pinch out growing tips regularly; discard when no longer attractive
Ferocactus latispinus	Barrel cactus, fish-hook cactus, devil's tongue	Succulent stem	Globular	Sparing	Full sun	16°–21°C/60°–70°F	Beware of the sharp, hooked spines
Ficus benjamina	Weeping fig	Foliage	Tree-like	Moderate	Bright; some direct sun	16°–21°C/60°–70°F	Many named varieties exist
Ficus deltoidea var. deversifolia	Mistletoe fig	Foliage and fruit	Tree-like	Moderate	Bright; some direct sun	16°–21°C/60°–70°F	Fruit is inedible
Ficus elastica 'Robusta'	Rubber plant	Foliage	Tree-like	Moderate	Bright; some direct sun	16°–21°C/60°–70°F	Clean leaves regularly
Ficus lyrata	Fiddle leaf fig	Foliage	Tree-like	Moderate	Bright; some direct sun	16°–21°C/60°–70°F	Pinch out the growing tip to encourage branching

PLANT	COMMON NAMES	FEATURES	SHAPE	WATERING	LIGHT	IDEAL INDOOR TEMPERATURE	SPECIAL POINTS
Ficus pumila	Creeping fig	Foliage	Creeping/ trailing	Plentiful to moderate	Medium light or light shade	13°–21°C/55°–70°F	Never allow the compost to dry out
Fittonia verschaffeltii argyroneura	Silver net leaf, mosaic plant	Foliage	Creeping	Plentiful to moderate	Bright light or light shade	18°–24°C/65°–75°F	High humidity essential; ideal for a bottle garden
Freesia	Freesia	Scented flowers	Grassy	Plentiful while flowering; moderate before drying corms off completely	Bright; some direct sun	13°–18°C/55°–65°F	Support flowering stems with split canes
Fuchsia	Fuchsia	Flowers	Bushy	Moderate; more sparingly in winter	Bright; some direct sun	16°C/60°F	Pinch out growing tips to encourage bushy growth

G

PLANT	COMMON NAMES	FEATURES	SHAPE	WATERING	LIGHT	IDEAL INDOOR TEMPERATURE	SPECIAL POINTS
Gardenia augusta (*G. jasminoides*, *G. grandiflora*)	Gardenia	Scented flowers	Bushy	Moderate; more sparingly in winter	Bright; some direct sun in winter	16°–21°C/60°–70°F	Protect from draughts, especially when buds are forming
Genista x *spachiana*	Genista	Scented flowers	Upright/ bushy	Plentiful while flowering; otherwise moderate to sparing	Bright	10°–16°C/50°–60°F	Stand the plant outdoors during summer
Geogenanthus undatus (*G. poeppegii*)	Seersucker plant	Foliage	Rosette-forming	Moderate; more sparingly in winter	Bright; no direct sun	21°C/70°F	High humidity essential
Gerbera jamesonii	Barberton daisy, Transvaal daisy	Flowers	Rosette-forming	Plentiful to moderate	Bright; some direct sun	10°–21°C/50°–70°F	Discard after flowering
Glechoma hederacea 'Variegata'	Ground ivy	Foliage	Trailing	Plentiful; sparingly in winter	Bright; no direct sun	13°–18°C/55°–65°F; 10°C/50°F in winter	Good for a hanging basket
Gloriosa superba 'Rothschildiana'	Glory lily	Flowers	Climbing	Moderate; dry tubers off after flowering	Bright; no strong direct sun	16°–21°C/60°–70°F	Provide support for climbing stems
Gomphrena globosa	Globe amaranth, bachelor's button	Flowers	Bushy	Plentiful	Bright; some direct sun	13°–18°C/55°–65°F	Discard when no longer attractive
Graptophyllum pictum	Caricature plant	Foliage and flowers	Shrubby	Plentiful	Bright; some direct sun	18°–24°C/65°–75°F	Pinch growing tips regularly to keep the plant compact
Grevillea robusta	Silky oak	Foliage	Tree-like	Moderate	Bright; some direct sun	13°–16°C/55°–60°F	Large specimens are suitable for conservatories
Guzmania dissitiflora	Guzmania	Foliage and flowers (bracts)	Rosette-forming	Moderate; keep the 'vase' full of water	Bright; no direct sun	18°–24°C/65°–75°F	High humidity required
Guzmania lingulata	Scarlet star	Foliage and flowers (bracts)	Rosette-forming	Moderate; keep the 'vase' full of water	Bright; no direct sun	18°–24°C/65°–75°F	High humidity required
Gymnocalycium mihanovichii 'Red Cap'	Gymnocalycium	Grafted stems; flowers	Upright	Plentiful in summer; sparing in winter	Bright	18–24°C/65°–75°F; 4°C–40°F in winter	Needs a cool winter rest period to encourage flowering
Gynura 'Purple Passion'	Purple passion vine, velvet plant	Foliage	Trailing	Moderate; more sparingly in winter	Bright; some sun, but not summer sun	16°–21°C/60°–70°F	Remove flowers as they appear

H

PLANT	COMMON NAMES	FEATURES	SHAPE	WATERING	LIGHT	IDEAL INDOOR TEMPERATURE	SPECIAL POINTS
Haemanthus humilis 'Wilsonii'	Haemanthus	Flowers	Upright	Freely in summer; more sparingly in winter	Bright; some direct sun	16°–21°C/60°–70°F	Repot only when essential
Haworthia pumila (*H. margaritifera*)	Pearl plant	Succulent leaves	Rosette-forming	Moderate; more sparingly in winter	Medium to bright; no direct sun	16°–21°C/60°–70°F	Never allow the compost to dry out completely
Hebe x *andersonii*	Hebe	Flowers and foliage	Shrubby	Plentiful to moderate	Bright; no direct strong sun	13°–18°C/55°–65°F; cooler in winter	Stand plants outside in summer

PLANT	COMMON NAMES	FEATURES	SHAPE	WATERING	LIGHT	IDEAL INDOOR TEMPERATURE	SPECIAL POINTS
Hedera helix	English ivy	Foliage	Climbing	Moderate	Bright; some direct sun	10°–13°C/50°–55°F	Provide supports for the climbing stems
Hedychium coronarium	Butterfly ginger, ginger lily	Fragrant flowers	Upright/bushy	Moderate; sparingly in winter	Bright; no direct sun	18°–24°C/65°–75°F	Most suitable for a conservatory
Heliconia schiedeana	Lobster claws	Flowers and foliage	Tree-like	Moderate	Semi-shade	18°–24°C/65°–75°F	High humidity required
Hemigraphis colorata (*H. alternata*)	Red ivy, red-flame ivy	Foliage	Creeping	Moderate	Bright; no direct sun	16°–21°C/60°–70°F	Free-draining compost and high humidity required
Hibiscus rosa-sinensis	Rose of China	Flowers	Shrubby	Plentiful in spring and summer; otherwise moderate	Bright; some direct sun	16°–21°C/60°–70°F; 13°C/55°F in winter	Do not move plant while buds are forming
Hippeastrum x ackermannii (*H. x acramannii*)	Amaryllis	Flowers	Upright	Moderate; allow bulb to dry out in autumn	Bright; some direct sun	13°–18°C/55°–65°F	A rest period is required in autumn and winter
Hoffmannia regalis 'Roezlii'	Taffeta plant	Coloured foliage	Shrubby	Moderate to sparing	Bright, filtered	18°–24°C/65°–75°F	Protect from draughts
Howea belmoreana	Sentry palm, curly palm	Foliage	Bushy	Plentiful in growing season; more sparingly in winter	Bright, filtered	16°–21°C/60°–70°F	Tolerates shade well
Hoya carnosa	Wax plant	Flowers	Trailing	Moderate; sparingly in winter	Bright; some direct sun	16°–21°C/60°–70°F	Stems can be trained around a wire hoop
Hoya lanceolata spp. *bella*	Miniature wax plant	Flowers	Trailing	Moderate; sparingly in winter	Bright; some direct sun	21°–24°C/70°–75°F	Avoid moving plants while buds are forming
Hyacinthus orientalis	Hyacinth	Flowers	Upright	Moderate	Bright	16°C/60°F while flowering	Bulbs require cool, dark forcing period
Hydrangea macrophylla (*H. hortensis*)	Hydrangea	Flowers	Shrubby	Plentiful in growing season; sparingly in winter	Bright; no direct sun	13°–16°C/55°–60°F	Ericaceous compost required for blue flowers
Hymenocallis littoralis	Spider lily	Scented flowers	Upright	Plentiful in the growing season; otherwise moderate	Bright; no direct sun	18°–27°C/65°–80°F	Best grown in a greenhouse and brought indoors for flowering
Hypoestes phyllostachya	Polka dot plant, freckle face	Coloured foliage	Bushy	Moderate to sparing	Bright; some direct sun	16°–21°C/60°–70°F	Discard when leggy and replace with cuttings

I

PLANT	COMMON NAMES	FEATURES	SHAPE	WATERING	LIGHT	IDEAL INDOOR TEMPERATURE	SPECIAL POINTS
Impatiens walleriana	Busy Lizzy	Flowers	Bushy	Plentiful to moderate	Bright	16°–21°C/60°–70°F	Flowers carried all year if temperature is maintained above 16°C/60°F
Ipheion uniflorum	Spring star flower	Flowers	Grassy	Moderate; reduce after flowering until the leaves die down	Bright; some direct sun	10°–16°C/50°–60°F	Keep in a cold greenhouse and bring indoors for flowering
Ipomoea tricolor	Morning glory	Flowers	Climber	Moderate	Full sun or light shade	16°–21°C/60°–70°F	Discard after flowering
Iresine herbstii	Bloodleaf, beefsteak plant	Coloured foliage	Bushy	Plentiful to moderate	Bright; no direct strong sun	16°–21°C/60°–70°F	Pinch out growing tips regularly to keep plants bushy
Ixora coccinea	Flame-of-the-woods	Flowers	Shrubby	Plentiful; more sparingly in winter	Full sun	18°–24°C/65°–75°F	Protect plants from draughts

J

PLANT	COMMON NAMES	FEATURES	SHAPE	WATERING	LIGHT	IDEAL INDOOR TEMPERATURE	SPECIAL POINTS
Jacaranda mimosifolia	Jacaranda	Foliage	Tree-like/bushy	Moderate; more sparingly in winter	Bright; no direct sun	16°–21°C/60°–70°F	Plants can be cut back hard when they become leggy
Jasminum mesnyi	Primrose jasmine	Flowers	Scrambling	Moderate	Bright; some direct sun	13°–18°C/55°–65°F	Tie stems to a support
Jasminum polyanthum	Chinese jasmine	Scented flowers	Twining	Moderate; more sparingly in winter	Bright; some direct sun	16°–18°C/60°–65°F	Can be trained around a wire hoop

PLANT	COMMON NAMES	FEATURES	SHAPE	WATERING	LIGHT	IDEAL INDOOR TEMPERATURE	SPECIAL POINTS
Jatropha podagrica	Gout plant, tartogo	Swollen bottle-shaped stem, flowers	Upright	Very sparingly, particularly in winter	Bright, filtered light or semi-shade	18°–24°C/65°–75°F	Good drainage essential
Justicia carnea (*Jacobinia carnea*)	King's crown, Brazilian plume flower	Flowers	Bushy	Moderate in summer; sparing in winter	Bright; some direct sun	16°–21°C/60°–70°F; 13°C/55°F in winter	Cut back stems by half after flowering
Justicia pauciflora (*J. rizzinii*)	Justicia	Flowers	Bushy	Moderate to sparingly in the rest period	Bright filtered light; some direct sun	16°–21°C/60°–70°F; 13°C/55°F in the rest period	Pinch out growing tips to promote bushiness

K

PLANT	COMMON NAMES	FEATURES	SHAPE	WATERING	LIGHT	IDEAL INDOOR TEMPERATURE	SPECIAL POINTS
Kalanchoe blossfeldiana	Flaming Katy	Flowers	Bushy	Moderate to sparingly	Bright; some direct sun	16°–21°C/60°–70°F	Flowers in short days
Kalanchoe manginii	Kalanchoe	Flowers	Semi-trailing	Moderate to sparingly	Bright; some direct sun	16°–21°C/60°–70°F	Good for hanging baskets
Kalanchoe marmorata	Penwiper	Foliage	Rosette-forming	Moderate to sparingly	Bright; some direct sun	16°–21°C/60°–70°F	Provide a winter rest at 50°F/10°C
Kalanchoe pumila	Kalanchoe	Foliage and flowers	Semi-trailing	Moderate to sparingly	Bright; some direct sun	16°–21°C/60°–70°F	Good for hanging baskets
Kalanchoe tomentosa	Panda plant, pussy ears	Foliage	Rosette-forming	Moderate to sparingly	Bright; some direct sun	16°–21°C/60°–70°F	Provide a winter rest at 10°C/50°F
Kohleria eriantha and hybrids	Kohleria	Flowers	Upright	Moderate; sparingly in winter	Bright, filtered	16°–21°C/60°–70°F	High humidity required; do not mist the leaves directly

L

PLANT	COMMON NAMES	FEATURES	SHAPE	WATERING	LIGHT	IDEAL INDOOR TEMPERATURE	SPECIAL POINTS
Lachenalia aloides	Cape cowslip	Flowers	Upright	Moderate; reduce after flowering to allow bulbs to dry	Full sun or light shade	10°–16°C/50°–60°F	Plant bulbs in late summer
Lantana camara	Yellow sage	Flowers	Bushy	Moderate; sparingly in winter	Bright; some direct sun	16°–21°C/60°–70°F	Prone to infestation by whiteflies
Leea coccinea	West Indian holly	Foliage	Bushy/tree-like	Moderate	Bright; no direct sun	18°–24°C/65°–75°F	Protect from draughts
Lilium spp.	Trumpet lilies	Flowers	Upright	Plentiful in growth; reduce after flowering to allow bulbs to dry	Bright; no direct sun	10°–16°C/50°–60°F	Support the flowering stems with canes
Liriope muscari (*L. graminifolia densiflora*)	Big blue lily-turf	Flowers	Upright	Moderate	Bright	16°–21°C/60°–70°F; cooler in winter	Tolerant of shade; keep out of draughts
Lithops lesliei	Living stones	Flowers and succulent leaves	Pebble-shaped	Sparingly in the growing season; keep dry through winter	Full sun	16°–21°C/60°–70°F	Old leaves die after flowering and are replaced by new ones

M

PLANT	COMMON NAMES	FEATURES	SHAPE	WATERING	LIGHT	IDEAL INDOOR TEMPERATURE	SPECIAL POINTS
Mammillaria bocasana	Powder puff cactus	Hairy stems, flowers	Cylindrical	Moderate to sparingly	Full sun	18°–21°C/65°–70°F	Mealybugs may be a problem
Mandevilla x *amoena* 'Alice du Pont'	Mandevilla	Flowers	Climbing	Moderate	Bright; no direct sun	16°–21°C/60°–70°F	Prune back stems after flowering
Manettia inflata	Firecracker vine	Flowers	Climbing/trailing	Moderate	Bright; some direct sun	16°–21°C/60°–70°F	Repot this vigorous plant as necessary
Maranta leuconeura	Prayer plant	Foliage	Bushy	Moderate	Medium; no direct sun	16°–18°C/60°–65°F	Requires high humidity
Medinilla magnifica	Rose grape	Flowers	Bushy	Moderate; more sparingly in winter	Bright, filtered	21°C/70°F	Difficult to keep after flowering
Mikania dentata (*M. ternata*)	Plush vine	Foliage	Trailing	Moderate	Bright; some direct sun	16°–21°C/60°–70°F	Do not mist the foliage directly

PLANT	COMMON NAMES	FEATURES	SHAPE	WATERING	LIGHT	IDEAL INDOOR TEMPERATURE	SPECIAL POINTS
Miltonia spp.	Pansy orchid	Flowers	Upright	Plentiful in spring and summer; more sparingly in winter	Medium; full sun in winter	18°–21°C/65°–70°F	Protect from temperature fluctuations
Mimosa pudica	Sensitive plant	Foliage and flowers	Bushy	Moderate	Bright; some direct sun	16°–21°C/60°–70°F	Leaflets fold up rapidly when they are touched
Monstera deliciosa	Swiss cheese plant, split leaf, window plant, Mexican breadfruit, fruit salad plant	Foliage	Climbing	Moderate	Medium to bright; no direct sun	18°–21°C/65°–70°F	Characteristic splits and holes develop on older leaves

N

PLANT	COMMON NAMES	FEATURES	SHAPE	WATERING	LIGHT	IDEAL INDOOR TEMPERATURE	SPECIAL POINTS
Narcissus spp.	Daffodil, narcissus	Flowers	Upright	Moderate; allow bulbs to dry out as leaves fade	Bright; no direct sun	10°–16°C/50°–60°F	Bulbs need a cool, dark forcing period after planting
Nematanthus gregarius (*Hypocyrta radicans*)	Nematanthus	Flowers	Bushy	Moderate; more sparingly in winter	Bright; some direct sun	16°–21°C/60°–70°F; cooler in winter	Benefits from being placed outdoors in summer
Neoregelia carolinae 'Tricolor'	Blushing bromeliad	Foliage and flowers	Rosette-forming	Moderate to sparing	Bright; some direct sun	16°–21°C/60°–70°F	Keep the central 'vase' filled with water
Neoregelia 'Meyendorffii'	Neoregelia	Foliage and flowers	Rosette-forming	Moderate to sparing; keep the vase full	Bright; some direct sun	16°–21°C/60°–70°F	An attractive cultivar
Nephrolepis exaltata 'Bostoniensis'	Sword fern, Boston fern, ladder fern	Foliage	Upright/arching	Plentiful to moderate	Bright; no direct sun	16°–21°C/60°–70°F	Good for hanging baskets
Nepenthes x *hookeriana*	Pitcher plant	Insect-catching traps	Climbing	Plentiful to moderate, using lime-free water	Medium; no direct sun	18–24°C/65°–75°F	Best in a warm, humid greenhouse
Nerine bowdenii	Nerine	Flowers	Upright	Plentiful during growth; otherwise not at all	Bright light; some sun	10°–16°C/50°–60°F	Can stand a temperature as low as -15°C/-5°F
Nerium oleander	Oleander	Flowers	Tree-like	Plentiful to moderate	Bright; some direct sun	16°–21°C/60°–70°F; 13°C/55°F during the winter rest period	All parts of the plant are very poisonous
Nertera granadensis	Bead plant, coral moss	Berries	Creeping	Moderate	Full sun	10°–16°C/50°–60°F	Placing plants outdoors while flowering ensures a good set of berries
Nidularium billbergioides	Nidularium	Foliage and flowers	Upright rosette	Moderate; less in winter; keep the 'vase' filled with water	Bright; no direct sun	16°–21°C/60°–70°F	Terrestrial bromeliad
Nidularium innocentii 'Striatum'	Bird's nest bromeliad	Foliage and flowers	Rosette-forming	Moderate; sparingly in winter	Bright; no direct sun	16°–21°C/60°–70°F	Keep the central 'vase' filled with water

O

PLANT	COMMON NAMES	FEATURES	SHAPE	WATERING	LIGHT	IDEAL INDOOR TEMPERATURE	SPECIAL POINTS
Ocimum basilicum	Sweet basil	Aromatic foliage	Bushy	Moderate	Bright; no direct strong sunlight	16°–21°C/60°–70°F	Pinch out growing tips regularly
Odontoglossum grande	Tiger orchid	Flowers	Upright/arching	Moderate; sparingly in winter rest period	Bright, filtered	16°C/60°F	Use special orchid compost
Olea europaea	Olive	Foliage	Shrubby	Moderate	Full sun	16°–24°C/60°–75°F	Benefits from a spell outdoors in summer
Oncidium spp.	Oncidiums	Flowers	Upright/arching	Sparing in period of active growth; keep almost dry in rest period	Direct sun, except midday summer sun	18°C/65°F; 13°C/55°F during rest period	Mist-spray and stand pot on a tray of moist pebbles when temperature is over 21°C/70°F
Ophiopogon jaburan	White lily-turf	Flowers and foliage	Grassy	Moderate to sparing	Bright; no direct sun	13°–18°C/55°–65°F	Tolerant of shade
Oplismenus hirtellus	Basket grass	Foliage	Trailing	Moderate	Bright; some direct winter sun	16°–21°C/60°–70°F	Best replaced every year or two

PLANT	COMMON NAMES	FEATURES	SHAPE	WATERING	LIGHT	IDEAL INDOOR TEMPERATURE	SPECIAL POINTS
Opuntia microdasys	Prickly pear cactus, bunny ears	Succulent stems	Branching, flattened stems	Sparing	Full sun	16°–21°C/60°–70°F	Bristly spines can be irritating to the skin
Osmanthus heterophyllus 'Variegatus'	Variegated false holly	Foliage	Shrubby	Moderate	Full sun	10°–13°C/50°–55°F	Pinch out growing points to encourage bushiness
Oxalis deppei (*O. tetraphylla*)	Lucky clover	Flowers and foliage	Spreading	Moderate to sparing	Bright; some direct sun	10°–18°C/50°–65°F	Discard when plants become too leggy

P

PLANT	COMMON NAMES	FEATURES	SHAPE	WATERING	LIGHT	IDEAL INDOOR TEMPERATURE	SPECIAL POINTS
Pachystachys lutea	Lollipop plant	Flowers (bracts)	Upright/ bushy	Plentiful to moderate	Bright; no direct sun	16°–21°C/60°–70°F	Prune stems by one-third in early spring
Pandanus veitchii	Screw pine	Foliage	Upright	Moderate	Bright; some direct sun	18°–24°C/65°–75°F	High humidity required
Paphiopedilum spp.	Slipper orchids	Flowers	Upright	Moderate to sparing	Bright; direct sun in winter only	18°–24°C/65°–75°F	High humidity essential; mist-spray daily
Passiflora caerulea	Common passion flower	Flowers	Climber	Plentiful; more sparingly in winter	Full sun	21°C/70°F; cooler in winter	Train pot plants around a wire hoop or on a trellis
Pelargonium x *hortorum*	Geranium, zonal pelargonium	Flowers	Bushy	Moderate; very sparingly in winter	Full sun	13°–18°C/55°–65°F	Prune stems back hard in early spring
Pelargonium peltatum	Ivy-leafed geranium	Flowers; foliage (some varieties)	Trailing	Moderate; very sparingly in winter	Full sun	13°–18°C/55°–65°F	Good for hanging baskets
Pelargonium spp.	Scented-leafed geraniums	Aromatic foliage	Mainly bushy	Moderate; sparingly in winter	Full sun	13°–18°C/55°–65°F	Many different species with different fragrances exist
Pellaea rotundifolia	Button fern	Foliage	Trailing	Moderate	Bright; no direct sun	16°–21°C/60°–70°F	Protect from fluctuating temperatures
Pellionia daveauana (*P. repens*)	Watermelon begonia	Foliage	Trailing	Plentiful to moderate	Bright or semi-shaded	21°–27°C/70°–80°F	High humidity and protection from draughts required
Pentas lanceolata (*P. carnea*)	Egyptian star cluster	Flowers and foliage	Bushy	Moderate; more sparingly after flowering	Bright; some direct sun	18°–24°C/65°–75°F	Pinch out growing tips to keep plant bushy
Peperomia caperata	Emerald ripple	Foliage and flower spikes	Bushy	Sparing	Medium; no direct sun	16°–21°C/60°–70°F	Take care not to overwater in winter
Peperomia magnoliifolia	Desert privet	Foliage	Bushy	Sparing	Bright; no direct sun	16°–21°C/60°–70°F	High humidity required
Peperomia scandens	Cupid peperomia	Foliage	Trailing	Sparing to moderate	Bright; no direct strong sun	16°–21°C/60°–70°F	High humidity required
Phalaenopsis spp.	Moth orchid	Flowers	Upright	Moderate to plentiful	Light shade	21°C/70°F	Likes a well-ventilated atmosphere
Philodendron bipinnatifidum	Tree philodendron	Foliage	Bushy	Moderate; more sparingly in winter	Medium; no direct sun	16°–21°C/60°–70°F	Requires plenty of space
Philodendron erubescens	Blushing philodendron	Foliage	Climbing	Moderate	Medium; no direct sun	16°–21°C/60°–70°F	Provide a moss pole or similar support
Philodendron scandens	Heartleaf philodendron, sweetheart plant	Foliage	Climbing/ trailing	Moderate	Bright; no direct sun	16°–21°C/60°–70°F	Tie stems to their support
Phoenix roebelenii	Pygmy date palm	Foliage	Bushy	Plentiful in growing season; sparingly in winter	Bright; some direct sun	16°–21°C/60°–70°F	High humidity required
Pilea cadierei	Aluminium plant	Foliage	Bushy	Moderate	Medium; no direct sun	16°–21°C/60°–70°F	Discard when leggy
Pilea peperonioides	Pilea	Foliage	Bushy	Moderate to sparing	Medium to bright; no direct sun	18°–24°C/65°–75°F	Pinch out growing tips regularly to keep plants compact; keep out of draughts

PLANT	COMMON NAMES	FEATURES	SHAPE	WATERING	LIGHT	IDEAL INDOOR TEMPERATURE	SPECIAL POINTS
Piper nigrum	Black pepper	Foliage and fruits	Climbing	Moderate	Bright; no direct strong sun	18°–24°C/65°–75°F	High humidity and even temperature essential
Piper ornatum	Celebes pepper	Foliage	Climbing/ creeping	Moderate	Bright; no direct sun	16°–21°C/60°–70°F	Cut out weak shoots in early spring; provide a support for the plant to climb on
Pisonia umbellifera 'Variegata'	Bird-catcher tree	Foliage	Bushy	Moderate; more sparingly in winter	Full sun or light shade	18°–24°C/65°–75°F	Prune to shape when repotting; leaves lose colour in poor light
Pittosporum tobira	Japanese pittosporum, Australian laurel	Foliage and flowers	Bushy	Moderate; sparingly in winter	Bright; no diect sunlight	16°–21°C/60°–70°F	Needs bright conditions to flower
Platycerium bifurcatum	Staghorn fern	Foliage	Spreading	Mist-spray, or plunge as necessary	Bright; some direct sun	16°–18°C/60°–65°F	Epiphyte that is best in slatted orchid basket or mounted on bark
Plectranthus coleoides 'Marginatus'	Candle plant	Foliage	Bushy	Plentiful; more sparingly in winter	Bright; some direct sun	16°–21°C/60°–70°F	Best discarded at the end of the season and replaced with cuttings
Plumbago auriculata	Cape leadwort	Flowers	Semi-climbing	Moderate; more sparingly in winter	Bright; some direct sun	10°–18°C/50°–65°F	Prune hard in spring; provide supports or a wire hoop
Plumeria rubra (*P. acuminata*)	Frangipani, temple tree, nosegay, West Indian jasmine, pagoda tree	Scented flowers	Tree-like	Plentiful in growing season; sparingly in winter	Bright; some direct sun	18°–24°C/65°–75°F	Needs plenty of space
Podocarpus macrophyllus	Buddhist pine, Japanese yew, Kusamaki	Foliage	Tree-like	Moderate; sparingly in winter	Partial shade	10°–18°C/50°–65°F	Tolerates draughty conditions
Polyscias scutellaria 'Balfourii'	Ming aralia	Foliage	Bushy	Moderate; more sparingly in winter	Bright; no direct sun	18°–24°C/65°–75°F	High humidity essential
Primula denticulata	Drumstick primula	Flowers	Bushy	Plentiful	Bright; some direct sun	10°–16°C/50°–60°F	Can be planted outdoors after flowering
Primula 'Kewensis'	Primula	Flowers	Bushy	Plentiful	Bright; some direct sun	10°–16°C/50°–60°F	Leaves and stems are covered with white meal
Primula malacoides	Fairy primrose	Flowers	Bushy	Plentiful	Bright	10°–16°C/50°–60°F	Best discarded after flowering
Primula obconica	Poison primrose	Flowers	Bushy	Plentiful while flowering; otherwise moderate to sparingly	Bright; some direct sun	10°–16°C/50°–60°F	Foliage can cause adverse skin reactions in some people
Primula sinensis	Chinese primrose	Flowers	Bushy	Plentiful to moderate	Bright	10°–16°C/50°–60°F	Plants benefit from spending summer outside
Primula vulgaris	Common primrose	Flowers	Bushy	Plentiful	Bright; some direct sun	10°–16°C/50°–60°F	Can be planted outdoors in the garden after flowering
Pseuderanthemum atropurpureum	Pseuderanthemum	Foliage and flowers	Upright	Moderate	Bright light or partial shade	18°–24°C/65°–75°F	High humidity essential
Pteris cretica	Table fern, Cretan brake, ribbon fern	Foliage	Rosette-forming	Moderate to plentiful	Bright; no direct sun	13°–21°C/55°–70°F	High humidity required
Punica granatum 'Nana'	Dwarf pomegranate	Flowers and fruit	Bushy	Moderate	Bright; some direct sun	16°–21°C/60°–70°F	Hand-pollinate flowers to encourage fruiting

R

PLANT	COMMON NAMES	FEATURES	SHAPE	WATERING	LIGHT	IDEAL INDOOR TEMPERATURE	SPECIAL POINTS
Radermachera sinica (*Stereospermum sinicum*)	Emerald tree, Asian bell tree	Foliage	Tree-like	Moderate	Bright; no direct sun	16°–21°C/60°–70°F	Tolerates dry air well, but will not tolerate a smoky atmosphere
Rebutia minuscula	Red crown cactus, Mexican sunball	Flowers, succulent stems	Globular	Moderate in spring and summer; otherwise sparingly	Full sun	16°–24°C/60°–75°F	A cool winter rest period encourages flowering

PLANT	COMMON NAMES	FEATURES	SHAPE	WATERING	LIGHT	IDEAL INDOOR TEMPERATURE	SPECIAL POINTS
Rhapis excelsa	Miniature fan palm, little lady palm	Foliage	Bushy	Moderate; more sparingly in winter	Bright; some direct winter sun	16°–21°C/60°–70°F	High humidity required
Rhipsalidopsis gaertneri	Easter cactus	Flowers	Trailing	Moderate while flowering; sparingly afterwards	Bright; no direct sun	16°–21°C/60°–70°F	Give a short, cool rest period after flowering
Rhipsalis baccifera (*R. cassutha*)	Mistletoe cactus	Succulent stems, fruits	Trailing	Moderate; more sparingly in winter	Bright; no direct sun	16°–24°C/60°–75°F	Provide a cool winter rest period
Rhipsalis cereuscula	Rhipsalis	Branching, succulent stems	Trailing	Moderate; less in winter	Bright; no direct midday summer sun	16°–24°C/60°–75°F	Needs a cool winter rest period
Rhododendron simsii and hybrids	Indian azalea	Flowers	Shrubby	Plentiful	Bright; no direct sun	50°–55°F/10°–13°C	Use ericaceous (lime-free) compost
Rhoeo spathacea 'Variegata'	Boat lily, Moses in the cradle	Foliage and flowers	Rosette-forming	Plentiful in growing season; sparingly in winter	Medium; no direct sun	16°–21°C/60°–70°F	High humidity required
Rochea coccinea (*Crassula coccinea*)	Rochea	Flowers and foliage	Upright	Moderate; more sparingly in winter	Bright; some direct sun	13°–18°C/55°–65°F	Requires a well-ventilated position
Rosa	Miniature rose	Flowers	Bushy	Moderate to plentiful	Full sun or light shade	13°–18°C/55°–65°F	Move plants outdoors after flowering until mid-winter
Ruellia makoyana	Monkey plant, trailing velvet plant	Flowers and foliage	Trailing	Moderate	Bright; no direct sun	16°–21°C/60°–70°F	A good plant for hanging baskets

S

PLANT	COMMON NAMES	FEATURES	SHAPE	WATERING	LIGHT	IDEAL INDOOR TEMPERATURE	SPECIAL POINTS
Saintpaulia	African violet	Flowers, foliage (some varieties)	Rosette-forming	Moderate	Bright; no direct sun	18°–21°C/65°–70°F	Avoid splashing water in the centre of the plant
Salpiglossis sinuata	Painted tongue	Flowers	Bushy	Plentiful; allow to dry out between waterings	Bright; some direct sun	10°–18°C/50°–65°C	Discard after flowering
Sanchezia speciosa (*S. nobilis*)	Sanchezia	Foliage and flowers	Shrubby	Plentiful in growing season; more sparingly in winter	Bright; no direct summer sun	16°–21°C/60°–70°F	Prune in spring to maintain compact shape
Sansevieria trifasciata 'Laurentii'	Mother-in-law's tongue, snakeskin or snake plant	Foliage	Tall, upright rosette	Moderate; very sparingly in winter	Full sun	18°–21°C/65°–70°F	Use heavy clay pots to provide stability
Sarracenia flava	Yellow pitcher plant	Liquid-filled insect traps	Upright	Plentiful during the period of active growth	Bright; some direct sun	13°–16°C/55°–60°F	Needs some humidity
Saxifraga stolonifera	Mother of thousands	Foliage and plantlets	Rosette-forming with trailing plantlets	Moderate; sparingly in winter	Bright; some direct sun	10°–16°C/50°–60°F	Good for hanging baskets
Schefflera arboricola	Umbrella tree	Foliage	Upright/tree-like	Moderate	Bright; some direct sun	16°–21°C/60°–70°F	Pinch out the growing tips for a bushy plant; otherwise provide a moss pole for support
Schizanthus pinnatus	Poor man's orchid, butterfly flower	Flowers	Bushy	Moderate to plentiful	Full sun	13°–18°C/55°–65°F	Discard after flowering
Schlumbergera x *buckleyi*	Christmas cactus	Flowers	Trailing	Moderate; sparingly during rest period	Bright; some direct winter sun	16°–21°C/60°–70°F; cooler during rest period	Provide a cool, fairly dry rest period of eight weeks after flowering
Schlumbergera truncata	Crab cactus	Flowers	Trailing	Moderate; sparing in rest period	Bright; some direct winter sun	16°–21°C/60°–70°F; cooler in the rest period	Needs a fairly dry, cool rest period after flowering
Scilla siberica	Siberian squill	Flowers	Grassy	Moderate	Bright; no direct sun	10°–13°C/50°–55°F	Place newly potted bulbs outdoors until shoots develop
Sedum morganianum	Donkey's tail	Foliage	Trailing	Moderate; sparingly in winter	Bright; some direct sun	16°–21°C/60°–70°F	Take care not to overwater

PLANT	COMMON NAMES	FEATURES	SHAPE	WATERING	LIGHT	IDEAL INDOOR TEMPERATURE	SPECIAL POINTS
Sedum sieboldii (*Hylotelephium sieboldii*)	Stonecrop	Foliage and flowers	Trailing	Moderate to sparing	Full sun	10°–16°C/50°–60°F	Good for hanging baskets
Selaginella kraussiana	Spreading clubmoss	Foliage	Creeping	Plentiful	Medium light or light shade; no direct sun	16°–21°C/60°–70°F	High humidity essential; ideal for a bottle garden
Senecio x *hybridus* (*Pericallis* x *hybridus*)	Cineraria	Flowers	Bushy	Moderate	Bright; some direct sun	10°–16°C/50°–60°F	Discard after flowering
Senecio rowleyanus	String-of-beads	Foliage	Trailing	Moderate to sparing	Bright; some direct sun	16°–21°C/60°–70°F	Discard when leggy and replace with cuttings
Setcreasea purpurea (*Tradescantia pallida*)	Purple heart	Foliage	Trailing, creeping	Moderate	Bright; some direct sun	16°–21°C/60°–70°F	Discard when leggy and replace with cuttings
Siderasis fuscata	Brown spiderwort	Foliage	Rosette-forming	Moderate	Medium to bright; no direct sun	21°C/70°F	Protect from fluctuating temperatures
Sinningia cardinalis	Cardinal flower, helmet flower	Flowers	Bushy	Plentiful while flowering; reduce to allow tubers to dry out	Bright; no direct sun	21°C/70°F; under 10°C/50°F when dormant	Tubers become dormant shortly after flowering
Sinningia speciosa	Gloxinia	Flowers	Bushy	Plentiful to moderate; reduce after flowering and allow tubers to dry out	Bright; no direct sun	16°–21°C/60°–70°F	Tubers become dormant shortly after flowering
Smithiantha hybrids	Temple bells	Flowers	Bushy	Moderate; reduce after flowering and allow tubers to dry out	Light shade	21°C/70°F	Tubers become dormant shortly after flowering
Solanum capsicastrum	False Jerusalem cherry	Berries	Bushy	Moderate	Full sun	10°–16°C/50°–60°F	Place plants outdoors in summer to encourage formation of berries
Soleirolia soleirolii	Mind-your-own-business	Foliage	Creeping	Plentiful to moderate	Medium to bright	16°–18°C /60°–65°F	Can be invasive
Sonerila margaritacea	Pearl plant	Foliage	Bushy	Moderate	Bright; no direct sun	21°C/70°F	High humidity essential
Sparmannia africana	African hemp, indoor lime, linden tree	Foliage and flowers	Tree-like	Plentiful to moderate	Bright; no direct strong sun	13°–16°C/55°–65°F	Replace plants annually with cuttings
Spathiphyllum wallisii	Peace lily, white sails	Flowers and foliage	Bushy	Moderate; more sparingly in winter	Bright light; no direct sun	16°–21°C/60°–70°F	High humidity required
Stapelia variegata (*Orebea variegata*)	Carrion flower	Flowers	Upright	Sparing to moderate	Full sun	16°–21°C/60°–70°F	Flowers have an unpleasant smell
Stenotaphrum secundatum 'Variegatum'	Buffalo grass, St. Augustine grass	Foliage	Grassy	Plentiful in growing season; more sparingly in winter	Bright; some direct sun	16°–21°C/60°–70°F	Good for hanging baskets
Stephanotis floribunda	Madagascar jasmine	Scented flowers	Climbing	Plentiful in growing season; sparingly in winter	Bright; no direct summer sun	18°–21°C/65°–70°F	Avoid fluctuating temperatures
Strelitzia nicolai	White bird-of-paradise	Flowers (bracts) and foliage	Upright	Moderate to sparing	Bright; some direct sun	16°–21°C/60°–70°F; below 16°C/60°F in winter	Requires plenty of space
Strelitzia reginae	Bird-of-paradise, crane flower	Flowers (bracts) and foliage	Upright	Moderate to sparing	Bright; some direct sun essential for flowering	16°–21°C/60°–70°F; around 13°C/55°F in winter	Plants do not flower until they are around five years old
Streptocarpus x *hybridus*	Cape primrose	Flowers	Rosette-forming	Moderate	Bright; no direct sun	16°–21°C/60°–70°F	Remove faded flowers before seeds form
Streptosolen jamesonii	Marmalade bush, fire bush	Flowers	Scrambling	Plentiful to moderate in growing season; sparingly in winter	Bright; some direct sun	16°–21°C/60°–70°F	Best trained against a wall
Strobilanthes dyeranus	Persian shield	Foliage	Upright	Moderate to sparing	Bright, filtered	16°–21°C/60°–70°F	Replace annually by cuttings

PLANT	COMMON NAMES	FEATURES	SHAPE	WATERING	LIGHT	IDEAL INDOOR TEMPERATURE	SPECIAL POINTS
Stromanthe amabilis (*Calathea amabilis*)	Stromanthe	Foliage	Bushy	Moderate	Medium to bright; no direct sun	18°–24°C/65°–75°F	High humidity required
Syagrus weddelliana	Weddel palm	Foliage	Bushy	Moderate to sparing	Bright; no direct sun	21°–24°C/70°–75°F	High humidity essential
Syngonium podophyllum	Arrowhead plant, goosefoot plant	Foliage	Bushy/semi-climbing	Moderate	Bright; no direct sun	16°–21°C/60°–70°F	Leaves change shape as the plant matures
T							
Tetrastigma voinieranum	Chestnut vine	Foliage	Climbing	Plentiful to moderate	Bright; no direct sun	16°–21°C/60°–70°F	Avoid fluctuating temperatures; provide sturdy support
Thunbergia alata	Black-eyed Susan	Flowers	Climbing	Plentiful	Bright; sun direct sun	13°–18°C/55°– 65°F	Annual, raised from seed in spring
Thymus vulgaris	Wild thyme	Aromatic foliage, flowers	Upright or spreading	Moderate	Bright; some direct sun	13°–18°C/55°– 65°F	Place plants outdoors in summer
Tillandsia cyanea (*T. lindenii*)	Air plant	Foliage and flowers	Grass-like	Mist-spray twice weekly in summer; less in winter	Bright; no direct sun	16°–21°C/60°–70°F	Epiphyte, often mounted on wood, but also grown in compost
Tillandsia ionantha	Air plant	Foliage and flowers	Rosette-forming	Mist-spray twice weekly in summer; less frequently in winter	Bright; no direct sun	16°–21°C/60°–70°F	Epiphyte, usually mounted on wood or a similar substance
Tolmiea menziesii	Piggyback plant	Foliage	Bushy/semi-trailing	Moderate	Bright; some direct sun	13°–18°C/55°–65°F	Plantlets are produced on the leaves
Trachycarpus fortunei	Windmill palm	Foliage	Bushy	Moderate; sparingly in winter	Full sun	16°–21°C/60°–70°F	Benefits from a spell outdoors in summer
Tradescantia fluminensis 'Variegata'	Wandering Jew, spiderwort, speeding Jenny	Foliage	Trailing	Plentiful in growing season; moderate in winter	Bright; some direct sun	16°–21°C/60°–70°F	Replace leggy plants with cuttings
Tulipa hybrids	Tulips	Flowers	Upright	Moderate	Bright	13°–16°C/55°–60°F	Bulbs require a cool, dark forcing period after planting
V							
Vallota speciosa (*Cyrtanthus elatus*)	Scarborough lily	Flowers	Upright	Moderate; sparingly in winter and early spring	Bright; some direct sun	16°–21°C/60°–70°F; about 10°C/50°F in winter	Repot only when essential
Vriesea splendens	Flaming sword	Foliage and flowers	Rosette	Sparing to moderate	Bright; some direct sun	16°–21°C/60°–70°F	Main rosette dies after flowering
W							
Washingtonia filifera	Desert fan palm, petticoat palm	Foliage	Upright	Plentiful to moderate	Bright; plenty of direct sun	21°–24°C/70°–75°F; about 10°C/50°F in winter	Benefits from a spell outdoors in summer
Y							
Yucca elephantipes	Spineless yucca	Foliage	Tree-like or rosette-forming	Moderate; very sparingly in winter	Full sun	16°–21°C/60°–70°F	Use clay pots for extra stability with tall plants
Z							
Zantedeschia aethiopica (*Z. africana*)	Calla lily, arum lily	Flowers	Upright/bushy	Plentiful when flowering; reduce to sparing as leaves begin to die back	Bright; some direct sun	13°–18°C/55°–65°F	Stand plants outdoors in summer
Zebrina pendula	Silvery inch plant, wandering Jew	Foliage	Trailing	Plentiful to moderate; more sparingly in winter	Bright; some direct sun	16°–21°C/60°–70°F	Tolerant of shade, though leaf colour will be reduced

GLOSSARY

Some of the botanical terms used in this book are explained here.
A word appearing in bold italics refers to another related entry,
and the two entries should be read in conjunction.

Acid Of soils and *compost*: below pH 7; containing no lime. (See *alkaline, ericaceous, pH*)

Active growth period The time when a plant makes new growth, producing leaves and flowers; compare *dormant* and *rest period*.

Aerial roots Roots produced from the stems of a plant which can often absorb moisture from the air.

Alkaline Of soils and *compost*: above pH 7; usually containing lime. (See *acid, pH*)

Annual A plant that grows from seed, produces flowers and seeds and dies in one growing season.

Anther The male, pollen-bearing part of a flower.

Architectural Refers to plants, usually with bold outlines, that are grown for their dramatic appearance.

Areole A modified side shoot on cacti that carries spines. Flowers and offsets arise from the areole.

Axil The angle between a leafstalk and the stem from which it grows.

Biennial A plant that grows from seed in one season and produces flowers and seeds and dies the following season; compare *annual*.

Biological control The deliberate use of natural enemies to control plant pests and diseases.

Blade The flat part of a leaf.

Bottom heat Warmth provided at the base of the compost in a propagator to encourage cuttings to root.

Bract A modified leaf that forms part of a flower; it may be brightly coloured and decorative, as in bougainvillea. Bracts are sometimes confused with petals.

Bulb An underground storage organ that contains embryo leaves and/or flowers.

Bulbil A miniature bulb that develops around the base of mature bulbs or on the stem of plants such as lilies, often in the leaf axil.

Calyx The outer covering of a flower bud, consisting of modified leaves, or *sepals*. These are often green but are sometimes colourful and decorative.

Carnivorous Describes plants, also known as insectivorous, that capture and digest insects to obtain nutrients.

Chlorophyll The green pigment in leaves that is important for *photosynthesis*.

Chlorosis Yellowing of foliage due to loss of *chlorophyll*; often caused by nutrient *deficiency*. It may cause distinctive patterns on the leaf.

Compost Growing medium specially prepared for plants in pots. Also waste organic matter rotted down in the garden.

Corm Solid underground storage organ, as in crocus, developed from the base of a stem.

Corolla The petals of a flower. They may be fused to form a tube, bell or another shape, or they may be separate.

Crocks Broken pieces of clay pot used as a layer in the bottom of a plant container to provide thorough drainage.

Crown The part of a non-woody plant from which the shoots and roots arise.

Cultivar A variety that has been bred in cultivation rather than arising in the wild; compare *variety*.

Deadheading Removing faded flowers to prevent the production of seeds and improve a plant's appearance.

Deciduous Refers to plants that lose their leaves at the end of the *active growth period*.

Deficiency Shortage of a specific *nutrient* which causes adverse symptoms in the plant.

Diffuse light Light that is screened and filtered, by a blind or curtain for example.

Dormant Refers to a plant in a temporary period of inactivity, normally when all top growth and roots die back; compare *rest period*.

Double Flowers with more than one layer of petals.

Entire Refers to leaves that are not divided.

Epiphytic Refers to a plant that in nature grows on the branch of a tree or a rock, rather than in soil. Such plants absorb water and nutrients from the air and from rain and use aerial roots for support.

Ericaceous Of plants: those that cannot tolerate lime in the growing medium; includes azaleas and heathers. Of compost, suitable for lime-hating plants.

Evergreen Refers to plants that retain their leaves year round; compare *deciduous*.

Family A botanical grouping of plants that share some of the same characteristics: e.g. cactaceae, bromeliaceae. Families are subdivided into *genus*, species and *variety* (or *cultivar*): e.g. family Bromeliaceae, genus *Aechema*, species *fasciata*, cultivar 'Variegata'.

Flower The reproductive, seed-forming organ of a plant.

Forcing Bringing plants into flower or growth earlier than their natural season by manipulating temperature, etc.

Frond The leaf of a fern or palm.

Genus A subdivision of a botanical *family*.

Growing point The tip of a shoot where growth occurs.

Habit The overall shape and form of a plant, such as bushy, spreading, creeping.

Hardy Describes a plant that can survive in the open without protection year round, including periods of drought or frost.

Heel A small strip of bark or older wood torn away with a side shoot when it is taken to form a cutting. Some plants root better when a heel is present.

Herbaceous Refers to plants that die down in winter and have no woody stems. (See *perennial*)

Humidity The amount of water vapour present in the air.

Humus Rotted organic matter in the soil which improves its structure.

Hybrid A plant resulting from a cross between two non-identical parents. Most hybrids are the result of crossing two different varieties, although some arise from crossing two different species (interspecific hybrids) or, more rarely, two different genera (bigeneric or intergeneric hybrids). Interspecific and bigeneric hybrids are indicated by an 'x' in the botanical name, for example, *Schlumbergera* x *buckleyii* (interspecific hybrid between *S. russelliana* and *S. truncata*) and x *Fatshedera lizei*, a bigeneric hybrid between *Fatsia japonica* 'Moseri' and *Hedera helix* var. *hibernica*.

The Sheffield
College
Hillsborough LRC

Hydroponics A method of growing plants in water rather than soil by adding all nutrients to the water.

Larva The caterpillar stage in the life cycle of an insect. Since it is the feeding stage, larvae can be very damaging to plants.

Lateral A side shoot; a sublateral is a shoot arising from the side shoot.

Leaf Usually the main area of a plant in which photosynthesis takes place. Leaves occur in many shapes and sizes; a few plants, such as some cacti, have no leaves.

Leaflet A single segment of a compound (divided) leaf.

Loam Soil, originally from rotted-down turf. Good loam is a mixture of sand, clay and humus and forms the basis of soil-based *compost*.

Lobe Part of a leaf, bract or petal partly but not entirely separated from the whole.

Microclimate The atmospheric conditions created within a small area that differ from those of the general area around it: e.g. the relatively humid atmosphere immediately around a group of plants within a drier room.

Midrib The usually large, central vein of a leaf, generally raised on the underside of the leaf.

Mist A very fine spray of water applied to or around the foliage. The tiny droplets of water will not damage the leaves.

Node The part of a plant where the leaf joins the stem. Many cuttings root most readily from nodes.

Nutrients Minerals required by the plant and usually taken up in solution from compost. Nitrogen, phosphorus and potassium are the major nutrients (macronutrients), but plants need many others, some in tiny quantities (micronutrients). Plants that are not receiving enough nutrients will show *deficiency* symptoms.

Offset A small, new plant, usually produced at the base of the parent, which can be separated for propagation purposes. Several cacti, succulents, bulbs and bromeliads produce offsets.

Ovate Of a leaf: broad and round at the bottom and tapering towards the tip.

Palmate Of a leaf: shaped like a spread hand, generally with five lobes.

Peat Decomposed vegetable matter, usually moss and sedges, used as a potting medium. Peat substitutes such as coir can often be used instead.

Pendant Applied to flowers which hang down, usually from slender flower stalks.

Perennial A plant that persists from year to year; usually applied to *herbaceous* plants; compare *annual*.

Petal A modified leaf that forms part of the *flower* and is often decorative and brightly coloured.

Petiole The leafstalk.

pH The scale on which acidity and alkalinity of soil is measured. pH 7 is neutral; soil is alkaline above this point and acid below it.

Phloem The transportation system for nutrients in plants.

Photoperiodism The reaction of plants to variation in day length; often important in the initiation of flower buds.

Photosynthesis The process by which plants convert light to usable energy. (See *chlorophyll*)

Pinnate Refers to compound leaves with leaflets in opposite pairs on each side of the midrib.

Pistil The female part of a *flower*, consisting of *style*, *stigma* and ovary.

Pricking out Moving small plants (usually seedlings) from one container to another where they can be spaced more widely.

Pseudobulb A thickened stem base on some orchids that acts as a storage organ and from which the leaves arise.

Rest period The time when plants make little or no growth but, unlike *dormant* plants, retain their leaves.

Rhizome A normally fleshy underground stem bearing shoots and roots.

Root ball The near-complete root system of a plant, together with the compost that clings around the roots.

Rosette An arrangement of leaves that radiate in a circle from a single point.

Runner A long, slender stem bearing a new plant at intervals along it or at the tip.

Sepal A modified leaf that covers the flower bud. (See *calyx*)

Shrub A plant that produces a permanent framework of *woody* stems, usually branching from the base.

Slow release Refers to fertilisers that break down gradually to release their nutrient content over an extended period.

Spadix A club-shaped, fleshy flower spike with small flowers on the surface; usually surrounded by a *spathe*.

Spathe A relatively large single *bract* surrounding a *spadix*. Often brightly coloured.

Species A subdivision of a *genus*. (See *family*)

Spur A short branch carrying flowers; also a long, slender projection from some flowers.

Stamen The male part of a flower, consisting of a pollen-bearing *anther* on a filament.

Stigma The tip of the female part of the flower (the *pistil*) that receives pollen from the male.

Stolon A creeping stem that grows along the ground and roots where the *nodes* touch the soil.

Stopping Pinching off the growing tips to stimulate the production of side shoots.

Style The stem joining the *stigma* of a flower with the ovary.

Succulent A plant that stores water in its stems and/or leaves and is adapted to growing in a dry environment.

Sucker A shoot arising directly from the roots of a plant.

Tender Of plants: damaged by frost or low or high temperature; not *hardy*.

Tendril A slender, thread-like shoot that twines around objects to support a climbing plant.

Terrarium A decorative miniature greenhouse which provides ideal conditions for plants requiring high humidity and protection from draughts, etc.

Terrestrial Of orchids: species that grow in soil as opposed to being *epiphytic*.

Top-dress To apply compost and fertilisers on the soil surface of a potted plant. This usually entails removing the top 5–8cm/2–3in of old compost and replacing it with fresh. It is carried out instead of repotting when a plant is already in the largest convenient pot.

Trace elements Essential minerals needed in very small quantities by plants; also known as micronutrients. (See *nutrients*)

Tuber An underground storage organ produced by stems or roots.

Tubercle A wart-like projection on a plant; common on the stems of cacti.

Undulate Of leaves or petals: wavy edged.

Variegation Different-coloured markings on green leaves; usually white, cream or yellow, but other colours occur.

Variety A subdivision of a plant species; strictly applied to forms arising in the wild but also widely used of forms arising in cultivation. (See *cultivar*)

Vein Conductive tissues used to transport food and water within plants.

Woody Applied to plant tissue and stems that become hardened and persist after leaf fall.

Xylem Water-conducting tissue within the plant. (See *phloem*)

*I*NDEX

The index should be used in conjunction with the Buyer's Guide and the Glossary.

ACKNOWLEDGMENTS

PHOTOGRAPHIC CREDITS

b=bottom; *c*=centre; *l*=left; *r*=right; *t*=top

10 The Interior Archive; 11–13 Chas Wilder; 14–15*l* Spike Powell; 15*tr* Spike Powell; 15*br* Chas Wilder; 16*l* Elizabeth Whiting & Associates; 16*r* Robert Harding Picture Library; 17*t* Elizabeth Whiting & Associates; 17*b* Camera Press; 20 Robert Harding Picture Library; 21 Elizabeth Whiting & Associates; 22 Spike Powell; 23*t* Linda Burgess/The Garden Picture Library; 23*b* Spike Powell; 24 Linda Burgess/The Garden Picture Library; 25 Spike Powell; 26*t* Chas Wilder; 26*b* Spike Powell; 30 Chas Wilder; 31*l* John Freeman/Lorenz Books; 31*r* Harry Smith Collection; 32*l* Photos Horticultural; 32*r* Chas Wilder; 33*t* Harry Smith Collection; 33*b*–35 Chas Wilder; 36 Robert Harding Syndication; 37*l* Chas Wilder; 37*r* Peter McHoy; 38 Chas Wilder; 39*t* Flower Council of Holland; 39*b* Chas Wilder; 40*l* A–Z Botanical Collection; 40*r*–41*l* Chas Wilder; 41*r* Peter McHoy; 42–43 Chas Wilder; 44*l*–44*cl* Andrew Payne; 44*cr*–44*r* Peter Rauter; 45 Harry Smith Collection, 46–47*t* Chas Wilder; 47*b* Andrew Payne; 48*l* Photos Horticultural; 48*cl* Chas Wilder; 48*cr* Harry Smith Collection; 48*r* Chas Wilder; 49–50*l* Andrew Payne; 50*r* Peter McHoy; 51*t* Chas Wilder; 51*b* Andrew Payne; 52*l* Chas Wilder; 52*r* Myer/Le Scanff/The Garden Picture Library; 53*l* Robert Harding Syndication; 53*r* Andrew Payne; 54 Chas Wilder; 55 Harry Smith Collection; 56*l* Peter McHoy; 56*r* Andrew Payne; 57*l* Chas Wilder; 57*r* Harry Smith Collection; 58–59*l* Chas Wilder; 59*r* Jacqui Hurst/Kyle Cathie; 60*l* Peter Rauter; 60*r*–61*t* Chas Wilder; 61*b* Peter Rauter; 62*l* Chas Wilder; 62*r* Andrew Payne; 63*l* Chas Wilder; 63*r* Andrew Payne; 64*t* Peter Rauter; 64*b* Chas Wilder; 65 Harry Smith Collection; 66*t* John Freeman/Lorenz Books; 66*b* Peter Rauter; 67–68 Chas Wilder; 69*l* Harry Smith Collection; 69*r* A–Z Botanical Collection; 70*l* Harry Smith Collection; 70*r* Chas Wilder; 71*l* Andrew Payne; 71*r*–72*cl* Chas Wilder; 72*cr* Harry Smith Collection; 72*r* Chas Wilder; 73*l* Harry Smith Collection; 73*r*–74*l* Chas Wilder; 74*r* Elizabeth Whiting & Associates; 75*l* John Freeman/Lorenz Books; 75*r*–76 Chas Wilder; 77 Harry Smith Collection; 78–79 Chas Wilder; 80*l* Andrew Payne; 80*r* Mark Gatehouse; 81 Chas Wilder; 82*l* Harry Smith Collection; 82*r*–83 Chas Wilder; 84*l* Andrew Payne; 84*r*–85*l* Chas Wilder; 85*r* Andrew Payne; 86*l* Harry Smith Collection; 86*cl* Chas Wilder; 86*cr* Peter H. Hallett/A–Z Botanical Collection; 86*r*–87*l* Chas Wilder; 87*r* Harry Smith Collection; 88*l* Chas Wilder; 88*r* Peter McHoy; 89*l* John Freeman/Lorenz Books; 89*r* Andrew Payne; 90 Chas Wilder; 91*l* A–Z Botanical Collection; 91*r* Harry Smith Collection; 92*l* Chas Wilder; 92*r* Harry Smith Collection; 93 Chas Wilder; 94*l* John Freeman/Lorenz Books; 94*r* Mark Gatehouse; 95*t* John Glover/The Garden Picture Library; 95*b* Chas Wilder; 96*l* Charles Marden Fitch; 96*r* Chas Wilder; 97*l* Harry Smith Collection; 97*r* Peter McHoy; 98–99*l* Chas Wilder; 99*r* Andrew Payne; 100*l* Harry Smith Collection; 100*r*–101*l* Chas Wilder; 101*r* Andrew Payne; 102*l*–102*cl* Chas Wilder; 102*cr* Christopher Fairweather/The Garden Picture Library; 102*r*–103 Chas Wilder; 104*l* Andrew Payne; 104*r* Chas Wilder; 105*l* Harry Smith Collection; 105*r* Andrew Payne; 106 Andrew Payne; 107–109 Chas Wilder; 110*l* Andrew Payne; 110*r* Chas Wilder; 110*l* Andrew Payne; 110*r* John Freeman/Lorenz Books; 112*l* Andrew Payne; 112*r*–113*t* Harry Smith Collection; 113*b* Andrew Payne; 114*l* Peter McHoy; 114*cl*–115 Chas Wilder; 116 Andrew Payne; 117*t* Chas Wilder; 117*b* Andrew Payne; 118–119 Chas Wilder; 120*l* Andrew Payne; 120*r* Harry Smith Collection; 121*l* Robert Harding Syndication; 121*r*–122 Chas Wilder; 123*l* Robert Harding Picture Library; 123*r* Harry Smith Collection; 124*l* Chas Wilder; 124*r* John Freeman/Lorenz Books; 125*l* Peter McHoy; 125*r* Andrew Payne; 126*l*–126*cl* Chas Wilder; 126*cr* Elizabeth Whiting & Associates; 126*r* Mark Gatehouse; 127*l* Harry Smith Collection; 127*r* Chas Wilder; 128*l* Harry Smith Collection; 128*r* Mark Gatehouse; 129*l* Chas Wilder; 129*r* Peter McHoy; 130–133*l* Chas Wilder; 133*r* Andrew Payne; 134–135 Chas Wilder; 136*l* Robert Harding Syndication; 136*r*–138 Chas Wilder; 139 Andrew Payne; 140*l*–140*cl* Chas Wilder; 140*cr* Andrew Payne; 140*r*–141*l* Chas Wilder; 141*r* Andrew Payne; 142*l* Chas Wilder; 142*r* Andrew Payne; 143 Chas Wilder; 144*r* Jacqui Hurst/Kyle Cathie; 145*l* Chas Wilder; 145*r* John Freeman/Lorenz Books; 146*l* Peter McHoy; 146*r*–148 Harry Smith Collection; 149*l* Chas Wilder; 149*r* Peter McHoy; 150*l* Chas Wilder; 150*r* Steven Wooster/The Garden Picture Library; 151 Peter McHoy; 152*t* Pam Collins/A–Z Botanical Collection; 153*t* John Freeman/Lorenz Books; 153*b* Peter McHoy; 154*l*–154*c* Chas Wilder; 154*r*–155*l* Robert Harding Syndication; 155*r*–156*l* Harry Smith Collection; 156*r* Peter McHoy; 157 Chas Wilder; 158*l* Photos Horticultural; 158*r* Derek Fell; 159*l* Harry Smith Collection; 159*r*–161*t* Chas Wilder; 161*b* Mark Gatehouse; 162 Chas Wilder; 163 John Freeman/Lorenz Books; 163*r*–164 Chas Wilder; 165*t* Bjorn Svensson/A–Z Botanical Collection; 165*b* Chas Wilder; 166*l* Charles Marden Fitch; 166*c* Brigitte Thomas/The Garden Picture Library; 166*r*–167*t* Harry Smith Collection; 167*b*–168*l* Peter McHoy; 168*r* Chas Wilder; 169 Harry Smith Collection; 170*t* Derek Fell; 170*b* Charles Marden Fitch; 171 Derek Fell; 172–173*l* Chas Wilder; 173*r* Gary Rogers/The Garden Picture Library; 174–176*l* Chas Wilder; 176*r*–177*l* Peter McHoy; 177*c* Chas Wilder; 177*r* Peter McHoy; 178*l* Chas Wilder; 178*r* Harry Smith Collection; 179 Mark Gatehouse; 180*l* Chas Wilder; 180*r* Harry Smith Collection, 181 Neil Davies/A–Z Botanical Collection; 182–183*t* Chas Wilder; 183*b*–185 Harry Smith Collection; 186–187*t* Chas Wilder; 187*b* Flower Council of Holland; 188–191 Chas Wilder; 194 Robert Harding Picture Library; 195*t* Stan Osolinski/Oxford Scientific Films; 195*c* Mr P. Clement/Bruce Coleman; 195*b* M.P.L. Fogden/Bruce Coleman; 198–240 Chas Wilder.

ARTWORK CREDITS

David Ashby 210–211
Lynn Chadwick 114–115, 126–127, 190
Chris Forsey Endpapers, 18–19, 192–193
Roger Kent 44–45, 48–49, 72–73, 86–87, 102–103, 140–141
Kuo Kang Chen 27, 196–197, 198–199, 204–205, 206–207, 208–209, 210–211, 212–213, 214–215.

The publishers wish to thank the following for providing plants for photography. Their kind cooperation is much appreciated.

Alexandra Palace Garden Centre, Alexandra Palace, London N22 4AY Tel: 0181 444 2555

Architectural Plants, Cooks Farm, Nuthurst, Horsham, West Sussex RH13 6LH Tel: 01403 89772

Arnott & Mason, New Covent Garden Market, London SW8 5NA Tel: 0171 720 7651

Europlants, The Great North Road, A1000, Bell Bar, Hatfield, Herts. AL9 6DA Tel: 01707 649996

Holly Gate Cactus Nursery, Billingshurst Road, Ashington, West Sussex RH20 3BB Tel: 01903 892930

McBeans Orchids, Cooksbridge, Lewis, Sussex BN8 4PR Tel: 01273 400228

Palm Centre, 563 Upper Richmond Road, London SW14 7ED Tel: 0181 876 1193

The Conservatory, Gomshall Gallery, Gomshall, Surrey GU5 9LB Tel: 01483 203019

The Dutch Nursery, A1000, Bell Bar, Hatfield, Herts. AL9 6ND Tel: 01707 653372

The publishers also wish to thank **Snapdragon Ltd,** 268 Lee High Road, Lewisham, London SE13 5PL, Tel: 0181 852 0296, for the loan of the pots used in the photographs on pages 14 and 25.